THE TLINGIT INDIANS

Results of a Trip to the Northwest Coast
of America and the Bering Straits

By Aurel Krause

Translated by Erna Gunther

UNIVERSITY OF WASHINGTON PRESS

Seattle and London

The original edition of this work, entitled *Die Tlinkit-Indianer*, was published in Jena in 1885.

This translation was first published in 1956 by the University of Washington Press as Monograph 26 of the American Ethnological Society.

Preface

As the ethnographic areas of the world become absorbed by
modern civilization, and the anthropologist must choose between
investigating acculturation or dealing with "memory" cultures,
an ethnographic report written by a trained scientist seventy
years ago gains in importance. Die Tlinkit-Indianer is one of
the many excellent studies of distant people produced by German
and other European scientists in the latter half of the nineteenth
century. None of them was an anthropologist, but their various
specialties brought them into contact with indigenous populations
in many parts of the world, with the result that many readable
and accurate accounts were published of these little-known cultures. Because of their scientific training they produced systematic records that are more useful than the casual remarks of many
observers who only mentioned exotic practices that appealed to
them. Franz Boas did his first ethnographic work while he was
on an expedition for the Geographical Society of Berlin, studying
the sea waters of the Arctic. The surrounding Eskimo interested
him as much as the problem in hand. In time his work was almost coincident with that of the Krause brothers.

Aurel and Arthur Krause were geographers sent by the Geographical Society of Bremen to follow up the work done by Nordenskiold on the Chukchee Peninsula in 1878 and 1879. This was the
third Arctic expedition undertaken by the society. After their
Siberian research was completed and Arthur had departed for
Europe, Aurel worked intensively with the Tlingit, settling at
Klukwan, which is still today one of the most aboriginally orient-
ed villages of southeastern Alaska.

Die Tlinkit-Indianer has not been superseded by any modern
ethnography. Many Tlingit studies have appeared since Krause's
publication, but each has been on a specific and limited subject.
In fact, because of the date of its writing and its comprehensive
coverage, this book is almost unique in the literature of the
northern area of the Northwest Coast.

Since Die Tlinkit-Indianer has been out of print for many years, it seemed highly desirable to translate it as a first step to getting it reprinted and thus providing for its greater use. The book was directed to the membership of the Bremen society and written in simple nontechnical German, but the scholarship of its author is always apparent. One outstanding chapter gives a resume of the history of Alaska with reference to the Tlingit, from the earliest Russian explorations to the purchase of the territory by the United States, and pictures the immediate consequences of the changes brought about by the new administration. In summarizing this history Krause cited many excellent Russian sources which were more readily available at the time of his writing than they are now; his footnotes have all been translated and retained. However, as the literature on the Tlingit has grown considerably since the original work appeared, references have been added when the translator felt that newer material would either correct Krause or supplement his statements. These references are indicated by underlined numbers. Krause used an assortment of geographical names, which in the translation have been checked with available gazetteers and brought up to date as accurately as possible.

It is a great satisfaction to bring this useful item in the literature of the Northwest Coast to a greater number of readers through translation and reprinting. Grateful acknowledgment is made here for the assistance given by the Research Fund of the Graduate School of the University of Washington for the typing of the final manuscript, and to the American Ethnological Society for its interest in making this valuable publication available to the scientific community.

University of Washington   Erna Gunther
Seattle
September 22, 1955

Contents

Illustrations

FIGURES

THE TLINGIT INDIANS

Introduction: The Journey

The Geographical Society of Bremen, which was formerly the German organization for polar exploration, set as a task for itself the direction of research expeditions for the expansion of geographic knowledge. Under this program they promoted through voluntary contributions from people in every walk of life, the first German Arctic expedition to East Greenland (1869-1870). Under the auspices of the society also, Dr. Finsch and Dr. A. Brehm went on a scientific expedition to western Siberia in 1876, the results of which were published by the former in a special travel account. As the goal of a third research expedition, it was decided to continue the Society's earlier work and further develop that done by Nordenskiold on the Chukchee Peninsula where he wintered from 1878 to 1879, and to follow the coastline of Bering Strait. My brother and I were honored by being asked to undertake this project.

The most certain and quickest way to reach the Tschuktschen (Chukchee) Peninsula seemed to be by way of San Francisco, since numerous whalers and trading vessels leave from there every year for Bering Strait, and thence to the Arctic Ocean. So San Francisco was chosen as the starting place for our expedition. After we had spent two days in Washington and enjoyed the most gracious hospitality and advice of Messrs. Baird, Bessel, Dall and Kennan, we arrived in San Francisco, May 5, 1881, four weeks after our departure from Europe. Thanks to our letters of introduction we received a friendly welcome. Unfortunately it developed that most of the shipping facilities on which we had counted were no longer available. We had to content ourselves with finding passage on a small vessel, a bark of 200 tons which took on oil and whalebone from the whaling vessels before they started into the Arctic Ocean for their late summer fishing season, and on this we made the trip north on the Pacific Ocean to the shores of Bering Strait. In addition to our equipment, we had a whaleboat with us and also a German-Russian sailor who, serving us as boatman and general helper, rendered excellent service and was thoroughly worthy of our trust.

The journey lasted eight weeks--a trip which under more favorable conditions could have been made in half the time. But calm and adverse winds, together with the small amount of sail were great handicaps, and, at the advanced season of the year, proved very uncomfortable.

After the first glimpse of the Asiatic continent at Cape Tschaplin[1] (Chaplin), the southeastern tip of the Chukchee Peninsula on the fourth of August, we landed at last on the sixth of August in St. Lawrence Bay. [2] Here we left the ship with our whaleboat to spend the next eight weeks in a nomadic life on the shores of the Chukchee Peninsula. Our experiences during this time have been recorded and sent to the Bremen Geographical Society and published in German geographical journals. Since they can be referred to, I will give here only briefly the most important occurrences of our stay on Bering Strait. First we succeeded in defining more exactly than heretofore the contours of East Cape, the eastern tip of the Old World, and in correcting errors which occur both on Russian and American maps. We also reached conclusions about the natives of the peninsula and their relations to the Reindeer Chukchee on the one hand and the Eskimos on the other, a chronic matter of dispute, which may now be brought to a satisfactory solution. Finally, in spite of our short stay and unfavorable conditions, we gathered an important collection of natural history specimens, especially plants and lower marine forms.

The thought of wintering on the Chukchee Peninsula was given up after the experiences we had and the information we secured, for the risks involved were not worth taking for our purposes. Therefore we decided to visit American Alaska since that was included in our instructions from the Society. Our attention was especially directed toward the southeastern portion, the territory of the Tlingit Indians. But, in order to get there, because of lack of transportation to other points on the American coast, we had to return to San Francisco. On the schooner Golden Fleece, which had just taken an American meteorological expedition to Point Barrow, we began our return journey from Bering Strait, which compared to the trip out was accomplished in a short time, only four weeks. On the fifth of November we arrived in San Francisco.

Arranging and shipping our collections took several days and then we equipped ourselves for the new trip north. Mr. Paul Schulze of Portland, the president of the Northwest Trading Company, a newly formed firm, invited us to spend the winter at one of their establishments in Tlingit territory, namely at Tschilkut[3] (Chilkoot) at the north end of Lynn Canal; and since this proposal offered us an opportunity to become acquainted with one of the most powerful Tlingit tribes, the Tschilkats[4] (Chilkat), the tribe

which has had the least contact with the whites, we accepted it
gratefully.

So we went from San Francisco to Portland where, through conversation with Mr. Schulze, we endeavored to inform ourselves
as fully as possible about conditions in Alaska. A steamer left
monthly from Portland to southeastern Alaska and we took it on
December 3, 1881. After a successful passage across the dangerous bar at the mouth of the Columbia River and past Cape
Flattery, at the entrance of the Strait of Juan de Fuca, we reached
Port Townsend, a flourishing town at the entrance of Puget Sound,
from which the steamer took us in a six-hour crossing to Vancouver Island and brought us to Victoria, the principal port of
British Columbia.

After many days of interesting sailing through narrow channels,
between countless heavily wooded islands which line the coast of
British Columbia, we arrived at Fort Wrangell, Alaska, on December 11, 1881, and there saw our first Tlingit Indians. The
next day we reached Sitka and then through the narrow Peril
Straits the journey continued to the recently established gold-
mining town of Harrisburg[5] which we reached December 15.
Here we left the vessel and proceeded toward our goal, the trading post Chilkoot, in our own boat. This trip, made in the company of a white man, his Indian wife and two other Indians, took
six days. Everywhere the ground was covered with several feet
of snow so that each evening when we were cold and soaked
through, we had to clear away enough snow to make camp before
we could enjoy the welcome warmth of a fire. On December 23
we fortunately arrived at the station where we prepared ourselves for an extended stay. The only white people we found
there were Willard, a missionary, and his wife, and Dickinson,
the trader in whose house we received a friendly welcome. Since
the Indians settled near the station spoke only broken English, it
was very important for us to have as interpreter and teacher, the
services of the trader's wife, a Tsimshian woman, who had been
educated in an English mission school and during her long stay
among the Tlingit had also learned their language fluently. This
woman had also lived for some time among the Haida and later
was active in missionary work at Fort Wrangell. Now at Chilkoot,
in addition to her housewifely duties, she taught at the mission
school. She was thoroughly conversant with the conditions of the
Indian population of the Northwest Coast from Yakutat Bay southward to Vancouver Island. We obtained information from her regarding the behavior, customs and traditions, especially the divisions of tribes and clans. In spite of her Christian education she
remained native to such a degree that she actively participated in
the affairs of the surrounding Indians and had a complete understanding of them, while her husband whom, by the way, she dom-

3

inated and psychologically overruled, regarded everything Indian
with contempt. Under these circumstances the trading station at
Chilkoot offered us the most favorable conditions for studying the
Tlingit people. During our joint winter stay we observed the Indians at their household tasks, attended their feasts and ceremonies, and became acquainted on short and long excursions with all
the settlements of the Chilkat tribe. We were somewhat restricted in our activities by the exceptional intensity and long duration
of the winter season, 1881-1882, when severe storms and days of
snowfall made communication difficult and even entirely impossible.

We were entirely cut off from the outside world for three and
one-half months until at last on April 5 a small steamer, the
Favorite, brought news from the civilized world. On that same
steamer I began my journey southward while my brother remained behind for a longer stay. The Favorite brought me to Gaudekan[6] on the northern shore of Tschitschagow (Chichagof) Island,
the principal village of the Huna. Here a mission station had also
been founded and on the invitation of Mr. Styles, the missionary,
I stayed for a few days in order to become acquainted with the
Huna tribe.

With the beginning of spring, the Huna were just in the process
of migrating to their hunting and fishing territories. Since that
ends the effectiveness of the missionary's work, he had decided
to go to Sitka for the summer months, which gave me an opportunity to continue my journey in his company. After we had engaged
a canoe and three Indians we went to Killisnu (Killisnoo) in Chatham Strait which we reached after a three-day canoe trip. Here
the Northwest Trading Company was just building a fish reduction
plant and so offered the Indians an opportunity for securing some
profitable employment. While I spent several days with Mr. Spuhn,
a countryman of mine, who, as an agent of the company, directed
the work, I had an opportunity to visit and acquaint myself with
the Chutsinus[7] tribe and their head village, Angun (Angoon), not
far from the station. While I stayed at Killisnoo I also had the interesting experience of seeing a whale, which had been killed with
a bomb, brought in and cut up to extract the oil.

A two-day canoe trip brought me from Killisnoo to Sitka. We
cut across Chatham Strait, famous for its high waves, in favorable weather and went into narrow Peril Strait whose dangerous
riptide we successfully traversed through the expert guidance of
our Indian companion. On April 26 I reached Sitka where along
the forest's edge there was still snow several feet deep, even
though in the town and its immediate vicinity it was cleared away.
I found a friendly welcome from the signal officer, Mr. McClean,
who had his home and station in the old Russian castle which Baranow (Baranof) had built high on a rock that overlooks Sitka. Fre-

quent visits to the nearby Indian village of the Sitka tribe acquainted me with them, and I also undertook more extensive trips from Sitka to Redoute, [8] to the hot sulphur springs and to Krusow Island. [9] Finally my stay in Sitka was especially valuable because I had an opportunity to glance through the large collection of new American books on Alaska which belonged to the customs officer, Mr. William Gouverneur Morris.

On May 13 I continued my journey south on the mail boat. In Chlowak (Klawak) [10] on the west coast of Prince of Wales Island, the first stop of the steamer, I gathered a few notes on the Hennega (Henya) [11] tribe; Wrangell was touched only briefly this time, but the steamer stopped longer at Kasan Bay where the inhabitants are Haida, the southern neighbors of the Tlingit.

On May 18 I left the mail boat at Departure Bay on the east coast of Vancouver Island in order to go on local boats to Victoria and thence through Puget Sound to Portland. After a brief stay I started my trip to San Francisco. For my journey to New York I chose the water route by way of Panama in order to have a glimpse of the tropical world. On July 27 I reached Bremen on the Donau after having been away from Europe fifteen months.

Meanwhile my brother spent the larger part of the summer, making natural history collections and carrying on geographical research. Of the longer trips which he took during this time the most important ones were those where he accompanied the Indians on their grease trails over the coastal mountains into the valley of the Yukon. The first of these he started in the company of two young Indians, on May 28 when the snow had not yet completely melted. After going to the north end of Deje Inlet [12] by canoe, he climbed into the valley of a rushing river that flows from the summit of the pass which he reached on May 28 after a steep climb under unfavorable snow conditions. A quick descent brought him to the shores of a small lake [13] whose outlet flows into the Yukon and following a chain of lakes which still could be crossed on the ice, he came to the first of the larger Yukon lakes, called Schutluchroa by the Indians, which Schwatka, a year later, going the same way to the Yukon named in honor of the secretary of the Bremen Geographical Society, Lindeman Lake. [14] Since this lake was also still covered with ice, my brother could not carry out his plan of going to the next settlements of the Gunanas [15] by canoe and had to content himself with finding a few camp sites which indeed proved very difficult on account of the adverse weather conditions. On the shores of Lindeman Lake he met a party of American gold miners who had just come the same way and were busy building two boats which they planned to use on the trip downstream.

On the first of June my brother started on the return trip. He accomplished the crossing of the pass and the difficult descent to

Chilkoot Inlet again under very severe weather conditions, rain and snow, as on the outward trip, but he reached the station on June 5 in good health. While crossing the coast range to the Yukon had been done before by prospectors, my brother was the first scientific traveler to pass this way and render an exact description and sketch maps of it. He started a second trip into the interior through entirely unknown territory on trails never before trod by a white man. On June 17 he left the station and started up the Chilkat River to the Chilkat village of Klokwan (Klukwan)[16] where he found comfortable quarters with the Chilkat chief, Tschartritsch, who sheltered us during the winter. From here he went out with two Indians whom he took as guide and packer into the valley of the Chilkat River and up its right tributary, the Tlehini,[17] to the high tundra which in contrast to the wild, almost impenetrable thicket in the valleys offered no hindrance beyond the numerous icy mountain streams which had to be forded at hip depth. On June 25 my brother reached the divide of the waters which flow to the Altsech[18] and those that flow into the Yukon. Unfortunately the illness of one of his Indian companions, the young son of Tschartritsch, forced him to turn back after he was within sight of Kussooa,[19] the largest lake through which the western source of the Yukon flows, and alone, while the Indians stayed behind, he followed beyond this lake for a short distance to the rushing waters of the Ssergoit.[20] The return was accomplished without delay and on July 2 they reached the station.

For further study of the geographic conditions in the headwaters of the Yukon, my brother planned one more long trip which would take him from the eastern to the western branch. Unfortunately these plans were spoiled right at the beginning because the Indians became discouraged with the weather and refused to go any further even before they came to the end of Chilkoot Inlet. Another misfortune brought the trip to the Alsek to an early end, when an Indian packer cut himself on the knee and the difficult climb into Klehini Valley could not be attempted.

On these trips, as well as on shorter excursions from the station, my brother directed his attention mainly to the collection of natural history materials; the herbarium which he gathered in the course of the summer consisted of five hundred specimens. The constant contact with the Indians moreover made him familiar with their customs and language, so that for the forthcoming description of the Tlingit tribe he could use whatever observations we made during our joint stay the preceding winter.

On August 6 my brother left the station and proceeded south. After a three-day canoe trip he reached Juneau where, during an eight-day wait for the mail boat, he observed life in the little mining town and the operation of the mine. Fron Juneau the steamer took him to Taku Bay at the foot of the mighty glaciers, then to Wrangell, Klawak and Kasan Bay. Fron Port Townsend, where he arrived on September 24, my brother went by way of Puget Sound to Portland. From there he followed the route of the still unfinished Northern Pacific Railroad where he did a stretch of about five hundred English miles in a stagecoach. On October 21 he left New York on the Oder which brought him to Bremen on November 2.

The following is a list of the published reports and accounts rendered by us both of our journeys:

1. The Scientific Expedition of the Geographical Society of Bremen to the Coastal Region of Bering Strait (Travel letters of the Krause Brothers). (Die wissenschaftliche Expedition der Bremer geographischen Gesellschaft nach den Küstengebieten der Bering-Strasse (Reisebriefe der Gebr. Dr. Krause) in "Deutsche Geographische Blätter," Jahrg. IV, Nr. 15, S. 245 bis 281, Bremen, 1881.)

2. The Scientific Expedition of the Geographical Society of Bremen to the Chukchee Peninsula. Summer 1881. Travel letters of the Krause Brothers. I, (With seven woodcuts). (Die wissenschaftliche Expedition der Bremer geographischien Gesellschaft nach der Tschuktschen-Halbinsel. Sommer 1881. Reisebriefe der Gebr. Dr. Krause. I. (Mit sieben Holzschnitten).Ebenda. Jahrgang V, Nr. 1, S. 1 bis 35. Bremen, 1882.)

3. The Expedition of the Bremen Geographical Society to the Chukchee Peninsula and Alaska. Travel letters of the Krause brothers. II. With maps, four cartoons and one woodcut. (Boat trips along the coast. Trip to St. Lawrence Island and return voyage to San Francisco. From San Francisco to Chilcoot). (Die Expedition der Bremer geographischen Gesellschaft nach der Tschuktschen-Halbinsel und Alaska. Reisebriefe der Gebr. Dr. Krause. II. Mit Karte, vier Cartons und einem Holzschnitt. (Bootreisen langs der Küste. Fahrt nach der Lorenz-Insel. Rückkehr nach San Franzisco. Von San Franzisco nach Chilkoot). Ebenda. Nr. 5, S. 111 bis 154.)

4. The Expedition of the Bremen Geographical Society to the Chukchee Peninsula and Alaska, 1881-1882. Travel letters of the Krause Brothers III. (Die Expedition der Bremer geographische Gesellschaft nach der Tschuktschen-Halbinsel und Alaska, 1881 bis 1882. Reisebriefe der Gebr. Dr. Krause. III.)

    1. Winter trip out of Chilcoot. (Winterausflüge von Chilcoot aus. Von Dr. Arthur Krause; ebenda S. 177 bis 189.)

    2. Spring trips out of Chilcoot. (Frühjahrsausflüge von

Chilcoot aus. Von Dr. Arthur Krause; ebenda S. 189
bis 202.)

3. From Chilcoot to Portland. Spring 1882. (Von Chilcoot
nach Portland, Frühjahr 1882. Von Dr. Aurel Krause;
ebenda S. 202 bis 223.)

5. The Expedition of the Bremen Geographical Society to the
Chukchee Peninsula and Alaska. 1881 to 1882. Travel letters of Dr. Arthur Krause IV. With two maps (sketches of
the trail from Deschu to the west side of Kusawa and
sketches of the trail from Deschu to the lakes of the Yukon
and the east side of Kusawa). (Die Expedition der Bremer
geographischen Gesellschaft nach der Tschuktschen-Halbinsel und Alaska. 1881 bis 1882. Reisebriefe des Dr.
Arthur Krause. IV. Mit zwei Karten (Skizze des Weges von
Deschu bis zum westlichen Kussooa und Skizze des Weges
von Deschu nach den Seen des Yukon und zum östlichen
Kussooa) von Dr. Arthur Krause; ebenda, S. 308 bis 326.)

6. A new way across North America. (Autumn 1882). By Dr.
Arthur Krause. With a map (Northern Pacific Railroad)
(Ein neuer Weg durch Nordamerika. (Herbst 1882). Von
Dr. Arthur Krause. Mit einer Karte (Nord-Pacific-Eisen-
bahn). Dtsch. geogr, Bl. Bd. VI, S. 1 bis 20.)

7. The Condition of the Population of the Chukchee Peninsula.
(Die Bevölkerungsverhältnisse der Tschuktschen-Halbinsel.
Von Dr. Aurel Krause, mit Karte; ebenda S. 248 bis 278.)

8. The Villages of the Tlingit Indians. By Dr. Arthur Krause.
With five sketches based on drawings by the author. (Ueber
die Dörfer der Tlinkit-Indianer. Von Dr. Arthur Krause.
Mit fünf Skizze nach Zeichnungen der Verfassers. Ebenda,
S. 334 bis 347.)

9. The Tlingit Indians of Southeastern Alaska. Lecture by Dr.
Aurel Krause. (Die Tlinkiten des südöstlichen Alaska, Vortrag von Dr. Aurel Krause. Verhandelungen der Gesellschaft für Erdkunde zu Berlin. Bd. IX, S. 489 bis 500.)

10. Travels in southern Alaska. Lecture by Dr. Arthur Krause.
(Reisen im südlichen Alaska. Vortrag von Dr. Arthur
Krause; ebenda, Bd. X, S. 284 bis 285.)

11. The Bremen Expedition to the Chukchee Peninsula. (Die
Bremer Expedition nach der Tschuktschen-Halbinsel. Von
Dr. Aurel Krause. Globus, Bd. XLIII, S. 107 bis 110 und
118 bis 120.)

12. The Tlingit. (Die Tlinkit. Von Dr. Aurel Krause. Globus,
Bd. XLIII, n. 14 und 15.)

13. The Villages of the Tlingit Indians. Lecture by Dr. Arthur
Krause. (Ueber die Dörfer der Tlinkit-Indianer. Vortrag
von Dr. Arthur Krause. Verhandelungen der. Berl.
Anthrop. Ges. 1883, S. 205 bis 208.)

14. The Condition of the Population of the Chukchee Peninsula. Lecture by Dr. Aurel Krause. (Ueber die Bevölkerungsver-hältnisse der Tschultschen-Halbinsel. Vortrag von Dr. Aurel Krause; ebenda S. 224 bis 227.)

15. Fishing, Hunting and Trade among the Tlingit Indians. Lecture by Dr. Aurel Krause. (Ueber Fischfang, Jagd und Handel bei den Tlinkit-Indianern. Vortrag von Dr. Aurel Krause; Verh, d. Berl. Anthrop. Ges. 1884, S. 232 bis 234.)

16. The Chilcat District in Alaska. (Das Chilcat-Gebiet in Alaska. Von Dr. Arthur Krause. Zeitschr. d. Ges. f. Erdkunde zu Berlin. Bd. XVIII, S. 344 bis 368. (Hierzu eine Karte Taf. IX.)

The collections we assembled have only been studied to a very slight degree. The following publications about them have appeared up to the present:

1. Catalog of Ethnological Specimens from the Chukchee area and Southeastern Alaska. Collected by Drs. Arthur and Aurel Krause during 1881-1882. (Katalog ethnologischer Gegenstände aus dem Tschuktschen-Lande und dem südöstlichen Alaska. Gesammelt von den Gebrüdern Dr. Dr. Arthur und Aurel Krause in den Jahren 1881 bis 1882. Anlage zu Heft 4, Bd. V d. dtsch. geogr. Bl. S. 1 bis 16.)

2. F. Kurtz, The collection of plants from the Chukchee Peninsula made by Drs. Arthur and Aurel Krause. (F. Kurtz; Ueber die von den Doktoren Aurel und Arthur Krause von der Tschuktschen-Halbinsel mitgebrachte Pflanzen-sammlungen. Dtsch. geogr. Bl. Bd. V, S. 326 bis 327.)

3. W. Peters, A New Kind of Lagomys from the Chukchee Peninsula. (W. Peters; Ueber eine neue Art von Lagomys von der Tschuktschen-Halbinsel. Sitzungsbericht der Ges. naturforschender Freunde, 1882, S. 95 bis 96.)

4. v. Martens, On some of the Mollusks collected by the Krause brothers on their return voyage. (v. Martens; Ueber einige von den Gebr. Krause auf der Rückreise gesammelten Conchylien; ebenda, S. 138 bis 143.)

5. Aurel Krause, Several land snails from the Chukchee Peninsula and Southeastern Alaska. (Aurel Krause; Ueber einige Landschnecken von der Tschultschen-Halbinsel und aus dem südlichen Alaska. Sitzungsber. d. Ges. naturf. Freunde zu Berlin, 1883, S. 31 bis 37.)

6. Reinhard, Varieties of Pupilla or Vertigo, Hyalina or Marginella and Vallonia collected by the Krause brothers on their journey. (Reinhard; Ueber die von den Herren Gebr. Krause auf ihrer Reise gesammelten Pupa-, Hyalina- und

Vallonia-Arten; ebenda, S. 37 bis 43.)

7. Arthur Krause, The deposits near Bering Strait. (Arthur Krause; Ueber quartäre Ablagerungen an der Bering-Strasse. Sitzungsber. d. Ges. naturf. Freunde zu Berlin, 1884, S. 14 bis 16.)

8. G. Hartlaub, Contribution to the Ornithology of Alaska. Based on collections and notes by Dr. Arthur Krause and Dr. Aurel Krause. (G. Hartlaub; Beitrag zur Ornithologie von Alaska. Nach Sammlungen und Noten von Dr. Arthur Krause und Dr. Aurel Krause. Cabanis Journal für Ornithologie, Jahrgang 1883, S. 257 bis 286.)

9. Carl Müller, Chukchee Mushrooms. (Carl Müller; Musci Tschuctschici. Botanisches Central-blatt. Bd. XVI, 1883, S. 1 bis 17.)

10. A. B. Meyer, Nephrite and similar material from Alaska. (A. B. Meyer; Ueber Nephrit und ähnliches Material aus Alaska. XXI. Jahresbericht des Vereins für Erdkunde zu Dresden (1884), S. 1 bis 21.)

11. Ferdinand Richters, Contribution to the crustaceans of Bering Sea. With one plate. (Ferdinand Richters; Beitrag zur Crustaceenfauna des Berings-Meeres. Mit einer Tafel. Abhandelungen der Senckenbergischen naturforschenden Gesellschaft. Frankfurt a. M. 1884, S. 1 bis 6.)

12. Arzruni, Several minerals from Alaska. (Arzruni; Ueber einige Mineralien aus Alaska. Schlesische Ges. für vater-ländische Kultur. Sitzung der naturwissensch. Sektion vom 14 Nov. 1883.)

13. S. A. Poppe, The free-living copepods of the northern Pacific Ocean and Bering Sea collected by Drs. Arthur and Aurel Krause. (S. A. Poppe; Ueber die von den Herren Dr. Arthur und Aurel Krause im nördlichen Stillen Ozean und Berings-Meer gesammelten freilebenden Copepoden. Archiv f. Naturgeschichte. L. Jahrg., 1. Bd. S. 281 bis 304, Taf. XX bis XXIV.)

14. Kirchenpauer, Northern species and varieties of Sertular-ids. (Kirchenpauer; Nordische Gattungen und Arten von Sertulariden. Abhandlungen des naturwissenschaftlichen Vereins in Hamburg. Bd. VIII, Abt. 1. 1884, S. 1 bis 54, Taf. XI bix XVI. (Mit Benutzung älterer Sammlungen, namentlich derjenigen Stellers.)

15. Arthur Krause, Contribution to the Molluscan forms of Bering Sea. (Arthur Krause; Beitrag zur Mollusken-Fauna des Bering-Meeres. Archiv f. Naturgeschichte 1885 (Im Erscheinen.))

1. Historical Survey

Period of expeditions of discovery, 1558 to 1794; Francisco Gali. Apocryphal journeys of Ferrer de Maldonado, Juan de Fuca and De Fonte. --Third large expedition to Kamchatka in 1741; Bering and Tschirikow (Chirikof), [1] the report of Steller. --Spanish, English and French expeditions of discovery 1774 to 1786, Juan Perez, Bodega, Cook, LaPerouse. Trips of the fur traders 1786 to 1790, Meares, Dixon, Portlock, Douglas, Gray, Marchand. -- New expeditions of the Spaniards, 1788 to 1791, Martinez, Fidalgo and Malaspina.

Vancouver's claim to the Northwest Coast, 1792 to 1794. Period of Russian rule: growth of the Russian-American Company, Schelechow (Shelikof) and Baranow (Baranof), founding of the settlements at Yakutat Bay and Sitka Bay. --Attacks of the Tlingit; founding of New Archangel after the conquest of the Sitkas. Uncertain relationship between the Russians and the Tlingit. -- Changes of administration after the death of Baranof. -- Condition of the colony according to the reports of Lütke and Wrangell. --The priest Weniaminow (Veniaminof). The smallpox epidemic of 1836. --Fair in New Archangel for the Tlingit. --Forty Stakhins (Stikines) killed. Uprising of the Sitkas in 1855. --Golowin's report.

Period of American domination; attitude of the Tlingit at the change of government. --Vacillating politics of the Americans. --Industrial enterprises.

As early as 1582 Francisco Gali (Franz Gualle)[2] is supposed to have touched the Northwest coast on a trip from Macoa to Acapulco. He had been commissioned by the King of Spain to investigate the truth of the statement that there was a passage to the east and north of Japan through which the Pacific joined the ocean

11

north of Asia. Gali reached the American shores at 57° 30' and admired the beauty of the majestic mountains whose peaks were covered with eternal snow while their bases were adorned with beautiful vegetation. It seems that he had no contact with the natives. Judging from the currents he decided that there must certainly be a canal or strait between New Spain and Tartary or Asia.[3]

After this expedition of Gali's it seems that the Spaniards made no attempt to press northward from their American possessions for almost two hundred years. The gap was filled by fantastic accounts of extensive voyages which are mentioned here only because they stimulated the great undertakings at the end of the eighteenth century.

In 1588 a Portuguese, Lorenzo Ferrer de Maldonado, claims he sailed from the Atlantic Ocean through the Strait of Anian into the "Great Ocean" (Pacific ?).

The year 1592 is assigned to the mythical voyage of the Greek pilot John or Juan de Fuca who came into a broad arm of the sea between 47° and and 48° latitude that led him into an extensive body of water where he sailed for twenty days.

Finally in 1640 the Spanish admiral de Fonte, de Fonta or de Fuentes, is supposed to have sailed along an archipelago which he named St. Lazarus, two hundred sixty leguas[4] wide with many winding channels, and on June 14 he came to a river which he named Rio de los Reyes.[5] This led him into an inland sea from which he traveled by boat along another river to a body of water that was visited by ships from the Atlantic Ocean.

The first definite accounts of the coast inhabited by the Tlingit, the Northwest Coast of America between 54° and 60° north latitude, came in 1741. In that year the so-called third great Kamchatka expedition under the command of the Dane, Vitus Bering, was organized with exploration of the American continent as its goal. On the 15/4 of June, 1741,[6] Bering left Awatscha (Avacha) Bay[7] on the coast of Kamchatka in the ship St. Peter, with his companion, Chirikof, in the St. Paul. In a storm on July 1/June 20 the ships were separated. Chirikof reached the American coast first and on July 26/15 he anchored at about 55° latitude. A boat with ten men under the command of the steersman Abraham Dementiew was sent ashore, but never returned; after two days another ten men in a second boat were sent in and they likewise failed to return. Then two fully manned canoes with natives approached crying, "Aga, agai." But when they saw the Russians on the forward deck, standing in readiness to meet them, they hastily rowed back to land and were not seen again. Since Chirikof did not have another boat at his disposal, he had to leave his companions to their fate. On August 7/July 27 he began his homeward journey and on October 20/9 arrived again at Avacha Bay.

12

On the following day, while they were still in the harbor, the astronomer of the expedition, Louis de l'Isle de la Croyère, a brother of the famous geographer, Guillaume de l'Isle de la Croyère, died.

Several days later than Chirikof, on July 29/18, Bering saw land and on July 31/20, St. Elias day of the year 1741, he anchored at about 60° between two capes which he named St. Elias and Hermogenes. [8] However he stayed here only one day, since the advanced season made the ailing commander decide upon a quick return. With difficulty our compatriot, George Wilhelm Steller, the doctor and naturalist on the expedition, obtained permission to go ashore with the water carriers. He used the brief time which he had at his disposal to become acquainted with nature in that long sought for and unknown land. From the interesting report of his discoveries which is included in the published diary of Pallas, I quote the following: "When I had arrived on the island with the protection and help of several Cossacks, I saw how precious time would be, so I bent every effort to do as much as possible quickly. I headed in the direction of the mainland in order to find people and habitations. I had scarcely gone one "werst"[9] from the shore before I found definite signs of inhabitants and their works. I found under a tree an old chopped down trunk, hollowed out like a trough, in which the natives, through lack of pots and pans, had a few hours before cooked meat with red hot stones in Kamchadal fashion, and bones were still lying around which indicated that the meat on them had been roasted on a fire. I looked at the bones carefully and determined that they were not those of a sea but a land animal, and thought that, according to the size and shape, they might be caribou bones, [10] even though this animal is not present on the island and would have to be brought from the mainland. In addition there were pieces of Jukola or dried bits of meat strewn about, similar to those which Kamchatkans use at every meal in place of bread. Also I saw a great mass of shells of the large Jacobs mussel, [11] more than eight inches broad, as well as blue mussels, similar to those found on Kamchatka, so without doubt they were eaten raw here as in Kamchatka. In several shells I found a kind of greens[12] prepared in regular Kamchadal style, arranged as in a dish with water poured over it to draw out the sweetness. Then I discovered a wooden firemaker, of the same workmanship as the ones in Kamchatka, beside a tree, where the fresh coals were still to be seen. The tinder which the Kamchatkans make of some kind of grass was different here, however, and seemed to be a kind of moss (Alga fontinalis) which bleached white in the sun and of which a sample was taken."[13]

From all these observations Steller came to the conclusion that the natives of this coast and the Kamchatkans must be of one origin and, therefore, sees further substantiation for his theory that America in a more northerly latitude must approach Asia much more closely.

In his wanderings he saw here and there felled tree trunks, which had been cut with stone and bone axes, as the many blunt blows indicated; he also saw many trees that had not long before been stripped of their bark. A little footpath led him to a spot covered with cut grass.

He continued:

"I at once removed the grass and found under it a cover of stones; after these had been put aside, we came upon bark which was laid over poles forming a rectangle about three fathoms[14] long and two wide. These covered a pit about two fathoms deep in which were found the following:

1. Wallets or receptacles made of bark, one and one-half "ellen"[15] high which were filled with a smoked fish that was a Kamchatkan variety of salmon, called "sterka" in the Tungus language at Okhotsk, but in Kamchatkan is commonly known as "Krasna ryba" (red fish).

2. A parcel of Slatka Trawa, or a sweet weed of which brandy is made in Kamchatka, well prepared and clean, in fact I have never seen it so well done in Kamchatka, nor did it taste so good.

3. Several kinds of fibers which have been peeled from a bark like flax, which I take to be nettles that grow in profusion here and perhaps are used for fish nets as they are in Kamchatka.

4. Dried inner bark of the larch or fir tree wrapped in rolls and dried, the same which is eaten to ward off starvation, when the need arises, not only in Kamchatka, but through all Siberia, even in Russia as far as Chlynow and on the Wjatka.

5. Large pack straps of seaweed, found by test to be of unusual strength and firmness. [16]

Among other things, I also found several arrows which were so large that they far outmeasured those of Kamchatka and were more like the arrows of the Tungus and Tartars, painted with black stripes and very smooth, considering that one cannot attribute the use of iron tools or knives to them."

Steller furthermore reported that Master (Steersman) Chytrew, who landed with his big boat, found a dwelling built of wood, whose sides were so smooth that they seemed to have been planed with a cutting tool. From this dwelling he brought various souvenirs: a wooden dish similar to those made of linden bark in Russia and used in place of boxes; a stone, which for lack of something better was used as a whetstone and on which streaks of copper were visible, as though the natives here, like the Siberians, formerly used copper for cutting tools; also a hollow ball of hard baked clay about two inches in diameter, with a little stone sealed in it as a rattle, which I considered a plaything for children, and finally a paddle and the tail of a gray-black fox."[17]

It has not been absolutely determined where Bering landed. Formerly it was believed on Vancouver's authority that the landing was made in Yakutat Bay, which was therefore named Bering's Bay by Vancouver. Newer investigations make it much more likely that Bering anchored in the neighborhood of the Copper River near Cape Suckling at Kajak (Kaye) or at Wingham Island.[18] Also there is uncertainty as to the exact part of the coast sighted by Chirikof.[19]

On August 1/July 21 Bering set out to sea again and since he now maintained a more northerly course, he came among various islands, landing on some but not examining them more closely. On August 13 the first man of the crew died and was buried on one of the Schumagin Islands[20] which was named for him. On November 15/4 land was sighted but not, as it was hoped, the coast of Kamchatka, but a desolate rocky island which in honor of the commander was called Bering Island.[21] The seafarers, racked by storm and scurvy decided to winter there; but the anchored ship was beaten to pieces on the rocks and on December 19/8 Bering succumbed to his illness. The rest of the crew however, were saved from starvation by the superabundance of sea mammals and, overcoming the hardships of wintering there, built from the wreckage of the stranded vessel a boat in which they returned to Kamchatka the following year.

So ended an expedition for which years of preparation had been made and into which, for those times, an enormous amount of money had been poured. Its immediate results were meager, but not the consequences. Through the reports which the returning sailors made of the wealth of furs in the newly discovered country, the Russian merchants were encouraged to undertake numerous commercial ventures which left Okhotsk and first were limited to the Aleutians, but later spread from island to island further east to the Alaska peninsula[22] and the neighboring coast of the American mainland. These traders were called promyschlenniks. They risked the dangerous voyage without a compass, in fragile craft, the planks of which were only bound to the ribs and the cracks stuffed with moss, from which they were called "Schitiken" or sewed ships. A trip lasted two to three years.[23] As early as 1761 Puschkarew spent the winter on the shores of the American continent in the false pass at the Alaska peninsula. However before the Russians reached the territory of the Tlingit in this way, voyagers of other nationalities came from the south, but without establishing any lasting relationships with the natives.

The advance of the Russians aroused the jealousy of the Spanish government and, after paying no attention to the coast north of California for almost two centuries, the fear that foreign powers might settle there instigated the dispatching of a string of expeditions which were to seek out the extent of the Russian penetration and establish their own supposed right to be there.

In 1774 Juan Perez was sent out from the harbor of San Blas in the corvette Santiago. [24] He reached the northern tip of the Queen Charlotte Islands and discovered Margarita Island[25] and the passage which separates Prince of Wales Island from the Queen Charlotte Islands. [26] On the return voyage he anchored at the harbor of Nootka on Vancouver Island, which later became so well known through Cook's stay there, and had a number of things stolen by the natives, a circumstance which explains the presence of the European articles found by Cook. After a journey of eight months the traveler returned to the harbor of Monterey.

In 1775 the Spaniards sent out a new expedition of three ships northwards under the command of Captain Bruno Heceta (Hezeta). In a storm the ships were separated and Hezeta returned, but Juan Francisco de la Bodega y Quadra with Maurelle (Mourelle) as pilot continued the journey in his little schooner Sonora. A sad misfortune befell the schooner on July 14, just below 47° latitude. Seven well-armed men who were sent ashore in a boat were killed by the natives when they tried to land. The Indians also acted as though they would take the vessel itself; the whole day they circled around it in great numbers.

Journeying on, the Spaniards saw on August 16 a beautiful, rounded, snow-covered mountain which they named San Jacinto because they saw it on the day of Saint Hyacinth. This is the same mountain which two years later Cook called Mt. Edgecumbe on Kruzof Island near Sitka. The bay to the north was called de Los Remedios[27] by the Spaniards, and the one to the south Guadelupe, now Sitka Sound. The Spaniards landed here in order to claim the land in the customary manner. While doing this, they were surrounded by a mob of natives who seemed more savage and determined than anywhere else on the coast, and with definite ideas about their rights to the land. They forced the Spaniards to pay not only for the fish which they brought but also for the water which they had to get themselves; the cross and other marks of possession were immediately removed as soon as they left in response to signs of disfavor from the natives.

Bodega continued his journey to 58° latitude, but then he had to start his return trip because the crew was weakening through weariness and illness and the winds took on great velocity. During this voyage he explored an extensive bay below 55-1/2° which he called Bucareli Harbor, [28] while the strait between Prince of Wales Island and Cape Margarita, [29] the limit of Perez' investigations, was named Entrada de Perez. [30] On November 20 the voyager returned to San Blas. [31]

Two years later, in 1778, Cook[32] sailed along the same coast to explore the possibility of a northerly passage through to the

Atlantic Ocean, in whose existence some geographers even then still believed on the basis of the mythical voyages of Maldonado, Fuca and de Fonte. Coming from the Sandwich Islands, Cook landed at Nootka Sound on the west coast of Vancouver Island during the end of March; going north from there, he saw, on the first of March, the mountain named San Jacinto by Bodega and which he called Mt. Edgecumbe; on March 3 he discovered Cross Sound and on March 4, Mt. St. Elias. According to his instructions, which directed him to explore the coast at higher latitudes, he attempted no landings; storm and fog prevented him for days from seeing the coastline so that he was not aware of its broken nature. Finally in Prince William Sound and Cook Inlet he began a more detailed study of the American coast.

In 1779 a new Spanish expedition went north to Prince William Sound under Arteaga and Bodega to explore Bucareli Bay more closely. Only very meager reports exist about this voyage, as well as the earlier and later ones, because the Spanish government kept all their discoveries secret on account of petty jealousy. We finally get more detailed accounts, especially about the natives, from La Perouse, who in 1786, coming from the Sandwich Islands (Hawaii), reached the American coast in the neighborhood of Mt. St. Elias, with an expedition outfitted at great cost and with great hopes by Louis XVI, and anchored in the harbor at 58° latitude which he called Port of France, but which is on the maps by the native name Lituja Bay. [33] He stayed here, July 4-30, busy with the repair of his ships and constantly in lively intercourse with the natives, who it seems had never been in contact with white people. In the barter which was organized at once and in which the Indians to the astonishment of La Perouse were very shrewd, iron was the most sought for article. Moreover it was already well known to them, and almost everyone carried an iron dagger in a leather sheath around the neck, and only occasionally was the blade copper, a metal used freely in all kinds of decoration. La Perouse draws a very unfavorable picture of the character and customs of the natives, while he recognizes their spiritual achievements and their skill in art. "Their arts," he said, "are well developed and their civilization has made great progress in this respect, but those traits which refine behavior and soften savagery are still in their infancy. Their mode of life excludes all sense of order, and fear of or desire for revenge makes them constantly uneasy. I have seen them always with a dagger in hand, stand against each other. During the winter they are in fear of starvation if hunting is not successful; while in summer they are in the midst of untold plenty, when in less than an hour more fish can be caught than are needed for their families; at leisure for the rest of the day, they pass the time in gambling for which they have as much liking as some of the inhabitants of our large cities; this is also the great source of their quarrels. I will predict without fear, that these people will destroy themselves if, in addition to all the disturbing factors they already have, they should have the misfortune to learn the use of intoxicating liquor.

"They were ceaselessly around our frigates in their canoes; they lingered three to four hours before they would begin to exchange a few fish or some fish otter skins. They took every opportunity to rob us; they tore iron loose which was easy to take away, and they always tried to see if they could find us off guard at night. I allowed the head men to come aboard my frigate and showered them with presents and even these same people whom I had so honored never missed the chance to steal a nail or an old stocking. Whenever they presented a smiling and ingratiating appearance I was sure that they had stolen something, and very often I acted as though I noticed nothing.

"I gave special orders to caress the children and give them little presents; the parents are usually won over by such signs of good will in all countries; but the only thanks shown by them were that they took the opportunity to rob us while they accompanied their children when we allowed them to come aboard; and for my own benefit I noticed that often, just when we were busy with his own child, the father would secrete under his skin blanket whatever he could lay his hands on. "[34]

The settlements visited by La Perouse seem to have been merely summer camps, closed only on the windward side and furnishing a bare shelter to the Indians who hurried to the bay fishing. He gives a graphic account of the terrible filth of these huts and their surroundings and the lack of sensitivity of the natives about this, as well as their own personal uncleanliness. [35]

During his stay in the harbor La Perouse had the misfortune to lose two of his boats and twenty-one men who, at the entrance of the bay, were pulled into a strong tide and swamped.

On the homeward journey both ships of the expedition, the Astrolabe and the Boussole, ran aground after the commander Delangle and the naturalist Lamanon had met death in a fight with natives. The ships were last seen in Botany Bay; their fate was finally revealed in 1827 through the report of the English Captain Dillon, who found parts of the shattered vessels on Santa Cruz Island. These statements were verified and further remains of the expedition were found by a French party under the command of Dumont d'Urville. According to reports of the natives, the survivors of the shipwreck tried to build another vessel, but all died a natural death before its completion. Only one member returned safely, Jean Baptiste Barthelemy, Baron de Lesseps, who accompanied the expedition as Russian interpreter and returned home overland from Kamchatka with the reports of the commander.

After Cook was killed on February 16, 1779, by a Sandwich islander and his successor, Clerke, who once more pressed forward into the Arctic Ocean through Bering Strait, had died of a chest ailment, Captains Gore and King led the expedition home On the return trip they landed in the harbor of Macao in China where the crew, who had exchanged worthless trinkets with the natives on the North American coast for furs, sold them for high prices to the Chinese. Especially prized were the skins of the sea otter, and this fact caused Captain King, who edited the report of the voyage after his return, to intimate to his countrymen the auspicious possibility of profitable trade. This appeal to English enterprise was not unheeded. Immediately trading companies were founded and in a few years we see ships from China, Calcutta, Bombay, from England itself and even from the young republic, the United States, go to the Northwest Coast of America where they not only followed the tracks of the above mentioned explorers but sought new ways to undiminished abundance of fur-bearing animals and uninflated demands of the natives as a means to greater profits. A whole series of travel accounts give us information about the discoveries of these traders and the geography of Northwestern America was greatly enriched, but one still gets only meager reports about the population; at most a few obvious peculiarities of bodily appearance or costume, as well as their behavior in trading, are mentioned in detail. Generally there are complaints about the greedy character of the northern Indians, their tendency to theft and their overbearing attitude, if they believe themselves to be stronger. Their willingness in the beginning to give valuable furs in return for a few pieces of iron soon gave way to a more selective mood. The choice varied by time and place; here one demanded "Tohis,"[36] others, beads, elsewhere, tin or copper pots, knives, hatchets, or axes. Soon also woolen blankets as articles of trade came into demand, which replaced the skins of which their former clothing consisted.

Following will be listed in chronological order the most important trade voyages of this period, which extended as far north as the Alexander Archipelago:

In 1786 Captains Lowrie and Guise sailed in two vessels, the Cook and the Experiment, from Bombay to Nootka and along the coast to Prince William Sound. The coastline of the Queen Charlotte Islands was first determined by them.

In the same year Captains Meares and Tipping left Calcutta in two ships, the Nutka and the Sea Otter, for the Northwest Coast. After Meares had sailed to the Aleutians, he went through the strait between Kodiak and the mainland [37] to Cook Inlet and thence to Prince William Sound where during a hard winter he lost twenty-three men, half of his crew, from scurvy. In the spring of 1787, he sailed south along the coast. As he approached the coast near Mt. Edgecumbe he was visited by many natives who were distinguished from the inhabitants of Prince William Sound by the use of wooden canoes and peculiar lip ornamentation on the women. From Nootka, Meares returned to Macao by way of the Sandwich Islands, while his companion Tipping, with the Sea Otter disappeared from sight, last being seen in Prince William Sound.

In 1785 there was organized in England the King George's Sound Company, headed by the Etches Brothers, which outfitted two vessels, the Queen Charlotte and the King George, the former under the command of Captain Dixon, the latter under Nathanial Portlock, who was also the leader of the whole expedition. Both men had accompanied Cook on his last voyage. The ships, after sailing around Cape Horn went to the Sandwich Islands, and from there in 1786 to Cook Inlet where they met a hunting party of Kadiak (Kodiak) Indians organized by the Russians. From there they went south to Nootka because adverse winds constantly kept them from running into the coast elsewhere. Much dissatisfied with the results of their voyage, they went to the Sandwich Islands, a favorite wintering place and restocking port for ships cruising in the Pacific since Cook's discovery.

In 1787 both vessels again went north. In Prince William Sound they met the Nutka with Captain Meares and by transfer of fresh food supplies saved them from want. The ships then separated to seek their fortunes independently, Dixon going southwards and landing next at Yakutat Bay (which he called Admiralty Bay). There he put in at a harbor which he named Port Mulgrave, [38] where he saw countless natives in miserable summer camps. Contrary to his expectations he found few skins for trading. After a ten-day stay he discovered that the meager supply which the natives had, was completely exhausted. He had been entirely fooled by the manner in which the Indians bartered. "Four or five people," he said in his report, "come in a conoe to the side of the ship, and wait at least an hour before they give the slightest indication that they have anything to sell. Then by a meaningful shrug of the shoulder or some other sign they indicate that they brought something of value to trade and demand to see what one has to offer them in return before showing their wares. If this trick does not succeed, they bring out their own goods (after long consideration) which consist of a few poor old sea otter skins. And then also much time passes before the bargain is made so that one often needs a whole day to obtain some trifles." [39]

Dixon estimated the number of natives in the bay at about seventy. He found them well built, and one girl, who was persuaded to clean herself of paint and filth, had features that were pretty even according to English standards, except for the lip plug. He

also does not give any pleasant description of their summer
camps. "More miserable huts than their dwellings," he writes,
"one can scarcely imagine. Several poles stuck in the ground
without any order or pattern, enclosed and covered by loose
boards, constitute such a hut, which does not even give protection from the rain and snow. Instead the many chinks and openings in these huts serve to let the smoke escape, for no other
opening is provided. The inside of one of these huts is a complete picture of dirt and filth, indolence and laziness. In one corner are thrown all the bones and other remnants of meals of the
inhabitants, in another lay piles of fish, pieces of rotting meat,
fat, oil, etc."

After Dixon left Port Mulgrave, he landed below the fifty-
seventh parallel in a bay which he called Norfolk Sound.[40] Here
he found the same people he had found in Admiralty Bay (Yakutat
Bay). He estimated their number at four hundred and fifty at most.
Barter was carried on by the natives with a certain formality and
ceremony. Every morning at daybreak they came to the ship and
they spent more than half an hour singing, before starting business. By midday they left the ship in order to eat their meal a-
shore but returned in about one hour. Toward evening when the
trading was finished, songs were started again and at last with
the fall of darkness they left the ship.

On further travel southward, Dixon landed next in a bay at 56-
1/2° latitude without seeing any sign of natives. Not until he
reached the shores of the Queen Charlotte Islands did he meet a
numerous native population again and one which had not been
touched, seemingly, by traders. They had a large supply of sea
otter and beaver skins which they traded easily and quickly. Very
pleased with his transactions, Dixon returned to England by way
of the Sandwich Islands and China.

Meanwhile Captain Portlock, after parting from Dixon, stayed
in Cook Inlet and Prince William Sound until July 25 and then
likewise directed his course southward until below Cross Sound
he found a harbor which he named Portlock Harbor,[41] and where
he stayed at anchor from August 2 to 22. In order to dispel the
mistrust of the natives he had accustomed himself to send a hostage to them ashore, and in return the Indians in groups of two or
more were allowed aboard the ship. He also found the numbers
of natives very small. The frequency of pock-marked faces led
him to believe that smallpox decimated the population, and because no marks were discernible on children under twelve years,
the conclusion might be drawn that the terrible disease was
brought in by the Spaniards who wintered in 1775 in the harbors
of Guadelupe (Sitka Sound) and Salisbury Sound slightly to the
south.

During his stay in Portlock Harbor, Portlock was visited by a

number of natives who came from the northwest. In the usual
greeting ceremony the leader played several roles in each of
which he changed his costume. "Every time this happened,"
writes Portlock, "some of his companions held a mat around him
so that we could not see what was going on. Once he appeared as
a warrior with all the ferocity of an Indian hero. He showed us
how they attack their enemies, how they fight, and how they treat
the conquered. Thereupon he appeared as a woman and to make
the illusion complete, he carried a mask[42] which represented a
feminine face with the customary decoration."[43]

After Portlock had sent a boat expedition into Sitka Sound to determine whether Mt. Edgecumbe was on an island, he went by
way of the Sandwich Islands to China where he met Dixon with
whom he finished the trip to England around the Cape of Good
Hope.

The King George's Sound Company sent two more ships out in
1786, the Prince of Wales under James Colnett and the Princess
Royal under Charles Duncan. These men also had once been
Cook's officers. In 1787 both vessels arrived on the Northwest
Coast of America. Captain Duncan made important geographical
discoveries on the east side of the Queen Charlotte Islands and
there named Princess Royal Island after his ship.

Soon after his return from his first voyage Meares outfitted a
new expedition. For this purpose he became associated with William Douglas and in 1788 the latter in the Iphigenie sailed to
Cook Inlet and Prince William Sound while Meares in the Felice
went to Nootka. On the trip south Douglas went to Cross Sound
where he witnessed the mistreatment suffered by an Indian at the
hands of his wife who considered herself offended. The authority
of wives goes so far, according to his report that no Indian dares
sell a skin until he has secured permission from his wife. [44]

The number of ships engaged in the fur trade on the Northwest
Coast was increased in 1788 by two: the Washington under the
command of Robert Gray and the Columbia under John Kendrick,
outfitted by merchants in Boston the previous year. Later Gray
commanded the Columbia, 1789-1790, the first American boat to
circumnavigate the globe, by way of China back to Boston,
whence he was sent again in four different craft to the Northwest
Coast. The American ships visited stretches of coastline as yet
untouched by Europeans, especially in the Strait of Juan de Fuca
and on the east coast of the Queen Charlotte Islands. In 1791
Gray explored countless bays and straits between 54° and 56°
north latitude, and cruised in one, probably Portland Canal, from
its mouth below 54° north latitude, one hundred English miles
without reaching its head. In one part of this arm of the sea,
which he took to be the Rio de los Reyes of Admiral de Fonte, he
lost his second steersman and two sailors who were murdered by

the natives. [45]

A French boat also took part in the fur trade, the Solide, which under the command of Captain Etienne Marchand, was sent out by the commercial firm of Baux at Marseilles on December 14, 1790. Marchand saw Mt. Edgecumbe on August 7, 1791, and from August 12 to 21 he lay at anchor in Sitka Sound to which he gave the misunderstood native name of Tschinkitane (probably) Tlinkitani, meaning earth; see glossary). The description of the voyage prepared by Fleurier from the diaries of the Captain and Roblet, the ship's doctor, is especially interesting because it discloses how rapidly European wares were diffused among the natives, how demand for them had increased, and how unprofitable the fur trade had become on account of the lack of supply of skins on the part of the natives and also in consequence of the high prices they asked. Good sea otter skins could only be obtained by Marchand in return for pieces of European clothing, and since he was not supplied with these for trading purposes, he had to use the supply carried for the crew.

On the coast of the Queen Charlotte Islands which he visited he also discovered that the English and Americans had gotten ahead of him. After a final unsuccessful attempt in the Fuca Strait (Strait of Juan de Fuca), he came to the conclusion that the coast of America was poorly supplied with furs. In addition he found that in China the market value of sea otter skins had fallen because of the heavy supplies, from seventy Spanish piastres in 1778 to fifteen, so that he decided to take his cargo to Europe with him.

Meanwhile the friendly competition of the nations in the fur trade was disturbed when the Spanish formally took possession of Nootka Sound in 1789 and built a fort there which was then besieged by Meares and three English ships. Three Spanish expeditions, the first under Estevan Martinez and Gonzalo Haro, 1788-1789, [46] the second under Salvador Fidalgo, 1790, [47] and the third under Alessandro Malaspina in the Atrevida, 1791, were sent north to Prince William Sound and Cook Inlet to come to an agreement with the Russians on their claims to the same territory. For the advancement of geographical knowledge, the last expedition only left a contribution, in that Malaspina examined the coast between Prince William Sound and Mt. Fairweather, entering, specifically, Admiralty Bay (Yakutat Bay), [48] where below 60° latitude, according to a report signed by Maldonado, there was to be found the entrance to the Straits of Anian, the long-sought-for passage between the Atlantic and the Great Ocean. After his return to Spain, Malaspina fell into disfavor with Minister Godoy, and for six years the notable seafarer languished in prison, being finally freed through the intercession of Napoleon. His ship's log was not published except for a short excerpt which was given without mentioning his name, in the introduction of the travel accounts of the Sutil y Mexicana. [49] Finally in 1849 his diary was included in a collection of unpublished documents issued by Salva and Baranda. One finds in this an extensive description of the Yakutat with whom, during his stay in Yakutat Bay, Malaspina established friendly relations which were threatened only once by a theft. Malaspina received favorable impressions of the moral standards and industrial capabilities of these natives; among their industrial achievements, their canoes and woven blankets aroused his astonishment.

The previously mentioned show of power on the part of the Spaniards, claiming the Northwest Coast to Prince William Sound, was not quietly accepted in England. Satisfaction and damages were claimed and preparations were made for war, when at last in 1790 a convention was called in which the Spaniards pledged the restitution of English possessions and freedom of trade on the coast. To settle the remaining differences and to continue the investigations begun by Cook on the Northwest Coast, an expedition was sent out under Vancouver, an astute protégé of Cook, who sailed from England in 1791 and arrived in the area the following year. Vancouver's accurate observations on the coast north from the Strait of Juan de Fuca to Cook Inlet still stand today as the foundation of modern cartography. As with Cook, one must admire in Vancouver, beside his skill as a seafarer and his courage as an explorer, his alertness and powers of observation. The account of his voyages, which unfortunately he did not live to see published, since he died in May 1798, bears witness to his powers of observation. Like Cook he showed constant interest in the savage population and since he was the first to penetrate the tortuous straits of the Alexander Archipelago, or at least had them explored by boat expeditions, his observations on the natives of this region are of special interest. In the following pages we will often have recourse to them, so at this point only a brief reference to his investigations in 1792-94 will be made.

In 1792 Vancouver in the Discovery and his companion, Broughton, in the Chatham explored the Strait of Juan de Fuca and Puget Sound, after which they went through the Gulf of Georgia and Queen Charlotte Sound back to Nootka, having circumnavigated the island named for him. From Nootka Sound he sailed south to Monterey, everywhere noting carefully the position of points of importance, while Broughton in the same year explored more closely the mouth of the Columbia River discovered by Gray. After Vancouver had finished his dealings with the Spanish plenipotentiary, Bodega y Quadra, and had sent Broughton to Europe, he betook himself to the Sandwich Islands in order that in the spring of 1793 he might continue his work on the American coast.

In that year he explored the coast from 52° to 54° latitude and re-
turned by way of the west coast of the Queen Charlotte Islands to
California where for the second time he set sail for the Sandwich
Islands.

In the summer of 1794 he went north to Cook River which he
changed to Cook Inlet and to Prince William Sound. In Cook Inlet
he met the Russians of whom he said that they lived in the same
way as the Indians only that they did not imitate their artistic
decorations. Furthermore he obtained the impression that they
were on good terms with the natives and that the latter were quite
satisfied with their subjection to the Russians. [50] From there he
sailed in the Discovery to Cross Sound while Puget in the Chatham undertook a careful examination of the coastline, especially
of Yakutat Bay. On July 7 Vancouver went into Cross Sound and
anchored at Port Althrop. [51] After his officer, Lieut. Whidbey,
had explored Lynn Canal and Chatham Strait in a sixteen-day
boat expedition, he sailed along the west coast of the archipelago
to Port Conclusion below 56° 15' north latitude, [52] where the
great undertaking was completed by two other boat expeditions
under Whidbey and Johnston who between August 2 and 19 explored Prince Frederick Sound[53] and Stephens Passage.

The relations which Vancouver had with the natives were not
always of a friendly nature. Even though the large vessels never
experienced open hostilities on the part of the Indians, the leaders of the boat expeditions had to be on their guard whenever they
saw themselves outnumbered. Through the wisdom and discretion
of the leader, it was possible to avoid bloodshed in large proportions, but Vancouver mentions in his account the fact that often
firearms seen in the possession of the natives who knew how to
use them made him realize that he did this work just in time, for
several years later, when the Indians had been more widely supplied with weapons by the traders, his defense would not have
been adequate.

Vancouver was convinced of the unreliable and treacherous
dealings of the natives as soon as he went beyond the 55th parallel north latitude. When he undertook the exploration of Portland
Canal in a boat expedition, on July 27, 1793, he met fifteen Indians in two boats who had a more savage appearance than anything
he had yet seen. Their faces were painted red, white and black
and this heightened their ugliness. "I offered them," said Vancouver, "such presents as I was accustomed to give in these circumstances, but they were refused by several with disdain and
accepted by a few with a cold unrelenting attitude. In the company
was a woman who was further disfigured with the astonishing lip
plug which served to accentuate her sullen and ugly face. I offered her a mirror and other trifles, but at the prompting of the
wildest young man in the group, she refused them. This Indian

then laid his spears, six or eight of them, so that the points just protruded beyond the prow of the canoe and beside himself he put his bow and several arrows; then he put on his armor and drew his dagger."[54] This time Vancouver was successful in pacifying these Indians, but several days later on August 12, on the west coast of Revilla Gigedo Island he saved himself only by the timely use of firearms after two of his men were wounded by Indian spears. On this occasion the natives made a show of friendliness, until, when they found themselves in the majority, they turned to open theft and violence. Again, it was an old woman with a large lip plug who incited her companions and seems to have had the strongest influence over them.[55]

When Vancouver stayed the following year in Cross Sound, he also had to resort to hostages in order to allay the suspicion of the Indians, for only then did they dare come aboard his vessel where they behaved themselves well, after, however, several attempts at theft were drastically punished.

In Lynn Canal Lieut. Whidbey again experienced the treachery of the natives. According to the Indians, eight important chiefs lived at the upper end of the canal. One of them, described as a tall, lean, older man, who was dressed more gorgeously and tastefully than any other chief on the Northwest Coast and who also was very conscious of his importance, met Whidbey as he was turning southwards after finishing his observations and indicated the friendliest feeling toward him. On the following day, however, July 17, his conduct and that of his followers was quite different. After new arrivals had increased their number to two hundred warriors, they seemed to want to attack openly and plunder the boats, and only the cautious, careful procedure at the right time on Whidbey's part prevented the success of their plan. One chief was especially aggressive with his large, well manned canoe that was equipped not only with spears but also with seven rifles and several blunderbusses, all of which were in the best condition. "He moved forward and shouted to the yawl through a megaphone which he held in one hand, while he had a telescope in the other; a powder horn hung from his shoulders and beside him lay a shining brass blunderbuss which he picked up frequently and aimed at Whidbey."

The next day, again, at the northern point of Admiralty Island, Whidbey could only avoid a clash with the Indians by giving up the exploration of the inlet which led to the east. When he reached the same region again on August 8, having left Port Conclusion[56] on the second expedition, the savages followed him in several canoes until a shot was fired at the foremost. Then they slowly pulled back until their canoes were in a line with one boat and, paddling slowly backwards, they protected themselves with the tall prows of their canoes. A new attack greeted Whidbey in

26

Frederick Sound by a horde that likewise at first made friendly demonstrations.

Otherwise, the reports of Vancouver and his officers indicate that in their period the population of the archipelago was small. Meetings with natives occurred relatively infrequently, and even more seldom did they meet many at a time, while settlements on the coast were seen only at long intervals.

With Vancouver's investigations which demonstrated the nonexistence of a strait, of reasonable width, to Hudson's Bay or the Atlantic Ocean, the interest of the English in the Northwest Coast dwindled, since at the same time the fur trade became less profitable. The Spaniards also gave up their claims to the area and San Francisco Bay continued to be their northernmost harbor. Only the young American republic continued to send a few trading vessels around Cape Horn, and making use of Vancouver's discoveries, penetrated all the canals and bays of the archipelago for furs which they traded from the natives and took to the Chinese market. The sea otter was still to be found in large numbers on the rocky coast, but the Russians already planned to expand their way of extermination to the Alexander Archipelago since through their reckless killing the numbers of fur bearing animals on the Aleutians and Kodiak had been greatly reduced. Since the enterprises of the Russians led to their permanent possession of the coast, a brief survey of the historical development and organization of the fur trade between America and Asia should be included.

For a number of years, the fur trade in the newly discovered lands was conducted mostly by promyschlenniks on their own or on account with the buyers in Okhotsk and other Siberian towns. In 1781 Gregor Schelechow (Shelikof), an enterprising Siberian merchant, joined with his partner, Ivan Golikof, to found a company with the object of discovering new lands to help out the fur trade which was already diminishing. Three ships were outfitted at Okhotsk and with them Shelikof came to the coast of America where, partly by persuasion and partly by violence, he brought Kodiak Island under Russian rule. In 1788, by a ukase of Empress Catherine II, the company was given the support of the Russian government in their enterprises and through a second ukase, in 1790, the natives were exempt from the "Jassaks" or yearly tribute, but instead must furnish the company with a certain number of baidarkas[57] and could sell their skins only to them.

The enterprises of the company were especially successful, when in 1790 Alexander Baranof, a merchant from Kargopol in the government of Olonetz, who had moved to Siberia in 1780 and there became acquainted with Shelikof, was entrusted with the direction of business of the American possessions. On the ship The Three Apostles, Baranof started for Kodiak right after the conclusion of these arrangements, but on account of a shortage of water the captain considered it necessary to land in Unalaska where, in a storm, the ship with its cargo went aground. So Baranof endured a winter of hardship and finally reached his goal, Kodiak Island, in baidarkas, in August of 1791. Here he immediately acted with his usual efficiency and, in constant effort to expand the fur trade, he turned his eyes toward the east where the almost untouched coast of the mainland of America seemed to offer inexhaustible hunting grounds. In this way Baranof came in contact with the inhabitants of this stretch of coast, the Tlingit, or as the Russians called them, the Kolosch, [58] when they made their acquaintance several years earlier.

In 1788 the administrator of the Shelikof Company, the Greek Delarof, sent out two steersmen, Ismailof and Bocharof, to make discoveries along the American coast and to bring the natives under the rule of the Russian empire. In Yakutat Bay they found the Kolushans in summer camp and among them Chief Ilchak from the Chilcat River, [59] who was supposed to rule over all Kolushans who live along the coast to Yakutat Bay, and who, this year, as was annually their practice, with one hundred and seventy souls of both sexes, excluding children, came in baidarkas to this place for trade and to see his people. To Ilchak the Russian gave as a token of esteem a Russian crest in copper and a picture of the heir to the throne on which the following was inscribed in Russian and German: "In the year 1788, in the month of June, seamen of the Shelikof and Golikof Company, steersmen Gerassim Ismailof and Dmitrii Bocharof, in their galleon The Three Apostles with forty men on board, found themselves in the bay called Yakutat by the heathen, where, through the kindly and friendly relations with Chief Ilchak and his subjects, the Kolushan people, they carried on an agreeable trade and at last brought them under the protection of the Russian Imperial throne; in commemoration of which they gave the estimable chief a Russian copper crest and a copper engraving of the likeness of his Imperial Highness, the heir to the Russian crown; therefore all Russian and alien ships coming here are warned to establish friendly relationship with this chief, using only such caution as is necessary; the steersmen who lay here from the 11th to the 21st of June with their galleon noticed no ill-natured behavior on the part of the chief and his people and happily returned to sea." [60]

In continuing their journey, the Russians came to the Antlin, Kalcho, Alzech and Kakan-in Rivers, [61] named for them by a Kolushan boy they took along, and landed in Ltua Gulf [62] where, as they had surmised there had been a ship two years earlier, obviously the French expedition under La Perouse. Here a copper crest was also handed over to the chief, Taik-nuch-tachtu-

28

jach, and as a sign of possession of the land, a copper plate was buried in the ground.

Baranof first met the Tlingit in 1793. In that year he went with a few Russians and a small group of Aleut in baidarkas to Tschugat Bay[63] in order to become acquainted with the Chugach who live there and to examine the neighborhood with the view of establishing a new settlement, when he was suddenly attacked in the middle of the night by Kolushans from Yakutat, outnumbering them five to one.[64] They were on the warpath against the Chugach and unexpectedly stumbled on the Russians of whose presence they had no inkling. Chliebnikof writes about this encounter as follows: "The Kolushans wore their armor which consisted of wooden rods bound together with leather thongs. Their faces were protected with masks which represented the heads of bears, dogfish and other animals and gave a frightening appearance. On their heads they wore large wooden hats which were fastened to the rest of their armor with thongs. Their weapons consisted of lances, bows, and two pointed daggers. The Russians aimed directly at their heads, but the bullets did not penetrate the thick head covering. The more intense the fire of the Russians became, the more vigorous was the storming of new hordes of attackers."[65] Finally the superiority of weapons won the victory for the Russians. Leaving twelve dead behind, the Tlingit fled, but the Russians had also suffered considerable losses; two Russians and nine Aleuts had fallen and more than fifteen men were wounded.

The same year that Vancouver concluded his investigations on the Northwest Coast, 1794, Baranof sent a flotilla of seven hundred baidarkas with 1460 Aleuts and seven Russians to Bering Bay (Yakutat Bay) for sea otter hunting. Puget in the Chatham met this assemblage and was witness to the dealings of Purtoff,[66] the leader, with the Yakutat Indians to bring about friendly relations. With great care the chief analyzed the situation; that the land belonged to them and the Russians were in the wrong to kill sea otter and take them away without offering them the slightest compensation. Their friendly intentions were explained, but Purtoff feared for his safety, although the Indians did not number more than seventy and at that time he had nine hundred Aleut with him, but he could not trust the courage of his people very much and he greatly feared the treachery of the Indians.

Nevertheless Purtoff finally succeeded in completing negotiations with the natives, and from the inhabitants of Cape St. Elias and from Yakutat Bay and Lituya Bay fifteen men went along as hostages, who during their stay at Kodiak Island allowed themselves to be baptized. [67]

In the following year Baranof went to Yakutat Bay in the ship Olga and after he had pacified the hostile natives, he planted a

Russian flag and the crest of the Russian Empire, claiming the coastline, amid the fire of cannon, the roll of drums and the shouts of his men. Leaving thirty men behind, he sailed further into Chilcat Bay where he placed crosses at all prominent points inscribed: "Russian Territory." The attitude of the natives in this bay was not a friendly one. While they were trading with the Russians they tried to lure their ship into a narrow passage where they would have found themselves at great disadvantage.

In 1796 Baranof went to Yakutat Bay the second time in order to establish a Russian colony there. During his two months' stay he settled about eighty colonists (deportees) and promyschlenniks and their wives and children and called the place "New Russia."

Even the most prominent chiefs flattered Baranof with a ceremonial visit and showed their friendly attitude by bringing as hostages some of their own children and relatives. At the wishes of the natives, the old chief's nephew was elected to fill his place and, in confirmation of his position, Baranof gave him a signed document.

Meanwhile Shelikof, the founder of the company, died in 1795, and for two years his widow carried on the management of the business, organizing new trading companies which interlocked with the Shelikof Company. In 1798 these combined into óne firm, the United American Company which, the following year, under the name of the Russian-American Company obtained extended privileges for twenty years through an ukase of Emperor Paul. By this decree the entire coast north of the 55th parallel was turned over to them for their free use. They were empowered to establish settlements, carry on agriculture and commerce, spread the Greek faith and extend Russian territory as long as they did not come in conflict with any other power. The Aleut were conscripted for a three-year term of service for the company, and from the natives of Cook Inlet and Prince William Sound a yearly tribute of skins was demanded.

Baranof remained the chief administrator of the colonies. Seeking to extend his power, he went in 1799 on the ship Olga, accompanied by many Aleut in their baidarkas, to Sitka Bay where he wanted to establish new factories. Although he had first consulted the natives about the settlement and the choice of a location and had obtained their consent, they later became very unfriendly. They even insulted the interpreter sent by Baranof to invite them to the celebration of the dedication of the fort named after the Archangel Michael. Baranof went at once with only twenty men to their village where three hundred armed natives were assembled to demand satisfaction for the offense, and this courage had such an effect on the Sitka that while Baranof was there they made no further attempt to drive the Russians away. However, Baranof did not succeed in trading with them, since

they would rather sell their furs to the English and Americans
who provided them with ammunition and weapons at better terms
than the Russians could.

When construction was completed and peace with the natives
seemed assured, Baranof returned to Kodiak in 1801, leaving
Medwiednikof in command of the fort. Even after his departure,
the friendly relationship with the natives seemed to continue until suddenly, while a number of the Russians and Aleut were
busy with the sea otter hunt and other tasks, about six hundred
Sitka Indians came from all sides, on land through the forest, on
the water along the various straits, and united to attack the fort.
The attack began at noon and after a few hours the fort was taken
and demolished.

The Russians, about fifteen of them, offered hopeless resistance, but when the enemy succeeded in firing the building, they
had to surrender. They were all killed without mercy. The promyschlenniks and Aleut who hurried to assist came too late and
with few exceptions also met their death. Altogether it was supposed that twenty Russians, including their commander Medwiednikof, and one hundred and thirty Aleut perished; in addition,
three thousand sea otter and other skins were plundered and a
ship built for the company burned. Through the intercession of an
English ship three Russians, five Aleut, eighteen women and six
children were released by the natives and delivered to Baranof,
but for high ransom. Among the attackers, who were well supplied with firearms, were supposed to be three sailors, who,
after deserting from United States ships and being taken into the
Russian service, now made common cause with the natives.

The success of the attack on Sitka encouraged the Yakutat to
attack an Aleut hunting party quartered in Yakutat Bay under the
leadership of Kuskof. The chief sought out Kuskof in his tent and
made the accusation that the hunters of the company not only rob-
bed them of their fur-bearing animals but also took the skins
which ornamented their graves. Kuskof tried unsuccessfully to
pacify them, but they became more and more wrought up until
they opened attack on the Russians. They withdrew to their boats
in good order and took a firm position nearby which, with the
help of a few cannon, they defended against a second attack of the
natives. Because of lack of ammunition Kuskof had to come to an
agreement with the enemy.

Less fortunate was another hunting party of ninety baidarkas
under the leadership of Urbanof which in Kek Strait (Kake) was almost entirely annihilated by the Kake and Kuju tribes. Only Urbanof and twenty Aleut succeeded in escaping.

Baranof could not let these attacks go unpunished. With four
small ships together with one hundred and twenty Russians and
four hundred baidarkas and about nine hundred Aleut he went to

the Alexander Archipelago in the spring of 1804. On a mission of hunting and revenge, he went with part of his forces into Cross Sound, Stephens Passage and Chatham Strait and took 1600 sea otter skins and destroyed the villages of the Kake and Kujus Indians. The latter, on hearing of the approach of Nanok, the name by which Baranof was known along the entire coast, became frightened and fled. [68] On September 19/8 he reached Sitka where for over one month the Neva with Captain Lisiansky had been at anchor, the first Russian ship which had made the trip from Europe to the colonies. The Neva belonged to the Krusenstern expedition and had come from the Sandwich Islands to Kodiak to deliver provisions to the Russian colonies, but Lisiansky had heard of the projected dealings with the Sitka Indians and at the suggestion of Baranof sailed hastily to Sitka Sound.

During a storm Baranof was separated from his Aleut retainers and only gradually did they arrive in the harbor in groups. Now there were only three hundred and fifty baidarkas and eight hundred Aleut, the remainder either having perished or on account of illness having been sent back to Yakutat Bay. This horde was led by thirty-six chiefs who received their orders from the officers of the company.

On September 27/18 the whole force was gathered together and it was decided to attack if the natives would not allow the peaceful establishment of the new settlement. They had left the steep isolated hill, their old home, where later the Russian castle was built, and had withdrawn to the mouth of the river which later the Russians called Kolushan but is now known as Indian River. On September 28/17, in quiet weather, the ships were escorted by the baidarkas close to the settlement and in the evening rode at anchor there, while alarms could be heard on land. On 29/18 the hill, which received the name of "New Archangel" was occupied by the Russians and several cannon were emplanted. Toward evening a messenger arrived from the Sitka Indians with friendly offers to which the reply was made that negotiations would be opened as soon as the chiefs themselves appeared.

The next morning the same messenger came again with another Indian who was sent by his people as a hostage. Both sang a melancholy song as they approached in a canoe. On landing the Indian who was sent as hostage threw himself on the ground in the shallow water and stayed in this position until he was picked up and with his companion led into the Russian camp. This time the messenger brought a sea otter skin as a gift for Baranof, who gave him in return a suit of warm clothing and sent the same answer which he had given the previous day. At noon thirty Indians equipped with firearms approached the hill within musket shot and began negotiations. Baranof demanded two more prominent persons as hostages and permission to retain the hill upon which to establish his fort. The Tlingit would not agree to this. Frequently repeating the shout, "uh, uh, uh," they rose and returned to their people, after the interpreter had informed them that an attack on their encampment would follow.

On October 1/September 20 the four ships, Neva, Jermak, Katharina, and Alexander took up their positions in a line in front of these encampments. Lisiansky had a white flag on board the Neva and immediately a similar one appeared on the enemy's fort. Lieut. Arbusof was sent with two boats and a four pounder to destroy the canoes on the beach, some of which were large enough to carry sixty men; since, however, he could not do much from the water, he landed and moved toward the fort with his artillery. When Baranof saw this he also landed with one hundred and fifty men and several light guns, and misled by quiet on the part of the enemy, which was only broken occasionally by musket shots, he ordered an attack on the fortification about six o'clock in the evening.

When the attachers reached the walls, they suddenly were met with well aimed fire which frightened the Aleut to such a degree that they quickly turned in flight and deserted their guns. At the same time the Tlingit broke out in strength, and only a small party of Russians managed to retreat to safety under cover of the fire of the Neva. On the Neva alone in this encounter, fourteen men were wounded and two killed. Baranof himself sustained an arm wound and thus was prevented from leading further expeditions. One of the dead Russians was held up on spears by the Tlingit for his compatriots to see. On the following day another of the wounded sailors died.

Lisiansky, who now led the action, ordered the opening of lively fire from the ships on the enemy's position, which had the result that by afternoon the Tlingit made peace offers. They agreed to yield the place, leave some members of prominent families as hostages, and give up the Aleut prisoners in their hands. That same evening a young man was sent as hostage and others, as well as a few prisoners, were delivered the next day. When Lisiansky discovered from these that the Tlingit had sent to the inhabitants of Husnoff (Killisnoo) for aid, he demanded the complete clearance of the fort which the head chief agreed to accomplish by October 6. However, by that date nothing had been done toward fulfulling this agreement so Lisiansky opened fire again. About eight o'clock that night one could hear aboard ship the "Uh, uh, uh" of the natives, the sign agreed upon to signify their willingness to submit, which was answered by a hurrah from the Russians. Thereupon the Tlingit started a song.

On the following morning October 7/September 26 a number of ravens were seen flying around the fort and a messenger was dispatched to find out the cause of this. He reported that the natives had left the fort except two old women and a little boy. Through this unexpected flight the Russians gained an abundance of food and twenty large canoes. When Lisiansky went into the fort he was surprised to find the bodies of little children and dogs, probably killed by the savages in order to cover their flight better.

The fort formed an irregular square with its longest side toward the sea. The walls were of wood but so thick and heavy that the cannon balls of the Neva had not penetrated them. On the beach side there was a gate and two openings for two cannon which the natives possessed and which caused considerable damage in the rigging of the Neva, while other exits led to the woods on the opposite side. In the stockade were fourteen houses which, according to Lisiansky's judgment, could have contained eight hundred men. Lack of ammunition seemed to be the principal reason for evacuation.

Baranof had the fort razed at once and for this work he brought three hundred men ashore. After everything had been removed which was usable, it was burned to the ground. On the following day the Russians, who had lost six of their number together with a few Aleut, withdrew to New Archangel and started at once on their building activities.

Lisiansky reported further that about two hundred graves of the natives were desecrated by the embittered Russians and only one, belonging to a chief who had always been kindly toward them, was spared.

For the fallen Russians a memorial was erected on the Indian River, which was still mentioned by Holmberg. Until recent years the remains of the stockade were still there but on all our visits we were not able to find them. Perhaps excavation would bring forth mementoes of this remarkable episode in Tlingit history.

The following year, 1805, when Lisiansky returned from Kodiak, where he had wintered, to Sitka, he found eight fine buildings and land cleared for fifteen kitchen gardens. The Tlingit had lived in scattered places during the winter, but now they gathered again and built a new fort at Chatham Strait, opposite Killisnoo. At the invitation of Baranof they sent a delegation to discuss definite peace terms which Lisiansky, on his arrival at New Archangel, described in the following words: "About four o'clock in the afternoon, five boats approached, rowing toward the fort. Shortly before arrival they began to sing and our Aleut hurried toward them, while the Chugach, who were supposed to guide them in, hastily prepared themselves by sprinkling eagle down on their hair and dressing themselves in their best finery. Many were dressed only in a threadbare jacket and others went forth proudly covered only by an old hat or dressed in a pair of torn trousers. In these rags, however, they carried themselves as proud-

ly as the most bedecked dandy in Europe. Close to shore the
company halted and began a dance in the boats. The chief himself made the most extraordinary leaps, while fanning himself
with large feathers. Finally the messenger was lifted out of the
boat on a carpet and was carried to the place agreed upon for him
and his followers."[69]

Kotlian, the bitterest enemy of the Russians who instigated the
destruction of the old settlement, now paid Baranof a visit to assure him of his good will. The ceremonial reception on which he
had counted, however, could not be tendered him, much to his
grief, because the Aleut had in the meantime gone out sea otter
hunting. However, he was carried ashore by several people.
Such visits from the Tlingit are also described by Langsdorff, who
as companion of Baron Resanof spent the winter of 1805 to 1806
in Sitka. "They generally come," he said, "in a party of several
persons of both sexes, traveling in large canoes, which are made
of a single log and artistically finished and decorated, and approaching the Russian establishment singing and paddling rhythmically. When they have almost reached the landing place they
halt and one of their number makes a long speech. They will not
come ashore until Nanok, that is Baranof, or his representative
has come forward and given them permission to land and assured
them of a friendly reception. Through an interpreter I heard that
these speeches which are delivered with rhetorical skill and seem
to consist of long, connected periods are a constant repetition of
one and the same idea, often in the same words, namely; we
were your enemies, we were your enemies, we injured you; you
were our enemies, you injured us; we want to be good friends; we
want to forget the past; we do not seek to injure you again; do us
no more harm also; be our good friends, and so on. This and
similar speeches lasted about half an hour and only then after as-
surances of friendship and good intentions did they step ashore.
Baranof, who had studied the customs of these people for many
years, had a tent set up for them at once and a plentiful meal
prepared. Only the head chief and the most important visitors,
but no others, were allowed to come up the hill where the fort is
located."

The visit of the Kolushans was usually linked with a little barter; they brought sea otter skins along and gave them to Baranof,
asking in return necessities of the same value. If they were dissatisfied with them they would take back the skins which they had
already prsented. [70]

At the end of October Langsdorff, accompanied by an American
trader, Wolf, a number of Aleut and a female interpreter, visited a new settlement of the Tlingit on Chatham Strait. Here he
was received in a friendly fashion by the chief, Dlchätin, the
father of his interpreter. The visitors were carried part of the

way by hand and brought with their baggage to the house of Dlchätin, without the smallest piece missing. The fort lay, according
to Langsdorff, on the northeastern tip of the opening of Peril
Straits into Chatham Strait, on a steep cliff which hung several
hundred feet over the water. The only approach was made very
difficult by an obstruction of large tree trunks. The rock itself
was protected against enemy action by a double palisade twelve
to fifteen feet high and three to four feet thick, made of tree
trunks set side by side. An even higher earth wall protected the
houses within so that they could not be seen by an approaching
ship.

The number of inhabitants of the fort was estimated by Langsdorff at 1300 to 1400. In the house of his host alone lived thirty to
forty people. He described the inside of the houses as well as the
people as exceptionally dirty. "The smoke, the smell of fish and
fish oil and the aspect of faces, smeared with soot and dirt, and
disfigured with a lip plug, is distasteful and many unbelievable
customs aroused disgust and horror. Many picked insects from
their smelly fur garments and ate them alive. "[71]

The capture of Sitka did not completely discourage the Tlingit.
As late as 1805 the fort at Yakutat was attacked and the head man,
Larionof, with twelve promyschlenniks who were scattered at
their tasks were killed. [72] Encouraged by this success, they planned an attack on the Russian settlements at Prince William Sound
and Kenai Bay.

They went in eight boats to the mouth of the Copper River,
where six remained behind while two went on to the fortification
at Konstantowski. The leader of the expedition was Fedor, a god-
son of Baranof and regarded as a friend of the Russians. He pretended to the head man at Konstantowski, Uwarof, that they had
come to trade with the Chugach. Uwarof, however, knew of the
planned attack through a Chugach slave who had escaped from the
Tlingit camp at the mouth of the Copper River, and he took Fedor prisoner. The Chugach, who had also been notified, invited
the Yakutat to a feast where they unexpectedly attacked them and
killed all but one or two. Fedor committed suicide during the
night. The remaining Tlingit who were still at the mouth of the
Copper River, fearing the Chugach, took flight in spite of the
rough sea, and when their boats grounded on the shore at the
mouth of the river, those who had escaped death by drowning
and had saved themselves on the shore of Ugalachmut were killed
by their age-old enemies who lived there. So the Yakutat who
once numbered two hundred warriors were reduced to scarcely
one. [73]

The destruction of the settlement at Yakutat, furthermore, resulted in another great loss for the Russians. In the fall of 1805
the Aleut hunters, who had been brought to Sitka during previous

years under the leadership of Demjanenkof, were sent back to
Kodiak. When they received word during the journey that the fort
at Yakutat Bay had fallen into the hands of the Tlingit, all but
thirty baidarkas that risked landing continued their trip in spite
of great weariness and stormy weather and with few exceptions
all two hundred of them met their death.[74]

As long as Baranof remained at New Archangel, fear of him
kept the Tlingit from new attacks. When, however, he returned
to Kodiak in the fall of 1806, they gathered in a threatening manner on the surrounding islands, and through the addition of the
Chilkat, Stikine, Auk and still others, their numbers rose to two
thousand people and four hundred boats. Kuskof to whom Baranof
had entrusted the place, found out from Tlingit girls who lived at
the fort about the planned attack of the enemy and realized the
impossibility of defending himself against their combined strength.
He, therefore, invited the important chiefs, including the Chilkat
chief and his following, to the fort, welcomed them with great
honor, feasted them royally, and gave them presents. This had
the desired result. The Chilkat called Kuskof his friend and
pledged himself to return home to allay all suspicion. Indeed, he
did this, and his influence was so great that all the other tribes
followed his example.[75]

In 1808 Baranof moved the seat of administration from Kodiak
to New Archangel. But all his pains to maintain friendly relations
with the Tlingit had no lasting results, and because of their
treachery the inhabitants of New Archangel lived in constant fear
of attack. The hostile attitude of the natives toward the Russians
showed itself especially in 1809 and 1813. In the latter year they
joined with the neighboring tribes in overrunning the fort. For
some time they had been supplying themselves secretly with quantities of weapons, armor and other provisions for war, when the
plans of the attack were discovered by the administration just in
time for proper measures to be taken against it. However they
continued through occasional theft and murderous attacks to make
the vicinity of Sitka unsafe. Even in 1818, when a well manned
Russian warship lay at anchor in the harbor of Sitka, substantial
revolts occurred among the natives. When hostages were demanded of them, they answered that they would only accede if the Russians did likewise. As a token the administration consented to
this and turned over two young Creoles[76] in exchange for a nephew of the chief. The delivery of the hostages was accompanied
with much ceremony and festivities lasting several days. Actually
with this the hostilities of the natives stopped for a long time and
even fur trading with the Russians was resumed. When they
brought back the Russian hostages, they demanded the return of
theirs, which was willingly granted.[77]

At that time Baranof himself was no longer chief administrator, for early in 1818 he had turned his post over to the person designated as his successor by the office in St. Petersburg after he had conducted the business of the colonies with great efficiency and unselfishness for thirty years.

Baranof belonged to the great of his day. "Without means," said Lütke, [78] "and with people who were more capable of wrecking an organization than founding one, Baranof organized and developed the fur hunt and the trading of skins in spite of hostile natives who were constantly incited by civilized people, and fought obstruction through personal sacrifice, when for some years he had not only no support but not even communication with Russia. Even though, in some respects, improvements and changes were later necessary, the plan of operation has been changed little to the present time."

In the last years of his administration Baranof did not show the old energy and, weakened by age, and bowed down by constant annoyances, he frequently asked for his retirement. The first selected as his successor, Koch, a native of Hamburg, died during the passage from Petropavlovsk in 1811. Then Bornowolokof was sent with the Neva, but at the entrance of Sitka Harbor the ship was wrecked at Mt. Edgecumbe and he met his death. At last in 1818 Baranof found a successor in Captain Hagemeister. But he was no longer in condition to stand the changed life and different climate, so he left the colonies on the Kutusof in the fall of the same year and died April 28/16, 1819, at the age of 72 in the roadstead of Batavia. Even though Baranof had administered the colonies without any accounting, he did not leave a fortune. [79]

The most important change in the administration of the colonies undertaken by Baranof's successor was discontinuing the practice of paying the promyschlenniks a proportion of the returns of the catch; from now on they received a stated wage, living quarters, fuel and light on condition that they did not trade on their own. Their situation was very much improved by this; while formerly only a few returned home with any savings, it was reported that in the twelve-year period from 1818 to 1830, of five hundred and seventy-six Russians who had come to the colonies with debts amounting to 367,650 rubles, four hundred and eleven returned home with 248,000 rubles capital. [80]

The strict military discipline established by Baranof was continued. Everyone was prepared in case of attack on the part of the natives or the outbreak of fire to be at a definite station, and regular inspection and frequent drills did not allow these orders to be forgotten. [81]

For some Tlingit who had put themselves under the protection of the company Hagemeister provided settlements outside the fort, and he also tried to win them over to doing some household work.

Hagemeister made an agreement with the French trader, Roquefeuil, who visited the Northwest Coast at this time, according to which he gave him thirty baidarkas with two Kodiak to each and supervised by two agents in return for half the catch. This hunting expedition had an unfortunate end. In Bucareli Bay, near Klawak, the hunters, who had camped on the beach, were suddenly attacked by the natives. In the fight twenty Kodiak lost their lives and twelve were wounded, of whom one died later. The rest, except two who probably drowned, saved themselves by swimming. As a result of this mishap, Roquefeuil returned to Sitka without accomplishing his purpose. One clause of the agreement was that he had to pay two hundred piastres as damages for each Kodiak killed. Roquefeuil then gave up hunting altogether and only carried on trade with the natives of Chatham Strait, but he had poor returns since his stock did not suit the taste of the Indians. They wanted guns, ammunition and blankets, but only of good quality, also axes, files, knives, small mirrors, glass beads, handkerchiefs and other goods of linen and wool. For a good sea otter skin they demanded and received a gun. Biscuits, rice, molasses and liquor served as bonus.

In the fall of 1819 Hagemeister turned over the administration to Janowski who retained the post until 1821. In that year by a decree of Emperor Alexander I the privileges of the company were extended for another twenty years.

From 1821 to 1826, Murawief administered the colonies. Under his leadership a great change was made in the relations between the Tlingit and the Russians. Up to that time, except for the provisions made by Hagemeister, no Tlingit were allowed to live near the fort. In the spring during the herring run about one thousand people assembled there and perhaps as many again on the neighboring islands to gather the eggs; but for some time very few were allowed to build their camps near the fort, and then only after they were disarmed. Murawief, however, allowed them to build a large camp close to the fort in the belief that when they had their wives, children and goods, all under the reach of his cannon, he had much better control over them and could more easily find out any evil intentions. Actually the Tlingit became more relaxed; and the intercourse of the Russians with Tlingit women brought knowledge of their actions, just as it had given warning of attacks in the past. [82]

To prevent the American ships from trading in firearms in the Russian colonies, warships were sent out from Kronstadt in 1821 and the following four years, but only the corvette Apollo under Captain Schabelski actually crossed the straits, and it was not of sufficient strength to seize the many American smugglers who were about. It was impossible to prevent the introduction of firearms, for their use was already widespread. For twenty years

Americans and Englishmen had carried on constant trade so that
the sea otter were exterminated and all the surrounding tribes
were fully supplied with firearms to the point where they had
forgotten the use of their old weapons, and without a gun could
not kill a single animal. [83]

Kotzebue, the son of the well-known poet, made his second cir-
cumnavigation of the globe from 1823 to 1826 on one of the ships
sent from Kronstadt. During this trip he anchored twice at Sitka,
in 1824 and 1825, and during their stay his scientific companions,
Hofmann and Eschscholtz, took the opportunity to make geological, botanical, and zoological studies. The description of the
Tlingit which Kotzebue gave in his travel account is entirely
worthless, since it was filled with exaggerations and unfounded
statements, facts and fancy hopelessly intermingled.

Murawief's successor in the administration of the colonies
was Tschistakof, 1826 to 1831. During his regime, Lütke visited
the colonies on the corvette Seniavin. Although he stayed in New
Archangel only five weeks, he and his scientific companions, Kittlitz, Mertens, and Postels, had many opportunities for observations. In his travel account published in 1835, Lütke could give,
beside statistical information about the administration of the colonies for which he thanked Tschistakof's successor, Baron von
Wrangell, also a good description of the land and its natives,
which he secured with the use of the manuscript reports of
Chliebnikof, the former bureau chief at New Archangel who lived
in the colonies for fifteen years. Through the use of this material, Lütke's account became a much more important source for
the study of the Tlingit because many of the earlier and even later reports were unsatisfactory on account of their short stay or
the unfamiliarity with the native tongue, as well as with the Russian people. In the following chapters we will have many occasions to refer to statements regarding the Tlingit in Lütke's reports, but at present only that which relates to the attitude of the
Russians to the Tlingit will be included.

About the changed relations between the Russians and the Tlingit Lütke has the following to say. "The Kolushans are not the
same today as ten to fifteen years ago. Then it was dangerous
for a man to go alone beyond the cannon range of the fort, since
murder without provocation was very common, but today one
does not hear of any such thing. The inhabitants of New Archangel go around in the neighborhood without danger and visit the
warm springs. Formerly the simplest quarrel was not settled
without bloodshed. Even now at the slightest disturbance they put
their hands on their guns and rush to their canoes, but the disputes in which the women take part are generally brought to a
peaceful conclusion. Just before our arrival a Kolushan who did
not answer the sentry's challenge at night was shot and killed,

and during our stay an insane promyschlennik shattered the head
of a native by throwing a stone, but both incidents had no consequences. According to the latest reports, two slaves who were to
be sacrificed at a ceremony escaped and fled to the fort. The
governor took them under his protection and refused to surrender
them to the chief, who did not take this unkindly."[84]

The association with the Russians was also an advantage to the
natives. The chiefs liked to dress themselves in uniforms and
were so vain that when they noticed the different cut of Lütke's
clothing on his arrival they did not rest until they had imitated
him. In the past year Nauschket or Nauschketl, the chief of the
Sitka Indians embraced Christianity without being urged by the
Russians.[85]

The trade of the Russians with the natives was carried on almost exclusively at Sitka, since the danger of direct trade in the
various channels was not worth the results. The caution which
had to be taken in trading in these tortuous straits according to
Lütke was unprecedented. "The forward part of the ships was
closed off by a spread of sails to a man's height. Behind this
wall, the armed crew took their places, supported by several
cannon loaded with grapeshot cartridges and ignited fuses. All
around the ship to the height of the bower a net was spread which
had an entrance only at one place for a single person. Before
trading began, the commander of the ship allowed the chiefs to
come aboard and be shown these preparations and given to understand that no more than a certain number of buyers would be allowed on the ship at one time. No one would be allowed more than
ten steps from the rail and if anyone were killed transgressing
these rules, it should not be looked upon as breaking the peace.
After these directions were laid out the supercargo could begin
trading without danger, but the slightest relaxation of these pre-
cautions could bring about the most serious consequences."[86]

This trade, however, could not compete with the ships from
the United States, because their prices were fixed by the administration in St. Petersburg, and finally it was driven out altogether. The average yearly return decreased to thirty sea otter,
ten beaver and the same number of land or fish otter. Raising
the price from one hundred to one hundred and fifty rubles helped
the trade a little so that in 1826 to 1829 the average was eighty
sea otter, four hundred beaver, three hundred foxes and sixty
black bears.

The ease with which the Tlingit could satisfy their needs at the
market which was held between the walls of the fort and the nearest Indian houses at Sitka was one of the difficulties of the fur
trade. "When there was a lack of fish the Russians bought a few
halibut from them, or some whale blubber or porpoise. In the
spring they brought bark to cover sheds, barracks and other

buildings, the eggs of gulls, auks, and other birds, like ducks
and geese, wood hens, roots and weeds of various kinds; in summer they sold berries and in winter, mountain sheep, crabs,
shellfish and the like; also things of their own manufacture like
hats, blankets, masks, pipes, and other trifles. For these they
received from the Russians and Aleut tobacco, iron cooking pots,
axes, glassware, linen, quantities of potatoes and even flour."[87]
In addition to these they received from the company woolen blankets, copper pots, sea lion whiskers as decoration on their hats,
ermine skins and so forth, for which they paid with dentalium at
the rate of one hundred for twenty rubles, a commodity which the
company used in trading with the Indians of the interior.

Another hindrance to the fur trade came from the relations of
the Russians with the native women. "The Kolushan courtesan
understands as thoroughly as the European dancer how to rob her
admirer and one often sees a promyschlennik bankrupt himself to
provide fine clothes for her, in spite of the efforts of the officers
to try to prevent such mischief."[88]

From 1831 to 1836 Baron Wrangell (died 1870), who was famous for his trips as a marine lieutenant along the Arctic coast of
Siberia, was administrator of the colonies. Through his reports,
published by Baer, we have very good information about conditions in the Russian colonies during that period.[89] At that time
there were seven administrative districts: 1. the region of the
Kuriles; 2. the region of Atka; 3. the vicinity of Unalaska; 4. the
district of Kodiak; 5. the northern district; 6. the colony of Ross;
7. the district of Sitka. In the principal factory of New Archangel
or Sitka the head supervisor had his office. The population of
this place in 1883 was four hundred and six Europeans, three
hundred and seven Creoles and one hundred and thirty-four Aleut
(from Kodiak) and "Kolushans." In addition there were from time
to time one thousand independent Kolushans in the neighborhood.
The market at New Archangel was abundantly supplied with food
at all times of the year, the value of which in goods traded to the
Kolushans ran to eight hundred rubles in 1831, according to colonial prices. Altogether the relations between the Russians and
the natives maintained themselves very favorably so that Wrangell no longer had anything to fear from them.

At Wrangell's suggestion the priest Veniaminof who had been in
Unalaska was transferred to Sitka in 1834 in order that he might
have the opportunity to become familiar with the customs of the
American Northwest Coast through the Tlingit.

Ivan Veniaminof was educated in the seminary at Irkutsk. As
a young man he came to the Aleutian Islands in 1824 where he
soon learned the Aleut language and through this as well as his
friendly and understanding ways won the favor of the islanders.
In his leisure time he made meteorological and natural observa-

tions, the instruments for which he constructed himself. [90] His
efforts to establish a school and convert the natives will be discussed in a later chapter. He was effective here, not only because of his zeal but also on account of his personality.

Belcher, who visited Sitka under Kupreanof's administration,
was surprised at the herculean size of the Father who officiated
in high boots and shining vestments and was about six feet three
inches tall and about forty-five years old. He also praised his
skillful address from the pulpit. [91]

In 1839 Veniaminof went to the Synod at St. Petersburg where
he presented a survey of the Orthodox Church of the Aleutians,
the Kuriles and in America. After he was elected Bishop in 1840
he returned to New Archangel where he worked until 1850.

More than anyone else Veniaminof was concerned with gaining
an understanding of the character, customs, and habits of the natives. We have him to thank for the most complete collection of
the mythology of the Tlingit and also for knowledge of the language. His publications in Russian are witness to his endeavors.
In spite of the naive style which Erman ascribes to him, he
shows himself to be a good observer and a conscientious report-
er and only occasionally his theological point of view leads him
to make bold hypotheses and draw attenuated conclusions. We
have substantiated his material descriptions almost everywhere,
whenever there was opportunity for checking them.

From 1836 to 1840 Kupreanof was director. During his administration, in 1836, smallpox broke out in New Archangel and in
three months about four hundred of the adult natives, that is,
about half of the whole population, who in spite of the efforts of
Veniaminof and Blaschke, the doctor in the service of the Company, stubbornly refused vaccination, died, while among the Russians there was only one death. In March of 1837 the epidemic
abated and in April it had stopped. Among the other tribes, especially the Killisnoo, the epidemic raged, though it was not as
virulent. According to Veniaminof the epidemic had one good result, in that it convinced the Tlingit of the superior knowledge of
the Russians and destroyed their faith in the power of their shamans. While this helped bring the Russians and the Tlingit closer
together, this was even more the case because of the ever increasing intercourse between the Russians and Tlingit women.

Veniaminof expressed himself very favorably about this matter;
"Almost all of them," he said, "are very decent women; and
even the worst are no worse than an ordinary Aleut woman.
Many of them are living with promyschlenniks and have several
children whom, in spite of their poverty, they keep very well,
and in general better than many Creoles. In their housekeeping
they are efficient and industrious and very much concerned with
the welfare of their men. It is not infrequent that the woman, in-

stead of being supported, through her work feeds them both. I also knew a Kolushan woman, who, living with one of the crudest Russians, did not leave him in spite of his inconsiderate treatment of her, even though she could have returned to her parents."[92] Also the Creoles of Kolushan extraction are more orderly than the Aleut. While among ten of them four orderly ones can be found, it would take twenty Aleut to get the same number.

In 1834 an expedition was outfitted by the Hudson's Bay Company to establish a factory at the mouth of the Stikine River, but Wrangell, at that time director of the Russian-American Company, prevented the Englishmen from carrying out their plan by sending a Russian ship to intercept them. However, the English claimed the right to travel on the rivers flowing through Russian territory according to a treaty made with Russia in 1825; so, after lengthy negotiations in 1839, an agreement was made with the English government according to which the stretch of coast from 54° 40' to Cape Spencer was open to the Hudson's Bay Company for ten years starting June 1, 1840, in return for two thousand Columbia sea otter annually.[93]

In 1849 this agreement was extended for ten years more. By that time the Hudson's Bay Company had built thirty-six hunting stations in this stretch of coast.[94] The contract was extended twice more, first for four years and then for two years more, ending June 1, 1865.

From 1840 to 1845 Etolin administered the colonies. He set a precedent which helped to promote even more friendly relations between the Russians and the natives. In 1841 he invited the natives to a fair at New Archangel which was to have ceremonial feasts for the guests. After advance notice had been sent to all the neighboring settlements, five hundred of the most prominent Tlingit gathered in a building set up in the fort for the occasion. According to an edict from the head officials, these markets were to be held from time to time.

In 1841 to 1842, George Simpson made an inspection tour through the Hudson's Bay Company territory during which he also visited the Russian holdings in America with Freimann, his companion and guide from the Russian-American Company. Simpson made the trip through Canada overland to Fort Vancouver on the Columbia River, and from there he went north by steam packet to inspect the factories on the coast, especially the newly established Fort Stikine and Fort Taco on the stretch of coast leased to the English by the Russian-American Company. After two long visits at Sitka, Simpson returned to Europe through Siberia. His travel account gives some observations about the native tribes and some very interesting comments on the Sitkas, the Stikines, and the Takus.

One important result of Simpson's journey was the prohibition issued by the head administrator, Etolin, against the sale of liquor to the natives. Since 1832 the Russians had not used brandy as an article of trade, and it was hoped that the cooperation of the Americans could be secured, for the neighboring Hudson's Bay posts adopted a similar practice. According to agreement, this trade was to stop in 1843. But since there were outbreaks among the Sitka Indians and at Fort Stikine through drunkenness, Etolin put the prohibition against liquor into effect immediately. At Fort Stikine the personnel of the Hudson's Bay Company started a fight with each other in which the chief of the fort, McLoughlin, was killed by gunshot. This encouraged the neighboring Indian tribes to an attack and only through the intervention of Simpson who arrived on a Russian ship was the threatening affair averted. [95]

In order to associate the Tlingit more closely with the Russians, the post of head chief of the Kolushans was created during Etolin's administration. For this office Michael Kuchkan who belonged to a highly esteemed clan and was a baptised Tlingit was selected at the suggestion of the colonial administration. In 1862 a head chief was also introduced among the Stikines. [96]

The privileges of the company were extended in 1844 for another twenty years.

From 1840 to 1850 Tebenkof administered the colonies. The efforts of Etolin to pave the way for friendly relations with the Tlingit, it seems, were not continued by him and his successor, Rosenberg, 1851-1853, who through excessive fear is supposed to have broken off relations altogether. In 1852 forty Stikines who had come to the Sitkas in order to make peace with them were treacherously murdered by the latter without any effort being made by the Russians, under whose very eyes the crime was committed, to hinder them. In order to satisfy their desire for revenge, the Stikines destroyed the hospital which the Russians had built at the sulphur springs. The situation became even worse in 1855 when Wojewodskof (1854-1859) was director. The Tlingit would not allow a messenger to take away the firewood intended for the company and attacked him with daggers and wounded him. The orders of the director to turn over the guilty ones were answered by the natives with threats, and two cannon shots fired from the beach at Wojewodskof's command had no results; furthermore, a horde of armed Tlingit moved against the stockade and made threats to destroy it. When a Russian had also been wounded by a shot, Wojewodskof ordered the opening of fire, but still the Tlingit held their stand, with a few trying to penetrate the harbor while others took possession of the wooden church which had been erected outside the palisade for worship in the native language, and began to shoot through the windows. Only after a two-hour exchange of fire had reduced their ranks, did they give up the fight and agree to give hostages. Their loss in dead and wounded was about sixty men and the Russians lost two dead and nineteen wounded. [97] However, the fight again convinced the Tlingit of the strength and skill of the Russians and consequently put them in a more peaceful frame of mind.

Meanwhile many complaints about the administration of the colonies reached St. Petersburg, and in 1860, while Furuhelm (1860-1863) was director, Captain Lieutenant Golowin was sent out to inspect the situation. As a result of the report which was unfavorable to the company, their privileges were not renewed and the crown took over the administration. Maksutof was the first imperial director in 1864. However, in 1867 the Russian government relieved itself of its American possessions which had become so troublesome and sold them to the United States government for $7,200,000.00. The natives barely received mention in the transaction, only the Russians who wanted to remain were assured protection by the American government.

The ceremonial transfer of the fort of New Archangel to the American troops took place on October 18. The Indians followed the ceremony with great interest. Since they were not allowed in town, they embarked in their canoes and took positions in the harbor from which, in spite of the distance, they had a good view of the proceedings. They had only a vague idea of the implications and because of their acquaintance with American whalers they were not inclined to regard it favorably. They watched the lowering and raising of the flags and listened to the thunder of the cannons and then quietly withdrew. [98]

As a result of the change of government the Russian calendar which had been used in Alaska was no longer official. In order to coordinate it with American time reckoning a calendar day had to be skipped, since the Russians, coming from the east, had brought their date system with them. New Archangel, the principal town, changed its name to Sitka, of Tlingit origin, which had already been in use among the English and Americans instead of the Russian name.

A new spirit moved in with American possession which destroyed that individuality of the native tribes which had up to that time been fairly well maintained. The Russians who lived among the natives adapted themselves to their customs and habits of living so that, as Vancouver remarked, they differed little from them. The Americans, on the other hand, who now poured into the country to seek their fortunes, concerned themselves very little about the customs of the Indian population and pursued their own purposes with no consideration of them even when they lived in blockhouses in their midst as traders and prospectors. The material consequence was that also among the natives their customs, which the strangers regarded with such disdain, fell more

and more into disuse and instead they took up ways of the whites
of questionable advantage to them. The Americans exploited the
resources of the country through various industrial developments
and brought the Indian into this industrial sphere which gave him
more numerous and varied contacts than he had had under the
Russians. At many places trading posts and salmon canneries
were set up and in 1882 even a fish-reduction plant was built at
Killisnoo. Above all, though, the discovery of gold-bearing
quartz in the mountains brought an influx of adventurers, who, in
search of the precious metal, swept through the whole country
and by their unbridled living had a bad influence on the natives.

The first gold was found in British Columbia in 1858. In 1872
the Cassiar mine which yielded richly in its first years, was discovered below 59° north latitude, at the source of the Dease River, near Dease Lake, the upper end of which is only a few miles
of level country away from the Stikine River where active traffic
developed in which the Indians had their share. In 1875 there
were already eight hundred gold seekers in the Cassiar area and
by 1877 the number had risen to twelve hundred, among them
three hundred to four hundred Chinese. [99]

The extraordinarily severe winter weather in the gold district
made the prospectors seek the milder climate of the coast for
their winter quarters, and several hundred usually stayed in Fort
Wrangell where they lived with Indian women and whiled the time
away with card playing and drinking.

In 1871 gold-bearing veins were also found near Sitka by a former soldier, named Doyle, but since they did not prove produc-
tive, work on them was abandoned. Then in 1880 a richer field
was found on the mainland in the vicinity of Taku Inlet and opposite Douglas Island. The settlement which developed rapidly
there was called Harrisburg after the founder and later was
changed to Juneau. In 1881, eighty prospectors had settled in
forty log cabins and, seeing the chance for easy gains, two hundred Indians set up their camps in the neighborhood.

After the transfer of Alaska to the United States, the land was
declared Indian Territory. [100] Only at Sitka, Fort Wrangell, and
for a time also in Fort Tongass weak American garrisons were
maintained for a short time to preserve order and protect the
white population from Indian attacks. When the military was withdrawn in 1877 and no authority remained in the country except the
customs officers, the Tlingit took courage again and their menacing attitude raised fears of serious outbreaks.

In July 1878 a boat from the schooner San Diego engaged in
fishing on the Alaska coast, overturned with the captain and five
Sitka Indians. A young chief in Sitka, Katlian, put in a claim for
this loss as well as the death of another Indian, who, in the company of a white man, had drunk himself to death, asking one

The Russian castle at Sitka

thousand dollars damages. His demand was recognized by a coun-
teroffer of two hundred fifty dollars. Even though Katlian accepted the sum offered, he later came back to his original claim.
Then he tried with violence to free two Indians who, accused of
the murder of a white man, were being taken to Portland, Oregon,
by mail boat to stand trial. He further tried to incite his tribe to
plunder the town and massacre the inhabitants. Since he got little
attention in Sitka, he went to the neighboring tribes, even to Chilcat to get their support for his projected fight. Meanwhile the
frightened whites not only turned to the American government in
Washington, but on account of their imminent danger asked that
an English warship be sent from Victoria in British Columbia.
After inquiring by telegraph to Washington whether English help
would be acceptable, the warship Osprey sailed at once and arrived in Sitka the same day that the much feared Chilcat came
down. Serious disorders were averted, but among the Indians
hostilities broke out between those friendly to the whites and those
opposed to them, during which the leader of the former group
was wounded and one Indian killed. The Osprey was soon released by an American man-of-war. Since that time in 1879, an
American warship has constantly cruised in the Sitka Archipelago
and all Tlingit towns are sufficiently aware of its presence to a-
void any wholesale outbreak.
   In Sitka itself the old ordinance that no Indian was allowed in
the white town overnight was put into effect again, and to maintain it a few trustworthy Indians were taken into the police force.
The houses of the Indians were inspected, and the inhabitants
were forced to clean them and their surroundings; and children,
under threat of punishment, were forced to go to mission schools.

In one census it was found that there were thirteen persons held as slaves, and in the presence of their masters, they were freed. Also all distilling apparatus, found in almost every native house for making "hutschinu," was destroyed. These and many other arbitrary orders by the commander of the warship contributed to the deterioration of the natives and had no lasting effect in advancing their civilization. Whether the civilizing effects of the Presbyterian missionary society which will be mentioned in another chapter can retard the decline of the Tlingit people, seems doubtful. It would be better if one could hope for the establishment of an organized government to end the present state of lawlessness.

2. The Territory of the Tlingit

Extent and geographical description of territory -- The
broken coastline; islands and straits -- Advantages and
dangers of navigation -- The innermost islands still unknown and hard to reach -- Mountains and volcanic phe-
nomena -- Hot springs and earthquakes -- Geological
structure; ores and minerals -- River valleys and passes
to the interior of the continent.

Climatic conditions -- Contrast between east and west
coasts of America -- Frequency of precipitation -- Glaciers -- Thunderstorms -- Northern lights -- The vegetation -- Abundant plant life -- Tree growth in the forests -- Thick underbrush -- Moss and muskeag tundra --
Berry bushes -- Salt water vegetation -- Attempts at
cultivation.

Animal life; predatory animals and fur bearers -- The
sea mammals -- The characteristic birds; eagle, raven,
hummingbird -- Wealth of fish in waters -- The lower
forms of marine life -- Insect pests.

The following description of the territory of the Tlingit in its
main outlines applies to the whole coast south to the Fuca Strait
(Strait of Juan de Fuca). [1] In spite of the expanse, covering
twelve degrees of latitude, the climatic conditions do not differ,
as one might expect, since the same current tempers the cold of
the northern winter and the heat of the southern summer.

The territory of the Tlingit stretches from 55 to 60 degrees
latitude. The broken coastline which begins north of the Strait of
Juan de Fuca continues to Cross Sound at the 58th parallel.
Countless islands, large and small, are separated by narrow
channels from the mainland. Vancouver recognized the most important and grouped them under special names. He gave the
name of King George Third's Archipelago[2] to the group consisting of Baranof and Chichagof islands which is bounded by Cross

Sound on the north and by Chatham Strait on the east, while narrow Peril Strait divided the two islands. Kruzof Island with Mt.
Edgecumbe and Iacoby (Yakobi) Island with Cape Cross, as well
as numerous small islands also belong to the same group.

East of King George Third's Archipelago and separated from it
by Chatham Strait is Admiralty Island which is cut off from the
mainland by Stephens Passage and which is bordered on the
south by Prince Frederick Sound (Frederick Sound). Kootznahoo, [3]
a narrow inlet, not yet fully explored, cuts this island in two.
North is Douglas Island, separated from the mainland by Gasti-
neau Canal.

South of Admiralty Island, across Frederick Sound, lies a
group of very much dismembered islands, part of which was regarded by Vancouver as belonging to the mainland because of his
oversight of Wrangell Strait and Suchoi Canal (Sukoi Inlet). These
islands are Ku or Kuju, Kuprianow (Kupreanof), Mitkow (Mitkof),
Sarembo (Zarembo), Wrangell and Etolin. The Duke of Clarence
Strait (Clarence Strait) separates these islands from Prince of
Wales Island and numerous small neighboring islets. Eastward,
separated by Behm Canal from the mainland, lies a larger island,
Revilla Gigedo.

The straits which separate the island groups just listed are almost all navigable by the largest ships and offer numerous good
harbors, but in foggy weather many hidden rocks and lack of correct maps make great care necessary. Especially noteworthy is
Chatham Strait which, with its apparent extension, Lynn Canal,
extend through three degrees latitude, maintaining an average
width of ten to twelve kilometers, and is more than one hundred
fathoms deep in some places. The canals navigable by small
boats and canoes are countless. Many of them are not well
marked even on the newest maps and are known only to the natives who use them for fishing and hunting. A more favorable territory for canoe travel can hardly be imagined, fjords penetrate
deep into the mainland and the larger island groups, and many
portages shorten distances where there are no direct connections
from one inlet to another. Of the fjords which extend into the
mainland and open into Cross Sound, the most important are:
Glacier Bay, roomy but not fully known, Lynn Canal, one hundred thirty kilometers long, and already mentioned, Taku Inlet,
Bradfield Canal, Boca de Quadra and above all, Portland Canal,
through which the boundary of British Columbia is drawn and its
important tributary, Observation Bay. Vancouver devoted a
whole week, from July 27 to August 2, 1793, to the exploration of
this narrow inlet.

All these channels remain open all year to shipping since the
high salinity of the water even in the coldest weather prevents the
formation of ice except at the far end of the inlet at the mouth of

a river. On the other hand, loose masses of ice from the glaciers can render entrance into some bays difficult even in summer, as in Glacier Bay and Taku Inlet.

Through the change of tide which has a mean difference of six
meters in the narrow inlets, strong rip tides and eddies are
created, which also tend to make navigation difficult. Especially
heavy is the rip tide in Peril Strait where even large craft can
only pass at certain times.

North of Cross Sound to Copper River the coast of the mainland
is unbroken. This region is the most inhospitable of the whole
Northwest coast. Here the continental mountain ranges come
down directly to the seashore and only two bays, Lituya and Yakutat, offer the navigator a safe harbor.

It is just as hard to penetrate the interior of the islands and the
mainland as it is easy for ships to travel along the coast except
for the region just mentioned. The whole archipelago and the
coast of the mainland is mountainous, nearly everywhere the
waves dash against a rocky shore so that for long stretches
beaches are found only at the mouths of rivers. The mountains
rise to over one thousand meters on the islands, in the north generally higher than in the south. The continental coast ranges,
however, reach far beyond the snow line in many places. Tower-
ing over all is the Elias range (St. Elias Alps) which extends
from Cross Sound northward to the Alaska peninsula, where its
lofty peaks, Mt. Fairweather, La Perouse, and St. Elias aroused
the astonishment of the first explorers. Only thirty kilometers
from the coast Mt. St. Elias rises, the highest peak on the North
American continent, with its mantle of ice and snow, a glittering
beacon to coastwise travelers. [4]

Beyond the steep coastal mountains, similar to the Norwegian
fjords, there stretches a bare rolling plateau, that gradually falls
off toward the interior and on which the sources of the Yukon and
the Mackenzie have their origin.

There are no active volcanos in Tlingit territory such as are
found in the western continuation of the coast range on the Alaska
peninsula and the whole chain of the Aleutian Islands. Because of
its regular contours, Mt. St. Elias might be regarded as an ex-
tinct volcano, even though there is no evidence of any former activity. Lisiansky, who climbed Mt. Edgecumbe, [5] another sym-
metrical mountain, in 1804, found an undoubted crater on its
summit. A column of smoke was supposed to have risen from it
in 1796. [6]

Indication of underground activity is the presence of hot springs
of which the sulphur springs at Sitka are best known. They rise
at the seashore from fissures in syenite rocks and are about 60°
C. Before the coming of the whites they were used by the Indians
to cure various ailments; later the Russians built some accomo-

dations to make the use of the springs more comfortable for the colonists. [7]

At various times earthquakes have been felt in the Sitka district. Blaschke records an earthquake in 1832; quite strong shocks occurred in December 1832 and in March 1848, [8] and the most recent were in October and November of 1880.

The mountain masses consist principally of granite and crystalline slate with rich ore deposits of gold, silver, lead, copper, iron, zinc, and others. The gold-bearing veins of Sitka, on the Cassiar, and at Juneau have in recent years been the scene of great mining activity. The natives have always known of the occurrence of native copper in the Copper River, of graphite at Sitka, and of large, well-developed garnets at Wrangell. Deposits of beautiful white marble which the natives used for pestles and small sculptures are found at various places in this territory. In the future the stone quarries which exist in great numbers on Admiralty Island in the neighborhood of Angoon (village of the Killisnoo) and on Kake Strait might become important.

With a few exceptions no important rivers flow into the sea between 55° and 60° latitude on the Northwest coast. Since the watershed is most everywhere only a short distance from the coast, there is no space for the formation of large rivers; however, as natural means of communication into the interior, even the small ones are important.

The Copper River, which gets its name from the presence of native copper just mentioned, flows just beyond the boundary of our territory to the north.

The Altsech, [9] a small stream in the valley through which the Chilkat travel to the sea, empties south of Yakutat Bay. [10]

The Chilcat River flows into the northwest arm of Lynn Canal and from its territory several passes lead into the Alsek, to Yakutat Bay and to the sources of the Yukon. The last could be reached by a shorter but more difficult route through the valley of the Deje which runs into a fjord of the same name in Northwest Lynn Canal.

The Taku River flows into glaciated Taku Bay and through its valley the Indians cross to the Yukon. The most important river, however, is the Stikine[11] or Stakin, as it is called by the natives, which below 56°40' empties into Sukoi Inlet and is navigable for some boats one hundred and forty kilometers upstream, not measuring its winding. Passes go over to the Mackenzie from its tributaries.

At the southern boundary of our territory the Nass River flows into Portland Canal where the Tsimshian, the southern neighbors of the Tlingit, live. [12]

The climatic conditions of southern Alaska invite comparison with the Norwegian coast. The yearly average temperatures are

53

considerably higher than at places of the same altitude on the east coast, resulting in the mild winters which this coastal region enjoys. By way of comparison, Sitka is below 57° north latitude and Bergen, 60°21'. In the former place flowers are said to bloom in February. [13]

On the Norwegian coast, as here, the mild climate is limited to a narrow coastal strip. While the temperature at Sitka in occasional winters falls a few degrees below zero, on the Cassiar it reaches the freezing point of mercury.

The whole coast has the heaviest precipitation in the world. The dampness which the prevailing south and southeast wind condenses against the high mountains turns into constant rainfall in summer and occasional snow in the long winter. During the second half of the winter of 1881-1882, which seems to have been an exceptionally severe one, three to four meters of snow lay in the Chilcat territory most of the time; in early June there was still snow in the valleys and early in September fresh snow fell at the timberline. Even in Sitka the ground was covered with snow in early May.

The most complete survey of the meteorology of Alaska is to be found in Appendix I of the Coast Pilot of Alaska, 1879, by Dall. The following facts are taken largely from this work which also reviews the older literature.

We are best acquainted with the climatic conditions of Sitka. Except for occasional older observations[14] we have almost continuous meteorological reports since 1832. The credit for beginning these is due to Admiral Wrangell. On the basis of his meteorological diary Baer gave a survey of the climate of Sitka in 1839 in which he also commented on the sharp distinction between the east and west coast of America in regard to temperature. Later Kupffer used the observations made in Sitka in a more extensive work.

The mean average annual temperature according to Dall (Fahrenheit degrees reduce to centigrade, divide by 6.3°). [15]

The average temperature of the seasons is: 5.1° C for spring (41.18° F), 12.6° C for summer (59.72° F), 7.2° C for fall (47.8° F), 0.4° C for winter (32.7° F).

The coldest month is January with an average temperature of 0.4° C; the warmest is August with 13.3° C.

The extremes noted in forty-five years of observation are 31° C and - 20° C.

The annual average of precipitation was ca. 2050 mm., the greatest rainfall being in October, the least, in June.

On the average it rains or snows two hundred days of the year or in a proportion of 166 to 34. The most favorable year during the observation period was 1833 with eighty-two rainy days and thirty-two days of snowfall; the most unfavorable, 1856, with two hundred fifty-eight days of rain and twenty-seven of snow.

At Fort Wrangell, 47' south of Sitka the observation period of 3-2/3 years gave these results: annual mean temperature, 5.7° C (44.54° F); maximum warmth, 33° C; minimum temperature, -23° C; annual rainfall, ca. 1650 mm.

In Fort Tongass, 2°17' further south than Sitka the observations extend only through 2-1/3 years. The data read: average annual temperature, 8.1° C; maximum, 33° C; minimum, -19° C. The annual rainfall was more than 3090 mm., or one-third more than in Sitka.

The extraordinarily heavy snowfall is related to the frequency of glaciers in the northern part of the territory. Especially heavily glaciated is the coast north of Cross Sound; great masses of ice break away from Mt. Fairweather and from the St. Elias group and slide into the sea. Also Glacier Bay which opens into Cross Sound is filled with large and smaller icebergs from the glacial streams that flow into it. Vancouver mentioned the difficulties caused by the icebergs. Another glacier which opens into the sea is found at the northern end of Taku Inlet. Also the glaciers in the Chilcat territory are very numerous, even though none of them reach the sea. In practically every valley of the mountains that hem in Lynn Canal one can catch a glimpse of glistening ice masses, sometimes in the upper reaches and often close to the water. In the valleys that lead into the fjords one finds glaciers, especially on the north and east sides. The passes to the interior which rise to a height of one thousand to fifteen hundred meters are covered with snow late into the summer and are surrounded by glaciers.

Conforming to the contours of the floor of the valley and the surrounding rock structures, the glaciers assume great variety of forms. One plunges in several cascades into the depth, while another flows down in a long winding course. Now they are a clean bluish shimmering surface, and again the edges and the middle have regularly spaced hummocks; the surface of some is closely covered with gravel so that they look black and from the distance more like a muddy crevasse than a sheet of ice. Another will have an opening at the end through which a sizable stream pours forth; another spreads fanwise in the valley and gives rise to several swift creeks.

Thunderstorms are an infrequent phenomenon in southeastern Alaska. During a stay of ten months we did not witness a single one. According to Langsdorff and Erman, they are more apt to occur in winter. [16] More frequently there is a display of northern lights which we generally saw in the form of the so called rays or drapery northern lights, and more seldom as a single or double lightbow.

As a consequence of the heavy precipitation the vegetation of

the coastal area develops to such an amazing abundance that it
has a tropical aspect. An unbroken coniferous forest rises to a
height of about eight hundred meters and is only occasionally broken in damp places by a light growth of alder, poplar and willow
or, on rugged precipices, by birch. There are two principal conifers, the Sitka spruce (Picea Sitchensis Carr.)[17] and a hemlock
(Tsuga Mertensiana Bong.). [18] The former is a stately tree which
in its habitat reminds one of the "Rottanne" since great trunks
more than a meter thick and fifty meters high are not infrequent.
One tree we measured had a circumference of 5.82 meters at a
height of two meters from the ground. Such trunks, when they
have grown straight, are used by the natives for their canoes and
for strong posts and planks in their houses. The hemlock never
reaches the size of the Sitka spruce, and only occasionally would
the circumference of a trunk be as much as 4.34 meters, two
meters from the ground. Its wood is not very useful. In unfertile,
swampy areas or places exposed to the wind from the sea one
finds small stands of a pine (Pinus contorta Dougl.)[19] and on the
mountains near the timberline the common Tsuga is replaced by
another variety (Tsuga Pattoniana Engelm.). Even higher than
this is Abies subalpina Engelm., [20] a prettier, taller tree that reminds one of the Canadian balsam fir, both in appearance and because of the large bubbles which contain pitch under the smooth
bark. On the coast it occurs only here and there in small clusters
while on the other side of the passes it is predominant. The so-
called red cedar (Thuja gigantea Nutt.)[21] is scattered or to be
found in small groups on all the islands, but only further south on
the Queen Charlotte Islands does this beautiful and useful tree
reach its best development. The yellow cedar (Chamaecyparis
nutkaensis Lamb.), [22] also found singly near Sitka, has a splen-
did wood for carving but really belongs to the southern portion of
the territory.

These two trees are often confused, so that one cannot always
tell in accounts which tree is meant. As a special quality of the
cedar, it is said to be light, close grained and durable. The
strong aromatic odor is supposed to be protection against moths
and other harmful insects. For this quality it was highly prized
in China where it was formerly imported and made into trunks under the name of camphor wood by the Chinese. The ship worm,
the teredo, is also supposed not to touch cedar. Davidson found
that the parts of a ship made of cedar thirty-two years ago and lying as a wreck for many years were not eaten. [23]

Few deciduous trees, except those mentioned above, as well as
the maple (Acer glabrum Tor.), [24] the service tree (Sorbus sambucifolia Cham. and Schl.), [25] and a kind of crabapple (Pirus riv-
ularis Dougl.), are scattered in the coniferous forest, but they
usually only form an undergrowth which in the deeper forests is

well developed and becomes an almost impenetrable thicket like
the creepers in a tropical forest. Fallen tree trunks lie crisscross, some half-rotted and all covered with moss. Even the living trees are thickly covered with lichen and moss. Man-high
ferns and even taller huckleberry bushes and rhododendron are
associated with the peculiar west coast Araliacea (Fatsia horrida
Smith.), [26] called devil's walking stick by the Americans, whose
slender stem is surrounded by a circle of large, handshaped
leaves which, like the stems, have countless fine spines that with
careless handling penetrate the skin and cause unpleasant sore-
ness. It is almost impossible to leave the narrow trails made by
the Indians. An eagle that was shot and fell just a short distance
from the shore in this forest undergrowth could be reached only
after hours of effort, and hunting for small birds in this primeval
forest is almost useless for even if one can reach the place where
the bird fell it is impossible to find it. Only in winter when there
is a heavy cover of snow is this wilderness easily passable, for
on snowshoes one can stride over all the hindrances just mentioned.

The dampness in the deeper forests is so great that a fire,
either deliberately set or caused by accident, cannot develop into
a conflagration. Baranof tried in vain to burn down the close
stand of conifers around Sitka because they gave the Indians bent
on attack such a good hiding place, [27] but he finally had to resort to
the axe to achieve his purpose. Today the place is surrounded
by a forest of stumps overgrown abundantly by shrubs, a witness
to Baranof's unsuccessful fight against the fecundity of nature.

At greater heights above sea level the coniferous forest thins
out where, through a subalpine region, the transition is made to
the bare high plateau which is reminiscent of the Norwegian
fields. Here, as there, snowfields alternate with rock formations,
moss, and lichen tundra; dwarf birches and creeping willows are
the meager representatives of the tree world.

The many uses to which the Tlingit put plant life will be discussed in a later chapter; here only the berry bushes used in
housekeeping will be mentioned. In the pine woods there grow two
shrub forms of Vaccinia (Vaccinium ovalifolium Smith and V.
sp.), blue huckleberry, with fruit tasting like our blueberries; on
the margin of the forest and on the mountain slopes are two kinds
of currants (Ribes laxiflorum Pursh. and Ribes lacustre Poir.),
trailing currant and swamp currant or gooseberry, and several
kinds of blackberries and raspberries of which Rubus Nutkanus
Lindl.[28] has a very tasty and fragrant fruit. On sunny river
banks are two shrubs, Shepherdia canadensis Nutt. (Buffalo or
soapberry) and Amelanchier ovalis Ser. [29] Their berries are
boiled in water and the thick pulp then laid in the sun or dried
over a fire. In the fall the berries of several varieties of low

vaccinium ripen above the timberline (V. Vitus idaea L. , rock cranberry, V. uliginosum L. , bog huckleberry, V. caespitosum Michx. , dwarf huckleberry, V. myrtilloides Hooker), [30] Kinni-kinnick (Arctostaphylus uva ursi and alpina) [31] and crowberries (Empetrum nigrum L.) are gathered. By far the most important berry is the snowberry (Viburnum acerifolium L.) which grows profusely in low lying, deep woodsy spots.

Salt water vegetation also makes its contribution to the Tlingit household. On the seashore there are edible algae (Alaria esculenta Grev.) of which square black cakes are made by pressing them into a wooden box. Very noticeable also is a giant kelp (Macrocystis pyrifera Ag.) whose long stem is agitated by the waves like a great sea serpent. The long, hollow stem, which at the far end is no more than a finger thick, ends in a ball about the size of a child's head on which there are long, thin leaves. The natives use the thin, whiplike part of the stem, which is very tough, for fishing lines and boat lines.

The climate is not suitable for cultivation. The Russians tried to introduce grains and fruit, but with little success. It is, how-ever, not impossible that, with continued effort, better results could be gained, since the climatic conditions are not much more unfavorable than in southern Norway. At least a number of vege-tables like cabbage, rutabagas, radishes, and peas prosper. The Indians have adopted the cultivation of the potato in many places, and even though they are small and watery the crop is quite large despite the slight amount of care expended on them.

In the dark depths of the forest a rich animal life is hidden. Two kinds of bears, the feared grizzly (Ursus cinereus Desm.) [32] and the black American bear, are plentiful. In winter they both hibernate in dens which they find under the roots of huge trees in the valleys, and they sleep until awakened by the sun of spring. Foxes, black and gray wolves, as well as the American wolver-ine, land otter, and ermine are not infrequent. The cat family is represented only by the lynx.

The most valuable fur-bearing animal, the sea otter (Enhydra marina F. Cuv.), [33] can now only be found in inaccessible places on the outer coast, on the Forrester Islands, west of Prince of Wales Island, and on the coast north of Cross Sound. In Vancou-ver's time they were plentiful in Chatham Strait and their pres-ence in Norfolk Sound was the reason for the founding of Sitka. Here, as in the whole archipelago, they were completely exter-minated by the devastating hunt of the Russians, who, in 1804 alone, took two thousand skins in one expedition through Cross Sound and Chatham Strait.

The half-wild dogs that are found in every Indian village, and make themselves very objectionable through their howling and thievery, belong to the race of Eskimo dogs; they have no relationship to the Indian dogs of British Columbia and Puget Sound who could be confused in their appearance with coyotes (Canis latrans Sm.). [34] They are never used as draft animals, but occasionally taken hunting.

Rodents are plentiful in the forests, represented by the squirrel (Sciurus hudsonicus Pall.), [35] the snow rabbit and the porcupine (Erethizon epixanthus Brdt.). [36] Along streams one finds the muskrat (Fiber zibethicus Cuv.), [37] and a few beaver, though these are more frequent in the interior and along the southern coast of the mainland. In the forests of the islands a small Columbian deer is common, while on the neighboring coasts of the mainland it is absent. The caribou is only found on the high plateaus of the mainland; in the coastal ranges live the mountain sheep (Ovis montana Cuv.), [38] and the mountain goat (Haplocerus americanus Blainv.), [39] whose white wool is used by the natives for weaving their peculiar dance blankets. Here also is the home of the ubiquitous ground squirrel (Spermophilus parryi Rich.) and the marmot (Arctomys sp.)[40] which attracts the attention of travelers with a long-drawn-out whistle.

And finally, an important addition to the mammals are the sea mammals, the whales, porpoises and hair seals, which, following the fish runs, penetrate the bays and straits of the archipelago, while the sea lions, sea otter, and fur seals confine themselves to the outer coast.

Among the characteristic birds of the area are the eagle (Haliaetos leucocephalus), [41] a beautiful, stately bird that can be seen from afar as it sits on a lonesome treetop. It is used in several ways by the Tlingit. Its meat is eaten, especially by the old people; even the Russians, in the first years after the founding of Sitka, when rations were short, are supposed to have killed two hundred eagles and eaten them. Langsdorff himself claims often to have satisfied his hunger with the meat of this bird and to have found it tasty. [42] In addition the Tlingit use the down feathers of this bird in their dances and ceremonies to sprinkle on the head and blow into the air. The tail and wings are used for fans for the same occasions, the wing bones are made into drinking tubes, as will be told later in the description of the rituals.

The raven (Corvus carnivorus Bartr.), [43] a sacred bird among the Tlingit, stays in great numbers near the villages in winter and makes itself very noticeable through its extraordinary trickiness. In Sitka it was hunted down by the Russians since it proved dangerous to poultry and, as Lütke reports, even tore the tails off pigs. [44] However, it proved its usefulness as a scavenger, earning itself the title of the "police" of Sitka.

Another winter visitor in the villages is the magpie (Pica hudsonica Bp.)[45] which in its appearance and habits resembles ours. A constant inhabitant of the forest is the beautiful bluejay (Cyano-

Landscape along Indian River near Sitka

citta Stelleri Gm.). [46] Among the owls, the snowy owl and the
great horned owl [47] are most noticeable, while several kinds of
fowl, the ptarmigan and grouse, bring welcome relief in winter
from a fish diet. Ducks, geese and cormorants are among the
large numbers of waterfowl living in the fjords, and during their
migrations swans and geese are also present.

The number of summer-nesting birds is not great; among them,
however, is one that attracted our attention, the California hummingbird (Selasphorus rufus Gmel.), that even in the snow and
ice of the northern part of the territory is not inhibited in its wonderful activity, as it flits from tree to tree, like a ray of sunshine, like a bee winging from roses to raspberry blossoms. On
the coast his range extends to the mouth of the Atna River [48] and
to the south side of the narrow Alaska peninsula, on whose north
shores the walrus is found.

Of greatest importance to the household of the natives is the
abundance of fish in the local waters. The salmon, the staff of
life of the Indians, goes upstream in untold numbers. Various
kinds come at certain seasons of the year. A very tasty fish from
which a fine oil can be rendered is Thaleichthys pacificus Gir. or
(Rich.), one of the smelt varieties, [49] which appear at the mouths
of rivers early in the spring. Haddock and halibut of extraordinary size can be caught the year round; in April and May great
masses of herring come into shallow bays and deposit their
spawn, greatly prized by the natives.

The lower forms of marine life are also represented in great
numbers and are not unimportant to the economy of the native.
Large crabs, sea urchins, and especially several kinds of mul-

lusks, among them the mussel and the cockle (Cardium Nuttallii Conr.), [50] furnish a nutritious diet and one easily gotten. The eating of the mussel is not without danger, for at certain times they are regarded as poisonous by the natives. Vancouver lost one of his men who ate some of these mussels, while another became ill, and in 1789 a group of more than one hundred Aleut (Konjagen) who, during a rest period in Peril Straits, ate some of these mussels died within two hours in terrible agony. [51] In memory of this the Russians called the strait, Sound of the Unfortunates.

The customary plague of northern lands, the hordes of bloodthirsty mosquitoes and gnats are not missing in the damp country of southern Alaska. They occur in greater numbers as one leaves the coast and goes farther up the fjords and inlets. Only the bare, high plateaus are comparatively free and offer the grazing caribou a refuge in summer.

Otherwise the insect life is noticeably meager. Especially lacking are a large number of wood-boring beetles, and therefore the rotting of fallen trees goes on at a slow rate.

3. The Tlingit People

Sparse population and scattered settlements in Vancouver's time -- Various estimates of population figures -- Meaning and orthography of the word "Tlingit" -- Other names of the Tlingit -- Origin of the word "Koloschen" -- Division into tribes; their leadership -- Division into clans; the groups of Raven and Wolf clans. Tables of the tribes and clans according to several authors -- The so-called nobility of the Tlingit -- The position and rights of a chief.

The territory described in the foregoing chapter is not capable of maintaining a large population. On account of the mountainous nature of the country, agriculture can only be practised in a few places, and also because of the rigorous climate with long winters and wet summers, late spring and early fall frost, few plants can be cultivated. For extensive cattle raising adequate meadows are not available, and the wet climate makes the preparation of necessary winter fodder exceptionally difficult. Hunting can feed only a very sparse population, and great activity in it would also soon exterminate the game in the forests, as has already been done with the sea otter. That leaves only the abundance of fish in the sea as a seemingly inexhaustible source of food, but that these can also be dangerously depleted has been seen in the past. A meager population can easily find abundant nourishment in this territory, and actually the first visitors to the Northwest coast found a sparse population. The English and American fur traders who were looking for natives and anxious to attract their attention by every means, often landed in inlets without the slightest sign of occupation. During the extensive exploring trips taken by Vancouver and his officers through the straits of the archipelago they seldom came upon natives and then usually in small hunting parties with a few canoes, and even more seldom did they notice their villages. According to Vancouver's Journal he and his men saw only the following villages: on August 11, 1793, on Behm Canal at Point Whaley, [1] a very large village, apparently deserted a few months before, which could have sheltered three hundred to four hundred people; on August 14, 1793, on a high isolated rock on a little island in Revilla Gigedo Canal, south of Cape Northumberland, ruins of an unimportant village;[2] on August 27, 1793, ruins of a second large Indian village discovered by Whidbey on Behm Canal; on July 22, 1794, some new houses observed by Whidbey south of Point Parker on Chatham Strait; on July 29, 1794, an uninhabited Indian village in which about fifty dogs were found, visited by Puget in Yakutat Bay; on August 8, 1794, a village seen by Whidbey on the north shore of Admiralty Island and a second one on the opposite shore of Douglas Island;[3] on August 10, 1794, four houses counted by Johnston on Ku Island at the upper end of Port Cambden; on August 13, 1794, on Kekou Island in Hamilton Bay,[4] eight deserted and partly ruined villages noted by Johnston, all on steep prominences or rocky points almost impregnable by nature but in addition fortified by art.

In addition to these settlements seen by Vancouver and his men during two summers, a few others were mentioned, knowledge of whose existence was only obtained through native hearsay. If many of these villages were deserted, the reason may have been that the inhabitants with their families had gone hunting or fishing in the woods and inlets as they are accustomed to do in the summer, although several places looked as though they had been unoccupied for a longer period of time. It would be hasty to deduce from this evidence a decrease in the population; rather, these observations seem to point to the nomadic nature of these people.

We would scarcely be wrong to assume that during Vancouver's time the native population of this territory was not much greater than it is at the present time. Actually there are very little reliable data available for judging population figures, for even today the estimates show considerable variation. However, the entire Tlingit group can scarcely total more than 8000 to 10,000 people.

Before the great smallpox epidemic in 1836, there were, according to Veniaminof, about 10,000, including the Kaigani of Haida origin on Prince of Wales Island, but the number fell to about 6000. The census report of 1880, excluding the Kaigani, was 6763. [5]

This sparse population was spread along a coastal strip, which, if drawn in a straight line, even disregarding the many inlets, would be almost as long as the German shore line of the North Sea from Memel to Kiel. Through similar speech and customs and by active intercourse, even though not always friendly, the Tlingit presented a homogeneity which distinguished them from neighboring tribes.

The name "Tlingit" by which the natives call themselves[6]
means the "people." The word has been written many different
ways. Langsdorff, who seems to have been the first person to use
it, wrote "G-tinkit" or "S-chinkit."[7] According to the pronuncia-
tion of the Chilkat Indians it seemed to us that the spelling of
"Chtlingit" or "Chlingit" was most accurate. Generally it has
been customary to follow the orthography of Holmberg who, according to Veniaminof, renders it "Thlinkith." Since it is almost
impossible to transcribe the unusual sounds of the Tlingit language accurately in our system of orthography, we have adopted
the transcription of Holmberg, only omiting the unnecessary cir-
cumflexes, as others, like Erman, have also done.[8]

The Tlingit were called Kaljusch, Kalosch or Kolosch[9] by the
Russians, a name which has found a place for itself in the literature and which, in ignorance of the differences among the tribes
living on the Northwest Coast, as Tlinkit or Thlinkithen, has
been used to designate not only the Tlingit themselves, following
Veniaminof and Holmberg, but the entire Indian population from
Mt. St. Elias to the Columbia River. The name is supposed, according to Veniaminof, to come from the Aleutian word "kaluga"
which means a dish or wooden utensil. The Aleuts who were taken
by the Russians to Sitka saw in the labret worn by the Tlingit
women a resemblance to the wooden dishes used at home and on
account of these labrets called the Tlingit, Kaluga. From this the
Russians formed the diminutive Kaluschka which gradually became current as the name for the whole group.[10] Erman tries to
show that the word is derived from the Russian kolotj, meaning
"to bore through or split," but Veniaminof does not follow him in
this explanation.[11] The oldest use of the word in the form "Koli-
uschen" I found in a report made by the two steersmen Ismailof
and Bocharof on Shelikof's voyage.[12] According to Erman's
translation[13] the passage reads as follows: "These people were
called Koljuschi. They live on the mainland along certain small
rivers. They have in addition to a number of petty chiefs also one
head chief whom they all obey." From this one might draw the
conclusion that it was not the Russians who on first contact gave
them this name but that the natives themselves used it, probably
the Konjagen[14] who accompanied them as interpreters.

Even more obscure is the origin of another name used by the
Russians for the Tlingit, namely, "schnjaga" which Holmberg
uses synonomously with "Kolosch" and uses quite as often. Since
this same word was used by the Tlingit when they called to a Russian, Holmberg claims as its meaning, "Friend, good friend,
listen."[15]

The Americans who have wandered in call the Tlingit categori-
cally, like all indigenous peoples, "natives" or "Indians" or also
Siwashes with the addition of their place of origin as Sitka Indians

or Sitka Siwashes. [16]

The entire Tlingit people are divided into a number of distinct tribes, called "kon,"[17] each of which has its permanent village and its hunting and fishing grounds. These tribes were called after the river or the bay upon which their villages were situated, as the Chilkat-kon and the Yakutat-kon, or after the island on which they lived, as the Sitka-kon.

The northernmost tribe of the Tlingit is the Yakutat whose principal village, "chlach-a-jek,"[18] is situated on Tsuska Island in Yakutat Bay.[19] The Yakutat tribe was never very large. Dixon counted only seventy natives here in 1787, but it must be taken into consideration that it was during the summer when most of the population is away hunting or on trading expeditions. Chliebnikof states that in 1805 the tribe had two hundred warriors. It seems that earlier they were somewhat dependent on the Chilkat tribe. The Russian steersmen Ismailof and Bocharof here met Ilchak the head chief whose own residence was on the Tschitschat (Tatshenshini) River,[20] but who had come in the spring of that year to Yakutat Bay by boat for a trading trip and also to visit his subjects. The local people traded with the Tschitschat to the east and the Ugalachmut[21] and Chugach to the west.[22]

Until very recent times the Chilkat and the Sitka carried on active trade with the Yakutat who are now almost the only people who can get sea otter. In spite of this the Sitka have claimed the privilege of this trade for themselves alone, and while we were there in the winter of 1881-1882 it was extended to the Chilkat after long negotiation.

The Yakutat have repeatedly shown themselves hostile and treacherous toward the whites. The Russian colony founded in 1799, as we have seen, was destroyed by them in 1805. After that no new stations were established in Yakutat Bay and only rarely did traders enter it until very recently when prospectors for gold visited there. Two of the latter were treacherously murdered by a native in 1881. The murderer, however, was later turned over to an American warship and taken to Portland where he was executed.

In more recent times the Yakutat seem to have pushed westward along the coast or they have intermingled with the Ugalent or Ugalakmut[23] with whom, according to Wrangell and Veniaminof, they are closely related both by marriage and blood. Petroff and Jacobsen met Tlingit at the mouth of the Copper River. According to oral information from the latter, there are in that region the villages of Tschilkat (Chilkat) and Allaganak[24] (Alaghanik on the maps of Holmberg)[25] which are inhabited by Tlingit who are subject to the chiefs of Yakutat Bay and who return there generally in the winter. A few scattered settlements are along the coast between Yakutat Bay and Cape Spencer which seem to be used only for hunting and fishing in summer and which have few or no permanent residents.

The Yakutat tribe differs from the other Tlingit in some peculiar customs, probably in consequence of their active intercourse with the neighboring tribes to the north. According to Veniaminof the Yakutat are the only Tlingit who do not hesitate to hunt whales; and he also insists that their women do not wear labrets, a statement contradicted by others. [26] Also their speech seems to have some strange elements in it. Veniaminof even claims that their language is independent and is divided into two dialects, the Yakutat and the Ugalent, each being spoken by about three hundred people. [27]

In the census of June 1, 1880, [28] the Yakutat tribe had eight hundred and twenty people who were distributed in the following villages: Chilkhaat village at the mouth of the Copper River, one hundred and seventy inhabitants; [29] Yaktag villages at the foot of Mt. St. Elias with one hundred and fifty inhabitants; [30] scattered villages between Yakutat Bay and Cape Spencer with two hundred inhabitants; Yakutat with five hundred inhabitants.

At the north end of Lynn Canal the Chilkat [31] tribe, the Chilkcat-kon (Tschishl-thatkhoan of Holmberg), the most powerful of all the Tlingit tribes, lives in four separate villages.

The principal village is Klukwan [32] on the Chilkat River about thirty kilometers from its mouth with sixty-five houses and from five hundred to six hundred inhabitants; about eight kilometers [33] below is Katkwaltu [34] with eight houses and one hundred and twenty-five inhabitants; and at the mouth itself is Iendestake [35] with sixteen houses and one hundred and fifty to two hundred inhabitants. The fourth village Tschilkut [36] with eight houses and about one hundred and twenty inhabitants, lies on the north arm of Lynn Canal at the opening of Tschilkut Bay (Chilkat). The Chilkat have always been held in high esteem by the other Tlingit as well as by their other neighbors, and they also seem to have a certain domination over some of them. The chief Ilchak, mentioned above as from the Tatshenshini River was probably a Chilkat. Vancouver's lieutenant, Whidbey, learned as he entered Lynn Canal of eight powerful chiefs who were supposed to live up the Chilkat River, and nowhere in his extensive investigations had he found as large a population as here; much to his discomfort this group of natives grew to the number of about two hundred warriors who were well armed and assumed a hostile attitude. [37] In demonstrations of the Sitka against the Russians, the Chilkat played a large role both as participants and as instigators. Through the wise winning over of the Chilkat chief, Kuskof succeeded in 1806 in persuading the Tlingit gathered on the islands around Sitka to move away. They also held tyrannical sway, in the interior, over the neighboring tribes of the Tinne family whom they called Gunana.[38] They did not allow them to carry on their own trade. Their trading expeditions went as far as Fort Selkirk on the Yukon which was destroyed by them in 1851. They took up trading into Yakutat Bay recently as was stated above.

Chilkat Indian on a trading expedition

The location of the main village above the mouth of a river which was navigable only by canoe in itself prevented the Europeans from reaching them and also gave the inhabitants a feeling of safety which prompted them to acts of violence and gave them an overbearing attitude toward the whites.

In 1880 a commercial company, the Northwest Trading Company, established a factory on the northwest arm of Lynn Canal, and the following year a mission was built. A second station was set up in the summer of 1882 in the Chilkat village of Klukwan. The trading center was recently moved to the Chilkat side of Labouchère Bay. [39]

According to the census of 1880, the Chilkat tribe consisted of nine hundred and eighty-eight, of whom five hundred and sixty-five were at Klukwan, one hundred and twenty-five at Kutkwutlu, one hundred and seventy-one at Yondestuk, and one hundred and twenty-seven in Chilkoot.

Chiefs of the Auks

A third tribe of the Tlingit is the Ak-kon who are in several villages on the north shore of Admiralty Island and on the mainland southeast of the opening of Lynn Canal. [40] Many Auks have settled near the new prospector's town of Juneau[41] where they can work for the whites as diggers, carriers, or woodcutters for fairly high wages of one to two dollars a day.

The census of 1880 counted three villages of the Auks, one on Stephens Passage with two hundred inhabitants, another on the north shore of Admiralty Island with three hundred inhabitants, a third on Douglas Island with fifty inhabitants, so that the whole tribe comprises six hundred and forty people.

Juneau City named after the discoverer of gold there, and formerly also called Harrisburg and Rockwell, already had in 1883 a population of over one hundred and had a post office and regular monthly steamship service to San Francisco.[42]

As neighbors, the Auks have the Taku-kon[43] who have settled on Stephens Passage at the entrance to Taku Bay and on Taku River. From these places the Taku Indians live upstream and trade with the Indians of the interior over reasonably high passes to the tributaries of the Yukon, just as the Chilkat do. In 1840 the Hudson's Bay Company founded a trading post on Stephens Passage at Taku Harbor, but it was later discontinued.[44]

According to the census of 1880 the Taku tribe consisted of two hundred and sixty-nine people, who lived in four villages on Taku River and Taku Bay. These are designated by the names of the chiefs, as follows: (1) Tokeatl's village with twenty-six natives; (2) Chitklin's village with one hundred and thirteen natives; (3) Katlany's village with one hundred and six natives; (4) Fotshou's village with twenty-four natives. The Samdans are occasionally added to the Taku or, according to some authors the Sundowns, about whom we obtained no additional information.[45] [46]

The Taku have, just like the Auks, settled in large numbers near the prospectors' town of Juneau. Named after the swift river running through the valley[47] there, the latter place is known to the Tlingit as Tsenta-ka-hini.

On Cross Sound there live the Hūna or Chūna; their principal village is Hūna-kŏn, belonging to the eastern people (chūn-east) and on the north coast of Chichagof Island[48] is the village of Gaudēkan[49] which had thirteen houses with about six hundred to eight hundred people. On the opposite shore of the mainland is supposed to be another village Chlulchagu with five houses. In summer the Huna leave their village to go fishing and sea otter hunting, the latter activity being carried on along the coast between Cape Spencer and Yakutat Bay. In 1880 a trading establishment was erected at Gaudēkan and the following year a mission, the former being moved in 1881.

According to the census of 1880, the Huna tribe numbered nine hundred and eight who lived in two villages, in Koudekan (Gaudēkan) with eight hundred and Klughagge with one hundred and eight inhabitants.

The Chūts-ta-kŏn on Chūtsinū (Killisnoo), which means Bear Island or Bear Fort, as Admiralty Island was known to the Tlingit,[50] had their principal settlement, Angoon on Chatham Strait[51] opposite Kănăs-nū Island.[52] There were twelve houses; to the south lay a second village, Neltūschk-ăn.[53] The Killisnoo helped the Sitka in 1804 against Baranof. Now many of these people find employment at a factory set up by the Northwest Trading Company in 1882 for the rendering of fish and whale oil at Killisnoo.

In the census of 1880 the Killisnoo tribe[54] had six hundred and sixty-six people of whom four hundred and twenty lived in Angoon and two hundred and forty-six in Scutskon.

The Killisnoo have lived peaceably in general with the whites, but in spite of this in 1882 the American warship Corwin bombarded the town of Angoon and partly destroyed it because the Indians tried to avenge the accidental death of an Indian who was in the employ of the trading company.

Chief of the Huna

Of all the Tlingit, the Sitka, Schita-kŏn (Schit-cha-chon of Langsdorff, Schitkhahóan of Holmberg), who live on Baranof Island which is called Sitka, meaning "Forested Island" by the Tlingit, have had the most contact with the whites. After the Russians took possession of their old homesite in 1804 and had also taken their fortification on Indian River, the Sitka settled, as we have said above, on Chatham Strait opposite the village of the Killisnoo. About 1822 they were invited by Murawiew to settle once again near the Russian colony, and so they built their present village under the cannons of the fort and separated from the Rus-

sians only by a strong palisaded fence. But they showed themselves several times as unruly neighbors, even later under
American rule. In fact in 1879 the frightened whites even called
for English help from Victoria against the Indians who, under the
leadership of a young chief, Katlian, and with the support of the
Chilkat, threatened to plunder the city. This unrest led to the
stationing of an American warship in the Sitka archipelago and to
the rigorous rules laid down by the commander which were discussed in the first chapter. The Indian village consisted of fifty
houses occupied by twelve hundred people. In the midst of the
usual Tlingit houses there were a few houses of European design.
Sitka has lost many of its unique qualities under American rule.

House in Angoon with a painted gable

In place of the many officials of the Russian American Company
who left as soon as the land was given over, only few Americans
have come in with the expectations of carrying on a large trade,
in which they were soon disappointed. The community now numbers only about three hundred. A census in 1879 listed two hundred and sixty-seven Russians and Creoles, the latter being the
descendants of Russians and Aleut or Tlingit women, and fifty
Americans, in total, three hundred and seventeen. According to
the census of 1880 there were one hundred and fifty-seven whites
and two hundred and nineteen Creoles, the latter being in very
deplorable condition. The old Russian structures, above all the
castle itself which under the regime of Wrangell and the later di-
rectors saw great magnificence, have fallen into decay. The palisade erected by the Russians against the Indians is only partly

standing, not through any hostile actions of the Indians but because the lazy Creoles find it a convenient place to get firewood.

About twelve kilometers from the present day Sitka, on Kotleana Bay, was situated the old Russian fort, Archangel Michael, founded by Baranof in 1799, which the Tlingit destroyed in 1802. Here at "Old Sitka" the Americans started a salmon cannery, but it was maintained only a few years. A few Indians have now settled there.

The hot springs are about five kilometers south of Sitka. The old bathhouse which the Russians built here was destroyed by the Stikine in 1852. Thereupon new structures were erected which were kept in condition until the troops left. These are now deserted and have fallen into decay since the last resident, a deserting soldier, was murdered by the Indians. Only a few Indians have houses in the neighborhood.

In the vicinity of the hot springs there is "Deep Lake"[55] on which the Russians erected a small bastion, for protection during salmon fishing, and later a flour mill, a saw mill, and a tannery. All these structures, as well as a little Russian chapel, are now in decay. In 1882 they were inhabited only by an old Russian and a few Indians.

According to the census of 1880 the Sitka tribe consisted of nine hundred and two, of whom seven hundred and twenty-one lived in the Indian village of Sitka itself, while thirty-nine were at Silver Bay, twenty-six at the hot springs, forty-three on Indian River and seventy-three at Old Sitka.

On Kupreanof Island and on part of Ku Island live the Keks[56] or Kĕkchkŏn,[57] a fairly numerous and restless tribe. Baranof had partly destroyed their dwellings in reprisal for their attack and almost complete annihilation of a group of Aleut hunters under Urbanof. Later a settlement of Kek and Stikine at Point Gambier where they were employed as workmen was cannonaded by an American warship and the chief of the Kek killed. In revenge for this a large group, heavily armed, went in canoes all the way south to Washington Territory in 1857 and killed Ebey, the customs inspector at Port Townsend. Also in 1868 when two of their number were shot in Sitka in a dispute they in turn killed two whites, feeling justified according to their own custom. As retribution, one of their villages was laid in ashes by the American warship Saginaw in 1869.[58]

In the census report of 1880 five villages were listed for the Kek tribe with five hundred and sixty-eight inhabitants: (1) Klukwan (identical in name with the Chilkat village) on Kupreanof Island with two hundred and sixty-one inhabitants; (2) a second village on Kupreanof Island with eighty-two inhabitants; (3) a village on Ku Island with one hundred inhabitants; (4) a settlement in Port Houghton with fifty inhabitants; (5) a village on Seymour

Canal with seventy-five inhabitants.

Roquefeuil also listed the village of Iknou on the west coast of little Kek Island. He saw there some palisades and a small piece of land planted with potatoes.

On one part of Ku Island which the Tlingit called Kuju[59] live the Kŭju-kŏn in several villages which are situated in the deep bays and fjords on the east shore. The Kuju seem also to have established themselves on the opposite shore of Prince of Wales Island. According to some reports there are supposed to have been about eight hundred people although the census report gives only sixty inhabitants to the Kuju tribe on the west coast of Prince of Wales Island.

On the Stikine River and on the islands at its mouth live the Stikine who number about one thousand. Vancouver was visited by O-non-nis-toy, the U-en-smoket or head chief of the U-en Stikine, on August 31, 1794, at Port Steward on the Behm Canal.[60] In 1834 the Russians built a redoubt, called the Dionysian, on Wrangell Island opposite the mouth of the Stikine River, which was taken over by the Hudson's Bay Company in 1839. In 1846 the Englishmen abandoned the fort again and it was later destroyed by the Stikine. After the sale of Alaska to the Americans, a military post was established at Fort Wrangell from 1867 to 1870 and again from 1875 to 1877. Through the development of the Cassiar mines and the consequent travel on the Stikine River, which in 1863 was explored by a Russian expedition under Bassarguine and Blake, the importance of Wrangell grew to the disadvantage of Sitka as it became increasingly popular as the wintering place for the gold miners. In Wrangell also began the missionary activities of the Americans among the Tlingit, which will be discussed later. The neighboring Tlingit tribes visited Wrangell in great numbers. When, during the winter of 1879-1880, a number of Killisnoo stayed there, a fight began between them and the Stikine through the overzealousness of the missionaries, which resulted in several deaths and some wounded on each side. As a result of this, even in 1882, these tribes were still hostile to each other.

When American troops were first placed there in 1869, the murder of the trader in the locality led to the bombardment of the Indian village. The circumstances were as follows: during the forcible arrest of an Indian who had bitten a finger off a laundress, resistance was offered, and in consequence an Indian was killed and several wounded. Thereupon the Indians revenged themselves by killing the trader and since they were all in accord they refused to deliver up the murderer. They were brought to terms by a long bombardment of the village and, after conviction, the murderer was hanged in the presence of the Indians.[61]

In the census of 1880, there are listed eight Stikine settlements named after their chiefs and numbering three hundred and seven-

teen people. They are as follows: (1) Shustak's village on Etolin
Island with thirty-eight people; (2) Kash's village on Etolin Island with forty people; (3) Shake's village on Etolin Island with
thirty-eight people; (4) Towayat's village on Etolin Island with
eighty-two people; (5) Kohltiene's village on Stikine River with
twenty-eight people; (6) Hinauhan's village on Stikine River with
thirty-one people; (7) Kadishan's village on Stikine River with
twenty-seven people; (8) Shallyany's village on Stikine River with
fourteen people.

According to the same report the white population of Fort
Wrangell was one hundred and five whites and one Creole.

The Stikine, like the Chilkat and the Taku, formerly carried on
an active trade with the Indians of the interior but, since the increased white population has offered them easier ways of making
a living, this has almost stopped. The Stikine are also supposed
to have gone to Fort Simpson by using the Iskut River, a tributary of the Stikine and the Nass River and then overland, reaching Fort Simpson in six days.[62]

The north end of Prince of Wales Island was inhabited by the
Henja-kŏn or Hennegas[63] with a count of about five hundred. The
census report which also calls them Hanega gives the same count.

South of the Henya on Bucareli Harbor and on the island at its
entrance, the Chlắwāk-kŏn had their homes, a small tribe which
according to the census of 1880 is listed as the Klawak with twenty-seven people. Frequently these census reports cannot be trusted, and in this case they are obviously mistaken. Far in this
winding inlet, dotted with islands, is a village consisting of a few
poor huts near an American salmon cannery.

On the islands opposite the opening of Portland Canal live the
Tungāss or Tongas. Their principal villäge is on Tongas Island,[64]
and in the census of 1880 it had one hundred and seventy-three
people. Formerly this tribe was supposed to be large and warlike.
On account of the closeness to the British border there was a customs house here until 1878 and also a fort was built here but after two years' occupation by American troops it was abandoned.[65]

The Ssang-ha[66] who live on the mainland near Cape Fox are
counted with the Tongas and, according to the census of 1880,
which erroneously puts these people on Prince of Wales Island,
there were one hundred of them.

Each of these thirteen listed tribes of the Tlingit[67] is divided
into several clans which have animal crests and which are
grouped into two divisions, one, represented by the Raven or
Jēlch phratry and the other by the Wolf or Kanuk phratry. The
former, according to Veniaminof, call themselves Kiksáti, the
latter Zitkujati.[68] The animals which are used as crests by the
first group are: the raven (jēlch), the frog (chichtsch), the goose
(táwok), the sea lion (tān), the "uhu" (tsüsk), the salmon (chrāt);

in the second group: the wolf (gūtsch), the bear (chūts), the eagle (tschāk), the whale (kĭt), the shark (tūss), and the "alk" (tschi). [69]

According to Veniaminof the Tlingit call all who do not belong to these clans kunjétkanagi which means "not here" or "stranger." In their presence they address such people as achssani, "uncle," or achkani, "son-in-law or brother-in-law," since they ordinarily have become related through marriage. People of the same clan call each other achchani, "countryman," or achgakau, "friend."

Veniaminof did not list the clans of the Raven group but instead he gives several clans of the Wolf group which are given here with their animal crests and comparative names from our own notes:

Veniaminof	Krause	Translation
kauakanit'tan or kuchontan	kagontan	wolf and eagle
tekujeti	tē-kuē-dĭ	bear
nangagi	nan-gche-āri	bear
	nanch-agētan	
taklkujeti	talch-kŭēdi	whale (Delphinus
	takla-uedi	whale orca)
kaschkikit'tān	karáschkidetān	whale
nuschkit'tān	nuschkē-tān	eagle and murrelet
hitlentan [70]	?	eagle and murrelet
tutsit'tan	ták-ssi-kān(?)	shark

The most important of all clans is the Wolf and Eagle (Kagontān), (Kauakanittān or Kuch'ontan of Veniaminof and what Holmberg calls (Kwawhakhanischthān or Koch'anthan), and they had their principal site at Klukwan, the largest of the Chilkat villages. According to Veniaminof, the Chilkat Kagontān (Wolf and Eagle) lived formerly in the neighborhood of the foothills of Ledjanow in a village called kaknau [71] which can probably be identified with the present Gaudēkan of the Huna. The present chiefs of the Wolf and Eagle clan in Klukwan, according to old Tschartritsch, are descendants of people who came over from Sitka. On account of their large numbers, the Wolf and Eagle clan has been divided into the following subgroups: kutschitān (xuts!hit - Grizzly Bear house); [72] anikigaittan (center (of village) house people); [73] kukittan (kŭkettān); kauuittán; kchakchanttan.

The name kauakanittan, declares Veniaminof, is derived from kauakan meaning "fire flaring up," hit, "house," and tan, "occupant," as "the occupant of the house which the fire lights up." According to Lütke, koukhontan or kokvontan means "soldier." [74]

For comparative purposes I will give the list of settlements and their population as recorded by Veniaminof.

The following sixteen places were listed by him:[75]

Veniaminof			Krause	Modern
1. Yakutat	with	150	Yakŭtat-kŏn	Yakutat
2. Ltua or Akwe	"	200	"	"
3. Kaknáu	"	200	Hūna-kŏn (possibly)	Huna
4. Tschilkat	"	200	Tschilkāt-kŏn	Chilkat
5. Aku	"	100	Ak-kŏn	Auk
6. Sitka	"	750	Schitka-kŏn	Sitka
7. Taku	"	150	Taku-kŏn	Taku
8. Kuzno	"	300	Chūts-ta-kŏn	Hutsnuwu
9. Keku	"	200	Kēkch-kŏn	Kake
10. Kuju	"	150	Kŭju-kŏn	Kuiu
11. Genuw	"	300	Henne-ga-kŏn (?)	Henya
12. Stachin	"	1500	Stakhĭn-kŏn	Stikine
13. Tangass	"	150	Tungāss-kŏn	Tongas
14. Kaigan	"	1200	Kaigani (Haidas)	Kaigani
15. Tschassin	"	150	Tschaseni (Chasen or Chasina) Haidas	Kasaan
16. Ssanach	"	100	Ssang-ha-kŏn	Sanya

As one can see, this list agrees substantially with the one given above, only the figures are not trustworthy.

Names of the individual settlements and tribes of the Tlingit and more or less complete enumeration of the population can also be found in the following authors:

Chliebnikof mentioned Yakutat, Sitka, Chilkat, Kuznow or Chuznow, Kaknaut, Konkontan, Akku, Taku, Zultana, Stachin, Kek, Kuju.

According to the diary of the American, Captain William Bryant, there were listed in the second volume of "Archaeologia Americana" ten tribes which speak the Sitka language, namely: the Chilcart, Sitka, Hoodsunhoo, Ark, Kake, Eeliknoo on Chatham Straits, Kooyou, Hennega, Stickeen, Tumgarse.[76]

Roquefeuil mentions Ako, Houtsnau, Kekh, Iknou, Haniga, Kowalt.

Veniaminof lists the above mentioned places as Tlingit, but has among them two which are Haida.

Dunn mentions the Chilcast, Stikein, and Tongarsse.

Scouler, following Tolmie, lists several tribes but only the last five are Tlingit.[77]

Simpson lists in his comparative section places already mentioned.

Schoolcraft gives in his list also the names of eight clans of the Stikine.[78]

Holmberg gives in his map, which is copied from the atlas

prepared by Tebenkof, the nine Tlingit places which are in his comparative table. [79]

Tikhmenief has a list which is based on the reports of Werman and which agrees, except for the population figures, with that of Veniaminof. [80]

Lieut. Scott gives a fairly complete count of the tribes in the report of Major Halleck. [81]

Vincent Colyer published the lists of Mahony and Louthan. [82]

Petroff gives a complete but not always trustworthy count of the settlements and tribes in the census report of 1880.

Other accounts like those of Anderson[83] are mostly drawn from sources just mentioned, but frequently there are errors in the transcription of the names.

The following table gives a survey of the tribes and clans. It is not complete and not always trustworthy, especially for the southern tribes, since the bulk of the information was secured only among the Chilkat. Nevertheless it is more complete than anything published in the past and the sources are indicated wherever there is any possibility of securing supplementary data, as with the Chilkat, the Huna, the Killisnoo and the Sitka.

The division of the Tlingit into clans is entirely independent of their geographical distribution. One finds the same clan in different places as the Wolf and Eagle (Kagontán) clan with the Sitka, the Yakutat, the Huna and the Chilkat. By reciprocal marriages and through the rule of maternal inheritance, as we shall see later, the unusual situation explains itself, that several clans, even from the Bear and Wolf phratries, live in every settlement while, on the other hand, a clan is also spread through several villages.

The several clans do not enjoy the same esteem. On account of their large numbers and the wealth of their members, the Wolf and Eagle clan is the most important.

Within the clan again individual families are ranked; they form a sort of aristocracy which bases its position not so much on birth as on the possession of wealth. Even the rank of chief is tied up with the possession of wealth, largely the ownership of slaves. According to custom this passes from uncle to nephew, but it happens frequently that instead of inheritance of the office, a new chief is appointed. In almost every place there are several chiefs, called amkáu, one of whom is looked upon as the head. The power of the chief is very limited and the direction which it takes depends on the personality of the individual. Only in cooperative undertakings and in council is he a leader; in everything else every family head is entirely free to do anything which is not counter to custom and which does not infringe on the rights of others.

Krause 1882 Chtlingit or Tlinkit	Veniaminof 1840 Tlinkit	Holmberg 1856 Thlinkithen	Tikhmenief 1863
I Jakŭtat-kŏn Village: Chlach-ä-jĕk	Jakutat-kuán	Jakhutháth- khóän	Jakutats (380, incl. 49 slaves)
Clan: 1. kǎschke-kon 2. kagontän 3. tĕ-kuĕ-dĭ 4. gŭnǎchokon (lives separately)	Ltua or Akwe-kuán	Shltúja or Akwetz-khóän	
II Tschilkät-kŏn Village: Klokwán	Tschilkat-kuán	Tschishlkháth- khóän	Tschilkats (1616, (incl. 160 slaves)
Clan: 1. kagontän (Bear) 2. takástina (Eagle and Wolf) 3. schengo-kĕdi (Thunder and Eagle) 4. taklá-uĕdi (Whale) 5. kanach-tĕdi (Raven) 6. rcháketan (Raven) Village: Kat-kwaltú 7. nŭschĕ-kǎári (Salmon) Village: Jen-dĕstáke 8. chlukŏach-adí (Raven) 9. kädŭwot-kĕdi (Raven) Village: Tschilkŭt 10. Kǎ-jĕch-adí (Raven)			
III Āk-kŏn Village: Ak'-än (from Ak'u Sea)	Aku-kuán		On Akan Bay (118 incl. 6 slaves)
Clan: 1. tlĕnĕdi			
IV Taku-kŏn	Taku-kuán	Thakhu-khóän	Takus (712, incl. 40 slaves)
Clan: tsata-hĕni (?) (Name perhaps identical with the following) Village: Tsenta-ka-hĭni			

Simpson 1847 Thlinkitt	Schoolcraft 1851 Concerning the klen- eekate language	Scott 1870	Census for 1880
			Yakutat
	Chilcat (267 men)	Chilcates, Chilkahts or Chilcahs (1200)	Chilkhat Kluckquan
			Kutkwutlu
			Yondestuk
			Chilcoot
Auckes	Auke (72 men)	Awks (700)	Auk
Taco	Taco Samdan	Tacos (300) Sundowns (150)	Tacoo

Krause 1882 Chtlingit or Tlinkit	Veniaminof 1840 Tlinkit	Holmberg 1856 Thlinkithen	Tikhmenief 1863
V Hūna or Chūna-kŏn	Kaknáu-kuán[84]		On Icy Point (331, incl. 23 slaves)
Village: Gaudēkān			
Clan: 1. taktēn-tān (Raven, 6 houses) 2. kusch-kē-ti (schkǎ-tā-rĭn-āri, after the schkā-tǎri-hĭn, 3 houses) 3. kagontān (Wolf, 2 houses) 4. tschūkanḗdi, (Bear, 6 houses)			
Village: Chlŭl-chágu			
5. nuschkē-tān			
Village: Chlachǎ-ĭk			
6. taktēn-tān (4 houses)			
Village: ? stacháti-āni			
VI Chūts-ta-kŏn	Kuzno-kuán	Chútznou-khóān	Chuznows (600 incl. 40 slaves)
Village: Angūn			
Clan: 1. dēschǐtān (6 houses) 2. uǔschkētan (3 houses) 3. dǎklá-ẃēti (3 houses)			
Village: Neltūschk'-ān			
4. nanch-ágētan 5. tēkū-ēdi			
VII Schitka-kŏn	Sitcha-kuán or Schitka-kuán	Schĭtkha-khóān	Sitchas (1344, incl. 94 slaves)
Clan: 1. kagontān (Bear) 2. kiks-ádi (Raven) 3. klŭk-nachádi (Salmon) 4. kusk-ēdi 5. chrátka-āri 6. kūket-tān	kaǔakanittán kiksáti (Name Veniaminof uses to designate all Raven clans) kukittan		incl. 94 slaves)

Simpson 1847 Thlinkitt	Schoolcraft 1851 Concerning the klen-eekate language	Scott 1870	Census for 1880
	Huna cow (258 men)	Hunnos or Hooneahs, Hunnas or Hooneaks (1000)[85]	Hoonyah
			Koudekan
			Village: Klughuggue
	Hootsinoo (274 men)	Koutznous, Koushnous or Koidxnous (800)	Khootznahoo
			Village: Augoon Scutskon
Sitkaguouays	Sitka (127 men)	Sitkas	Sitka

Krause 1882 Chtlingit or Tlinkit	Veniaminof 1840 Tlinkit	Holmberg 1856 Thlinkithen	Tikhmenief 1863
VIII Kĕkch-kŏn	Keku-kuán	Khĕkhu-khóãn	Keks (455, incl. 25 slaves)
IX Kŭju-kŏn	Kuju-kuán		Kujus (262, incl. 10 slaves)
Clan: 1. kujĕĕdi 2. kŭn-hittan 3. nas-tĕdi			
X Stak-hĩn-kŏn	Stachin-kuán	Stach'ĩn-khóãn	Stachins (697, incl. 81 slaves)
Clan: 1. nãŋ-gche-ãri 2. tĭgĭtãn 3. kãtschădi 4. rchŭch-ĕdi 5. kã-rásch-kidetan 6. chrĕlch-kŏn 7. kassra-kŭĕdi 8. talch-kŭĕdi 9. ssĭk-nachădi			
XI Hennĕ-gã-kŏn or Hen-ja-kŏn	Genuw (?)		Genuws (411, incl. 19 slaves)
Village: Tsĭchoãn			
Clan: 1. uĕch-ĕ-nĕĕti			
Village: Chlå-wãk		Thlewhákhkhóãn	
2. ták-ssi-kãn			
XII Tungãss-kŏn	Tangãss		Tangass (333, incl. 25 slaves)
Clan: 1. tĕkŭĕdi 2. kanách-ădi 3. taktla-uĕdi			
XIII Ssángha-kŏn	Ssanach		

The ending "an" in a place name means village or dwelling

The ending "tan" found on many clan names means, according to Veniaminof, the inhabitants of a certain place; and frequently the combination "itan" occurs which he says means the inhabitant of a certain house (from "hit," house and "tan," inhabitant).

Simpson 1847 Thlinkitt	Schoolcraft 1851 Concerning the kleneekate language	Scott 1870	Census for 1880
Kayk	Kake (169 men)	Kakus, Kakes, Kekous (800)	Kehk
			Village:
Kooyan		Kous	Klukwan
			Kouyou
Stikine	Stikeen	Stikeens (1000)	Stakhin
	naa nee aa ghee ta ee tee tan kaadg ett ee kook a tee		
	kaas ka qua tee tal qua tee		
Secatquonays	sick naa hutty kick sa tee (cp. kiksadi in Sitka)		
Hanego	Hanago (82 men)	Hennegas (500)	Hanega
	A he alt near Ft. Stuart (50 men)		Klawak
	Tongass (85 men) kee tah hon neet	Tongass (200)	Tongas
	Lugh se le (45 men)	Cape Fox Indians (150)	Cape Fox Indians

In addition to the ending "tan," clan names also end in "edi," "eti," "adi," or "ati," but it must be remembered that words are recorded, sometimes with a "d," and sometimes with a "t."

Also the so-called aristocracy does not possess any particular privileges except the high esteem in which they are held by their tribesmen. At feasts they are given the places of honor and the richest presents are given them. For the death or injury of an important person greater compensation is demanded than for a person of lesser rank; two or more lives being payment for one chief.

4. Villages, Houses, and Inhabitants

Location and appearance of villages. Description of
dwellings. Interior furnishings -- Ceremonial houses --
Totem poles -- Fortifications -- Storehouses -- Shelters
for childbirth -- Gravehouses -- Racks for drying fish --
Unsanitary conditions -- Summer shelters and tents --
Description of inhabitants -- Bodily decorations -- Lip
plugs of the women -- Tattooing and painting -- Clothing
-- Ornamentation -- Hairdress.

Health of natives -- Conditioning of the body and physical capability -- Diseases.

Mental ability of the Tlingit -- Slight knowledge of
their natural environment -- Artistic talents.

The slaves; numbers, origin and condition.

Like all inhabitants of the Northwest Coast, the Tlingit are a
sedentary people. In the summer however, they lead a half nomadic life, for they scatter according to clan and family lines to
their hunting and fishing territories, or undertake extensive voyages, which sometimes last for months, in order to trade with
the whites or with neighboring Indians. With the approach of winter the various tribes reassemble in their villages and each clan
reoccupies its own house.

One of the larger Tlingit villages is an impressive sight if one
sees it from across the water and at a fair distance. The regular
row of solid wooden structures on the shore, which is covered
with canoes and fishing gear, presents in this wilderness, a
friendly picture of a civilization that would bring thoughts of
home, if the sight of an occasional totem pole or grave post and
Indian figures wrapped in woolen blankets did not again transpose
one into a strange world.

Since fishing supplies the principal subsistence of these people,
the choice of a place for settlement depends largely on the prox-
imity of good fishing grounds and safe landing places for canoes.

For this reason the villages are mostly situated on the flat, sandy beach of a bay sheltered from the tide, on quiet inlets, or at the mouth or the lower course of a river. Some consist of only a few houses which are set in a single row, others have as many as fifty to sixty houses of varying sizes which are arranged in two more or less regular rows, for the houses of each clan form a separate group. There are paths trodden through the rank growth of nettles from house to house and others leading behind the houses to the woods where the Indians get their fire wood. Near the older settlements the woods close in have been cut down and have been replaced by a thick growth of shrubs of willow, alder, and berry bushes. The houses themselves are built close to the shoreline, barely out of the reach of high tide. Almost without excep-

House in Klukwan belonging to the chief of the
Whale clan   a.   Little grave house

Totem of the Whale clan (kit, whale)

tion they are set with the gable end, in which the door is cut, facing the shore. Often one finds a platform in front of the gable end, which overhangs the shore so that one must mount several steps to reach it.

In building the house, great posts are first sunk into the ground at the four corners of a square, the sides of which are about ten meters long. These posts, called "gāt" by the Tlingit, stand about three meters out of the ground, and are seven to eight decimeters wide and two decimeters thick. They serve as the support of the plate beam with prominent projections and grooves. Then a

vertical post is set in the middle of each side wall and two others
at each gable end to be supports for the three rafters, at the gable and at the midpoint. The four corner posts protrude slightly
above the roof and are especially well worked. The gable end between the vertical corner posts is enclosed with planks called
"Chrangejĕt" which are 1.5 decimeters thick and four to six decimeters wide, laid horizontally. They are lapped so that they fit
together like the logs of a blockhouse. Four round beams which
extend from the four posts at the gable wall of the front to that of
the back form the framework of the roof. As a cover there lie on
these two to three courses of shorter boards like shingle which
are weighted down with stones, or are held in place by means of
thin poles laid lengthwise. Pieces of bark, used as wedges between the boards, further tighten the roof. The gable ridge post
has grooves cut into either side to hold the inner ends of the over-
lapping wall planks. In the middle of the low pitched roof a large

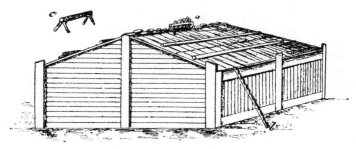

Small house about twelve steps (feet?) square at Jendestake
a. Smoke hole b. Ladder, dsĕt c. Trestle over smoke hole, gan-
ĕchli

square opening is left through which the light comes in and the
smoke goes out. A movable board covering which extends over
the opening on the windward side also offers some protection
from rain and snow. In order to set this according to the weather
there is usually a notched tree trunk which serves as a ladder
leaning against the sidewall of the house. [1]
   The only opening in the walls of the house is the door which is
always in the gable end facing the water and usually raised somewhat above the ground so that one must ascend a few steps to
reach it. This doorway was once only a round or oval hole which
was closed from the inside by a mat hung over it, but now one
sees in most houses square doors which, however, are so low
that one must bend over to enter. The door itself, which is provided with lock and bolt and made of strong boards, opens to the
inside.
   Only in smaller houses is the inside on a level with the ground.

In larger buildings the center is dug down about one meter so
that there is an earthen bank about two meters broad running the
length of the house and closed off from the excavated area with
boards or blankets and mats hanging from the beams. In this way
a vestibule is created which one enters and from which one de-
scends a few steps into the inner space. This also sets off separate sleeping quarters and storage rooms along the side and back
walls. Then there is also a second tier which is lined with planks
as well and serves the same purpose.

The innermost space has flooring also, except for the hearth in
the middle which is about one and one-half meters square. Above
this hangs a long iron chain which comes from the ridge post and
to which a large kettle is fastened, the common cooking vessel
for the inhabitants of the house. The older method of cooking in
wooden boxes by means of hot stones has long been abandoned.
Grotesque woodcarvings are often found in the corners of the living room and on both sides of the door.

Hunting and fishing gear, guns, paddles, salmon spears, snowshoes and the like lie on the beams. In practically every house a
space is reserved for a sweat bath, which is only large enough to
accomodate one person lying down. Steam is made by pouring water on hot stones.

One occasionally finds departures from the general type of
structure just described, sometimes in the way of outside decoration or in the care taken in carrying out the details of the construction, as well as in the extent of white influence. Even though
the ground plan of the house is not always an exact square, there
is never a great difference between the length of the two sides.
We saw a different type of gable structure in an old house of the
Killisnoo at Angoon where the triangular gable space was raised
and painted with bright, partly effaced mineral pigments. Langsdorff also mentions a similar painted gable.

Special ceremonial houses like the "kachima"[2] of the northern
Indians are supposed to have existed among the Tlingit according
to the evidence of Erman and Holmberg. In such a structure,
which served for ceremonial gatherings, for the housing and feeding of strangers, and for exceptional household chores that required much room, Erman noticed at about a man's height, above
the usual sleeping platform a second row of enclosures which
were used for the same purpose. [3]

Malaspina saw among the Yakutat a space surrounded by posts
inside of which stood painted columns and which he believed
could be made into a large ceremonial house by draping blankets
around them.

In smaller houses the inner subdivisions are lacking, as is the
excavated center. A few modern structures after European plans
were seen among the Sitka, among the Stikine at Fort Wrangell,

among the Killisnoo at Angoon and among the Huna at Guadēkan.
In other places the modernizations were limited to the introduction of windows in the gable front or to the building of a primitive
chimney.

An unusual decoration of the house is the heraldic column or
totem pole, [4] set up by wealthy chieftains and which is about fifteen meters tall. These poles are carved from single tree trunks
and show various combinations of animal and human forms,
brightly painted, the heraldic crests of the clans.

In the Tlingit villages these totem poles are not as numerous

Carved wooden figures at the sides of the inner
entrance of a house at Klukwan

as with their neighbors, the Haida and Tsimshian. Among the
Chilkat only one totem pole was found, in the form of two whales
lying on top of each other, which was repeated on both sides of a
house at Klukwan, belonging to the chief of the whale clan. Likewise only one totem pole was found at Gaudēkan, the village of
the Huna. It was of medium size and looked new, as though it had
been recently erected. The Sitka and the Killisnoo had no poles
at all, but a large number were seen in the Stikine settlement
near Wrangell where they attained considerable height.

These totem poles stood at the side of the doorway, never directly in front of it, like those of the Haida and Tsimshian, where the actual doorway is often a round hole cut at the base of the pole.

The house is not only a dwelling place for the Tlingit but also a fort. Its strong walls served as protection for tribe and clan groups against the arrows and spears of former enemies and even today ward off the weak bullets of the old flintlocks in their possession. Some houses still have a palisade fence which bars access to the door, as additional protection. We saw such a palisade among the Chilkat at Klukwan and the remains of such a fortification, which was surmounted with the head of a bird, were

Wood carving on a wall board inside a house
at Klukwan

in front of a Huna house at Gaudekan. Formerly these fences were much more widely used and not a single house but whole settlements were surrounded. In such a fortified place the Sitka defied the Russians for several days as we have seen, and in their new settlement at Chatham Straits they protected themselves again by a double palisade according to Langsdorff's description. Vancouver's Lieutenant Johnston saw in 1794 in Hamilton Bay on the west coast of Kupreanof Island the remains of eight fortified, deserted villages, each of which had been built on a steep rocky projecting point which from its very nature was almost impregnable. At these places a substantial platform occupied the top of the cliff and projected over the sides. Along the edge a barricade of piled up logs was erected.

In one Tlingit village there were, in addition to the dwellings described above, other small structures in which supplies were stored. [5] Small huts made of conifer branches served as shelter for women confined in childbirth. Other small houses, in a variety of forms and decorated with various symbols, are grave houses which contain the ashes of cremated bodies, and are set a little aside from the village either toward the woods or the beach. Everywhere in the village itself one finds racks for drying fish and along the beach, beyond the reach of high tide, stately rows of neat canoes which are covered with fir boughs or cedar-bark mats to protect them from the sun. The favorable impression which one gets of the industry and intelligence of the natives,

Carved wooden figures in a house at Klukwan

from all this, is much altered when one becomes aware of the indescribable filth on all sides, in the houses, and amid all the surroundings. Occasionally the influence of the whites seems to have made a slight improvement, but in general the drastic statements of La Perouse, Dixon, Langsdorff, and others still hold true. [6]

The Tlingit seek the protection of a well-built house only in winter. In summer most of the villages are deserted and the inhabitants are scattered for hunting and fishing. If they stay long in one place or come back to it year after year, as for salmon fishing, they build a house of planks, but naturally not with the care lavished on the winter dwelling. According to La Perouse the shelters of the natives at Lituya Bay were covered with boards or bark only on the windward side. [7] In Yakutat Bay Malaspina found six or seven structures so poorly done that the wind and rain drove through them, a fact all the more surprising when

91

one is aware of the native's distaste for cold and dampness, as well as a consciousness of their fine sense of workmanship exhibited in their canoes.[8]

If a shelter is to be made for a short time, the Tlingit wastes no time on it. A few staves and some cedar bark mats are always taken along on extensive canoe trips and of these or, lacking them, fir boughts, a cone-shaped tent is set up which truly offers but little protection from the rigors of the climate. Nowadays the natives often use canvas tents secured from the whites or pattern their own after them, a custom they became familiar with from

Carved wooden figure at the inner entrance
of a house in Klukwan

the prospectors who passed through their territory.

Now let us turn to the inhabitants themselves. The Tlingit generally are of medium stature, well built, strong, and in good proportions. The best physical types seem to be the Chilkat, which is perhaps due to the fact that they use canoes less than the other tribes. Among them we saw tall people quite frequently; Jēlchkuchu, the son of the old Chilkat chief, Tschartritsch, measured one hundred eighty-three and one-half centimeters.

The men have a proud and erect posture and a springy step, while the women, probably as consequence of the perpetual squatting at the family hearth, are generally bent over and in later years develop a waddling walk. The skin color of the natives is quite light, not darker than southern Europeans; to Erman the skin color of the men appeared to be a little more red than that of the women. [9] The young girls often have, as Portlock and Dixon noticed, a very delicate color and red cheeks. The features are generally regular and not unpleasant; but according to Lütke's description they have mostly an earnest, gloomy, and even an austere expression. [10] The eyes are medium large, deep set, and bright with a dark brown iris and short black eyebrows. The nose is mostly well developed, straight or sometimes also bent downwards, seldom flat with broadened nostrils. The cheekbones are somewhat prominent though not to a striking degree, the lips are full without being puffy. Two rows of dazzling white healthy teeth ornament a mouth which is not unusually large. The hair is pitch black, seldom reddish, coarse, long and shiny; in old age it turns grey, but not white. Since the hair covers the neck, it forms, as Lütke pointed out, a sort of hood from which the rain runs off. [11] The growth of beard is slight; and the young men usually pull it out, but men now and then wear cheek and chin whiskers as well as mustaches. Nowhere did we see a Tlingit who could be called stout. Malaspina speaks of a Yakutat chief who was corpulent but admitted that he was well proportioned. Large-boned, broad-shouldered individuals are not infrequent. Hands and feet are

Wooden post with carved figure inside a house at Klukwan

not large, and those of the women may be classed as small. However, individual variations from the bodily proportions of this general type are not infrequent; even head shape had considerable variety. The following measurements which were taken of three Chilkat Indians with the aid of Virchow's calipers will illustrate these differences. The four individuals were:

A. Jēlchkuchu, the son of the first Chilkat chief, Tschartritsch, about twenty-five years old.

B. Don-ē-wāk, chief in Yendestaq!e, about sixty years old.

C. Kasko, a relative of Tschartritsch, about forty years old.

D. A twelve-year-old son of Chlūnat, the second chief at Yen-destaq!e.

Jēlchkuchu (A) was the second tallest man in the whole village, Don-ē-wāk (B) had a very pronounced aquiline nose and Kasko (C) had an obviously thick head.

Bodily mutilations for the sake of decoration are limited among the men to the piercing of the septum of the nose and the rim of the ear, while the women in addition to these also pierce the low-er lip for a labret. The piercing of the septum takes place very early in boyhood, in fact Holmberg states that it is done to new-born babes. Usually a small silver ring is put in the septum; and since this interferes with cleaning the nose, it disfigures the face through the ensuing uncleanliness rather than ornament it through its presence. According to Holmberg these rings were often so large as to cover the mouth. [12] However, we saw only

Kī-dschūk - Goshawk

Ssāch - seal

Schā-kā-nāri - mythical personage

Kētl - dog

a.   b.

Totem pole (Kū-tī-ga) in Huna

a. Front view

b. Side view

	A mm	B mm	C mm	D mm
1. Greatest length of head	196	191	192	175
2. Greatest width of head	166	168	173	158
3. The whole face length from hairline to tip of chin	194	201	196	152
4. Total face height	133	127	115	103
5. Face width (molar width)[13]	93	98	97	68
6. Bigonial	131	119	119	113
7. Bizygomatic	162	172	160	137
8. Interocular	38	33	35	33
9. Biocular	99	95	115	85
10. Nose height (nasion to edge of upper tip)	56	59	50	41
11. Nose length (from nasion to tip)	54	60	48	38
12. Nose width	42	41	42	30
13. Length of mouth	63	64	67	42
14. Height of ear	133	137	---	120
15. Length of ear	71	---	72	64
16. Stature	1835	1683	1720	1300
17. Span between outspread arms	1920	1740	---	1290

small rings and often we found the use of the nose ring had disappeared completely. In the pierced ears ornaments made of stones, shells, and teeth were worn. Very much liked and very high in price were sharks' teeth which were secured through trade with southern Indians, as was the abalone shell which is found southward on the coast. Sometimes several holes were made in the rim of the ear and red wool or small feathers were drawn through. According to Veniaminof and Holmberg the number of holes determined the esteem in which a Tlingit was held and each hole signified a great deed done by him, like for instance the celebration of a great feast in memory of a dead hero. [14]

The women are apt to wear silver rings in their ears. But their most peculiar ornament is the wooden plug which is worn in an incision in the lower lip. Since this unusual ornament, the labret, is now almost entirely obsolete, we must discuss it through the evidence of some of the older informants who frequently contradict each other. La Perouse writes about the natives of Lituya Bay: "All the women, without exception, have the lower lip pierced the full length of the mouth and down to the gum, and in this incision they have a kind of wooden spoon without a handle, which rests against the gum and spreads the pierced lip into a roll so that the lower part of the mouth extends out two or three inches. The young girls just have a nail in the lower lip and the married women alone have the right to the spoon. We tried to persuade them to abandon this ornament. They agreed to it reluctantly. They made the same gestures and showed the same embarrassment which a European woman would show at baring her breast. The lower lip then fell to the chin and this second picture was little better than the first." [15]

Dixon said about it: "This peculiar operation of piercing the lower lip of women never occurred during childhood but appeared, according to all observations, to be associated with a certain period of life. When girls are about fourteen or fifteen years old, the center of the lower lip in the thick part near the mouth is pierced and a piece of copper wire inserted to prevent its growing together. The opening is lengthened from time to time, in line parallel to the mouth and the wooden plugs are increased in size accordingly, until they are three or even four inches long and approximately of the same width. Perhaps this is done so that when a matron ages and the muscular tone relaxes, her age is respected more than the exceptional ornament." [16]

Portlock writes about the custom of this ornament in Norfolk Sound, as follows: "One old woman who especially attracted my attention had one as large as the saucer of a tea cup. The weight of this ornament pulled down her lower lip so that it covered her chin and left exposed the teeth and gums of the lower jaw in a most disagreeable manner. In eating they usually take more in their mouths than can be swallowed at once. When they have chewed their food they are apt to use the labret for a plate on which to lay the masticated food and for this purpose it is occasionally removed. The custom of wearing this wooden labret seems to be a universal practise among the local women, even two-year-old girls already have the lower lip pierced and a piece of copper wire inserted. This remains there until they are thir-

teen or fourteen years old; then it is removed and a wooden labret put in, which at first is only the size of a button."[17] Also
Marchand reports that lip plugs are taken out at will and inserted
again. In some women he found the incision more than three inches long; in contrast to Dixon and others he asserts that girl ba-
bies still unweaned have their lips pierced and wire inserted.[18]

Vancouver repeatedly observes that women who had lip ornaments, some two and one-half to four inches long, were held in
great esteem and steered canoes. "In childhood," he writes fur-

Don-ē-wāk, chief of the Chilkat

ther, "a small incision is made and a brass or copper wire is
pulled through. This widens the hole by eating away the surrounding flesh until the opening is large enough for a lip plug."[19]

According to Langsdorff, when a girl is thirteen or fourteen
years old a small opening is made directly in the center close under the lower lip and at the beginning a thick wire is inserted,
then a wooden double button or a little cylinder, thickened at both

ends. This opening gradually becomes larger through months and years, and by the insertion of a small elliptical piece of wood or little dish the hole continuously widens and gives each woman the appearance of having a large, flat wooden soup spoon ingrown in the flesh of her lower lip. The outer rim of this little plate has a furrow into which the gradually expanding lip fits tightly. All women without exception have such a spoon whose size seems to be determined either by position or age. It is two to three inches wide and one-half inch thick. The wives of the head chiefs usually have them wider and longer. Langsdorf saw a lip plug worn by a very distinguished lady that was fully five inches long and three inches wide. Kissing is of course, as he intimated, made impossible by this ornament. [20]

A similar description of this custom is given by Holmberg: "As soon as the first signs of maturity appear in a girl her lower lip is pierced and usually a bone point is inserted in the opening, though sometimes silver is used. As long as she remains unmarried she wears this, but when she gets a husband, a larger ornament of bone or wood which is slightly grooved on the gum side is pressed into the opening. Through the years the ornament is enlarged so that the old women wear them over two inches long. In this way an enlarged lip develops which is eminently unattractive especially so, since it is impossible to shut the mouth and there is constantly a trickle of brown tobacco juice visible."[21]

Erman saw labrets or kaljugi of varying sizes used by the four wives of chief Nauschket; the eldest had a wooden plug about one-half an inch high and three inches long and rather round which filled the hole in the lower lip, while in the younger ones the hole was more elliptical. In the latter the upper surface of the plug was slightly concave while the round one was convex. Even the flanges of this cylindrical body were concave. In honor of the European foods which were served to the eminent Kolushans during a feast on board the ship (the frigate Krotkoi) the lip plug was removed in spite of the difficulty of contracting and expanding the lower lip. During the meal several old women laid the wooden plates they had removed from their lips beside the European plates from which they were eating.

Erman saw the twelve-year-old daughter of a chief who had just undergone the lip operation sitting on the upper level of the ceremonial house silent and motionless for passersby and visitors to see. She was fully and carefully clothed, while many boys and girls of equal age wandered around on the beach totally naked. The cut no longer bled, in fact it looked like a six "linien" long horizontal split, that gaped only noticably in the center but, since no insertion had been made, did not change the natural appearance of the mouth. [22] In another place Erman mentions that he saw the lip piercing of a girl scarcely six years old. [23]

Lisiansky also saw a child only about three months old with nose and lower lip pierced and strings of beads inserted. [24]

The accounts just related differ in the age at which the lower lip is pierced. While Portlock, Marchand, and Lisiansky declare that the operation takes place very early in life, Dixon, Langsdorff, Holmberg, and others agree that it was not done until puberty. The latter seems to be the case among the Chilkat where we both observed and inquired. The lip plug called "kéntaga" is,

Jēlchkuchu, son of Tschartritsch, first chief of the Chilkat

in fact, as mentioned before, almost completely out of use, but a silver or bone peg with a button end pressed against the gum and protruding about two to three centimeters from the chin is used quite regularly by adolescent girls. Most of them keep this silver peg after their marriage and wear it all their lives; even the wife of Tschartritsch, the Chilkat chief so frequently mentioned, wore one. Others set a plug of wood or bone like a double button in the slit but they never reach the dimensions of the former labrets. Even the simple silver peg is becoming less and less popular. Among the Huna according to hearsay several old women still wear labrets and in Klawak we had the privilege of seeing such an ornament on a very old woman, which bore out fully the unpleasant descriptions of Langsdorf, Holmberg, and the others.

At the beginning of this century the labret was still worn very commonly by Tlingit women. Veniaminof and Holmberg mention however that the Yakutat women disdained this decoration, [25] while Ismailof says specifically about them, "the lower lip is pierced along the entire mouth and a carved wooden plug almost the shape of a spoon about two inches long and one and one-half inches wide is inserted in the slit." [26] Belcher also found in Yakutat Bay the lip plug in general use.

As early as 1827 Lütke observed that the lip plug was seldom used. Possibly the distaste which the Russians had for this kind of ornament was the principal reason that the Tlingit women gave it up, while they retained many other strange customs and habits.

The labret, wooden plug, or silver peg could only be worn by free Tlingit women. Slaves did not have their lips pierced.

We never saw a tattooed body, but according to older reports it formerly occurred. Ismailof says of Yakutat women, "some decorate the chin," [26] which probably means that they did it in the same manner as the Eskimo women to the north who smear a piece of sinew with soot and draw it through just under the skin, making a thin blue line drawing. La Perouse also mentions that a few women had designs scratched into their arms and Marchand even said of the inhabitants of Norfolk Sound that some men had tattooing on their hands and shins and nearly all the women were tattooed.

La Perouse mentions other bodily mutilations though none from the Tlingit, namely, scars on the arms and chest caused by their iron tools which they sharpened by running them along their teeth, just as one would do on a whetstone; also they are supposed to file their teeth down to the gum, using a stone shaped like a pair of tongs. [27]

Both sexes among the Tlingit paint their faces red and black. First they prepare charcoal of fir pitch, soot, graphite, or molybdena by mixing it with seal grease, and they also use a brown powder which is obtained by burning a sponge (Polyporus sp.) to charcoal and pulverizing it. With the shiny black paint either the whole face is evenly covered or just the lower half and rings are also left around the eyes. The Tlingit can give several reasons for blackening the face. In winter it protects against the cold and the danger of snow blindness or the radiant heat of the open fire at which the women especially squat all day; in summer a sooty face is protection from insect plagues; on long sea voyages the glare from the water is more bearable and, while wandering in the mountains, it softens the breezes which come from the ice fields. Also to indicate mourning the face is blackened, and then especially, as Dawson pointed out among the Haida, a mixture of charcoal and grease is used.

The blackening of the face was formerly a widespread practice and done without any special occasion. Holmberg says that a wealthy Tlingit painted his face daily, but his arms only when the color needed renewing. According to the same author they used their own urine to wash the color off, which gave them a distinctly unpleasant odor for strangers. [28] On ceremonial occasions the Tlingit painted their faces red, as they also did for fishing, hunting, and war. Often they used both red and black at once and brought about variety in their designs by changing colors. [29] A few had red rings around their eyes with a completely black face, and Lisiansky saw a Tlingit who had a black ring from his forehead to his mouth and a red chin. [30] Instead of using the customary mineral pigments, cinnebar is used for coloring and is gotten from traders at high prices.

The aboriginal costume can no longer be found anywhere among the Tlingit. Not only European materials but also ready-made garments are found everywhere, as we learned from the accounts of the fur traders, since very early times. Even the worn-out clothing of sailors was traded for by the natives for their costly sea otter furs. Again we must turn to the descriptions of early travelers on the coast if we are to find out how the Tlingit dressed before they became acquainted with European clothing. "The clothing of men and women in Tschinkitane," says Marchand, "consists of a shirt or Dalmatian mantle of tanned skin, which is sewn down the sides and whose broad sleeve falls only a little below the shoulder, and a cape of fur with the hair on the outside. The women wore over the shirt an apron of the same skin which reached only to the waist, and a second cape of sea otter skin over the first one." [31] Dixon described the women's clothing as follows: "Their underclothing consists of finely tanned skin, covering the body from the neck to the ankles and is fastened along the sides so it will fit better. Over this in the form of an apron a piece of tanned skin is tied which reaches to the waist. The outer garment is made like the coat of the men and uniformly of tanned skins. [32]

The place of the skin shirts has been taken today by calico shirts of white and blue, and the fur cape which consisted of a blanket of skins sewn together is being crowded out by the woolen blanket. Blankets of marmot skin though are sill being worn by the Chilkat.

A woolen blanket now is the most indispensable piece of clothing of an Indian. It is thrown loosely over the shoulder and worn
in a togalike fashion. Blankets of blue and white are preferred
but even here fashion changes, much to the chagrin of the traders.

Trousers were first introduced to the Tlingit by the Europeans,
but today one sees few without them. Footgear and head covering
are missing. Holmberg says that in summer and winter they went
barefoot, but among the Chilkat, who were faced with much more
rigorous winters than the Sitka, the wearing of short or tall moccasins was quite general. The latter are used with snowshoes and
are made of moose or buckskin sewn with sinew and, fitting
closely, they reach to the knee or beyond. The skin or even the
finished moccasin is mostly secured from the interior Indians in
trade.

An unusual headgear found among the Tlingit since olden times
is a hat woven of roots and straw in the shape of a truncated cone.
Now they are only occasionally worn, for example, during the
summer fishing to protect the face from the sun and on ceremonial occasions.

In the vicinity of Sitka and Wrangell where the white people are,
one sees Tlingit very frequently fully clothed in European style,
the men with felt hats and white linen, the women in calico, wool-
en, and even silk dresses. Bright colors are most sought after.
Chiefs like to appear at ceremonial occasions in the discarded
uniforms of officers and officials whom they hold in great esteem.

As jewelry the women like to wear strings of beads and heavy
silver bracelets of native manufacture, often several on one arm
and rings of the same material on all fingers. Silver is the most
popular of the precious metals, gold being much less prized.

Quite generally we found the custom of wearing, as an amulet,
a little stone, a piece of mother of pearl, [33] or a piece of bone,
either in its natural state or tastefully carved. This was worn on
a leather thong on the bare breast or more recently in a little
skin bag. Among the inhabitants of Yakutat Bay, Ismailof and
Bocharof report that they saw a piece of iron shaped like a
crow's bill with eyebrows of copper which according to their experience they imagined had great influence on the wearer's health
and well being. [34]

An unusual hairdress is the wooden ring trimmed with beads
through which the young girls draw the braid and which they wear
at the nape of the neck. Not so common and more highly prized is
an ornament made of dentalium and beads which covers the braid
in a broad band and hangs almost to the ground.

The men wear their hair, which is well rubbed with grease,
loose, and let it fall to the neck; [35] only the hair of the shaman is
divided and braided and during a performance hangs down the
back, in one instance to the knees, but ordinarily it is fastened up

at the back of the head. The women wear their hair like the men, only longer and parted in the middle. As a sign of mourning it is also cut off at the neck. Among girls, we noticed in addition to the braid drawn through the ring at the back of the head, two small braids which were drawn from the forehead along the temples and so framed the hair.

Blaschke who was a physician in Sitka in 1836 comments favorably on the health of the natives. He states that because of their constant living outdoors with almost naked bodies and bare heads and through their custom of daily bathing in the sea, even in winter, they are so hardened that they seldom are subject to illness. However, infant mortality is high because newborn children are exposed to changing weather and cold baths even in icy water. Those who survived this treatment were strong and healthy and often attained a ripe old age. A particularly harmful influence, both physical and moral, is the use of alcohol. [36]

The ability to withstand rigors of climate, their bodily strength, and their endurance are considerable; and if some reports have been exaggerated, still their achievement compares favorably with anything Europeans could do under similar circumstances. When one sees the Tlingit carrying packs of one hundred pounds through the mountain passes to the interior and spending the night out with little covering in a temperature of 20° - 30° C., or what seems even more difficult, to bear without protest the smoke-filled houses with the scorching heat of the fire and the dreadful smell, we must not forget that, in the light of such everyday hardships, these achievements are no greater than those of our own laboring population; and also that when it comes to any unusual effort, the greater will power of the European will probably succeed.

Contagious diseases have repeatedly ravaged the Tlingit. Portlock in 1787 noticed the large number of pock-marked faces among the natives near Sitka and believed that the Spaniards who anchored there twelve years earlier brought the smallpox with them. According to the reports of Maurelle the disease is supposed to have been present among the Indians before the Europeans came. Lütke states that the disease assumed such proportions that in every family only one or two survived. [37]

Scarcely less extensive was the smallpox epidemic in 1836 in which at Sitka, alone, four hundred natives died. The disease appeared for a third time in 1862.

Typhoid fever raged in 1819, 1848, 1855. Measles and scarlet fever are common children's diseases.

Among the nonepidemic diseases the most prevalent are scrofulous ailments mostly caused by syphilis, which was not known before the advent of Europeans.

Eye trouble is very common, especially as a result of snow

blindness against which no precaution is known except blackening
the face or the occasional use of a headband which shades the
eyes a little. Total blindness is often found and now and then
deafness accompanies old age; and we encountered one deaf and
dumb person. One Indian who had been a cripple since birth and
had to be supported by his relatives, died while we were with the
Chilkat.

Veniaminof speaks very favorably of the intelligence of the
Tlingit; he calls them the most gifted of all the coastal people
from Bering Strait to California. A Kolushan boy who attended a
Russian school learned to understand Russian and speak a little
in five months when he was instructed by a teacher who understood no Tlingit. [38]

As a matter of fact the ability of these people is not to be under-
estimated. According to our experience it seems that Tlingit
children do not have as much difficulty in mastering the elemen-
tary disciplines like reading, writing, and arithmetic as the
European child. Neither do they lack the drive to learn. We saw
even adults go to the mission school to practice spelling and
arithmetic. On the other hand one would certainly make a mistake
to assert that these Indians need only education to put them in the
highest rank of intelligence. [39] Their power of understanding is
limited; the outlook which they have on their environment and
which is best expressed in their myths is childishly naive. The
tales of the origin of things are full of lively imagination, but
lack all sensible understanding and scarcely show any comprehension of the universe.

In spite of the fact that the Tlingit is constantly surrounded by
nature, he is only acquainted with it as it offers him the necessities of life. He knows every bay that lends itself to fishing or the
beaching of a canoe, every valley that offers a way to the interior
and for these he had names; but the mountain peaks themselves,
even though they are outstanding on account of their shape or
size, are scarcely noticed by him. Among plants and animals he
designates by name only those which are useful or harmful, all
others are included under the classification of bird, weed, etc.
Naturally those best known are the animals and plants that yield
food. In this way the many varieties of ducks and many berry-
bearing shrubs all have their individual names; but all the Indians
are not equally well acquainted with them and many contradic-
tions occur. As a general thing the ability to classify is not well
developed. A buzzard is confused with an owl. Some birds were
completely unknown to our guides; for instance they insisted that
they had never seen the beautiful little singer, the Arctic blue-
bird (Sialia arctica Swains) with its blue feathers.

The artistic skill of these people is decidedly advanced. Their
wood carving is outstanding not only for its technical perfection

but also for its good design and decorative quality. Their singing is also not to be overlooked. Their own songs show a fine development of rhythm and are much more expressive than one generally finds among primitive peoples. They learn foreign melodies very quickly.

A considerable portion of the native population consisted formerly of slaves, wealthy chiefs often possessing as many as twenty to thirty. [40] Now their numbers are few, even Tschartritsch, the most esteemed Chilkat chief has only two.

The slave, called "kuchu," was the sole property of his master who could do with him whatever he willed -- sell him, give him away, or even kill him. The children of slaves were also slaves.

The Russians called the slaves "kalgi." The origin of the word is not clear since it is neither from Aleut nor Tlingit. [41] According to Veniaminof the slaves of the Tlingit mostly belonged to the Columbia River people from Oregon. Their heads were generally pointed and the left side protruded. [42] They were war captives or obtained through purchase.

5. Household Life

Squatting at the hearth; securing and preparing food; spiritous beverages; smoking -- Occupations of men and women; division of labor -- Reciprocal relations of housemates; care of children -- The lot of slaves -- Behavior toward tribesmen and strangers -- Diversions of the Tlingit; the stick game; occupations of children -- Sitting on the cliff -- Slight care for cleanliness; sweat baths; sea and river baths -- Sleep -- Well developed sense of ownership -- Idea of individual use -- Gift giving -- Work done in anticipation of large rewards -- Vanity -- Letters of recommendation.

If we step through the narrow doorway into a Tlingit house, we will see the occupants squatting around the fire in the living quarters, occupied with various tasks, or giving themselves up to the luxury of idleness. Chairs or benches are nowhere to be seen; only matting lies here and there on the floor on which the Tlingit squat or lie stretched out with the head resting on one arm. He can maintain this position, which we would consider uncomfortable, for hours. Even outdoors he will forego leaning against a stone or tree stump and, when visiting whites, he uses a chair only with distinct discomfort. However, for his white guests he always quickly finds a seat, either in the recognized place of honor, opposite the door, or on a box used for storing household goods, which is set out and covered with a piece of cloth or a blanket.

The fire in the middle of the hearth is kept up all day, but in the houses of poor people it is very small. Usually fallen logs are burned. To build a fire uncut trunks, about a foot thick, are laid crosswise in pairs and piled up in more or less of a stack. Just as the Tlingit does not feel the cold so he also does not mind the scorching heat and thick smoke that fills the room and while we tried to move as far away from the fire as possible, he always came closer to it.

Obtaining wood for the fire is the duty of men and boys. Every day they go into the woods to get fallen pieces. In spite of the example of the whites, the Tlingit have not adopted the practice of laying in a supply of green wood and letting it season for a winter's supply, instead, only enough for each day is gotten.

The principal care of the day is the preparation and eating of food. Since, in some of the larger houses, there are several families numbering as many as thirty individuals, but all using just one fireplace, it is almost constantly in demand by men and women, preparing the greatest variety of dishes. The principal dish of every day is always fish, boiled, roasted, dried, but never raw. [1] Next in importance is the meat of land and sea mammals mentioned before, fowl, crabs, squid, shellfish, sea urchins and finally from the vegetable kingdom, berries, roots, bulbs, and other things. Wheat flour is being used more and more, either as porridge or with the addition of yeast, baked as bread in pans or on flat stones. Butter is also one of those items of diet now purchased from white traders.

Formerly cooking was done in wooden vessels or in baskets which were woven so closely of roots and split twigs that they were watertight. Accordingly Dixon says of the Yakutat; "They prepare their food by putting heated stones in a willow basket[2] with pieces of fish, seal, porpoise, etc. and closing it tightly. In the same way they prepare broths and fish soups, and they preferred this to cooking even though we at once gave them several copper pots and showed how they should be used."[3] Now almost everywhere they use iron or copper pots for cooking and only for the preparation of fish oil is the older method still used, as we shall see.

Fish and venison are roasted over an open fire by means of wooden sticks. At a campfire outdoors, several fish are stuck on a swordlike stick which is then set obliquely against the fire. Fowl are only partially plucked; but they are singed as are porcupine, the latter because it is too much trouble to skin them. For eating, spoons carved of bone or wood are used (Plate I, nos. 11, 12), the larger ones serving also as plates, being held in the left hand while the pieces of meat or fish are lifted out with the right. Knives and forks are seen only in a few Tlingit homes, fingers and teeth being used instead. The scraps of the meal, such as bones and fishbones, are thrown into the fire. The washing of dishes causes little trouble; scarcely are the scraps of one meal removed before the next one is started. They eat several times a day without binding themselves to any regular hours, though the principal meal is usually eaten at midday.

All dishes are prepared in a very rich manner, but we did not notice that fish oil was drunk from full wooden dishes as related by Lütke.[4] Much water is drunk with meals. Snow is eaten with special pleasure and even in summer it is brought home from the mountains. In the homes of the wealthy coffee and tea are occasionally used but they have not become items of daily consumption.

The Tlingit have a great desire for alcoholic beverages, although they only became acquainted with them through the Europeans. However, in his day Langsdorf says that they refused brandy, supposedly because they were afraid of losing their faculties and falling into the hands of the Russians,[5] but soon afterward alcohol became the most desirable item of trade and the greedy fur traders found that with it they could break down the shrewdness of the Indians in barter. Although later both the Russian and American governments positively prohibited the sale of liquor to the natives, they succeeded in gaining possession of it through bootlegging (smuggling), but the worst situation is that they have learned to prepare an intoxicating drink themselves. A white trader, named Brown, a discharged soldier, who had long manufactured liquor secretly, taught them the art. The distilling apparatus was made of a petroleum can, and either the hollow stem of giant kelp (Macrocystis pyrifera Ag.) or even angular pipes of tin pieced together served as tubes. When the agents of the Northwest Trading Company no longer gave the natives molasses, they used, in addition to sugar, potatoes and other products with starchy content for fermentation.[6] The Killisnoo were the first to manufacture this product called "hutschinu," and it was scarcely palatable to a European. It was made not only for private consumption but also for trade. The Chilkat took it as their costliest barter goods to the Interior Athapascans and received valuable furs in return. In Klukwan we found a "still" in almost every house. The results of the Indian's using alcohol are pernicious. He is easily intoxicated and then he is unable to control his wild passions and stops at no crime.

Less harmful is the use of tobacco to which the Tlingit are passionately addicted. Even before the advent of the Europeans they were acquainted with a tobaccolike plant. Vancouver's Lieut. Whidbey saw this plant cultivated by the natives of Chatham Straits, the only sign of agriculture which he encountered in the Alexander Archipelago. But it is not reported anywhere that they used this plant for smoking. According to Dixon they chewed a tobaccolike plant which they occasionally mixed with lime (probably from shells) and conifer bark and pitch. Today tobacco, generally obtained from traders in the form of leaf tobacco which is often mixed with dried and finely pulverized bark, is smoked in short, beautifully carved wooden pipes (Plate I, nos. 2, 3) or in clay pipes secured from traders, but only by men and in great moderation. At feasts, where supplying tobacco is part of the hospitality, attempts are made to rival one another in smoking, even to the point of reaching a stage similar to intoxication. The chewing of tobacco is widespread, even the women indulge in this practice. In addition both sexes still chew pitch, as mentioned before, and the root of the lupine "kantak," which also induces a form of intoxication.

The occupations of the Tlingit during the day are numerous, hunting and fishing taking the greater part of their time. Even in winter they have a great deal to do outside the house, such as setting traps and tendng them, cutting wood or building a conoe. At home a man spends his time making and repairing utensils both for the household and for the summer season. Long since a division of work has taken place so that individuals with a decided skill work for one another; accordingly in every community there are certain persons who engage in wood carving, silver work, and blacksmithing. [7] The women, in addition to tending to the cooking and caring for small children, do various kinds of hand-work. One sees them idle less frequently than the men. The pretty baskets, the colorful dance blankets, moccasins, and other pieces of clothing are all indications of women's industry, which aroused our admiration especially when one considers that they are made with little help and by the meager light of fish-oil lamps.

In summer there is even more work for the women. Wherever the cultivation of potatoes has been undertaken, the work has fallen upon them. During the fishing season they are busy from early until late storing and preserving the catch. Then again in the fall it is their duty to pick berries, gather bark, leaves and other plant materials, while at other times of the year they collect shellfish from the beaches.

The Tlingit developed an amazing patience and endurance in his work and he never hurried with it. In his ordinary actions he was slow, even sluggish; time did not press him since he scarcely thought of the future and lived entirely in the present. Also he saw no great virtue in work and only necessity and poverty drove him to it; the aristocrat thought he was lowering himself to do the work of slaves and common people.

The activity of each member of the household was regulated through habit and custom; even the children devoted their energy according to their strength to the general welfare, the boys as helpers for their fathers who early start to train them in all manly occupations, while the girls help their mothers. The behavior of the housemates toward each other and toward strangers is one of restraint and dignity. One seldom heard loud outbursts of joy or sorrow; at the departure of relatives one heard no expression of regret and no demonstration of pleasure was shown at the greeting of a friend after a long separation, not even between parents and children. When Lisiansky brought back the son of a Sitka chief, whom he had taken the year before as an apprentice to Kodiak, neither the father nor the son showed any sign of emotion. [8] Nevertheless small children are cared for in a kindly, even a tender, way. Nowhere did we see them receive blows and only seldom were they spoken to harshly as a matter of correction. [9]

Veniaminof states that the children receive corporal punishment only when they refuse to go into the cold water in the winter. Then they are punished by whipping which is done, not by the father, but by the uncle. [10]

The adolescent boys are very much restricted both in respect to food and clothing. They must give unconditional obedience to

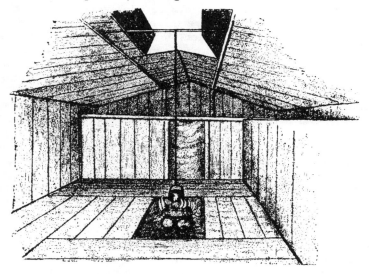

Inside a house at Klukwan

their parents but especially to their maternal uncle from whom they will inherit and to whom they stand in closer relation than to the father and whose requests for work must be carried out with no idea of recompense. Even when they are grown up they are still under the authority of the head of the family.

Even a woman's position is not unfavorable. She is not the slave of her husband; her rights are definite, and her influence considerable; often a business deal depends on her sanction. Douglas and Vancouver went so far as to report that there were some women who were held in such esteem among their people that they were the real leaders whose judgment the men willingly followed. [11]

In the past the slaves played an important part in the life of a Tlingit household; now their numbers are so few that they are no longer of significance. In regard to the treatment given slaves by their masters, diverse reports have been given. Lütke said that they were treated practically like children of the household; Veniaminof also finds that their position is not unfavorable since, he explains, a slave, even though a possession, is an expensive one. Also according to our own observations the relationship between masters and servants is a pleasant one; we never saw or heard of any mistreatment or oppression, also no complaints on the part of the slaves, who enjoyed a great measure of freedom. When Tschartritsch, the Chilkat chief lent us his slaves as guides, they were allowed to keep a specified part of the remuneration.

In contrast to Lütke, Schabelski, who visited the Northwest coast a few years earlier, described the condition of slaves as a very sad one. He related that they were forced to perform the hardest labor and lost their lives at the slightest whim of their masters. When a chief planned to build a new house, he strangled one his slaves in order to saturate the site with his blood. Every fifteen or twenty years according to the wishes of the shamans great feasts were held at which slaves were given their freedom, but first a slave was thrown from the roof of the house to be cut to pieces by the daggers waiting below. [12]

Simpson also pictures the lot of slaves, who, according to his doubtlessly exaggerated report, comprise one-third of the coast population, as a very sad one. "These unfortunate ones," he declares, "are constantly the victims of their cruelty and tools for malice and revenge. When his master orders him to kill a red or a white man, he must obey, for if he refuses or is not successful, he must pay for it with his own life. [13]

Furthermore Simpson tells that Shakes, the cruel Stikine chief, often killed his slaves to gain prestige and show what a great man he was. He is supposed, shortly before Simpson's visit, to have slaughtered five slaves at the dedication of a new house; and on another occasion when in a fit of drunkeness he fell into a quarrel with a white man who chastised him, he had one of his slaves shot, both to re-establish his injured prestige and to sooth his own hurt feelings. In spite of this, none of his slaves made any attempt to get away, knowing full well that, if recaptured, they would be cruelly tortured and killed. [14]

Belcher states that when a chief wanted to mortify another he would kill a number of slaves, which injury the other could only answer by killing at least as many, but, if possible, a few more. This would continue until the entire supply of slaves had been exhausted. [15]

Sacrifices of slaves were nevertheless customary until in

recent times, but only at the great feasts where custom demanded it. Veniaminof's accounts of this seem much more trustworthy than those of Simpson or Belcher who, because of their shorter visits in the country and their lack of knowledge of the native language as well as of Russian, were much less in a position to obtain accurate information. However their reports are probably based on isolated instances. Rival chiefs today still try to outdo each other at great feasts, and it is on such occasions that the sacrifice of slaves formerly took place. However, slaves were also given their freedom at such feasts and received all the rights of freeborn Tlingit.

In recent years there has been no report of the sacrifice of slaves, which may be due to the small numbers of slaves available as well as to the fact that expensive feasts are not often given. Also, the American authorities have made an effort to prevent such sacrifices, just as they have ordered the freeing of slaves in specific instances.

In intercourse with his own people and with strangers the Tlingit maintains equitable and quiet behavior. Without a greeting, without even a word to say, he enters the house of another, and without invitation squats down near the stove. If he has a request to make he does not come out with it for some time; and neither is he asked about the purpose of his coming. Haste or curiosity is regarded as unseemly. In spite of the gift of natural oratory, words come to him slowly, almost painfully; only through tragic emotion does his speech become lively and expressive. Conversation is generally monosyllabic, although the Tlingit is not averse to joking and in the evening when the tricky pranks of Jēlch, the Raven, are told, the listeners lay aside their stern expressions and join in the fun with gay laughter. Also, everyone does not have the same temperament, and here, too, one finds the professional prankster, who takes every opportunity usually through questionable jokes to arouse the laughter of his audience.

Among the forms of recreation to which the Tlingit are given during the daytime, games are very important. They play with small round sticks about one decimeter (four inches) long, marked with red lines, which are shuffled by being rolled in a bunch of ten to twenty between the palms of the hands, a feat accomplished with great skill, similar to that of card shuffling by an ardent card player. The sticks are then laid down and covered with some shredded cedar bark to hide the markings, and the game consists of guessing the marks. Only two individuals or parties can play. [16] La Perouse gives the following description of the game: "They have thirty sticks each of which is marked differently, like our dice. They hide seven of them; everyone plays in order and the one who comes closest to guessing the marks on the seven sticks wins the stake, which is usually a piece of iron

or an axe. These games make them sad or serious."[17] Dixon
saw that an Indian at Port Mulgrave, in this game, in less than
an hour lost a knife, a spear and several stone axes, [18, 19] but he
bore his bad luck with great patience and control. According to
Lütke the Tlingit are such desperate gamblers that they will bet
their clothes, furs, guns, slaves, even their wives. [20] In addition
to the stick game, in more recent times common playing cards
are being used in gambling games which they have learned from
the whites.

The children, in so far as they are not kept busy by the adults,
tend to amuse themselves in a harmless fashion. The girls play
with beach pebbles which they arrange in all kinds of figures; the
boys hunt and wrestle, play ball with one another, make bows and
arrows with which to hunt small birds, or float small bark canoes on the water. On warm days they play in the water and
practice swimming though they can only do the so-called dog paddle. Ball is played by the children as well as by adults. In one
game which is often played by the young people in the village, two
groups oppose each other and toss a thick leather ball back and
forth, the object being never to let it touch the ground.

When a Tlingit has finished the work of the day he enjoys a well
earned rest. Preferably he looks for a rocky point on the beach
and sits there, wrapped in his blanket, absolutely motionless, by
the hour. The Russians in Sitka were especially familiar with a
rock near their palisades as a favorite sitting place of the natives. [21] Erman attributes, probably without justification, some
religious significance to this sitting on a rocky point, though it
may have been for the purposes of weather observation. [22]

The Tlingit devotes little time to personal cleanliness or to the
care of his surroundings. But if one is to believe the reports of
earlier authors, some progress has been made in this direction.
More and more, soap is replacing the use of urine for washing.
In the household of Tschartritsch, the Chilkat chief, members of
the family washed their hands and face every morning, at least
superficially, and the planked floor was scrubbed clean by slaves.
But even before acquaintance with Europeans the need for thorough bodily cleanliness was not completely foreign to the Tlingit;
one acquired it in a very complete manner through sweat baths,
which still today, as we saw, are in use everywhere. Instead of
the space already described for indoor bathing, there was erected an outdoor arrangement which could easily be set up in summer in camp. A framework of poles set off a small space in
which a person could squat. After this space had been completely
closed off with woolen blankets, it was filled with steam which
was created by pouring water over stones that had been heated in
the enclosed space. After such a sweat bath the Tlingit were accustomed to plunge directly into the sea, even in the depth of

winter.

These sweat baths were also indulged in by several persons together and with the observance of special ceremonies. That is
what Erman saw in the month of November when, around an ordinary fireplace in a Tlingit house, a space was shut off with
hangings in which about ten men took a sweat bath, while singly
or in chorus they sang or shook wooden rattles. Thereupon,
streaming with perspiration and with dark red skin, they stepped
naked out of the enclosure, and screaming and singing plunged in-

Women at Huna, planting potatoes

to the icy cold sea water, where for a while they jumped and
danced, moving toward the shore and away from it, until altogether they at last ran back to the house. [23]

Bathing alone in the surf or in rivers was not the custom of
adolescents although they were all tireless swimmers and whenever it was necessary to take a cold bath or cross a stream to
reach a desired goal they did not shy away from it. The hot
springs found in various parts of the Tlingit territory were used
by them, and especially the sulphur springs at Sitka were in use
for illness long before white occupation. Simpson tells that the
natives came from afar to these springs and often stayed in them
for hours, with only the head projecting, and ate, drank, and often even slept (?) in them, occasionally refreshing themselves

114

with some snow, when it was available. [24]

When, with the finishing of the evening meal, the business of
the day was over, and a little time had been devoted to entertain-
ment or the playing of games, people finally sought rest. Carefully the fire was extinguished and then the occupants of the house
retired to the boarded sleeping compartments, hung with blankets,
at the rear and sides of the house, or covered only with a blanket
laid down on the plank covered floor, generally without removing
any clothing. They sleep until daybreak, but in winter no one
rises before eight or nine o'clock.

The Tlingit has a highly developed sense of ownership. He not
only has his own clothes, weapons and utensils, he also has his
own hunting grounds, his own trade trails which no one else may
use without his permission or without paying damages. Generally
everyone's property rights are respected by his tribesmen, less
from a sense of justice than from fear of revenge. Theft is not
considered a disgrace; the thief who is caught is ashamed of his
lack of skill and regrets that he must return his booty. He does
not have to fear any further punishment, nor does he lose the respect of his tribesmen. Even in his relationship with his friends
and his nearest relatives the Tlingit shows great selfishness. For
every service he renders, for every gift he gives, he expects a
return. Belcher had to get permission to get wood and water in
Yakutat Bay through giving gifts. [25]

When a Tlingit gives a present he expects a return in some
form. Therefore he is distrustful when he receives a gift. Either
he thinks he has a right to it or he thinks the donor intends to get
something from him. So Belcher says of the Yakutat that they accepted a gift as a debt, not as a present and operated on the principal of "nothing for nothing." [26]

When a Tlingit asks another for something with the intention of
returning or replacing it, one may not deny him his request. It
is then the custom that he return more than he received; "kēisch,"
the custom is called. Under these circumstances, a demand can
also be made for work on the part of another. For instance, at
the first signs of the gray dawn of a winter morning we were
awakened by the loud voice of a shaman as he went from house to
house, calling ceremonially on his friends of the bear clan to
help him build a new house. This call was not in vain, and during
the winter the friends prepared the posts and beams and dragged
them on the snow to the building site. In summer the building of
the house began and before it was finished the owner was obligated to give a feast at which the friends who had helped him were
entertained and given gifts according to their services.

Vanity is one of the leading traits of Tlingit character. Nothing
can hurt him more than injury to his self esteem. [27] Jealously he
is on guard to see that all his prerogatives and rights are recog-

nized, and he looks with disdain on anyone who has lost an advantage. He puts great value on letters of recommendation of such whites as are in his opinion in high and influential positions. Such letters are carefully put away and on occasion shown to strangers to impress them with the importance of the owner. Frankly, sometimes the contents of the letters are not such as to help give the desired impression. Among the documents of chief Don-ē-wāk, which in good Tlingit tradition he did not bring forth until the second or third day, there was a statement that he owed a certain firm so and so many dollars for tobacco; another mentioned his weakness for making love to white women.

Plate I

Household Utensils of the Tlingit

1. Long wooden dish, kalchlá; 2 and 3. Pipe bowls, kstā-kĕt; 4. Wooden vessel, kā-kă-nē; 5. Vessel of horn, with eagle face, chlinēt-tsik; 6. Vessel of horn, no carving; 7 and 8. Wooden vessels, with beaver head, tsikēdi-tsĭk; 9. Seal-shaped wooden vessel, tsa-tsĭk; 10. Lip plug of wood, klū-ú-chrĕn-tacha; 11 and 12. Wooden spoons, schetl; 13. Basket woven of straw and cedar roots (seen from above), kātă-chúk; 14. Knife, chlíta; 15. Slender horn spoon, chlinēt-schatl; 16. Paint brush, kū-chĭta

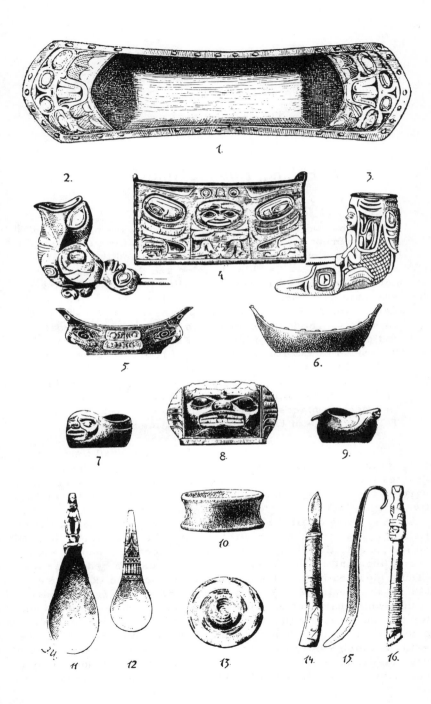

1.

2. 3.

4.

5. 6.

7. 8. 9.

10.

11. 12. 13. 14. 15. 16.

6. Fishing, Hunting, and Trade

Building and use of canoes -- Various ways of catching salmon; preparation and drying of salmon for winter use -- Catching flounders -- Catching smelts and the preparation of fish oil -- Catching herring and the gathering of herring spawn -- Haddock and halibut fishing -- Hunting sea mammals, sea otter, seal, dolphins and whales -- Land mammal hunting -- Traps for bears and fur-bearing animals -- The hunt for mountain sheep, mountain goat and caribou; hunting of birds -- Extensive trade before the advent of Europeans; articles of trade -- Slave trade -- Trading customs -- Present trade with Americans -- The Northwest Trading Company -- Trading trips of the Chilkat Indians to the interior Athapascans; preparation and meeting places -- Trading trips of the Stikine and Taku -- Trade of little profit to the Americans.

The Tlingit directs his attention primarily toward fishing; through this he gains the main part of his livelihood and to it he devotes the greatest part of his working hours. He lavishes great care on the making of the necessary equipment and has shown active imagination in its invention and development.

Most striking of all the equipment necessary for the Tlingit in fishing is his canoe, not only on account of its usefulness but also for its artistic construction. These canoes are usually made during the winter, the larger and better ones of a red cedar log (Thuja gigantea Nutt.)[1] the second grade ones of Sitka spruce (Picea Sitchensis Carr.), or of poplar trees. Strong and sound trunks which have not been bent or twisted spirally were sought for this purpose. Felling is still done in this fashion: with an axe a hole is cut on the windward side of the standing tree and a fire set in it which slowly eats its way through until after a number of days the trunk falls over.[2] Then it is first trimmed down with a hoe-shaped axe[3] and not until the desired outside shape is achieved is it hollowed out. To make a wall of even thickness, small holes are bored from the outside and wooden plugs about two to three decimeters[4] stuck in them. When the workman strikes them from within he knows that he has reached the right thickness. In order to make as large a canoe as possible from a given trunk, about two-thirds of its diameter is used, but such a canoe has a very clumsy shape, for the side walls bend inwards at the top and the bow and stern have little height so that the craft is easily overturned in the water. To obtain a more pleasing rounded body with greater stability, the canoe is spread. After the holes mentioned above have been closed with wooden plugs, the canoe is filled with water which is heated by means of dropping in hot stones; then cross pieces are set to spread the softening walls and gradually they are replaced with longer ones until finally an even and efficient shaping of the sides is achieved.

Canoes are made in varying sizes, the smallest are for only two or three people, the largest carry thirty or more men. Lisiansky saw several that were forty-five feet long and held about sixty men. [5] Among other things, the walls, according to Lütke, are extended with side planking. On the larger ones the bow is often ornamented with a carved figure and the side walls are gaily painted. According to Lütke, they also had names, such as Sun, Moon, Constellations, Earth, Island, Shaman, Whale, Otter, Eagle, Raven and similar ones, with the idea carried out in the figures on the bow and stern. [6]

In shape, canoes were alike, long, narrow and with high pointed bow and stern. Since neither a keel nor outriggers were used, it took all the skill a Tlingit had to keep the light craft from capsizing in stormy weather and high waves. In the smaller ones he had to sit on the bottom with his legs stretched out in front of him, or kneel in order to keep the center of gravity as low as possible; but even in the larger ones moving about had to be accomplished with the greatest of care. The canoes were propelled with short paddles about one and one-half milimeters (58-1/2") long. These had a crutch handle and were manipulated by one hand pushing the paddle forward, while the other hand, grasping the middle of the handle pulled the blade through the water. Similar, somewhat longer blades were used for steering. For celebrations brightly painted paddles were used.

In keeping with the amount of work necessary to make a good canoe, they were placed at a high value. In Holmberg's time a large, so-called war canoe had a value of eight hundred Banco-Rubles in Russian merchandise, [7] and now the Americans pay up to one hundred fifty dollars for the larger ones.

Such a valuable piece of property was handled with care by the Tlingit. In landing they tried to avoid running up on stones or rocks and carried, not dragged, it beyond reach of the tide.

During travel in the sunshine, the sides were kept damp by sprinkling water on them, and when idle on the beach, it was protected from the sun by a cover of woolen blankets or cedar bark mats. If however the boat is damaged, as may easily happen with its thin walls, only two to three centimeters thick, [8] the harm is repaired with great care by setting in a new piece of wall and sewing the break with roots of Sitka spruce or yellow cedar or by dovetailing in pieces of wood and making the joints watertight with pitch.

In spite of the skill with which the Tlingit handle their canoes they did not like to risk the open sea in stormy weather. If, however, they are overtaken by bad weather during a trip, they show themselves equal to the danger. With keen attention they watch every oncoming wave and, if an unusually high one threatens to overturn the light canoe, they strike it with flat paddles which gives the impression that they are pushing the sea down, while in reality they push the boat toward the crest of the wave.

It does not appear that the Tlingit knew the use of the sail before the coming of the Europeans. Now it is very common, but generally they sail only before the wind.

Even though the straits and bays on which the Tlingit have built their settlements are extraordinarily rich in fish, they nevertheless do not catch them right at home at all seasons of the year. They have to follow the wandering schools of fish, so they first make a summer camp at the mouth of a river, later on a shallow bay and with hook and line even follow the fish out into the open sea. This often makes the canoe a second home, for weeks and even months, and in it they carry all their household possessions, as well as the gear for fishing and hunting.

The Tlingit does not follow any other fish as eagerly as the salmon, because this is his main support in winter and on journeys when other foods are scarce. The method of catching salmon differs according to various kinds and localities. Following will be a description of methods we ourselves observed on the Chilkat River. Three kinds of salmon were distinguished here, the most prized of them being the red salmon which on an average weighed about fifteen pounds and attained a length of about twenty-nine inches. At the end of July the fish begin to ascend the river; but the principal catch is taken in July, August and September. The red salmon is followed by the white and, in some creeks, the humpback. The salmon is caught with salmon spears, with hooks, or in traps. The salmon spear consists of a shaft eleven to sixteen feet long, at the end of which is a long iron, formerly bone, point that has many barbs and rides loosely (Plate II, fig. 5). The fish is speared from a canoe. The point, which is fastened to the shaft by means of a leather thong, detaches itself and is held in the flesh of the fish by its many barbs. In this way the salmon does not break the shaft while thrashing around wildly.

The second, a very primitive way of catching salmon, is generally done from shore, but in shallow water a canoe can also be used. The fisherman lowers a long pole with an iron hook (Plate II, fig. 3) into the water and pulls it toward him over the pebbly bottom with a motion similar to that of raking. The muddy waters of the Chilkat River are not generally favorable for this method, but the numbers of ascending salmon are so great that often enough one of them is caught by the hook.

Most common is the salmon trap. Its erection is also very simple. A fence with some openings is stretched across a stream, preferably at rapids. In front of these, upstream, woven baskets are placed (Plate II, fig. 7), which are built very much like our fish weirs and serve the same purpose. This method of catching salmon was also observed by La Perouse at Lituya Bay. [9]

The fish are slit open on the ventral side after the heads, tails, and fins have been removed, and then are laid lengthwise on the back over a triangular wooden block (Plate II, fig. 9) so that both sides project in such a fashion that the entrails and backbone can easily be removed. While the fishing is done by the men, the women do the cleaning with the use of a crescentic knife set in a round handle (Plate II, fig. 10).

The clean salmon are then hung on a framework, also with the flesh side out. They are protected as much as possible from the rain and direct sunshine by green branches and during wet weather they are also hung inside the house and if necessary dried over the fire. The dried salmon are laid out flat on top of each other and tied together in bundles, which are stored away for later use.

After the winter's supply has been provided for in this fashion, the rest of the catch is used for the preparation of oil. For this purpose the white salmon is especially suitable, for it is very fat but not so tasty. The oil is prepared through rendering it in canoes in the same way as is done with the very oily candlefish, a description of which follows immediately.

Of much less importance than salmon fishing is the catching of flounders, which is done principally in winter and only to supply the needs of the moment. In the rivers, small holes are broken in the ice where the water is about a meter (3-3-1/2 feet) deep, and bait is sunk. Near these holes the Indian squats entirely wrapped in a woolen blanket which shuts out the direct daylight and makes it possible to peer into the dimly lighted depths where the fish hide from impending danger, and thus he sits motionless waiting with poised spear for the approach of a flounder which he will transfix with a swift and sure stroke. The spear used for this purpose has a short center prong of iron and two longer side prongs of wood, each of which has iron nails pointed inwards (Plate II, fig. 4). These prongs spread at the thrust whereby the obliquely set nails penetrate the fish.

At the end of February there appears in the rivers of the Chilkat territory a small fish belonging to the smelt family (Thaleichthys pacificus Gir.), which is called "ssag" by the natives and "smallfish" by the English and Americans. Since by this time the winter's supply is beginning to grow short, the coming of the "ssag" is jubilantly welcomed and young and old hasten to catch the tasty fish during its brief ascent. The use of this fish which is never too plentiful is only immediate. Two months later, from the end of April to the middle of May, the same fish appears again but in great numbers, also the individual fish is larger and fatter. Now the fishing takes on greater proportions, partly with traps and hooks, similar to the ones used in salmon fishing, only constructed closer and more lightly, partly with hand nets which during the winter are made of sinew by the women (Plate II, fig. 6). The fish catch is thrown into canoes to render the oil. The canoes are half buried in the sand and made secure by posts set in along their length and cords which cross the canoe and are pulled taut. Beside them stones of fist and head size are heated in a stong wood fire and by means of wooden tongs are put in the canoes filled with fish and water. The water gradually reaches a simmering temperature and as more heated stones are added maintains a boiling heat for several hours. The cooled stones are removed with a sievelike wooden shovel, and after they have been laid on a sort of wooden rack over a canoe they are washed off with warm water and heated again, whereupon the process described above is repeated several times more. The oil on the surface of the water is pushed toward the forward end of the canoe with a semicircular piece of cedar bark and here it is ladled into a large square box. By standing for some time and then being skimmed off into smaller containers it is purified. After cooling off, the oil has the appearance and consistency of goose grease, and when it is prepared from fresh fish it is supposed to be almost white and quite palatable. However, when it is made, as is frequently done, from fish which have been lying in a pit for ten to fourteen days, it is scarcely adapted to a more or less civilized palate. The mush of half-cooked fish left in the canoe, which still had lots of oil in it, is put to further use by being pressed through baskets woven of roots. [10] Also by trampling on them in a canoe with feet not especially cleaned for the purpose and by more boiling with hot stones, the last bit of oil is squeezed out.

A middle-sized canoe which would carry three men, when filled with fish would yield about five to six gallons of oil. In 1882 there were eight to twelve canoes of fish per man in the Chilkat territory. The oil is used exclusively for nourishment and enjoyed with dried salmon. In the autumn also various kinds of berries are put away for winter use with fish oil.

The middle of April is the time for the herring run, which in closely packed schools move into shallow bays to spawn, and only little effort is necessary to catch them. Poles about nine to ten feet long, provided with a row of sharp nails at the lower end are used (Plate II, fig. 1). They are propelled in the water like a sculling oar and the fish are impaled on the nails, often one on every nail. With a quick thrust on the side of the canoe, the fish are thrown off into the boat. In this simple way a canoe full is obtained in a short time. They are eaten fresh according to need or

Huna Indian building a canoe

dried on strings and stored for future use. Together with the catching of the herring their eggs are also gathered. In the bays in which they are known to spawn, hemlock boughs are laid during low tide on the exposed beach and fastened in various ways. After the fish have deposited their spawn the branches are collected again and hung on strings or spread on mats to dry. By scalding, the eggs are loosened from the branches and dried or mixed with fat and stored for winter use.

The haddock and halibut are especially plentiful on the outer coast, but are also found in Cross Sound and Chatham Strait. An unusually large wooden hook with an obliquely set iron nail and

generally ornamented with a more or less artistically carved figure (Plate II, fig. 8) is used for halibut and baited with any fish,
sometimes even with pieces of red salmon. The lines are made
of the fiber of red cedar (Thuja plicata Donn.) or of braided sinew, as well as the long, finger-thick stem of giant kelp (Macrocystis pyrifera Ag.) which has exceptional tensile strength. [11]
These lines are let down to the bottom by means of stone sinkers
and at their upper end is a wooden float in the form of an animal
which jerks when the fish is biting. The whole set is kept afloat
with inflated bladders. In this manner two people going out together in a canoe can keep several lines, as many as fifteen, out
and watch them. [12] When a fish bites, it is pulled up on the line
and as soon as it comes to the surface of the water it is clubbed
on the head. The club used for this purpose is made of very
heavy wood and carved with symbolic figures (Plate II, fig. 11).

In spite of the crude equipment a plentiful catch was obtained
in this fashion. Dixon remarked that his men with much finer
equipment did not have the results by far which two Indians obtained nearby with the gear described above. [13] There was no advantage for the native to give up his gear and fishing methods,
and generally he is still using the ways he employed before his
acquaintance with Europeans. This holds not only for the haddock
and halibut fishing but also for salmon, smelt and herring where
they still use their old gear. Only one innovation made quick
headway, the replacement of the bone and stone points with iron.

In contrast to fishing, hunting has not been carried on in the
native fashion for a long time. Here the old weapons, bows and
arrows, were crowded out completely by flintlocks and other
guns of older types, and, in place of the cleverly constructed
traps for various small animals, steel traps, more easily set,
are constantly coming into greater use. But also another change
has taken place: the hunt is no longer necessary to provide
clothing, but to exchange the skins of animals with white traders
for all kinds of new necessities. Almost all larger animals and
birds are hunted. Among the sea mammals, the sea otter formerly took first place, but now they are gotten only in small numbers
by the Huna and Yakutat. These, as well as the seal and dolphin,
are shot, a method that has contributed to their quick extinction.

Whale hunting is not now carried on by the Tlingit, and among
the older authors, only Marchand reports on it. "In whale hunting they use a barbed bone harpoon with a long shaft. When they
come to the spot where they last saw him dive, they slow up their
boats and play slowly on the surface of the water with their paddles and as soon as he appears, the harpooner reaches for his
harpoon and throws it at the monster." [14] Accordng to Veniaminof and Holmberg, the Tlingit, with the exception of the Yakutat,
disdain whale meat which the people to the north regard as a

treat. [15] We observed however, that the Killisnoo were very anxious to get the blubber from a whale caught by whites.

The hunting of land mammals offers nothing exceptional. The Tlingit Indian is generally a poor shot, and therefore he tries to come as close to his prey as possible, waiting for hours in a blind until the game approaches.

Holmberg tells that they seldom, and only of necessity, kill bears because they regard them as related to man. [16] This is perhaps not to the point, but the Tlingit shies away from encounters with the brown bear, and pursues the black bear whose skin he prizes highly. [17] In winter he hunts him with dogs in his lair, which he recognizes by the scratchings on the tree trunk, and in summer he lies in wait for him in the twilight when he comes down from the mountains to forest meadows to feast on young greens, and in autumn he finds him while he is fishing for salmon in shallow streams. He is also killed by deadfalls of simple construction. A strong tree is weighted down with a log or stones and held in a diagonal position by means of a support which is baited. A little horseshoe-shaped shelter with the floor covered with chips of wood attracts the attention of the bear toward the bait so that the weight of the falling log will break his back.

Another hunting device is a fairly strong sling made of caribou skin which is occasionally used by the Chilkat and probably comes from the Indians of the interior.

The dog is only of advantage to the Tlingit in hunting deer, for they chase the animals out of the forest tangle to the beach where they can be shot by the waiting hunters. Furthermore, the deer is also an easy prey when he is surprised while crossing from one island to another.

In order to get mountain goat and mountain sheep, the Tlingit must climb high in the mountains. Several Indians join in such a hunting expedition and while the best shots are left at vantage points, the others chase the timid game toward them. [18] It is similar to caribou hunting.

Wolves, foxes and other animals of prey are now taken only in steel traps, but occasionally deadfalls, similar to the one described above, are used for them. Carved-bone trap sticks are used to fasten the lines. The same type of trap is built for small animals, like squirrels and weasels. Marmots, ground squirrels and rabbits are caught in snares made of eagle quills and sinew.

Of the larger birds only one is safe from pursuit, the raven, "jělch," the ancestor of the Tlingit clan and the hero of a cycle of mythology. According to Holmberg, the albatross is also spared because his death is supposed to cause bad weather. [19] Likewise we were warned not to kill the long-tailed duck, but these superstitions seem to have lost their power, because one of these birds was brought to us by an Indian himself. With the exception of the ptarmigans and the gulls which are often caught in snares, most birds are shot, but never in flight. The hunter carefully approaches a flock of ducks or geese and waits motionless for hours behind a blind on the shore until one or more birds come within close range.

Besides hunting and fishing, the Tlingit devotes the greatest part of his energy to trade. Long before the coming of the Europeans this was carried on; not only the neighboring tribes ex-

Indian women and canoes in Taku harbor

changed different products of hunting and fishing, but there is evidence that more distant coastal territory and remote interior tribes carried on an active tribe to tribe trade through to the Tlingit. [20]

To their astonishment the first visitors to the Northwest Coast found the knowledge and use of iron spread everywhere, even though it was scarce and highly valued. In 1741 Steller saw iron knives, supposedly not of European manufacture, in the possession of two Indians on Shumagin Island. [21] In 1775[22] Cook found iron knives and arrow points in Nootka Sound, and La Perouse and Dixon observed in 1786 and 1787 iron lance points and daggers

126

among the natives of Yakutat and Lituya bays. This iron, as Steller suggests, may either have come through trade which the Chukchi carried on with the Russians at Anadyrsk or have been brought by American tribes on the Diomede Islands from Asia to America. According to Wrangell, who was the first to point out the meaning and spread of the trade through the Chukchi, Russian goods were diffused from the Arctic, south to Bristol Bay. [23] But when the opportunity was offered to the Tlingit to get European wares directly from trading vessels, they accepted it greedily, as we have already seen in the first chapter. After a few years iron utensils and other things of European manufacture were to be found on the entire coast and had found their way across the mountains into the interior. That this trade is not a new custom and that it moves along ancient trails and probably was only intensified by the interference of the Europeans can be seen from the reports of the fur traders who found the natives endowed with all the tricks of trading, and we can see it even today in the household possessions of the Tlingit, which are the products of many different places. The caribou skin which the Chilkat use for their clothing, the sinew with which they sew, the lichen with which they dye their dancing blankets are all secured through trade with the Athapascan-speaking Indians of the interior. The dentalium, the sharks' teeth and pieces of mother of pearl (haliotis) which they wear as jewelry in their ears or hang as pendants on a thong around the neck come from the south, principally from the Queen Charlotte Islands. The dentalium, called "tsuklis" by the Russians was especially prized formerly. The Russians, who used them for their trade with the northern peoples, paid in Lütke's time in the market at Sitka thirty rubles for one hundred pieces. [24] Also the carved utensils of wood or horn which one finds in every household come to a large degree from the south, although single artists are found among every tribe. The frequent ornamentation of these pieces with the operculum of a snail, one of the Turbo variety (Pachypoma gibberosum), points to the Queen Charlotte Islands where the northern boundary of this style is reached, although these opercula may have been independent items of trade.

Although canoe building is carried on everywhere the largest and finest canoes, made of red cedar logs, also come from the south. The Sitka and Huna make the best basketry and the Chilkat are famous for their celebrated dance blankets.

The heavier pieces of leather armor, which formerly were used all along the coast in fighting but are now freely sold to curio dealers as useless, are supposed to be made of buffalo skin or, according to Wrangell, of musk ox skin, which is obtained from the Indians of the interior. From the Copper River comes the native copper, which was worked into arrow points, lance points and daggers and, in a special form, was used as a treasured possession, [25] but today serves only for ornamentation or trimming on carved utensils and masks.

Food also was formerly an article of trade, as the oil of the candlefish which was rendered only in a few places. From the outer coast the cakes made of the leaves of Alaria esculentia were sent to the interior and from there came the conifer gum used for chewing.

A lively trade was also carried on with slaves. Originally prisoners of war, they were traded from tribe to tribe like personal possessions. So we read in the reports of Steersmen Ismailof and Bocharof that the inhabitants of Yakutat Bay brought two boys about twelve years old to the ship to sell; one was a native of Kodiak who before the establishment of the Company at Kodiak had been captured by the Kenai and sold by them to the people of Prince William Sound and then to the Ugalachmut and finally to the Kolushan or Tlingit. Because the boy understood the languages of the Tlingit and Kodiak the Russians bought him for four and one-half pounds of iron, a large coral and three fathoms of enamel. The other boy, a Chilkat by birth, the natives exchanged for a Prince William Sound native whom they found on shipboard.

The slave trade was still flourishing in Holmberg's time. The majority of slaves at that time consisted of Flatheads[26] whom the Tlingit secured in trade from their southern neighbors. Recently the slave trade has almost entirely stopped and only a few slaves are found in the possession of chiefs. But frequently we are still told about certain valuable pieces that formerly were equal to the price of a slave, so it is certain that slaves were valuable articles of trade. Lütke reports that for a little carved figure to put on a canoe a slave was given. [27] A slave, in Wrangell's time, was worth twenty-five beaver skins or two sea otter skins. [28]

Dixon, La Perouse and others give us some idea about the way trade was formerly conducted. The market was always opened with festivities and formality, usually beginning with song that

---

Plate II

Fishing Tackle

1. Herring rake, chitla; 2. Fishhook for salmon and eulachon, tíchrá; 3. The same, lower end; 4. Trout spear, tlakwá; 5. Salmon spear, kat; 6. Net for catching eulachon, dig-há; 7. Fish basket of fir withes for catching eulachon; 8. Fishhook for halibut, nǎ ch (according to Lisiansky); 9. Wooden rack on which the salmon were cleaned; 10. Crescent-shaped knife with wooden handle for cutting up the salmon; 11. Club for killing halibut

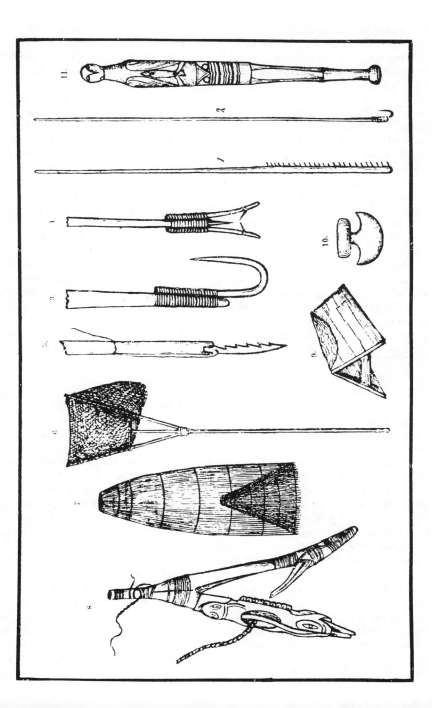

the natives started before they boarded the ship. In trading they showed themselves exceptionally concerned with pressing their advantage. "They showed," said La Perouse, "to our great astonishment, great familiarity with trading and they made bargains as astutely as European merchants." Dixon described an incident as follows: "The chief of the tribe always oversees all the trading of his people and puts himself to great pains to see that their skins are favorably presented. If another tribe comes to the ship to sell something, they wait patiently until he is finished and if in their opinion he made a good bargain, they use him to offer their skins also. Actually they are very jealous of each other and practice every kind of caution to keep their neighbors from knowing what they receive for their wares."[29] "At the second that a leader has closed a bargain he repeats the word "coocoo" three times and at once the people answer from the canoes with "hwoah" which is shouted with more or less volume according as to how the trade strikes them."[30]

Malaspina said, about these same Yakutat, that they would sit over an hour, looking at the things which had been set out before them, before they would bring out their own wares. An especially good skin they showed with great secrecy and immediately packed it away again. When a deal was finally closed, they tried to repudiate it again. Through it all there was not the slightest sign of disagreement to be detected among them, everything seemed to

---

Plate III

The Preparation of Fish Oil

In the canoe which is half-buried in the sand the fish are cooked with the help of hot stones. At the left in the foreground is the fire in which the stones are heated, at the right stands an Indian, with a wooden shovel, who puts the hot stones into the canoe and takes the cold ones out. The latter are washed off on a wooden rack by the woman squatting behind the canoe. In the background at the right is a woman engaged in ladling the fish oil, at the left two Indians are preparing a meal for which some fish impaled on a wooden stick are being roasted. In the background at the right center is the pit in which the fish are stored. In front of the canoe lie some tools: (1) wooden tongs with which the hot stones are taken out of the fire, (2) a wooden spoon, schīn, (3) the wooden shovel, tachū na, with which the stones to be washed are laid on the wooden grate which is above the canoe, (4) a piece of cedar bark, kotána, which is used for collecting the layer of oil. The larger boxes, tlākt, are used for the wash water, the smaller for the fish oil; the wicker baskets behind the middle of the canoe are used for pressing out the fish oil.

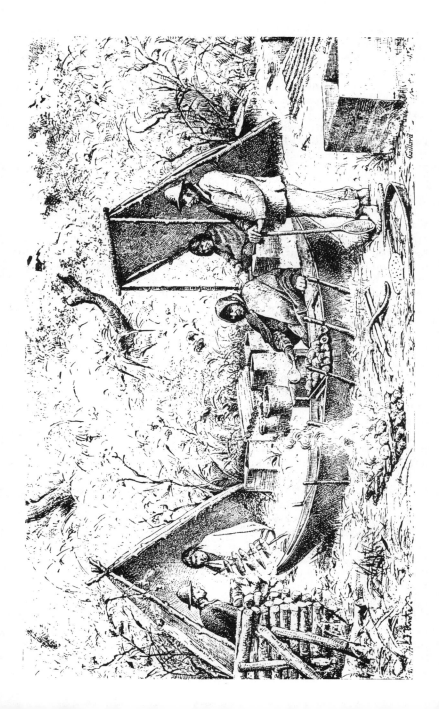

have been arranged beforehand. According to whether they considered the transaction more or less profitable, they approved it
with one, two, or three shouts. [31] In the report mentioned above
of the steersmen Ismailof and Bocharof they said, "In their sharp
and not well-founded trade they are especially greedy for Russian
wares in return for their own and demand with every exchange a
'lagniappe. '"

In the trade which the Tlingit have been conducting with the
Europeans since the end of the last century they have received
for the furs mentioned above a great variety of European goods.
Soon the needs of the small population were supplied and then the
traders had to plan to bring some new things every year. Beads
and other jewelry dropped rapidly in value, but iron bars, and
iron, tin and copper vessels were eagerly sought for a longer
time; knives, axes, guns, ammunition, calico, woolen blankets
and clothing are the principal items of trade today. Woolen blankets, the three or four dollar kind, are the standard of value; the
Indian buys them beyond his needs because possession of them
determines his wealth, and a rich chief may have several hundred piled up. Formerly caribou skins took their place and fifteen to twenty of them were given for one slave, five to six for a
sea otter and ten to fifteen for a good canoe. [32]

In food stuff, principally tobacco, hardtack, sugar and flour
were introduced, and the use of the last article rose from year
to year. In general the store of a trader among the Indians was
outfitted like a retail stall in a village, and the Indians accustomed themselves gradually to demand more and more European
made goods. Only two items could not be imported into Alaska,
liquor and breechloaders. These prohibitions were strictly enforced and with a large degree of success, since it was to the interest of the traders themselves, if they planned on continuing
business, to prevent the distribution of these wares which threatened the existence of the Indian population as well as the safety
of the whites. Actually, as we have seen, the natives themselves
learned the preparation of an intoxicating drink, called "hut -
schinu" which they derived from the distillation of molasses.

The Russian American Company traded with the natives principally in Sitka while in the inner archipelago the American and
English ships plied a trade, not really legal, but unhindered by
the Russians. In 1840 the difference, which arose through the
English demand for the right to navigate the Stikine which flows
into Russian territory, was set aside through the leasing of all
the trade on the coast from 54°40' north latitude to Cape Spencer,
to the Hudson's Bay Company in return for the delivery of two
thousand Columbia sea otter a year.

Now the trade with the Tlingit is largely in the hands of an American company, the Northwest Trading Company, which was or-

ganized in 1880 under President Paul Schulze in Portland. Six
factories were opened in southeastern Alaska by this company, in
Sitka, Juneau, Chilkoot, Huna (later abandoned), Killisnoo and on
Kenasnu Island opposite the village of Killisnoo and on the south
of Prince of Wales Island among the Haida at Howkan.

The price of goods is fixed by the company in American money
as well as the value of furs offered in exchange. However, they
are not paid in cash but given tickets of various colors, worth
one, one-half, one-fourth, one-eighth dollars, and which can be
exchanged for merchandise at any of the company's factories.
Since the goods were twenty-five to fifty percent above the prices
in Portland or San Francisco, the price actually paid for the furs
seemed greater than it really was. It was a common practice on
the part of the traders in dealing with the Indians to use substand-
ard weights and measures. An "Indian" yard had thirty-five inches (instead of thirty-six inches) and an "Indian" pound had fifteen
ounces (instead of sixteen).

In the following I will give an account of skins sold by a Chilkat
to a trader with the prices paid for them:

Item	Chilkat Dollars	San Francisco Dollars
Brown bear (Ursus arctos?)	1.00 - 5.00	1.00 - 4.00
Grizzly bear (Ursus horribilis Ord.)	1.00 - 6.00	
Black bear (Ursus americanus)	1.00 - 7.00	1.00 - 5.00
Wolf (so-called mountain wolf from the interior)	2.00	
Wolf ("prarie wolf" from the coast)	1.25	
Fox, red	.50 - 2.00	1.50 - 1.75
Fox, black	5.00 - 60.00	
Fox, silver	5.00 - 60.00	10.00 - 50.00
Fox, gray	8.00 - 15.00	
Fox, cross	2.00 - 8.00	3.00 - 5.00
Lynx	.50 - 2.00	
Marten	.50 - 5.00	1.50 - 3.00
Ermine	.125 - .25	.05 - .10
Sea otter (Enhydra lutris nereis Merriam) from Yakutat	10.00 - 70.00	20.00 - 200.00
Land otter	1.50 - 5.00	1.50 - 4.00
Seal	.25 - .50	
Beaver	1.00 - 7.00	1.00 - 3.00
Ground squirrel sewed together for blankets	.50 - 1.50	
Marmot, also as blankets	.50 - 1.50	
Also moose, caribou and moun- tain goat		

The larger number of the skins mentioned above were obtained by the Chilkat from the Indians of the interior with whom they have traded since ancient times. The Chilkat were the middlemen between the interior and the coast and they guarded this position so zealously that for a long time they would not allow any white man to go into the interior and they still try to prevent the American fur traders in every way from trading directly with the Athapascans. Several times during the winter of 1881 to 1882 these Athapascans came through the pass laden with the results of their

A Chilkat wolf trap

hunting, skins of all kinds, among them beautiful furs of black and silver fox which bring the highest prices. But only one among them, a blood relative of one of the Chilkat chiefs, was allowed to deal directly with the whites, the rest all had to leave their wares with the Chilkat for comparatively low prices. The Chilkat themselves undertook each year an extensive trading expedition on the route already given in the valley of the Yukon and to Yakutat Bay. For weeks ahead preparations went on, tobacco, sugar, flour, woolen blankets, colored materials, gunpowder, lead and other articles desired by the Athapascans were secured from the whites at the lowest prices possible and, together with their own dried salmon, fish oil, and flour as traveling rations, were packed in large bundles which were carried on the back by means of packstraps across the forehead and chest. The Tlingit manage perfectly astonishing loads of one hundred pounds and more on steep mountain trails and across broad snow fields on trips of several days far into the interior. Formerly they carried their trading expeditions as far as Fort Selkirk, three hundred seventy kilometers in a straight line from the coast. [33] In winter almost the whole trip is done on snowshoes, which are especially large to prevent the packer, who carries, in addition to his load, a gun and an axe, from sinking into the snow under his weight. Sleds were seldom used and the numerous wolflike dogs were nowhere pressed into service as draft animals. Each carrier was provided with a staff which he used in winter to knock the snow off his snowshoes and in summer to bend back the thick underbrush.

In summer an even more extensive trip was undertaken in the period between the end of the candlefish run and the appearance of the salmon. In addition smaller groups went over throughout the year as well as single individuals who went into the interior to hunt or set traps. Before going, dances were performed, thorough bodily cleansing was undertaken, and the face was freshly painted; during the journey no one washed.

The trail varies with the season. It leads up the valleys of the streams coming down to the coast and here it is well marked; on the plateau, however, where, on account of the snow one could lose the trail, markers are set. The campsites, which are chosen so that water and firewood are close at hand, could be recognized by an upright flat stone which marked the center of the circle. Climbing the snow covered cliffs is very difficult; as far as possible it is done by zigzaging up on snowshoes, but at the steeper places they take off the snowshoes and carry them on their backs. Rivers were usually crossed near the source. If the current threatened to sweep away the heavily laden Tlingit, a chain was formed of several people who braced themselves against the stream with poles and thus gave the person passing downstream from them something to cling to. As much as possible the food taken for the journey was saved by using whatever was secured by hunting or visiting trap sites during the trip.

With an empty stomach one broke camp in the morning and during the day only dried salmon is eaten if there are no ripe berries to add to the diet. The principal meal is eaten in the evening. Part of the food carried along is deposited in caches. To protect it from bears the grass is burnt off around the cache. The burnt smell is supposed to keep them away, and, as a matter of fact, our deposits were untouched in spite of the numerous bear tracks round about.

If a Tlingit is forced to make camp on a thick cover of snow, he first makes a foundation of hemlock twigs on which several larger branches are laid. Beside it a fire made of fallen wood gradually melts the snow on the ground.

Special places in the interior are designated as rendezvous points, as on the trail through the Chilkoot Valley a place called Tagish between two lakes in the Yukon area, Marsh and Teslin Lakes; on the Chilkat trail we met parties at Alsek or at the north end of Kusawa. Often the Chilkat Indians have to cover considerable territory before they secure sufficient skins from the nomadic Athapascans. Then they indicate their presence, as well as the trail which they have broken, by bending twigs in one direction. Such a method was followed also by our guide. He set three little sticks upright in the ground to indicate our numbers and then laid cut twigs in the direction of the trail which we intended to take. Smoke signals are also often used.

Simpson reports that the Secatquonays, [34] Tlingit living at the mouth of the Stikine River, also made trading expeditions into the interior to get skins. [35] Three or four times a year they are supposed to have gone to a trading place sixty English miles from Dease Lake and one hundred fifty miles from the coast, which was inhabited by the Niharnies. These people were under a female chief who assumed very friendly relations with Campbell when in the winter of 1838 to 1839 he had set up a new trading post at Dease Lake. This chieftainess undertook occasional trips to the coast and was, just like Campbell, the object of zealous attention on the part of the Secatquonays. [36]

The Taku also, at Simpson's time, carried on a profitable business as middlemen with the inhabitants of the interior since they could, in spite of the strong current, take their canoes the first one hundred English miles up the river and proceed about the same distance on foot to trading places in the interior. [37]

After returning home the Tlingit were in no rush to sell their skins to the white traders; weeks, even months passed before they brought their whole stock to market; they did not like to sell it all at once, piece by piece they bargained, often for hours over one skin. Several times the same heavy bearskin would be carried thirty kilometers from the village of Klukwan to the factory and back again while the owner would not agree on the price offered. Frequently the women carry on the trading and they are even more inclined to be stubborn than the men.

All tricks are allowable among the Tlingit in trading. The rare and costly black fox skins are imitated by dying the common red ones and if one is caught at it, he smiles in embarrassment, regretting, not the deceit, but the fact that he did not succeed. However these attempts at deceit are very clumsy. Thus during our stay, the Chilkat demanded that the Indian wife of Dickinson, the trader, should not be present during their transactions, supposedly because she encouraged her husband to pay very little for their skins, but actually because they could not deceive him as easily on account of her knowledge of the Tlingit language.

In consequence of the toughness of the natives in trading and their acting as middlemen for the hunting peoples of the interior, the fur trade of the company was not as lucrative as that of the Hudson's Bay Company. The price of the trade goods also could not be raised too much because the Chilkat did not hesitate to undertake the long and difficult canoe trip to the Hudson's Bay factories in British Columbia if they thought they could make even a little more profit. A visit on the part of a white man to the Athapascans to trade with them directly was regarded by the Chilkat as an infringement of their rights and likely to be prevented by force. Just as every tribe had its hunting and fishing territory, so they had their trading trails, the Chilkat went up the Chilkat River, the Chilkoot over Chilkoot Pass and it took lengthy negotiations to reverse the procedure. Also there existed a sort of contract or patronage relationship between the Tlingit and the Athapascans in which the latter delivered their skins only to a definite patron. The Athapascans were badly cheated in these dealings and the Tlingit treated them like slaves.

7. Arts and Handcrafts

Preparation of items of clothing; skin and basketry
work; weaving of woolen blankets; jewelry of silver,
bone and stone -- Description of ceremonial regalia;
masks, rattles and drums -- Household utensils; wood-
en boxes and dishes; spoons of wood and horn; stone
mortars and lamps; pipe bowls; snowshoes; woven baskets and mats -- Armor of thong and wooden rods --
Tools, knives and axes; painting equipment -- Blacksmithing, copper and iron -- Use of Indian manpower
by the whites -- Wages; wood cutting and freighting --
Smuggling -- Irresponsibility of the Indians -- Attitude
toward Chinese workmen.

In this chapter only a quick survey will be given of the techno-
logical achievements of the Tlingit with special attention to the
places where the ethnological collections were made. To give a
more complete discussion, it would be necessary to have a more
comprehensive collection at hand; also a study of such scope
would be beyond the limits of the present work.

The clothing of the natives is no longer entirely of aboriginal
manufacture. As we have seen, instead of blankets made of animal skins sewn together, woolen blankets are largely used, as
well as ready made pieces of European clothing. Equally widespread is the use of cotton underwear instead of the former skin
shirt. Cutting, sewing, mending, darning and so forth are carried on by the native women who have shown themselves adept at
all these skills. They learn all this in the mission schools as
well as knitting stockings, even though the need for these is still
slight.

To use with snowshoes and for traveling through the woods, the
women formerly made moccasins, called akūschtetích, which
were similar to house slippers and were trimmed with colored
patterns. They also made skin mittens, generally trimmed with

fur, called tsāg. On these as well as on all skin work including
pouches, sinew, especially that taken from the backbone of
moose or elk, was used instead of thread. The skin itself was
cut with a crescentic knife similar to the one used for cutting salmon. These things were usually very well made and durable and
were not unattractive with their ornamentation of colored ribbons,
braid and cloth appliqué. Split porcupine quills (Erethizon epixanthus) were also woven in for ornamentation.

The fur caps, which we saw in use occasionally, may have
been introduced through the whites. Of exceptional art, however,
are the hats which are woven of the roots of the Sitka spruce
(Picea Sitchensis Carr.) or the yellow or Alaska cedar (Chamaecyparis Nutkaensis), and are called tsāch. Bright painting is common on them and, if they belong to a chief or any other important
person, several cylinders woven the same way, called schátá-
kŭch, are set on top. When the Russians still had their colony at
Ross, California, they developed quite a trade with these hats. [1]

In order to prepare roots for weaving they are soaked in hot
water and the bark peeled off. In this state they are called chrat-
kassa-tūk. Then they are cut lengthwise and dyed gray. [2] In addition to roots, grasses, tschak-kadlet, and rushes, tschaga-
chlíti, are used as weaving materials. [3]
Wooden hats which are shaped like the woven ones with the
same cylinders on top are highly valued. At a Huna chief's we
saw such a hat very beautifully made with a whale design carved
on the front. The hat was regarded as especially valuable and
was worth more than two hundred dollars. It was wrapped in
cloth for safe keeping.

The art and sophisticated taste of the Tlingit are shown in
their ceremonial garb with its decoration and ornament more
than in their ordinary clothing. Above all should be mentioned
the dance blankets, called dschénu, which are artistically woven
of mountain goat wool. Among the southern tribes the Tsimshian
are noted for making these blankets, while among the Tlingit the
Chilkat are famous for them; in fact, the blankets are generally
known as Chilkat blankets. The making of such a blanket requires
as much as half a year or more. The wool is spun into thread
without the use of machinery. The spinner rests on her knees,
takes a bit of wool from the pile at her left and rolls it with her
right hand on her bare right thigh into a thread of the desired
thickness. Some of these threads are dyed black and yellow, the
latter color being derived from a yellow moss, probably Parme-
lia vulpina, [4] which they trade from the Indians in the interior.
The weaving of the blanket is done without a loom. From a round
stick which rests on two uprights of nicely carved wood, the
warps hang straight down and are gathered in small bundles into
animal bladder bags. The weaver, who squats in front of this

frame, puts the wefts through singly by hand. With colored wools the designs which are copied from a pattern board, are woven into the blanket. These are again the ever present crest figures, consisting of designs derived from the crest animals. Even though each blanket has its peculiar design they nevertheless have a striking similarity. They resemble a wide skin apron with

Chilkat woman weaving a dance blanket

long fringes and at ceremonial occasions they are worn by the chiefs and shamans around the waist like a skin apron. These blankets or dance aprons are highly valued by the natives; and to preserve them they are wrapped in cases made of bear intestines, which are slit and sewn together in strips and put in wooden boxes, which will be discussed later on. Even while they are being made they are covered by these protectors to prevent soiling.[5] Only a few women understand the weaving of these dance blankets.

Even at the factories (Hudson's Bay posts?) they are sold for
high prices ($25 - $30) and now they are very hard to get.

In the line of jewelry, silver bracelets and rings are outstanding because of their neat and tasteful execution, considering the
crude tools which are used. All silver work is done with American dollars (dana means silver as well as dollar) and, in addition
to the typical heraldic crests, the Indians also carve graceful
arabesques and personal names, if they are given a pattern to
follow. As was said before, there are only a few who are skillful
at this art.

Small ornaments, models, and toys are carved with more or
less skill from a variety of materials, such as stone, bone,
shell, or wood. Nephrite and other hard silicates like marble and
alabaster and a softer black slate from the Queen Charlotte Islands are all worked. Among the wooden ornaments, the labrets
have been previously described. Those which we secured do not
show any especially fine carving, the largest being five centimeters long, two and one-third centimeters wide and one and one-
fourth centimeters thick. According to Dixon and others much
larger lip plugs were formerly in use. In the past beautifully decorated combs were made of wood, bone, or whalebone, but they
have fallen into disuse because of European importations.

Masks, rattles, drums, and dance wands used for ceremonial
and shamanistic performances are found in extraordinarily large
numbers. The masks are either face masks with eye and mouth
holes or they represent the heads of animals, principally birds
or any fantastic combination with mechanical contrivances moving the wings and so forth. As an example we saw a mask which
was a model of a salmon trap; but the complicated masks do not
appear among the Tlingit often and seem to be importations from
the south. All masks are made of wood and generally painted
with red lines and often inlaid with mother-of-pearl. [6] Thongs fastened to the sides are put around the head to hold the mask on,
but sometimes a leather loop on the inside is held by the teeth.
The details are often crude but nevertheless in some of the older
pieces great care is shown in the work. Among the face masks
also are found some representing women with a copy of the labret
in the lower lip. A few masks are decked out with human hair.

The rattles tsche-schuch consist in their simplest form of two
equally large ovoid wooden forms, laid one upon the other so as
to enclose an empty space. In this space small pebbles are put;
the two halves are tied together with sinew or thong. A short
wooden handle is either added or is made in one piece with the
rattle itself. More often one finds the two parts of the rattle richly ornamented with carved symbolic figures. Repeatedly there is
a human being lying down, whose protruding tongue is held by a
froglike being. In addition to one such piece which we brought

with us, I find a similar one in Lisiansky[7] from the Tlingit and further in Belcher[8] and finally also a Haida rattle in Dawson.[9] Also in other details these four rattles just mentioned show many resemblances without being completely identical. In the presence of such rich material and with the knowledge of so many myths one must be able to find many other representations and interpretations which have not yet come to light.

Also used as rattles are rings hung with puffin bills, tschi-kå-chåta, which have been frequently described. Wands about four decimeters long, hung thickly with puffin bills and with the end carved in the form of a bird's head, are used as well. This kind of wand we saw only at Klawak. During the dance they are grasped in the middle and shaken with a quivering motion.

The drums, gau, are decorated in various ways. They are mostly painted red, and the wooden boxes which are used as drums are richly carved and painted with heraldic figures. Also the wands which are used by the heralds in the various feasts and with which they beat time on a board on the floor are often carved their full length.

Repeatedly we saw neatly made models of the shamanistic paraphernalia, especially the masks. Whether these have a special meaning we could not find out, but they were highly prized. Furthermore, models are made of other things too, canoes, houses, and household objects, whether just to pass the time, or as patterns, or toys for the children could not be determined.

Of the household utensils, the various ones made of wood, as the troughs, boxes, and dishes should have more specific descriptions. They are made in all sizes, from the smallest which serve as children's toys to the large containers in which ceremonial

Fishbone comb, gåkchēdu, carved with bear's head, from Huna

blankets and other costly things are stored. There is great variety also in shapes and decoration. Of the wooden containers, two kinds can be distinguished, the boxlike kind called kā-kǎ-nó which consists of two pieces, a bottom and the sides, but may also have a lid, and the dishlike one called tsīg which is worked from a single piece of wood. The former ones are made in the same way as our wooden boxes. A thin board is split from a cedar log and bent at right angles three times to form the sides, after kerfs have been cut on the inside to a depth of about half the thickness of the wood. The two edges that meet are carefully sewn together with tough, thin withes or roots. The bottom, which consists of a thicker rectangular board, is fastened at right angles to the sides in the same way. The sides are sometimes bent slightly outward with a regular and pleasing curve and are decorated with painting, or if thick enough, are carved. The upper edge is generally decorated with the operculum of the sea snail (Pachypoma gibberosum). [10] The large boxes have a lid which overhangs the box on all four sides and is made of one piece.

A greater variety of shapes is found among the dishes made of one piece; occasionally they are round, some are oval, and some are long and troughlike. Often the whole dish represents a bird, a frog, a beaver, a seal, or any other animal, lying either on its belly or its back, one end showing the head, the other, the tail of the animal, while feet or wings are indicated on the sides. In other cases figures are carved on opposite sides. Also on these vessels the rim is decorated with the operculum of the sea snail. These opercula look very much like teeth, and often it is erroneously stated that teeth are used to decorate these utensils, but in every case in which I could examine the object I found them to be opercula. Formerly wooden dishes were used as cooking vessels, but now they serve only as food dishes or lie around among the household unused. Smoke and grease has given them a fine, shiny, brown color. Some have inlay of abalone in the eyes and copper plates in the mouth as extra decoration.

Very pretty dishes are also made of mountain sheep horn. One which we brought back with us is boat-shaped, having a length of twenty-seven and one-half centimeters, a width of seventeen and one-fourth centimeters, and at each end there is a face with a bent-back beak forming a handle. A similar horn vessel is shown by Dawson. [11]

Spoons, called schatl, with pleasing shape and usually with long curved handles, richly decorated, are carved of horn as well as of wood. The little black spoons which are in most common use are made of mountain goat horn, while the larger light ones are of mountain sheep. Occasionally two pieces are combined in a spoon, the handle being of mountain goat and the bowl of mountain sheep horn.

Very large wooden or horn spoons are called schīn. One specimen in our collection, which nevertheless is not among the largest, has a handle thirty centimeters long and a bowl twenty-five centimeters long and seventeen centimeters wide. These large spoons are not used for eating but, as was mentioned before, are used as serving spoons and as plates.

Formerly mortars, gắe′t or kaje′t, made of various kinds of stone, were used to mash berries and to grind up tree bark which was mixed with tobacco. Now they are rarely used, but one still finds them in many households. Generally they are not decorated, but a few have various designs on them as, for instance, the one we saw in the form of a frog. The pestles used with them have a round head and a short thick handle. We secured one made of white marble.

Flat stone vessels, usually oval in shape, serve as lamps, tsi͗-na. These also are usually without any sculpture, but occasionally one is made in the form of a frog or some other animal. These lamps are filled with fish oil which is soaked up by a wick of peat moss or twisted wool. They give off only a meager light, but even by this the women can do the finest handwork.

Especially artistic are the pipe bowls, kstã-kêt, which are

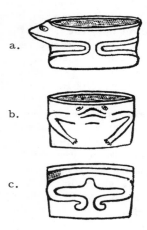

a.

b.

c.

Stone mortars, te-kajét, representing a frog, chichtsch, from Klukwan
a. side view
b. front view
c. back view

filled with tobacco and passed to guests at feasts. Most of them are carved of wood and lined with copper which is neatly carried over the rim, but a few are of stone. They have a variety of shapes, a bird, a chiton, a ship, or anything else that tempted the imitative skill of the maker. Just as carefully as the bowl is worked, just so careless is the preparation of the stem which is only a thin twig with the pith pushed out and which was rarely kept from one occasion to the next.

The snowshoes, which are especially used by the tribes who trade in the interior, are among the most important household articles and are another example, with their pleasing and functional shape and their neat execution, of the artistic skill of these people. The frames are made of maple or birch and are slowly bent into shape over the fire. The two sides of the frame, each made of one piece, are joined at the front by splicing and binding with strips of skin, the other ends being drawn together to an acute angle by means of sinew lashing. With three crosspieces the inner space is divided into four sections of which the front and two back ones are filled with a closemeshed net of thin rawhide strips while the second section, except for a rectangular opening behind the first crosspiece, is strung with heavier strips which serve as support for the foot. A medium-sized snowshoe is about one hundred eighteen centimeters long (measured along the convex side) while its greatest width at the front is twenty-five and one-half centimeters. Especially large snow-shoes are used for travel to the interior. The snowshoe is fastened to the foot by means of a thong so that the heel can move freely up and down while the front part of the foot rests on the netting and only the toes find play in the rectangular space mentioned above. If the thong is adjusted to fit the foot, it is very easy to put on and take off the snowshoes by means of a sideways movement of the foot toward the inside. Walking on these snowshoes over even ground and in open terrain takes no practice since one uses ordinary gait and only spreads one's legs to accommodate the width of the snowshoes. But a trip through underbrush or on uneven ground with these snowshoes is quite difficult as is any ascent of a snowy slope which must be done zigzag. One occasionally sees some deviations from the patterns mentioned above. For instance, snowshoes for use in open terrain and especially liked by the Indians of the interior, are pointed at the front as well as the back. Some snowshoes are further ornamented with woolen tufts which are attached to the frames. Men and women share in making snowshoes, the former making the frames and the foot mesh and the latter filling in the remaining sections with the fine-meshed rawhide netting.

Other examples of the skill of the women in weaving, besides the hats previously mentioned, are baskets and platelike trays woven of split cedar root, chrat, straw, tschak-kadlet, and rushes, tschaga-chliti. Thick bags, kak, which are water tight and can be used for carrying water, are woven of cedar root. Malaspina even saw the natives cooking the meat of sea lion and sea otter in these baskets by throwing in hot stones. [12]

At Sitka and Huna very pretty round baskets called kătă-chŭk are made with pleasing patterns created through the use of various weaving materials and different colors. The lids usually have a hollow space in which little pebbles are put as rattles. The platelike trays, talch, are made of the same materials and with the same designs. Even though these woven pieces are very pretty, nevertheless they do not have the variety present in the wood, bone, and stone carving where the realistic use of nature gives a greater range of design. In order to help out this dearth of design the missionaries and traders have recently given the natives new patterns for their weaving. Thus more shapes have been developed, but much of the original artistic value has been lost.

The fishing and hunting implements were described in the fifth chapter, but here the armor of which we have several examples in our collection needs to be discussed. In former times the customary garb for war consisted of thick leather armor worn, according to Dixon, in several layers. [13] Of the five specimens which we brought back, one, kēk-ke, reaches to the knees, the others, chlŭch-tschí-nē, are shorter and cover only the upper body. One of the latter, obviously of recent make, is cut like a jacket without sleeves and is buttoned down the front with brass buttons; the second consists of separate breast and shoulder pieces, the latter being fastened front and back like a broad packstrap. The left one of these packstraps is attached both front and back to the breast piece by means of wooden pegs which are put through loops. The breast piece itself is fastened in the front by means of thong lacings which are drawn through a row of eyelets. These were made by drawing strips of leather through cuts like buttonholes and knotting them on the inside. A similar loop is found on the left side of the breast, probably to slip through a knife.

Even more remarkable than these leather suits of armor are the suits of body armor, uó-nda, made of wooden rods. A very complicated suit of armor of this kind was described and illustrated by Lisiansky, Plate I, p. 150. Two which we brought back must be worn under the armpits since they have no opening for the arms and are therefore only part of a complete outfit. One suit is made of round staves, the other of flat ones. On the latter the staves gradually increase in length toward the middle being from sixty-four centimeters to seventy centimeters long. The middle staves are also the widest ones, being up to two and one-half centimeters thick, while the outer ones are almost round, their thickness being uniformly one centimeter. Altogether there are thirty-nine staves which are bound together with three broad bands of sinew cord, closely wound. On both sides there are leather laces to tie it together.

If one casts about for the tools with which the Tlingit produce this artistic work, build their canoes and their houses, and make their remarkable totem poles, one finds that they were very simple and mostly still are. It is scarcely to be doubted that in the past century the natives produced with stone knives and stone axes the same kind of work which they are producing today. When they first became acquainted with iron, they were very anxious to get it and use it in place of their stone tools, but they generally

---

Plate IV

Armor, Daggers and Various Weapons

1. Cuirass of wooden staves, uónda; 2. Leather cuirass, chlūcht-tschinē; 3-6. Rods of wood or bone for holding the trigger of fox traps; 7. Painted oar for use on festal occasions, úútsā-gá; 8. Knife with carved wooden hilt, chlíta; 9. Dagger with bear's head, chūts tschüchanat; 10. Double dagger; 11. Dagger with bird's head and inlaid mother-of-pearl; 12. Smaller dagger with bird's head; 13. Staff of bamboo and a carved wooden section, for use on festal occasions

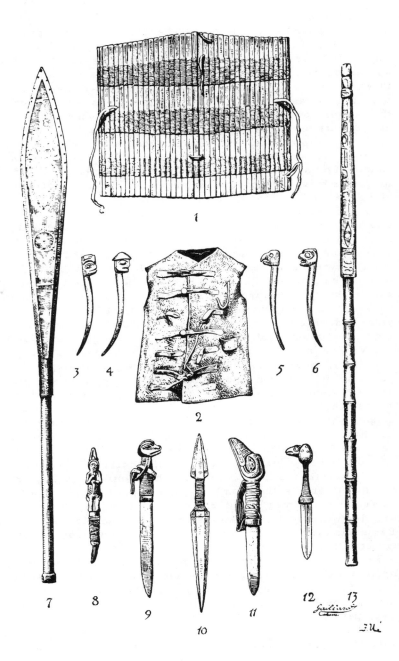

1

3   4   5   6

2

7   8   9   10   11   12   13

shaped it like the tools to which they were accustomed. [14] So
even today the customary knives and axes of the Tlingit remind
one of their former stone tools. The axes were described with
the building of canoes. The knives, which through filing, grind-
ing, and blacksmithing, are made from traded European knives
as well as files and other kinds of steelwork, are usually short,
three to four centimeters long, with a slight S-shaped curve to
the blade. These knives, chlita, are grasped so that the palm of
the hand is upward, the back of the hand being underneath. One
always cuts toward the body. The handle is usually made of wood
or bone and is carved. An important tool is the drill, kē-na,
which is made of a sharpened iron nail with a wooden or bone
handle. For skinning animals and scraping the fat from the skin,
long bone knives called krischá are used, which are ornamented
along their entire length with incised designs.

The colors which the Tlingit like to use for painting their utensils and carvings are ground on a stone, tlechiu-tát, which is
generally carved. Dawson illustrates such a stone in the shape of
a frog. One which we brought back with us is in the shape of a
palette, which may be purely accidental, just as the hole in it
may not be planned. The brushes, kūchi´ta, consist of a wooden
handle about two to three decimeters long, straight or slightly
curved, and carved at one end, and short, stiff bristles at the
other end. The colors are now mostly bought from traders, but
the yellow color mentioned above is still used. A dark blue to
black color is gotten from the juice of blueberries.

Pottery, an art found often among more primitive people, appears not to be known among the Tlingit, since they satisfied the
need for such vessels through the use of wood and basketry
wares. On the other hand, they understood the art of working
copper which, according to Veniaminof, a woman among the Chilkat discovered. On account of her skill she was called Schukas-
saka which means half man. [15] More probably the Chilkat obtained this art, which, according to Holmberg, [16] was kept a secret in certain families, from the inhabitants of the Copper River, the Ahtena, with whom they had contact through the Yakutat.

We have only meager information about the way these copper
articles were made. Ismailof said that the inhabitants of Yakutat
Bay made their daggers themselves (whether of iron or copper is
not stated) on a stone anvil.

Erman, who gives more information on the question, is of the
opinion that the Ahtena who found blocks and lumps of native copper in the Copper River worked them without any smelting
through mechanical means and that iron was used in the same
way, patience replacing technical knowledge. [17]

As long as the use of iron was not widely known, copper was
used for ornamentation of utensils and carvings and also for

148

daggers, lances, and arrowpoints. Considered as especially costly pieces were the copper plates or shields of a special shape which, according to Lisiansky who gives an illustration of one, are carried in front of masters and beaten by slaves on ceremonial occasions. [18] These shields came by trade to the Haida who, according to Dawson, paid ten slaves for one of them. [19] One which Dawson pictures is about two feet tall and is almost an exact duplicate of the one shown by Lisiansky.

It must be taken for granted that the iron used by the Tlingit before the advent of Europeans was a soft iron which they could shape by continuous hammering without heating. Later the native probably learned the smelting of red-hot iron from the European traders since, whenever they stayed any length of time, they set up a smithy on land and here in front of the natives made necessary repairs or manufactured chisel-shaped "tohis" [20] out of iron rods for trade purposes.

The unusual technical skill of the Tlingit could have easily been developed. Even in Lütke's time they undertook minor repairs on their guns; in fact we frequently saw them take the guns completely apart and put them together again. A broken butt was very skillfully replaced for us with a new one.

The labor of the Tlingit is used widely by the whites. In the industrial activities of salmon canning and gold washing many natives are employed. The average daily wage is from one to two dollars a day, which is generally paid in credit or merchandise, rarely in cash. The most common work done by the natives for the whites is the cutting and hauling of wood. For a cord, 8 x 4 x 4 English feet of wood cut and stacked, the price is two dollars. Since the wood is usually cut near the water and can be transported by canoe, the work is not too heavy and can be done by a skillful workman in a day.

Furthermore, Indian labor is largely used for the transportation of passengers and freight. During the great activity when communication between the Cassiar mine district and Wrangell was at its height, the natives offered the steamboats on the Stikine River lively competition by taking a ton of freight to Glenora Landing for thirty instead of forty dollars. [21] They also took an active part in the smuggling which took place between Alaska and British Columbia, by bringing woolen blankets into Alaska and taking back alcoholic beverages and syrup, duty free.

It is very difficult to employ Indian labor since they do not abide by their contracts and always try to get out of their agreements or ask for more pay. If the Indians see that one is totally dependent on them, it makes matters even worse. Through the irresponsibility of the natives we were frequently prevented from carrying out our plans. This lack of responsibility is also the reason why Chinese laborers were brought in. When the first

Chinese arrived in Sitka to make tin cans in the salmon canneries, the Indians protested vigorously because they had reserved
the right to this work for themselves. They allowed the Chinese
to land only after they had received the promise that as soon as
they learned how to make the tins the Chinese would be sent
back. [22]

8. *Birth, Education, Marriage, and Death*

Seclusion of the pregnant woman; midwives; care of
new born infants; cold baths; naming -- Seclusion of
girls during puberty; piercing of the lower lip -- Securing a bride and wedding customs; exchange marriages;
polygyny; divorces; custom of polyandry; chastity of
women -- Wailing at death; the four day mourning feast;
cremation ceremonies; preservation of the ashes; burial
of a shaman; variation in practices of the Yakutat according to Dixon; the little grave houses; treatment of
slave corpses; efforts of the missionaries to introduce
burial -- Laws of inheritance.

The reports of earlier authors differ greatly in regard to birth
customs. According to the account of Veniaminof, who is usually
well informed, women were aided in childbirth by midwives who
were called kakatuk. After the birth the new mother stayed for
ten days in the little hut erected for the purpose. [1] The newborn
infant was bathed in cold fresh water and put in a cradle of moss.
The child was not allowed to nurse until through manipulation and
pressure on the stomach it was forced to vomit all uncleanliness
which was regarded as the source of future illness. [2] According
to Langsdorff, when a woman felt her confinement approaching, a
little hut was built near her dwelling. Only a few women and no
men were allowed to be present at the birth while the woman's
mother or some other female relative delivered the child. [3] Lütke
reports that, after giving birth, the mother spends a whole month
without leaving the hut, after which she washes herself and the
child and puts on new clothing. [4] Less believable and probably
based on misunderstanding is Holmberg's statement, according
to which the women when about to be confined were chased into
the woods even in the depths of winter, in rain, in storm and
cold and here without any help in pain and suffering awaited their
time. [5] According to our information, the new mother stays only

five days in the confinement hut prepared for her, during which time she partakes only of warm water; during the birth she is aided by her female relatives. [6]

The nursing period is very lengthy. According to Veniaminof, it can be as much as ten to thirty months, but our observations indicate that it might even go into the fourth year. As long as children are unable to walk they are wrapped in moss and skins or, now, in cloth and bound to a board which the mother carries around in her arms or which by means of cords is hung from the beams of the house and so serves as a cradle. After a year the child is given food and, according to Lütke, the first morsels, which are always prechewed, [7] are dried fish; however, Veniaminof states that any kind of blubber of a sea mammal except whale is used. [8]

As soon as children learn to walk they are bathed daily in the cold sea or river water. The first bath is given by the parents themselves, but after that the place of the mother is taken by an uncle because he is less considerate and uses the rod on the disobedient children who do not stop crying. [9] Now, this practice of daily cold baths, on which Holmberg blames the high mortality of children and which only those with hardened bodies can survive, is no longer common. [10]

Soon after birth the child is given the name of a maternal ancestor. Later, by giving a great feast in honor of his dead relatives a Tlingit obtains the right to acquire a second name, one from his father's family. Wealthy chiefs are supposed to give this second name to their sons right after birth, thus obligating them to give great feasts.

The Tlingit take a third name when a son is born, calling themselves the father or mother of this or that son. Thus a father of the three or four year old Don-ĕ-wak is called Don-ē-wak-īisch and the mother Don-ē-wāk-tlā. A highly regarded chief in Sitka who had no son, according to Holmberg, was called after his dog, the father of such and such a dog. [11]

At the beginning of puberty a girl is secluded as unclean and, like the woman about to be confined, is put in a little hut of branches. Erman describes these huts as six to eight feet high with a barred opening toward the sea and the street and otherwise closely covered with green conifer branches. In several there were women sitting with averted faces, but in one a younger slender girl showed without shyness a face smeared and dirty with soot and charcoal. [12] Formerly this seclusion is supposed to have lasted a whole year, but Veniaminof reported that the Tlingit in the vicinity of Sitka had already shortened it to half or a quarter of that time. Now they are satisfied with even a shorter period or the practice is entirely abandoned. During the whole period of seclusion the girl was not allowed to leave her narrow

and dark prison except at night and then only when fully covered.
She had to wear a hat with a broad brim so that she would not
look at the heavens and make them unclean with her glance. Only
her mother and her slave or her nearest female relatives were
allowed to visit her and bring her food. [13]

Langsdorff indicates that during this period girls had to observe the greatest privation and were allowed to sip water only
through the wing bone of a white-headed eagle. [14]

At the beginning of the seclusion the piercing of the lower lip
for the later insertion of a labret is undertaken. At the conclu-

A woman from Huna and her slave

sion of the period, if the girl belongs to an important family, the
relatives give a feast at which the girl, clothed in new apparel,
is brought before the assembled guests whereupon the serving of
food commences. The slave whom the girl clothes for this feast
obtains her freedom and the old clothes are destroyed. During
the menstrual period[15] every woman is secluded for several days
(Veniaminof says three) in a special hut and regarded as unable
to perform any household duties. [16]

If a Tlingit desires a girl as his wife, he sends a go-between
to her parents or, if they are no longer alive, to her relatives.
If he gets the consent of the relatives and the girl herself, the
suitor sends as many presents as he can afford to his future
father-in-law, and prepares to go to the wedding. For the set

day, the father of the bride invites his and the bridegroom's relatives. The bridegroom himself, in ceremonial clothes, comes through the door and sits down in the middle of the floor after the guests have assembled. At once songs and dances begin which have as their purpose to lure the bride out of her hiding place in a corner of the house. Then cloth or skins are spread on the floor from her hiding place to the spot where the bridegroom is sitting, and on these the bride, ceremonially decked, walks out to seat herself beside the groom. During this whole time she keeps her head bowed. After she is seated the songs and dances start again without the bridal couple participating. At the close of the ceremony the guests are served, but the bridal couple do not partake, in fact they must fast the following two days. Then they are allowed some food and drink after which they must fast again for the same period. After this fasting the new couple are allowed to remain together, but only after four weeks are they regarded as husband and wife. [17]

If the bridegroom is wealthy, he also gives a feast after the marriage to which he invites the parents and relatives of his bride; however, a poor man ends the wedding ceremonies without such an occasion. A married man among the Tlingit always has the right to live with his father-in-law or to move to his own home. At leaving he receives, from his father-in-law and the relatives of his wife, presents which amount in value to at least as much as he brought to them or more. [18]

Marriage never takes place between the members of the same clan or tribe; a member of the Raven clan of the Tlingit must seek a wife from among the Wolf clan and vice versa.

A wealthy Tlingit can have several wives, as many as he can support, but the first wife always outranks the others. Among the Chilkat, however, we found only a few who had two or more wives, although Lütke reports that distinguished Kolushans formerly had five or more wives. [19]

Divorce, according to Veniaminof, occurs seldom among the Tlingit. If a separation takes place because of incompatibility and by mutual consent, the gifts exchanged at marriage are not returned. But if a man sends his wife home because he does not like her, he must return the gifts given him by her relatives after their marriage, although his father-in-law is under no obligation to give back the presents he received from the bridegroom. Should he leave his wife because she is unfaithful, he may keep the gifts he received and can demand those which he gave. In any case the children stay with the mother. [20]

The custom of polyandry also exists among the Tlingit, according to Veniaminof, though only a brother or a close relative is allowed as an extra husband. [21] The seducer of a married woman, if he escapes the dagger of her injured husband, must pay for his action by gifts. If he is a close relative, he assumes the position of a second husband and must contribute to the support of the woman.[22]

After a man's death his brother or the son of his sister is obligated to marry his widow. If neither of these relatives is available, the widow may choose any man in the clan of her deceased husband.[23]

With few exceptions, the earlier authors praise the chastity of the Tlingit. Langsdorff, who undoubtedly presents the natives in the most favorable light, says, "Good manners, modesty, affection and marital faithfulness generally characterize the women of this nation."[24] But Veniaminof already remarked that since contact with Europeans these virtues are not as common, since greed overshadows all other considerations, and it is now a commonplace to see men sell the favors of their wives and their older daughters to the prospectors and other whites. In this respect, however, the Chilkat still enjoy a good reputation. Unfaithfulness still occurs infrequently and is regarded as a serious offense. Also jealousy is not uncommon among both men and women.

Lütke declares that suicide is unknown among the Tlingit. He says that there is not even an instance of a slave taking his life.[25] According to our findings, suicide is not such an unknown act. An injured person who has no possibility of revenge, or someone who is pursued and sees no way out, takes his life with the thought that he is thereby injuring his enemy, for the person who drives another to suicide will still be held responsible by the dead man's friends and relatives, just as though he had killed him outright. A woman was accused by a shaman of the Stikine of causing the illness of another woman by witchcraft, and the relatives of the latter faced her with this accusation. This upset the accused woman so that she seized a knife and cut her throat. As a result the shaman, as well as the relatives of the sick woman who brought the accusation, were besieged by the relatives of the dead woman in their houses until they acknowledged their guilt. A way of seeking death by those who wish to end their lives is to commit themselves to the sea in a canoe without paddles. The story goes that a Chilkat Indian who was badly scratched up in a fight with his wife, through shame and anger, left without a word to commit suicide after spending the night sitting in the trader's house. However, this time it went no further than the attempt. After dark the following evening the supposed dead man returned and without much resistance allowed himself to be reconciled with his wife.

As soon as a Tlingit dies, his relatives start a loud wailing. The body is prepared by the women and placed in a sitting position opposite the door against the back wall of the house which has been ceremonially decorated. The mourning ceremonies last four days, or rather nights, which need not be consecutive, and consist of songs accompanied by rhythmical body motions as well as feasting and gift giving to guests who always represent a different tribe[26] from that of the deceased.

During our stay among the Chilkat we attended such a ceremony which was held for a woman from the Bear tribe. [27] Her relatives showed their grief by distributing among the members of the Raven tribe a large amount of cloth, woolen blankets, and similar things. The widower also gave away his entire fortune except a few woolen blankets which he held out for his future wife, a twelve-year-old girl, and so that his friends would not know about this he stored them with the white trader. The distribution of gifts as well as the whole ceremony took place in a recently built house, the largest in the community. It was packed with people for four nights, the men squatted around the fire, the women sat along the walls, while near the door a space was set apart for ten to twelve people of the Bear tribe who, during the general mourning songs, kept time by striking the floor with long poles grasped with both hands. Several women also held poles. They were close relatives of the deceased and they showed their sorrow further by having their hair cut short and their faces painted black. During the singing they rose several times and accompanied the songs with peculiar, but beautiful, motions, a rocking with the knees and the willowy bending of the upper body. Near the fire stood a small boy wrapped in a woolen blanket of the deceased.

An old Indian started, with a few words, the distribution of the gifts, which were brought from all sides and spread out so that everyone could see them. The cloth in pieces of ten to twenty meters was unrolled and was passed along close to the fire through a row of hands, care always being taken that there was no break between the unwinding of one piece and the start of the next. The actual distribution took place quickly. At once, after the pieces of cloth had been passed around they were cut into strips, measured only by eye, and all accompanied by a monotonous song. When a guest's name was loudly called his portion was thrown to him, though all did not receive like amounts, the chief, Don-ē-wak, getting the lion's share. During this action the guests were also being served berries, sugar and tobacco, the berries by the spoonful for immediate eating, while the tobacco was passed around in a large carved pipe which was smoked by the guests, one by one. In this manner goods worth several hundred dollars were distributed during the four evenings. The shaman of the Raven tribe expressed the thanks of his tribe in a lengthy speech after each of the principal donors had finished.

The cremation of the body took place usually before the end of the four days' festivities, generally on the third or fourth day after death, though sometimes later. According to Holmberg, poor people, who cannot afford the expense of the ceremonies just described, take the body to a remote cove and burn it. Otherwise the cremation takes place in the vicinity of the house of the deceased. The cremation of a Chilkat Indian which we attended took place in the early morning. Directly behind the house where the body had been lying, a funeral pyre of heavy tree trunks about two meters long was piled in regular crisscross fashion and the body which the women had wrapped in cloths was placed in the center. A pile of wood was kindled on top of it. Men and women stood or squatted around at random except a few Indians who stood in a row singing and pounding a board at their feet with long staffs. Then while the pyre was still in bright flames all the onlookers and mourners as well left quietly. After the pyre had burned down and the fire had been put out, a few women returned and picked some charred bones out of the ashes. These were wrapped in cloths and put in a little wooden box which was set in a grave house. This wrapping of the remains was done to protect the soul from cold. The whole ceremony had great dignity and the behavior of the onlookers was serious and quiet. [28]

The ceremonies observed at the death of a chief of the Sitka were described in a dispatch to the New York Herald of April 16, 1881, from which I will take the following. The corpse was ceremonially prepared and placed in a sitting position in the center of the back wall of the house. On his head he wore a wooden hat, carved with figures of the raven, his face was painted, and around his body a woolen blanket decorated with buttons was draped. Two beautiful Chilkat blankets were laid on his knees and on these was a package of letters of recommendation given him by the commanders and other important white people, and a dagger in a carved sheath. To one side of him lay his treasure, mostly woolen blankets packed in several trunks; on the other side stood his wife, wrapped in a woolen blanket. She was not allowed to speak and no one was allowed to address her for eight days after her husband's death. Before the cremation a part of the back wall of the house was removed and through this opening the body was carried out, followed by a live dog, who according to the belief of the Indians, was supposed to take out with him every trace of the illness which had caused this death. The funeral pyre to which the body was taken was prepared by placing five cedar logs on the ground, side by side, and on these others were piled to build an open square with room in the center for the body. Over it were placed several woolen blankets and finally a ceremonial blanket. Then the opening was covered with more cedar logs and the pyre was lighted. Ten mourning Indians who showed great grief squatted on the snow and ten or more men beat time with long poles on a board at their feet in a ritual manner, not in

157

the least unpleasant. Members of the family squatted on the ground also, with their backs to the fire. As a sign of mourning they all had their woolen blankets tied with a cord around the waist.

The cremation was followed by a large potlatch (the distribution of gifts). The costs of the cremation ran to about fifty to seventy dollars. At the potlatch woolen blankets to a value of five hundred dollars were torn and distributed by relatives. The ashes were gathered in a fine Chilkat blanket and put in a small wooden box.

In another account of a cremation at Sitka it was said that the pyre was constructed of four logs placed side by side and the body was laid on these, then more logs were used to build up the sides and finally across the top to fill the opening. During the burning a woman threw several blankets into the fire. Eight people sang and beat time with staffs on the ground. [29]

A variant is the description, given by Simpson, of a cremation of a Sitka Indian which was witnessed by him. The body, after it had been dressed in the best and laid in state for two or three days, was placed on a pyre about which the mourning relatives stood with faces painted black, hair cut short, and their heads sprinkled with eagle down. A pipe was passed around the circle two or three times; whereupon, at a secret signal, the pyre was lighted at several places, while drumming and wailing raised considerable clamor until the pyre had burned down. Finally the ashes were gathered in a small decorated box which was put on a scaffold or on the top of a post. [30]

We never observed the placing of the box of ashes on the top of a post, as reported by Simpson, but other witnesses did. Ismailof said of the Yakutat, "They do not bury their dead in the ground, but they burn them and gather the ashes and remaining bones in a box especially prepared for the purpose, which they put on a chopped-off, so-called imilasaby." [31]

Lisiansky reports that the ashes together with unburned bones are stored in a wooden container which is set on a post painted with various figures and carved according to the wealth of the deceased. [32] Malaspina saw the same at the burial place of the Yakutat, which was on an island, in the form of a monument that was a large and fearsome figure which held a box of ashes in its hands. [33]

Mourning, according to Lütke, is supposed to last a whole year.

In addition I wish to offer the report of Schabelski concerning the cremation of a chief, as an example of an earlier custom: "At the death of a chief," he said, "burial takes place with great ceremony, and the more slaves offered to his ghost, the more successful the occasion. When a notable man dies, a funeral pyre

is erected with great care and the body placed on it. All friends
and relatives attend the ceremony. The leading chiefs are provided with staffs which resemble lances without points, and the
faces of almost all attending are painted black. The nearest relatives light the pyre after they have poured oil on it. Then the
speaker steps in the center of the assemblage and delivers a eu-
logy on the deceased. If he was a rich man and had several
slaves, some of them with their hands and feet tied are thrown
on the pyre and cremated with their master, so that they may

Grave houses at Huna

serve him in the next world. During the whole ceremony terrible
wailing, in which the women distinguish themselves, rends the
air. "[34]

Quite different ceremonies are the custom at the death of a
shaman. When a shaman dies he is left lying the first night in the
corner of the house where his death occurred, the second night
he is carried to another corner, and so on, until he has been in
every corner of the house. During this time all the inhabitants of
the house must fast. On the fifth day the burial itself takes place.
The body is dressed in the bright-colored costume of the shaman,
with gloves on his hands and moccasins on his feet, and is laid
on a board with some holes along the sides through which it is

fastened down with straps. Of the two small bones used by the shaman in his practice, one is put through the septum of his nose and the other is stuck through the bound topknot of his hair. The head is covered with a large basket woven of branches. The body is then placed in a little grave house which stands on four posts and is erected at a spot that can be seen from the water. Every Tlingit who passes the grave of a shaman makes a small offering by throwing a little tobacco or a little dried salmon in the sea.[35]

The Yakutat separate the head from the body, according to Dixon.[36] "They wrap the body in skins and put it in an oblong box, while the head is put in a square box. At each end of the box con-

Grave houses at Klukwan

taining the body a heavy pole is driven diagonally into the ground so that the upper ends meet and are tied together with cord. The poles are connected about two feet below this tie by a crosspiece which is neatly fastened into each pole. On this crosspiece the box with the head is placed and tied to it with cord. The box is often ornamented with two or three rows of small shells and occasionally with teeth. These are placed in the wood very neatly and with considerable taste, also paintings of several colors are used as decoration. The poles are painted only in white. Occasionally they stand upright on all sides of the body, but the head is always in the position just described above."[37]

There is considerable variation in the grave houses in which the bodies of shaman are put, as well as those in which the ashes of cremated Tlingit are placed. In all cases they look like a small square house with a steep gabled roof, but the shamans' grave houses are distinct from the others in that they are raised on four posts. Poor families of the same clan use a common grave house, but for a chief or a wealthy Tlingit a special one is built and artistically decorated.[38] Sometimes the front wall is covered with a brightly colored painting, sometimes with a carved figure of a totemic animal of the deceased, and occasionally even a gay dance blanket woven of mountain goat wool is hung over it. In addition, totem poles stand near the graves. In modern times flag poles with small pennants are erected near the graves of the notables in imitation of European custom. Utensils are usually not sent along with the dead, only at Huna was a canoe seen lying near a grave. Wreaths of spruce boughs from the nearby trees were hung on it.

The bodies of slaves were not cremated, but without ceremony consigned to the sea.[39]

As a result of the efforts of the Christian missionaries, the Indians in a few places, especially Sitka and Wrangell, have been won over to burial of the dead, but still cremation is the customary procedure. Also at the trading post at Chilkoot an Indian child was buried in 1881 at the suggestion of the missionary. When, however, during the following winter, especially in the months of February and March, continuous bad weather, strong winds, and snow storms made hunting and fishing difficult so that famine faced the population, it was commonly believed that failure to cremate the child's body was the cause of the inclement weather and efforts were made to correct this neglect. Great fires were lighted on the beach and effigies were burnt in order symbolically to atone for the burial and, when this did not help, it was demanded of the missionary that he reveal the grave site of the child's burial. He refused to do this, and he interfered with the Indians who with the help of witnesses tried to find the site, not an easy thing to do with a blanket of snow several meters deep. For days men and women were busy locating the grave and exhuming the body. Through delayed cremation rites they hoped to regain the good graces of heaven.

The estate of a deceased Tlingit goes to the son of his sister or, if there is none, to a younger brother. Since the children follow the clan of the mother, the nephew belongs to the same clan as the uncle, and in this way family property remains in the clan. The presumptive heir is required during his youth to serve his uncle without payment, but the future inheritance is expected to repay him. He is also obliged at the death of his uncle to marry his widow even if he already has a wife. If there is no nephew or younger brother, Veniaminof states, the inheritance goes to relatives and the widow receives only her dowry.

9. Customs of Peace and War

The feasts; hospitality and gifts to guests, dances, ceremonial regalia, potlatch houses -- The three important feasts, cremation, memorial feast, and the feast for children -- Smaller festivities -- Greeting ceremonies -- Disputes and warfare; causes of disagreements; blood revenge; attacks; peaceful settlement of disputes; sham battles; duels -- Armor and weapons -- Treatment of the besieged -- Scalping; offering of hostages by the Tlingit in the morning and evening.

The long winter is the time for feasts, which play an important part in the life of the Tlingit and to which he responds with enthusiasm. Feasts are connected with the most diverse occasions: birth and death, successful hunting expeditions or war parties, the reconciliation between two quarreling factions, or the completion of a new house. These feasts usually begin after sundown, last the whole night, and often go on for several days. They consist of the performance of dances, the feeding of guests and the presentation of gifts to guests who belong to another tribe from that of the host. The apparent generosity of the host, which is contrary to the customary avarice of the Indians, is explained by the fact that at the next opportunity the guests are obliged to give at least the value of the gifts in return. The food now generally consists of bread, berries, sugar, dried salmon, and grease. In large part the food is put directly into the mouths of guests, seated around the fire, by friends of the host. They also fill pipes with tobacco, light and smoke them a little, and then pass them around. The gifts are largely colored cloth and woolen blankets which are shown to the assemblage with ceremony in their entirety before they are torn into pieces. The value of the gifts distributed in one evening is seldom less than a few hundred dollars. The dances are sometimes done by men and sometimes by both sexes, even children do their part. Rhythmical movements of the

162

body accompanied by expressive and not unmelodious singing make up the dances. The dancers decorate themselves with colored festive regalia, gaily paint their faces or wear grotesque masks, and sprinkle their hair with downlike powder and carry wooden clappers, carved staffs, or white tails and wings of the bald eagle. Ermine is also used for headgear or to decorate clothing.

Large feasts take place more seldom now than formerly; also we saw no special potlatch houses similar to the kachimas of the northern Eskimo people, which, according to the reports of Malaspina, Erman, and Holmberg, once existed among the Tlingit. These potlatch houses were like the winter houses, only larger. (Cp. Chap. IV, p. 88)

Veniaminof also mentions just three large feasts, the cremation ceremony, ukech ataschich, meaning the "feeding of the dead," then the anniversary feast, kchataschi, literally "the setting up of the dead," and third, the feast for the children, gischtaschigi. Each feast is supposed to have its own special songs. [1]
Since these feasts are no longer given with all their details as formerly, and since we ourselves did not have the opportunity to attend them all, I will give the descriptions of them rendered by Veniaminof who recorded the entire procedure in detail and with great trustworthiness.

The first feast, the cremation ceremony, is given at the burial of a chief or a notable person by his relatives. There is no special time set for this feast, for it begins when the hosts are ready, which is usually when the body, which is cremated during this feast, is in an advanced state of decomposition. The cremation takes place in the presence of relatives and friends, but all preparations are made by the members of the friendly tribe[2] while the nearest relatives wail in mourning for the dead. Many singe off their hair as a sign of mourning by putting their heads in reach of the flames.

After the body is burned, the guests go to the house of the deceased and seat themselves in a circle with the widow or widower, since he or she would belong to the same clan as the guests. When all the guests are seated, the people belonging to the house come in, with singed or cut hair and faces smeared with soot. In their hands they carry staffs and after they go into the living quarters of the house with bowed heads they start wailing for the dead and singing songs which the guests accompany. For four[3] evenings after the cremation this wailing is continued. During this time the relatives of the deceased slaughter one or two slaves to serve the deceased in the next world, these, however, not being taken from the slaves of the deceased, but from their own. These slaves are supposed to suffer the same death as the deceased. If he met his death at sea, they are drowned, but if he died of an illness, they are crushed by means of a log laid over the neck. [4] After the wailing ceases on the fourth night, the relatives of the deceased wash their faces, paint themselves with fresh paint and give presents to the guests, especially those who helped at the cremation. After that the final feast takes place and the whole ceremony is ended. [5]

The second large feast, the anniversary feast, Kchataschi, in memory of deceased relatives was seldom celebrated in Veniaminof's time because of its great expense. Guests were invited to it from far and near and the gifts given at this feast not only depleted the fortune of the host but also the dowry of his wife. For this reason the Tlingit say when they see an impoverished person, "You have probably celebrated the Kchataschi."

"The house intended for the celebration is scrupulously cleaned or, if possible, a new one is erected which is decorated with the crest of the host. After the guests have arrived the feast begins with songs and dances which are continued until dawn. Thereupon feasting follows in which only those guests participate who have the right to begin the ceremony. For several days these songs and dances continue, interrupted only by feasting, and this goes on as long as the owner of the house or the host of the ceremony is in position to satisfy his guests. On the evening of the last day of the ceremony, the host, who is usually a chief, goes, accompanied by a slave, to a compartment in the house and dresses himself in regalia handed down in the family for such occasions only. This costume differs in various clans and consists of parts or all of the name animal. In addition at present they are decorated with all kinds of ornamentation as, for example, scalps, human teeth, ribbons, thongs, ermine skins, and the like. The slave who helps clothe his master at this feast receives his freedom and is selected for this before the occasion.

"At the moment that the host, clothed in this manner and surrounded by his slaves, appears from his seclusion, the cry of the eponymous animal is taken up outside. After this cry which had been arranged for beforehand and is carried out by a member of the family, one or more slaves are killed. For the benefit of the sacrificed slaves the host sings the family songs, telling of the deeds of deceased ancestors and of the origin of the family. Thereupon the host seats himself and the articles to be given away are brought in and distributed. All the guests do not receive equal presents, the wealthy and important people get larger and more expensive gifts than the poor. For example, the former might receive slaves. With this the ceremony ends, but the following day it might be continued in another jurte, and so on, in case several families or settlements have helped in arranging the feast. The host, as we have already mentioned, has the right at such occasions to take the name of a deceased ancestor on his father's side."[6]

Another feast seldom given because of its cost, according to Veniaminof and Holmberg, is the one which gains social recognition for children. At this feast slaves are never killed; to the contrary, as many as there are children get their freedom. For the ceremony a new house is always built, and all who helped in the work receive gifts. Otherwise the feast resembles the ones described, except that at the close the children are brought for-

Chief of the Huna with his wife in ceremonial regalia
(with dance masks)

ward according to age and their ears are ceremonially pierced. This operation is always done by a woman who is selected by the father of the children and rewarded with rich presents. The ear lobe is pierced with a thorn and a thread drawn through it. During this operation all present emit a loud "ssss," which Holmberg thinks serves to ease the pain. When this is done, gifts are distributed and food served.[7]

According to Veniaminof, the Indians with pierced ears are called angaschi meaning "of the nobility," and similar honor is supposed to be enjoyed by their descendants, even if they do not have the means to attain this distinction themselves. The number of holes can total as many as eight, that is, four in each ear, though hardly any Tlingit was in a position to attain this, since eight feasts must be given for it. The piercing of the ear, especially common in Sitka among the ordinary Tlingit, does not confer the privileges of nobility. [8]

In contrast to the large feasts just mentioned, smaller ceremonies which consist only of singing and dancing take place frequently. In the winter of 1881-82, we had occasion to attend several such among the Chilkat, and since they all seem to be alike in type, it will suffice to describe just one. Shortly before moving out on a trading expedition to the interior, the Bear tribe[9] in Klukwan gave a dance. At dusk the preparations for dressing began with every participant receiving help from his friends and relatives in his house. Faces were painted with charcoal and cinnebar, the colorful designs being carefully applied with the use of mirrors. Meanwhile the house designated for the ceremony gradually filled with spectators, the women squatting down along the walls, while the men took up the space around the fire, leaving only one side, the right from the entrance, free for the dancers. About eighty to one hundred persons -- men, women and children -- gathered here. In the middle of the house a tremendous pile of wood with pieces a foot thick burned. The dancers, including the leaders of the community, among them old Tschartritsch, the most important chief, not only of the Chilkat Indians, but of all the Tlingit of Alaska, meanwhile had gathered outside and had begun a lively and expressive song in which the assemblage joined, accompanied by drums. One after another the dancers appeared, each one sticking his head in first and withdrawing again as though he wished to convince himself that there was no danger at hand. With constant hopping back and forth, they proceeded to the space left for them to the right of the fire, and took up their positions there in a row. At this time there were only eight dancers, and all were adults. The first carried a lance, the second, a gun, the third, a paddle, and so on. Both their regalia and their movements differed as they maintained the positions which they had taken. Vigorous movements of arms and feet and various twistings and bending of the body made up the dance. After a short time the participants were exhausted. At the finish one of the dancers made a loud speech in which he expressed various greetings and words of thanks to which one of the gathering, who had gone outside, answered from there. Thereupon the crowd dispersed, the festive costumes were taken off and packed away and the painted faces were washed clean.

Among the Chilkat we saw two kinds of dances, which were distinguished as those of the Haida and those of the Athapascans of the interior and which maintained their character even to the accompanying songs and the costuming. In the Athapascan dances only the men and boys took part, while in the others, the girls also participated. The melody of the Athapascan dances was somewhat like this:

Each time the dancers came in singly, as was described before, and placed themselves in a row and, while the spectators, men, women and children, sang in unison, they carried on vigorous arm and leg movements for quite a while. This choral singing did not sound unpleasant, but it surprises the stranger with frequent variations and expressive changes in tempo. A text is not at hand for the choral singing; however, a leader sings a phrase followed by a refrain from the chorus of the syllables "hi-ha" put together in various ways.

The dancers carry on their movements in exact time with the singing, which is accentuated by drumming, stamping the feet, and pounding on boards with wooden staffs. The drums are often wooden boxes, decorated with carving and painting, or are like our tambourines, and are beaten with the hand or a small stick. In addition at these performances the clappers mentioned before are used, or rattles which are made of

A wooden drum, about one meter high, a-niáti bigan (chief's drum) with carved front and painted side walls. From Huna

two pieces and filled with pebbles, also rings on which a large number of puffin bills are loosely tied so that they rattle against each other. Headgear and costumes also have many rattles attached to them such as puffin bills, small wooden sticks, dried berries, and similar things.

The participation of the audience in these ceremonies is a lively one even though it does not express itself in hilarious joy or applause. The space is filled to the last seat, and the odors arising from such a crowd as well as the heat and smoke from the fires which are stronger than usual create an atmosphere which for the civilized person is almost unbearable.

Tlingit dance rattle

In spite of this one sees the spectators follow the performance with great attentiveness to the very end, and from the outside others who could not get in look through cracks or climb the roof to get a glimpse through the smoke hole. Especially energetic in this are naturally the children who are introduced to the dances at an early age. For instance, a three or four year old, who in spite of his age was still nursing at his mother's breast, had learned all the steps of the Athapascan dance and one had only to hum the melody or beat the rhythm to have him start dancing with great seriousness and energy.

At the end of every ceremony one of the dancers gives a loud speech made up of short sentences, which is answered by one of the audience who has gone outside, and sometimes even from several directions answers are given in single words. We could only discover that this was an expression of greeting and thanks which members of one tribe extended to others, but any more exact meaning remained uncertain.

It is also in order here, in additon to the description of ceremonies conducted indoors, to mention the ceremonies and songs which are used as greeting on meeting strangers to assure friendly relations. These ceremonies are not conducted as frequently now as in former times, especially not for whites, probably because of their disregard for them, but when a tribe visits another in order to trade or for some other purpose, the formalities, which almost all the early travelers, such as Dixon, Malaspina, Vancouver and so on, describe, [10] are carefully carried out. They stop before a landing is made and the chiefs put on their ceremonial regalia. Then, standing up in a canoe and holding a rattle, they start to sing a song of peace which a chorus accompanies by raising the hands, palms forward, and the paddlers stroke rhythmically. From time to time they join the song of the leader. At the close of the ceremony, usually bird down is blown into the air.

It was also customary to greet Europeans this way as long as a large vessel was a rarity in these waters. Partly to satisfy their own desire to show off and partly to indicate their friendly intentions toward the natives the visiting Russian and other foreign warships established the custom of giving the Tlingit a feast. At such occasions the Indians brought forth all their traditional ritual. Dressed in fantastic regalia, singing and gesticulating, they proceeded around the ship before they went aboard. Here they were served, usually with rice and molasses, as well as with highly diluted grog (so called Sitka mixture in proportion of four to one), after which they expressed their thanks to their hosts by dancing. [11]

Not less important than the feasts, which express the peaceful side of Tlingit life, are the almost endless amenities between individuals as well as tribes and clans. The Indian cannot stand a peaceful, quiet existence. His great sensitivity and his strong sense of property rights are constant cause of resentment. For every bodily injury, for any damage to his goods and property, for any infringement by strangers on his hunting or trading territory, full compensation is demanded or exacted by force. Marital unfaithfulness, gambling, and drunkenness are also the causes of strife. A friendly settlement is generally the rule. After much threatening and long bargaining an agreement is reached on the amount of compensation established on the basis of value for value. A feast of reconciliation at which the defeated party distributes presents closes the incident. [12] Often the whole affair depends on high pressure methods, especially when exorbitant demands are made of timid whites, but the whole matter is dropped quietly as soon as a decisive refusal is met. [13] When an injured Tlingit is seriously intent on taking the life of his enemy, he does not eat or drink until his intention is carried out. Relatives of a victim at once prepare to revenge his death and until an equal amount of blood has been shed on both sides, the strife continues. Not only the amount of bloodshed is taken into consideration but also the quality, for an important person or a chief counts two or three times as much as an ordinary man and, since the two parties do not always agree as to the value of their dead, a new difficulty arises which also takes long deliberation to settle. These quarrels which are the result of the law of blood revenge are generally not fights in our sense of the term but a series of murders carried out by a lurking enemy from a safe ambush. Open warfare was usually avoided, but if one tribe made war on another, it was done mostly by setting up an ambush or attack by night and, in spite of the apparent eagerness to fight and extensive preparations, small losses were enough to bring about a decision.

According to Lütke, the preparations for an attack usually were kept secret, even from the women who often had parents and sisters among the enemy. When preparations were complete, the men went in their canoes to the enemy village and landed at the break of dawn. Before the attack they put on their wooden rod armor which protected their backs and chests, they covered their faces with masks representing the heads of animals, and put wooden coverings decorated in the same way on their heads. All these parts were fastened to the armor with strong sinew. Then they attacked the enemy suddenly and killed without mercy all the men who did not succeed in escaping; the women and children were taken prisoners. Then the roles changed and an opportunity arose for the defeated to attack and avenge the death of their tribesmen by killing an equal number of their recent enemy.[14]

The Tlingit does not have personal courage to face obvious danger, and therefore he rates it so much more highly in whites. A good example of how this disregard for danger impresses them is an experience of Veniaminof which he described fully. "During my stay in Sitka in 1824," he writes, "when the Kolushans were nearer their original state, a quarrel ensued between them and the Russians which was so severe that all Russians took up arms and the Russian frigate Kreisser which was then in the harbor was prepared to open fire on the first signal from the fort. The Kolushans, who had already taken to arms, took up their station on the surrounding rocks and tree stumps while a few of them made their way to a house near the edge of town where negotiations and markets were usually held. Then Nossow, an official of the company, unaccompanied, and with only his saber, went there to negotiate with the Kolushan chief. A bold Kolushan who found himself on the same path, threatened him with his gun, seemingly not to shoot him but just to scare him. Nossow, without paying any attention to the gun, walked right up to the Indian and gave him such a cuff on the ear that he dropped his gun in the mud. Whereupon Nossow continued quietly on his way. The Kolushan, embarrassing as the insult must have been to him, for all the officials of the company laughed at him, did not dare take vengeance against the Russian."[15]

In their fights with the Russians, the Tlingit showed great bravery, however, as we have seen (provided that the Russian

170

accounts have not exaggerated the bravery of their opponents in order to make their own greater), but also ignorance of the power of their opponents' weapons may have been responsible for their stubborn and courageous resistance. How quickly hostilities can break out among the natives, and how quickly they can be set aside, is apparent from a characteristic description given by G. Simpson who was an eye witness to a struggle among the Sitka Indians in 1842.

In the village of the natives directly under the cannons of the fort, an important chief became involved in a drinking bout quarrel with a man of high rank, but lower than the chief, and the former stabbed the latter with his dagger. The followers of the victim, about one hundred men strong, started out at once with terrific howling to avenge the death, all painted in the most frightening manner and armed with every kind of weapon -- spears, clubs, daggers and firearms -- while the women, possibly even wilder than the warriors, urged on the warring groups with wicked cries and gestures of violence. The fall of night prevented the outbreak of hostilities. On the following day several thousand of different ages and both sexes, most of them armed, who, by their own desire for revenge and the conjuring of the shamans had been transformed into demons, gathered for the attack. The life of the chief was demanded as atonement, but it was refused by his party because it was worth more than that of the murdered man. Then the Russian governor and the Bishop intervened for the chief for through baptism he had become a member of the Christian church and at the same time the artillery of the fort was prepared. This led to an agreement and for a minute or two the parties attacked each other with loud cries and a clash of weapons. When they withdrew one saw the bodies of two slaves who had met their death in place of the chief. [16]

The same kind of sham fighting was used, according to Lütke and Veniaminof, when, as result of an agreement, hostages who were to be held to secure the peace were captured. Lütke described the procedure as follows: "Both parties, both men and women, proceed to an open place. The foremost, who are supposed to capture the hostage who is always selected from the most important people, give the appearance of starting a fight by swinging vigorously with their lances and daggers. Finally they throw themselves into the midst of the opposite party and with loud cries seize the person designated as hostage, who has hidden himself in the crowd, and carry him back on their arms with shouts of joy. The same is done by the other side. The ceremony is closed with a feast. The hostages are taken to the houses of their new friends and after they have stayed there a year or longer, return to their own people while the union is further strengthened with a new feast." [17]

Quarrels between clans and families are frequently settled by duels, as Lütke and Holmberg report. For this the opposing sides arrange themselves in battle order. The chosen warriors are clothed in thick armor of tanned caribou hide and wooden helmets decorated with the totem of the tribe. The dagger is the only weapon used and the progress of the fight is followed with songs and dancing by the spectators. [18] In recent times the custom of duels seems to have been discontinued. The general use of firearms has also caused a change in fighting methods, since the old armor which protected against daggers and arrows is of no use against bullets. They are stored now only as relics or are sold to dealers as curios. In additon to the hide armor which looks like a vest and was worn over the left shoulder and under the right arm, a breast plate was also used which was made of wooden rods, neatly fastened together with sinew and in some cases with leather strips. (See p.145)

The dagger is the only one of the old weapons still in use. The form of the dagger is not always the same; occasionally it has two blades, the upper one being only about one quarter as long as the lower. The blades are stuck in leather sheaths which are worn around the neck on a leather strap. The handle is also wound with leather that continues in a long strap, which, according to Holmberg, is tied to the hand during combat and which Dixon reports is secured to the middle finger by means of a hole at the end. [19] Formerly there were also copper daggers; Erman saw them among the natives of Sitka. "These were about one and one-half feet long and four to five inches wide running to a point, some formed like a saber with a convex blade and some straight and two edged like the old Roman swords. Above the narrowed handle there was a wooden knob, often carved in the shape of a bird head or something similar, or the second smaller blade, sometimes the whole thing was smooth and carefully polished. [20]

One sees bows and arrows only in the hands of children. According to older descriptions and through what one can still find out today, they were never very artistic. The arrows had stone, bone, copper and iron tips, many of them barbed. The bow was held horizontally.

In addition to bows and arrows, long throwing spears with iron points were used in combat. However, no information could be secured about the use of stone or bone war clubs which are found here and there among old household possessions. The scalping of fallen foes appears to have been practiced, though perhaps only in isolated cases. According to Lisiansky the natives were guilty of horrible cruelty toward enemies, especially Europeans who fell into their hands. "Men, women and children fall upon the poor victim, some wound him, some stab and burn him, some cut off an arm or leg and others scalp him. The latter also hap-

172

pened to an enemy found dead on the battlefield. It is done by the shaman who first cuts the skin around the head and lifts the scalp off by the hair. The head is cut off and thrown away or stuck up somewhere as a marker."[21]

Holmberg also says that the captured enemy is made a slave, while the dead ones are scalped and the scalps kept as war trophies to be used as leg ornaments on ceremonial occasions.[22]

Now the custom of scalping is entirely given up. We were told that a Chilkat chief had a scalp among his trophies as a curiosity.

It was generally the practice to secure a peace treaty or a reconciliation by offering hostages. According to Veniaminof and Holmberg, they were allowed to eat only with the left hand for several days since the right one had carried weapons during the fighting. For every hostage two substitutes were furnished who also had to be guarded.[23]

The Kolushans formerly practiced flagellation to make themselves good warriors, though even in Veniaminof's time this seldom took place. This author reported that flagellation took place in winter during the heaviest frost, early in the morning. With supple whips in hand, the eldest of the tribe placed himself on the beach while the young men who were anxious to show their courage first bathed in the tides and then stood in front of him, allowing themselves to be whipped until they could no longer stand it or others pushed them away. This was not enough for some, who cut the flesh of their chests and hands with sharp stones until the blood flowed, then they sat down in the sea and stayed there until they were almost numb. Thereupon they went to their houses and stretched out on mats by the fire.

In addition to the whipping on the beach in the morning, whippings also took place in the house in the evening near the burning stove which, because of the greater sensitivity of the skin, were much more painful than the others. Veniaminof related that when all were gathered around the fire, at a secret signal the eldest was brought bare branches of which he picked several while the inmates of the house undressed themselves and then without emitting a cry of pain or even changing expression they allowed themselves to be severely whipped. Nobody who did not wish to be called a coward could withdraw from this whipping, but the whipping on the beach was voluntary. Veniaminof was convinced that one reason for the disappearance of the evening whippings since the closer contact of the Tlingit with the Russians was that fighting ability achieved in this way was no longer of any use against the firearms of the Europeans. Still the practice of whipping even today does not seem to have disappeared completely. We heard from the Chilkat Indians, at least, that on cold winter mornings they go to the beach and in pairs squat with bare bodies. With an alder switch one begins to beat the other and then they reverse the procedure.

173

10. Myths of the Tlingit

The birth of Raven -- His education and youth -- His
uncle waylays him and makes attacks on his life -- The
great flood -- Analysis of this myth by Veniaminof and
Lütke -- Raven secures drinking water from Petrel;
origin of lakes and rivers -- Raven liberates the heavenly bodies, the sun, moon and stars; origin of animals on
land, in the air and in the sea -- Raven gets fire -- Raven brings about a quarrel between the gull and the
crane and secures eulachon -- Raven and the fisherman
-- Raven catches salmon and deceives his nephews, the
jays -- Raven and pitch -- Raven goes with the bears to
catch salmon, pulls out the cormorant's tongue, kills
bear and his wives, all through crafty advice -- Veniaminof explains the personalities of Raven and Petrel --
Raven as a deity -- Parallels with Bible stories -- The
explanation of the differences between nations according
to the Tlingit belief -- The myth of the thunder and his
sister -- Mount Edgecumbe -- The tales of the origin of
the sun and moon, according to Veniaminof -- Tales of
the transformation of humans into animals -- Tales of
the Kuschta (Land Otter) people -- Tale of Jehuchklane
and the whale -- Tale of the origin of the Sitka Indians
according to Lisiansky -- Narrative of the jealous Athapascan wife -- Tales of the haunts and life of ghosts.

The mythology of the Tlingit revolves around the adventures
and deeds of Raven, about whom a large number of tales are told
among those people. These are the bases for ethics and customs
of the Tlingit, according to Veniaminof. The fundamental concept
is, "As Raven[1] lived and acted, so we must also behave."[2] The
most complete accounts are given by Lütke and Veniaminof and
almost all later reports, even those of Holmberg, are taken from
these sources.[3] In the following accounts I am adhering faithfully

to the transcriptions which we made during our stay at the trading post of Chilkoot. They are for the most part the narratives of an old blind Indian, named Kaschkoe, who made a habit of coming to the factory on winter evenings and entertaining a group of Indians, both men and women, with his stories. The listeners were attentive and often interrupted the narrator with hearty laughter when he told about the sly tricks and coarse jokes of Raven.

In the beginning, so we heard, there was a mighty chief, who had a young wife of whom he was very jealous. [4] He also had a sister [5] whose ten sons he killed one after another, so that they would not inherit his widow after his death, according to Tlingit custom. In sorrow over the death of her sons the sister went into the woods to kill herself. There she met an old man who asked her the reason for her sorrow, and after she had told him, he gave her the following advice: "Go to the beach at low tide and find a round pebble, make a large fire and heat the pebble in it, then take it out and swallow it without fear for it will not harm you." [6] The woman did everything according to the advice of the old man and when she became pregnant, she built herself a shelter on the same spot and there gave birth to a son who grew into a beautiful child. This was Raven. She placed a stone she had received from the old man under his throat and so made him invulnerable and she also bathed the child in the lagoon twice a day, as she had been told, to make him grow rapidly.

When the boy had grown a little his mother made a bow and arrows for him with which he shot his first little birds, whose skins his mother sewed together for a blanket. Then he shot rabbits, foxes, wolves, mountain sheep and other animals. The lucky hunter provided the shelter with large supplies of food; his mother always sewed the skins of all his game together for blankets. [7]

After he had grown up Raven once asked his mother where their friends and relatives were. She replied that she had none and when he pressed her further, saying that one could not originate out of nothing, she gave the impression that they had all died. One day, however two slaves of his uncle arrived, having been sent by him to collect the remains of his sister, and they had even brought a box to put them in. But they found the shelter filled with food when there was famine elsewhere. They reported this on their return to the uncle and also told him that his sister had a very handsome son. The uncle sent them out again at once to invite this son, his nephew, to visit him. When the slaves delivered the invitation, the mother warned her son not to accept it and told him that his uncle had killed his ten brothers. Raven declared that he would go nevertheless and she should not worry. Thereupon he followed the slaves and took a blanket of fox, one of marten, and an apron of caribou with him. His mother followed him. When Raven entered his uncle's house he saw his wife to whom he took a great fancy. The uncle was so jealous of his wife that when he went out he locked her in a box which he hung in the rafters of the house and tied a peculiar knot so that he could always tell whether anybody had untied it. [8]

The chief then invited his nephew to sit down beside him and had the slaves bring him the board on which he had killed all his brothers and the sawlike knife with a blade of glass (obsidian?). Then he had his nephew lie down on the board and tried to cut his throat. But all the teeth of the saw broke and the youth was unharmed. Then the chief said he was cold and ordered the boy to cut down a tree behind the house and make a fire with the wood. His mother warned him against doing this because under the tree he would find the remains of his brothers. But Raven went out and started to cut down the tree beside the remains of his brothers. Splinters of glass fell about his head, for the tree was of glass, but Raven did not heed them and they all broke on his head without injuring him. After he had felled the tree, he chopped the wood into small pieces in front of the house and, carrying it in on his shoulders, made such a great fire inside that the uncle feared his house would burn down.

Thereupon the chief said to Raven, "Come with me and help me spread my canoe." In spite of his mother's warning the youth followed his uncle this time, too, and at his request crawled under the canoe to spread the sides further apart. Then the chief quickly took out the crosspiece so that the sides collapsed and, leaving with the idea that his nephew could not free himself from under the canoe, went to his house. Raven however easily broke the canoe, took the two halves on his shoulders, and carried them to his uncle and threw them at his feet. Then the chief said that he would like to eat a squid. Raven secretly made himself a small canoe which he carried under his blanket when he went out with his uncle to catch a squid. When Raven stood in the bow of the canoe ready to catch the squid, his uncle made the boat rock so that the boy was thrown into the sea; he then returned home in the belief that his nephew had drowned. Since it had gotten dark he could not see that Raven had taken out the little canoe and put it under himself. Raven then caught the squid and rowed ashore. He took the squid to his uncle and threw it at his feet. Now the squid swelled up in size and got larger and larger until it filled the house. At the same time the water rose until there was a flood and all mankind perished. Raven however put on his birdskin and gave a second one to his mother who also put hers on and together they rose into the air. Raven flew so high that his beak stuck in the sky and he hung there for ten days while the flood rose high enough to reach his feet. After this the water subsided and he let go and came back to earth. But he fell directly on a pile of seaweed. [9]

The story of the origin of Raven is first found in Lütke[10] who obtained it from the notes of Chliebnikof. Even though the present recording is less complete, I am letting the oldest version stand because of certain special features.

"Kitkh-oughin-si (French orthography), [11] the first inhabitant of the earth, had several children by his sister whom he killed so that mankind would not multiply. His power extended over all inhabitants of earth and he punished them for their misbehavior by a flood. However he could not destroy them all, because they saved themselves in boats on the tops of mountains where one can still see the remains of the boats and the ropes by which they fastened themselves.

"The sister of Kit-ká-ositiyi-qā separated herself during the flood from her cruel brother and along a beach met a large and handsome man, who, when he discovered the reason for her flight, made her swallow a small round stone and promised her that she would bear a son whom nobody could kill. The result of this was the birth of Raven. His mother raised him with care, bathing him in the sea every morning and teaching him to shoot birds. Raven first killed a great number of hummingbirds and his mother made him a garment of them. Then he killed a large white bird, put on his skin and through his pleasure at having wings developed a burning desire to fly like a bird. At once he lifted himself into the air, but since he could not control his wings and was overcome with weariness, he could make no progress, so he cried ruefully, 'I would have done better to stay with my mother.' As soon as he had said this he found himself back in his house. When he had grown he asked permission of his mother to seek out Kit-ká-ositiyi-qā and punish him for cruelty. He found the dwelling of his uncle, seated himself on the roof and waited until he returned. After he had locked him in the house he called on the waters to rise and drown the evil one while he lifted himself into the air on his wings. He flew for a long time and finally when his strength was exhausted he fell on a stone, injuring himself so that he lay there for a while, unconscious. This is the origin of all sickness of mankind. When he came to he heard a voice that called him, but he saw nobody. Then he gathered all his strength and went to the beach where he noticed some land otter who were playing on the surface of the water. One of them said to him, 'Sit on me and I will take you to the place to which you are being called.' 'But you will drown me,' answered Raven. 'Do not fear, close your eyes, and seat yourself on me.' Raven seated himself on the land otter and soon glimpsed a settlement where there were many people. Here he met his mother and his uncle who had apparently reconciled themselves and here he became acquainted with Raven from whom he received the power to become the tribal ancestor of the Kolushan clans."

Lütke goes this far. According to the version told us, Raven went ashore after falling on the seaweed, but found no water anywhere until he came to the house of an old man, named Petrel. He had water in a small box which he always kept locked and on which he sat. Petrel gave Raven some to drink but not enough, so Raven now employed his wiles to get more water. When Petrel had fallen asleep, he laid dog excrement under his caribou skin blanket and woke him up and said, "My friend, you are dreaming and you have soiled your bed; go outside and wash it." Petrel actually followed this advice and Raven drank so much water while Petrel was outside that it rose up into his throat. Then he flew away and sat on a pitchy tree. The angry Petrel gathered pitch wood under the tree and kindled a large fire. Raven, who had been white, became black from the smoke. Then he flew away over all the mountains and spit a little water everywhere. Since that time the brooks and rivers come from the mountains.

According to Veniaminof, Petrel is a secretive person, without beginning or end, older and mightier than Raven himself. He had his home on a treeless island, "Tekinu," which means "sea fortification" and is east of Sitka Island[12] near the promontory Schigliutu, that is Sitka Point. On this island there was supposed to be a stone well, closed with a stone cover. The water of this well disappeared and came out on the beach if an unclean person washed his hands in it. Even in Veniaminof's time the water was still called "Kanuk-hīn," water of Petrel. Petrel had built his house over the well and slept on the stone cover. Veniaminof's description of the means by which Raven got possession of the water differs from the one given above and since it is more complete, I will repeat it here.

"One day while Petrel was out on the sea in his boat he met Raven and asked him, 'How long have you been in the world?' Raven answered that he was born in the world before the earth existed. 'How long have you lived in the world?' Raven countered. 'Since the time,' answered Petrel, 'when the liver came up from underneath.'[13] 'Then,' said Raven, 'you are older than I am.' While they were talking in this fashion, they were moving away from shore. Petrel, who wanted to show his power and control over Raven, took off his hat and laid it under him. At once so thick a fog spread over the surface of the water that one sitting in the back of the boat could not see the front. At this time Petrel separated himself from his companion. Raven now began to call to Petrel, 'Achkani, Achkani,' which means friend, my friend, but the latter maintained silence. After Raven had called in vain for a long time and did not know in which direction to turn, he finally, in tears, asked his companion to come to him. Then Petrel approached him and said, 'Why do you cry?' With these

178

words he put his hat on again and at once the fog disappeared. So Raven said, 'Now I see, Achkani, that you are mightier than I.' Thereupon Petrel invited Raven as a guest and they traveled to Tekinu Island where Petrel, among other things, also served Raven some sweet water. The water tasted so good to Raven that although he had not quenched his thirst he was ashamed to ask for more. After the meal Raven began to relate his deeds and the whole history of the world. Petrel at first listened with attention but regardless of how interesting Raven's story was, he began to nod and soon fell into a deep sleep on the cover of the well. Then Raven took dog excrement and secretly laid it beside Petrel. He moved away and began to call, 'Achkani, get up and look after yourself, you do not seem to be well.' Petrel woke up and since he believed the word of Raven, he took to the sea and washed himself. Raven hurriedly lifted the cover of the well and drank as much water as he could hold. After he had imbibed and with his mouth still full he changed himself into a raven and flew through the smoke hole. Here he was delayed by something. Then Petrel made a fire to smoke his guest as much as possible and through this Raven and all ravens with him became black, where he had formerly been white. At last Petrel ceased and Raven flew away to earth and let drops of water fall from his mouth on the land, and wherever they fell there now are springs and brooks and where the larger ones fell, seas and rivers originated." (Veniaminof, 53-55)

For the myths relating to the theft of the heavenly bodies and fire, I also follow Veniaminof's report.

"The heavenly bodies were kept by a powerful chief in three boxes which were carefully locked and which no one was allowed to approach. Raven had heard of them and formulated a plan to gain possession of them. The chief had an only daughter whom he loved very much and guarded so carefully that he did not allow her to eat or drink before he had examined the dishes. Raven, who saw that he could only obtain daylight from this chief if he were his grandson, conceived a plan to allow himself to be born by this daughter. It was not difficult for him to carry out this plan since he had the ability to change himself into any form. So one day he changed himself into a blade of grass and let himself down on the rim of a vessel from which the chief's daughter drank. When she drank, after careful examination of the vessel, he slipped into her throat. She at once realized that she had swallowed something and tried to get it out, but did not succeed. The result was that she became pregnant and when her time came, her father had beaver and other skins spread out for her, but she could not give birth. Finally an old woman led the girl into the woods and after a bed of moss had been prepared she lay down. At once she gave birth to a son whom no one suspected of being

Raven. The grandfather rejoiced over the birth of a grandchild and loved him even more than his daughter. When Raven began to gain understanding, he cried so badly one day that nothing would pacify him. Everything, when it was given him, he threw away, and crying harder than before, he pointed to the spot where the three boxes with the heavenly bodies were, but nobody was allowed to give these to him without the special permission of his grandfather. Finally he consented to give him one of the boxes. At once Raven quieted down when he received the box and began gleefully to play with it, without letting it out of his hands. He went out of the door with the box and when he saw that he was unobserved opened the lid and at once the stars appeared in the sky, leaving the box empty. The grandfather was very sad over the loss of his treasure but did not scold his grandson. Through the same wiles Raven obtained another box in which the moon was hidden. At last he tried to secure the third box, the costliest of them all, which contained the sun. But here the grandfather did not want to give in to the wishes of his grandchild so Raven did not stop crying and whining, refused food and drink and finally became ill, until at length the grandfather gave him the last box with strict orders to take care and not open it. After Raven had gone out of the door he changed himself into a raven or, according to others, into a grown man, and left the place with the box in order to return to earth. At one place he heard the voices of people but could not see them because there was no sun. Then Raven said to them, 'Do you want light?' They answered, 'You deceived us, for you are not Raven who alone can bring us light. In order to convince the disbelievers, Raven opened the box and at once the sun shone with all its radiance in the heavens. The people on whom it shone ran away in all directions, some to the mountains, others in the forest, some to the water and from them originated the animals, the birds and the fish.

"Fire was still on an island in the sea and had not yet come to earth. Raven flew there and after taking a firebrand in his mouth, came back quickly. But the distance was so great that by the time he had returned the firebrand was almost completely consumed and even his beak was half burned off. Raven let the burning coal drop at once on the earth and the scattered sparks fell on stones and wood and that is why fire can be obtained from both of these." (Veniaminof, 44-48)

Of the many adventures and deeds of Raven which are supposed to be so numerous that one person cannot know them all, only a few were told us among the Chilkat that Veniaminof did not already have and which we have therefore included here. [14]

Raven flew to Gull at Yakutat and asked her when she finished. She said right now in February she caught herring and as Raven pretended to doubt her, she flew out, caught a large fish and

180

swallowed it. Then Raven went to Crane who stayed on the Nass River and told him that Gull had spoken badly of him and called him a hollow-legged, long-necked scoundrel. He should not let such a thing be done to him, but should attack Gull and pierce her stomach, were she is very sensitive, with his bill. Then he flew back to Gull and told her that Crane spoke badly of her and so he wrought them up against each other. This developed into a quarrel. Crane flew to Yakutat and knocked down Gull and pushed her in the stomach so hard that she gave up the fish she had swallowed and Raven immediately took possession of it. So through his scheming he obtained the herring. Raven smeared his head, his canoe, and all his gear with the scales and gills of the herring which he cut into small pieces. When he came to a fisherman he told him that now there would be plenty of fish. The fisherman would not believe him at first, but his sons saw that Raven's canoe was full of scales and reported this to their father. He then divided his supplies and began to roast the fish in order to eat them. Raven went into the woods, as he said, to get pine boughs to caulk his canoe. Instead he pulled moss from the trees and wound it around his head and neck so that he looked like a bear. He rushed upon the diners who fled in fright, and gathering up all the fish he took it to the woods where he consumed it in peace. Then he returned and warned the fishermen, who had made a club with which to defend themselves against the bear, not to hit him on the head with it. When, however, he attacked them, again disguised as a bear, one of the men jumped on him and beat him about the arms, legs and back, but not on the head. Raven ran back into the woods and took off the moss; his arms and legs were badly swollen. The fishermen asked him when they saw him again what had happened to him; whereupon he answered that he fell out of a pine tree while he was getting some branches from it.

Once Raven went out with his nephews, the magpies, to get salmon. They saw a large salmon that was playing around in the water and Raven called to him, "Come close to shore so we can play with you." But the salmon said, "We were not born yesterday, we know your trickery." And he would not let himself be lured in, but all of a sudden he darted over to Raven and knocked him over with such force that he fell unconscious. When Raven recovered he made several holes along the beach. Then he flew far away. As soon as he was gone, the salmon came and jumped from one hole into the next until he came to the last one, and there was Raven who had quietly come back and he grabbed him and killed him. Raven now made a large fire to roast the salmon, and he sent out his nephews to get leaves to use as plates. They wanted to get them close by but Raven said, "Not from here, my friends, for here I cremated my wife; you must get them from across the mountains." While they flew there Raven ate the whole salmon except the tail which he hid. Then he stuck sticks in the ground around the fire and went to sleep. When his nephews came back and wakened him he asked them, "Where did you leave the salmon? You haven't eaten it all?" and with pretended anger he threw ashes on them which made the magpies black where they had once been white.

Once Raven came to Pitch who had a whole houseful of halibut. Raven asked him where he caught them. "Here, right under these projecting rocks," answered Pitch. "Come with me, dear friend," said Raven, "show me the place." Pitch had no desire to do this but finally let himself be persuaded and they went out together. It was a hot summer day and Pitch became softer and his voice weaker until he finally melted away. Then Raven returned to the house and gorged himself on the rich supply of dried halibut.

Another time Raven went to Brown Bear who had two wives and invited him to go halibut fishing with him since he knew a place where there was a great plenty of them. Bear was not anxious to go, since, he said, he had no bait. Raven promised to show him how one could get bait. At last Bear agreed to go along. They made themselves lines of spruce twigs, and when they came to the place designated by Raven, they threw them out. In a short time Raven, who had hidden some salmon under his feathers and had used it as bait, caught five halibut, but Bear, who had no bait, caught nothing. Then Raven told him that he should cut a little meat off his leg and, standing in a position as though he were going to do it himself, cut off some of the salmon which he had hidden under his feathers. Then he sharpened the knife to a keen point and gave it to Bear with the advice to cut hard and fast for then it did not hurt. Bear followed this suggestion and made such a deep cut in his leg that he screamed and ran away on three legs. He jumped in his canoe to follow Raven, but the latter flew back and forth until Bear weakened from pain and died.

Cormorant who was in the canoe with Raven and had watched everything was now anxious to tell the wives of Bear. Therefore he asked Raven to reach the shore quickly, but the latter said, "Oh my friend, a large louse is on your head. Come here and I will remove it." Cormorant laid his head in Raven's lap and Raven caught the louse, saying, "Now open your mouth and I will give you the louse." "Give it to me in my claws," replied Cormorant. Now Raven said, "No, she bit you, now you bite back. Just stick your tongue out far." Cormorant did this and Raven pulled his tongue out with force and then told him to speak. Cormorant tried it but could only babble unintelligibly. "Your ancestors spoke in the same way," said Raven. When Raven came to the wives of Bear he gave them the bladders of the halibut and told them to swallow them whole or he would not be able to catch any more halibut. The wives allowed themselves to be persuaded and then Raven advised them to drink water. They followed this advice too and the bladders swelled up and distended their stomachs until they burst.

Veniaminof sees in Raven and Petrel the two tribal ancestors of the Tlingit who later were deified. Raven, according to him, is the creator of the world since he existed before he was born, never aged, and never died. He liked mankind, but in his anger sent them illness and misfortune. He is supposed to have come from the east where the east wind blows. His home is called "Nass-schaki-jĕlch" and is at the source of the Nass River and is inaccessible to humans as well as ghosts. When Raven had accomplished his deeds on earth he is supposed to have returned there. A bold ghost once dared to penetrate to his house and as punishment his left side was paralyzed so that he could not turn around, and this miracle was performed at the same time to the mask of this spirit which was in the possession of a Chilkat shaman. [15] Raven is supposed to have a son who likes mankind even more than Raven himself and who often stands as sponsor for them. [16] But these observations, for which no further evidence is at hand, may be the results of Veniaminof's endeavors to parallel the stories of Raven with the New Testament. He is supposed to have brought dead boys to life again by tickling their noses with a girl's hair. [17] According to Holmberg, Raven as a deity had the name "Haschak hūn" which is also used for the God of the Christians.[18] Veniaminof also tells of a great flood during which the people saved themselves on a large floating structure. When the water receded the craft was stranded on a rock and when the flood had completely disappeared it broke in two on account of its own weight. In one half the Tlingit remained and in the other, all other peoples, and this accounts for the difference of speech among mankind. [19]

The following myth about the origin of thunder and earthquake I will give in the form rendered by Veniaminof.

Once there lived a brother and sister, the brother "Chetl" which means "sound," the sister "Agischanak," meaning a subterranean being. When for some reason they had to part, the brother said to his sister, "You will never see me again, but as long as I live you will hear me." Thereupon he put on the skin of a great bird and flew to the southwest into the clouds, where the Tlingit believe the Kijĕki live, but the sister climbed a mountain near Sitka (Mt. Edgecumbe) and suddenly let herself into the ground. Proof of this can still be seen today by the hollow near the peak of the mountain. [20] The brother, Chetl, comes to Sitka every year to bring news to his sister hidden in the ground. Thunder is the noise of his wings, and lightning, the glance of his eyes. When Chetl is angry he tears whole trees up with his tremendous claws or shatters them and burns the forests. His favorite food is whale, and to catch one or two whales is no more difficult for him than catching two herring for a Tlingit. He carries the whales in his claws to the top of a high mountain in the north and devours them there. He needs no less than a whole whale for a meal. [21]

The sister, Agischanak, is much more active in the interests of mankind. Ever since she went under the ground she has supported the column on which the earth rests, otherwise the earth would have fallen over into the sea long ago. Agischanak likes humans because they make fire on the earth by which she can warm herself. She is immortal, never sleeps, and is so strong that even Raven himself could not overpower her. Raven often in his anger at the disobedience and bloodthirstiness of man wishes to destroy him and tries to lure Agischanak away from her post, but he cannot force her. These fights are the causes of earthquakes.

A more complete version or a repetition of the myth related above was given us among the Chilkat Indians and runs as follows:

A great chief had a daughter who was desired by many men as a wife, but he was too proud to give her to anyone but another chief. He owned an ugly dog who one night in the guise of a man went to the daughter and asked her if she would have him as a husband. Since he had a handsome appearance, the girl agreed and later she gave birth to puppies, eight in all. The father flew into such a rage that he and his whole tribe abandoned the daughter, destroyed the food supplies, and put out the fires in order to leave her to starve. A sympathetic relative hid some embers and food under the threshold so that the chief's daughter could make a fire and have some food until she could catch salmon for herself and her dog children. As long as she was away from the house her children played with each other in human form, the seven boys around the fire, while the little girl watched at the door for their mother's return. When she saw her coming they all returned to their dog forms. But once the mother quietly stole home and saw her children in human form with their dog clothing hanging on the wall. She then threw these into the fire and the children remained human.

The youngest of the sons was Chlkajágo and he was a mighty hunter who killed all dangerous animals on land and in the sea. Once Chlkajágo persuaded his brothers to play with the ring of the great bear. This was a shiny ring with a sharp edge which attracted people toward it against their will. Chlkajágo and his brothers were cut in two by this ring, all except the eldest who was a shaman. He took the ring and broke it in two pieces and threw it into the sky where it became the rainbow. Then he gathered the remains of his brothers and brought them back to life.

Chlkajágo was in love with his sister and was ridiculed for it by his brothers who tried to cure him of it. One day they smeared their elder sister's bed with pitch and when the following day they found the buttocks of their brother covered with it, they laughed at him. In shame Chlkajágo fled to the peak of a high mountain near Sitka (Mt. Edgecumbe) and here said to his sister, "We must part, but you will hear my voice." The sister thereupon sank into a deep hole to the bottom of the mountain, and the brother transformed himself into a bird, and flew westward where, as the thunder, he speaks to his sister.

A somewhat similar story is told by Veniaminof about the origin of the sun and the moon. These were also brother and sister according to the belief of the Tlingit. [22] Since the sister had a lover she embarrassed the brother in such a painful manner that he left the house. She became one of the great heavenly bodies and the brother, the other. But her disgrace followed her and therefore she constantly tries to stay away from her brother. [23]

The sun is considered poor and the moon rich. An eclipse of the moon signifies that the moon has suffered a loss and therefore wealthy Tlingit on such occasions carry all their possessions outdoors and offer them to the moon, and when the eclipse is over they carry everything back except a small offering which they leave for the moon. At a total eclipse of the moon they believe the moon has lost his way. Then they all go outside and sing certain songs in order to bring the moon back on his proper path. [24] The spots on the moon are supposed to be two children who ridiculed him while they were getting water so he seized them and took them to him.

A local myth is connected with a rock in Dejah Valley which is supposed to be a woman turned to stone who, under the name of Kanuga, is regarded as the bringer of wind. In the months of February and March, 1882, when there were exceptionally strong winds, it was said among the Chilkat that Kanuga was angry at the whites and that the object of her wrath was the anemometer at the trader's at which the Indians cast awesome glances.

The long tailed ducks, Ja-á-une, are regarded as transformed children who went out in a canoe and drowned. They constantly cry, "ha āni ha āni" which means "our village." The little screech owls are ghosts of newborn children suffocated by their mothers in sleeping.

The brown bear is also regarded as a transformed human. According to a tale related by Veniaminof, one fall day some Tlingit girls, among them the daughter of the chief, went into the woods to pick berries. When they came across some bear tracks and then found some excrement, the chief's daughter, in spite of the warnings of her companions, began to ridicule the bear, calling him a slow, stupid, and blind fellow. On the way home she dropped the basket in which she had picked her berries and they spilled out. Her companions helped her to pick them up, but she always dropped them again until her friends grew angry and left the chief's daughter behind. After she had picked up her berries, she followed her companions, but lost her way as it became dark, and after wandering around aimlessly she laid herself down exhausted and soon fell asleep. When she suddenly awoke she saw a handsome young man standing before her who offered to show her the way. She followed him willingly but when they did not come upon the path, she became uncomfortable and afraid of her companion who tried in vain to quiet her. At last they came to a bear den and her guide asked her to enter it. When she stepped in she saw two bears inside, and, frightened, she wanted to flee, but her companion held her back, saying that she had made a mistake. Actually when she looked a second time she saw, in place of the bears, an old man and an old woman, who greeted her in a friendly way. Suddenly her companion assumed the form of a bear and explained to her that he had led her here because she had ridiculed him and laughed at him. Although at first the girl was very sad, she finally found the bear attractive and became his wife. When in the spring her tribesmen came to the den, they killed the bears and would have killed her too, for she had assumed the form of a bear, had she not made herself known to her brother and her relatives who were among the hunters. They brought her back home where she took on human form again. Now when women see the tracks of a bear they praise him and beg him not to be angry with them and not to steal them. The men cut the head off a dead bear before they skin him and decorate it with feathers like the head of a shaman and throw it into the fire while they sing certain songs in order to bring luck for future hunting. They dare not say anything bad about him, as what they call "t'likass."[25]

An important role is also played by the land otters, the "Kuschta people," in the myths of the Tlingit. Their significance for the shamans will be discussed in a later chapter, but here I want to tell a tale which we secured from the Chilkat.

In a village of the Kake Indians there was once a famine. One Indian, however, who had built himself a canoe set up a shelter some distance from the village and lived there with his wife and two children. Every day his wife gathered edible marine animals on the beach, while the children got mollusks and crabs. At first they still found enough nourishment, but later there was less and less until at last there was nothing. Gradually the man became so weak that he could scarcely work until one day when he was sitting in his shelter, full of care, with his back to the fire, the door opened and a woman passed in a basket full of all kinds of food -- seal meat, seal oil, halibut and many other things. She said she was his sister and that many years ago when they had an

accident on a canoe trip, she was rescued by the Land Otter people. She was now married and the mother of two sons. Since she
had heard of his need, she came to help him and his family. They
were to eat the food which she brought them. Then she disappeared without coming in the shelter and after three days when
they had eaten all the food she appeared again with a new supply
of sea lion meat, seal oil, halibut, and so on. Now her brother
invited her to come in and she did, but she hid her face with a
cloth. As she sat by the fire she saw a crab shell which the children had gathered on the beach, lying on the ground. At once she
asked where it had come from for nothing had as high a value
among the Land Otter people as the shells and mandibles of crabs
because they make dance rattles of them. That is why the Land
Otter people always try to rescue drowned Indians in the hope
that they may get crab shells and mandibles from them. The
brother wanted to give his sister a stone axe such as is used in
canoe making as a present for her husband in return for their
gifts, but she refused it in favor of the crab shells which she took
with pleasure. After a few days she appeared again, this time accompanied by her husband and her two sons who brought a supply
of food to exchange for crab shells. All the remaining Land Otter
people came to this man and bought crab shells from him so that
he became very wealthy and supplied the whole village with food.
One day the sister invited her brother to her home, called
"Kuschtakani," the root place. It lies not far away on the river
behind a little hill. The brother consented but asked his sister to
send her sons to help put his canoe into the water. The sister
promised this but warned her brother to go into the house and not
watch her sons at work. On the next day the nephews came. After
the uncle cautioned them to be careful with his canoe since he
was a poor man, he went into the house, as his sister had told
him, while his nephews transformed themselves into land otters
and pushing their tails under the canoe, brought it to the sandy
beach. When the uncle turned around to see what his nephews
were doing with his canoe, they changed themselves back into
young men and the canoe which they had supported with their tails
fell on the ground, but without damage since the beach was sandy.
The Indian now rode with his nephews to the village of the Land
Otter people where everything was changed and he found real
houses and people. His sister received him on the beach and led
him to her husband's house where he and his whole family were
hospitably entertained. When, however, the Land Otter woman
took her little niece on her lap she grew a long tail. Her mother
would not stand for this, and when she took the child back, the
tail disappeared. After a while the Kake Indians started on their
homeward trip. The sister advised her brother not to think back,
but put his mind on the trip home. However, after they had com-

187

pleted a large part of the journey, the brother thought again of the unusual Land Otter people and all at once the canoe was pulled back to the place they had just left. His sister who met him there told him that this was the result of his thinking of the Land Otter village. He was not to think of it, or else he would be pulled back repeatedly. So he did not do it again and arrived safely in his village where he found his tribesmen in dire need. He put on a great feast at which he divided the bountiful supplies which he had brought home and saved everyone from starvation.

All Tlingit girls are afraid to go in the woods alone for fear that the Land Otter people will seize them. A young girl who had had such an experience in the woods came back to the village half crazed and raging, she attacked everyone, struck and bit those who tried to hold her, and tearing off her own clothes, ran around naked. She even threw a stone at the shaman who tried to cure her by dancing before her with drum and rattle. Then her tribesmen made a medicine of the roots of a poisonous weed which they had scraped into a fine meal under the water. Then four cuts were made on the head of the sick girl and these were brushed with the medicine. At once the invalid became calmer and gradually she recalled her experience in the woods. Then she fell into a deep sleep from which she awoke after several hours completely recovered.

The following narrative, which we also secured during our travels, comes from the Tsimshian Indians, and is so characteristic of the beliefs of the whole coast population that I will give it here.

In Metlakatla[26] there lived a man named Jehuchklane who was famous far and wide as a hunter. Once he killed a white sea otter whose skin he allowed his wife to prepare. Since there was a little blood on the tip of the tail, the woman went to the beach to wash the skin. The waves tore the skin away and as she tried to recover it, she was pulled into deeper and deeper water till suddenly a whale came who took her on his back. At once the people prepared to rescue her, only her husband did not hurry, but carried on his preparations very deliberately. He bathed himself in devil's club (Oplopanax horrida), stuck eagle feathers in his hair, and painted his face. Then he took a large amount of tobacco and poison with him before he hastened after his companions. Soon he was so close to the whale that he could hear his wife's cries for help when it prepared to dive near the great cavern in the Nass River. Then the man tied a long tow rope around his middle and ordered his slaves to let him down gradually. A short distance below the surface he reached a cavern which was not full of water. Here he saw many geese who were feeding on the roots of a seaweed. When he approached them they raised a loud cry, saying, "What is this queer sound? It smells like a man; it smells like

188

Jehuchklane. " Since he knew that the geese were blind, he took
the roots away from them and they began to quarrel with each
other. Then Jehuchklane smeared their eyes with the roots
whereupon they could see and all began to cry, "The eyes are
opened, the eyes are opened. " And that is the way they still cry
today. Jehuchklane further increased their joy with a gift of tobacco which they chewed at once. It is from this that they got the
brown color of their bills. The geese now reported to the man
that the whale with the woman passed them a short time ago and
that he had asked them to keep watch. They also said they would
not consider harming him. He would, however, have a hard time
with the large mussel, the one-horned fish, and the halibut. On
his way back he should not be afraid of them if for appearances
they attacked him with clubs, but he should pass over quickly and
they would beat the sand behind him. Jehuchklane thereupon went
on and came to the great mussel into whose open shell he spit
some tobacco juice. Since then this shell always tastes like tobacco inside. The mussel closed up quickly when the tobacco
juice reached it so that Jehuchklane could pass by. Then he came
to the one-horned fish (cottus sp?) on which he also sprayed tobacco juice. While it crawled in between the rocks, he stepped
on its head and flattened it. After that Jehuchklane came to the
halibut who was so slippery that he could not cross over it. He
also gave the halibut tobacco, and she liked it so well she turned
over and had her rough side on top. Then he came to Crane who
was lying on his stomach in front of his little hut of twigs, facing
the fire. He blew ashes in his face which gives him the gray appearance of his belly. With a little tobacco he also made a friend
of him, but since he had to cough as a result of the smoke, the
whale people came up and asked about the cause of the disturbance. Crane took the man as a little louse under his wing and
when the whales looked for him, saying that they smelt a man, he
spread his wings to show that he was hiding nothing. After the
whales had left, Jehuchklane crept out of his hiding place. Now
Crane said to him, "Do not be afraid of me when you return. I
will strike at you but will always miss you. " In gratitude for this
the man gave him a nice sharp bone of which he could make himself a fine bill for probing deep into the water.

At last Jehuchklane came to the giant slaves of the whales who
had three dorsal fins. He found them busy making a fin for the
stolen wife of their master and for this purpose they were split-
ting a tree trunk with an axe. The man crawled under it and bit
off the edge of the axe. When the slave noticed this he took another and Jehuchklane bit that off too. Now the slave began to cry
and the man came out from under the tree and stepping up to him
explained the cause of his trouble. Then the slave said, "My
master beats me now without cause but when he sees the broken

axes which are worth more than his whole tribe, he will surely kill me." Thereupon the man took the axes in his mouth and replaced the pieces he had bitten off. Through this and with a gift of tobacco he made a friend of the slave who then promised to help in freeing his wife. After he had cut up some pitchy wood, he packed the man in it and carried him to the whales' house. The slave had four wives, fish otter, mink, marten and ermine, from whom he had to hide the man because he was familiar with their inclination to gossip. But they smelt him and hurried out to tell their master about it. However, when they came upon a sandbank they started cleaning their mouths with sand and forgot about their errand. When Jehuchklane finally arrived in the whales' house he found all the whales gathered there to attach the fin on the woman. Already stones had been heated in the fire. Across from the fire lay the woman with her bent back exposed where the fin was to be attached. The slave then went out to get water. When he returned he poured the water on the fire sending up a great cloud of vapor. The man took advantage of this moment and seized his wife and fled with her. At once the whole whale folk stormed after him, but the slave into whose mouth the man threw another piece of tobacco, laid himself across the door and swelled up so that nobody could pass. Then he also took part in the pursuit, but only to gain another piece of tobacco and block the way again. When Jehuchklane came to the Crane he struck at him with his bill, but without hitting him, and the geese likewise, as they had promised, beat the sand behind him and received much tobacco as reward. At last the pursued came to the rope which had been let down from the canoe. At a signal which had been agreed upon, they were quickly hoisted up and then they rowed as fast as possible to their home village. There, however, the whales had already arrived and came to the surface, surrounding the boat. Now Jehuchklane threw out the poison, which he had taken along, on the surface of the water, which caused the whales to die, some sinking and others floating, belly up, and one still lies on the beach today, near Ft. Simpson, turned into stone. Jehuchklane now reached home safely, but his wife retained the crooked back the whales had given her and her descendants have the same.

Here a myth recorded by Lisiansky about the origin of the Sitka Indians is also appropriate, even though it sounds suspiciously like the Old Testament version of Paradise. "In a small cove in the neighborhood of Sitka, the old settlement," Lisiansky heard from an Indian from Hoodsnoff (Killisnoo), "there once lived two brothers about whose origin nothing was known. They had a surplus of everything until one day while they were walking along the beach together, the younger one, Chat, found a seaweed, that looked like a cucumber and tasted it. When the elder one saw this he told him that he had eaten of a forbidden fruit and that as a result the surplus which they had enjoyed up to the present would stop and that from now on they must work for their living. They both began to bemoan their misfortune. Soon thereafter some inhabitants from Stikine visited this place and they wanted to take the two men as slaves but they told about their plight and helplessness and asked for their freedom and for permission to marry a few women from their country so that they could teach them how to live in this world. These wishes were granted by the Stikine and the two brothers had many children and became the tribal ancestors of the Sitka people."[27]

The following little tale is remarkable because it deals entirely with human relations and, until the denouement at the end, steers clear of the usual supernatural elements. We heard it at the trading post at Chilkoot.

A Gunana lived with his wife and little son in a hut at the base of a high mountain. During his hunting he came to the other side of the mountain and one day he found there in a cabin a woman to whom he felt so drawn that he lived with her and brought her his "bag." He visited his first wife and his child so seldom that they were in dire need. Once when he returned after a long absence bringing her some meat she gave it to her son, saying, "That is all which your father brought you." Then she secretly followed her husband and when she saw that he entered a strange house she hid herself in the neighborhood and waited until after a while he came out with new clothes and left. Then she entered the house and killed the interloper with her knife. After she had taken as much of the ample food supply as she could carry she set fire to the house and returned home with her booty. Her husband when he came back to his sweetheart found only a pile of ashes. He began to cry, and in sadness he went back to his wife. She asked him why he was so sad, but received no answer. Then she took her things and the child and returned to her father. Her father who was a shaman had seen his daughter in a dream wandering around in the prairie and guided her footsteps homeward. There she told him the cause of her sorrow and he turned her husband, who tried to follow her, into an elk.

The belief in a life after death is widespread among the Tlingit. Once there was a Tlingit, as we were told, who wandered along the way to the land of ghosts and came back to life and told his tribesmen what he experienced and saw. Right behind his house he found a wide and pretty path that led to the other side of the mountains where the ghosts of the dead stay. First he came to a wide river on whose shores many souls gathered. These were the unfortunate ones who had no friends among the dead who could take them across in their canoes. If one has many friends they come on call and take one across and ask about news from the other world, how their friends are and whether they are coming soon. Our man was warned by the ghosts on this side of the river that if he once crossed he could not return and that he should return while he still could, before his corpse was cremated. Their waiting place is a terrible one and their life is miserable, with much suffering from hunger and thirst. When he pointed to the river which had much water in it they said he must not drink of it for it tasted as bitter as gall. Then he saw that the ripples on the water were green like the gall of an animal. Even the fortunate ghosts who got to the other side did not lead an enviable life since they received only as much food and drink as was used by their friends on earth. That is why a Tlingit never fails to remember the dead during his meal and, calling their names, throws a little food into the fire.

Only when the survivors observe all the mourning rites carefully does a soul easily find the path to the land of shadows. Otherwise the soul must wander around a long time before it reaches its goal. The souls of those Tlingit whose bodies are cremated, according to Veniaminof, find it warm and light because they can always go to the fire, but the souls of those who are not cremated are dark and cold because they must always stand behind the others and can never get up to the fire. All ghosts must do their own work except those for whom slaves were sacrificed. These lead a comfortable life because the slaves do all the work for them. [28]

Veniaminof tells the following story which the Tlingit regard as the origin for the custom of throwing some food into the fire for the dead. "When Raven was still among mankind, he gathered the ghosts of the dead as his guests and set various dishes before them. But none of the guests touched them, even though the host urged them. At last one of the ghosts said to him, "Host, your guests cannot eat so set the food by the fire." The host did this and saw that the guests fell to and were well satisfied. But when they had left it was seen that the food had not been touched. Therefore, when the Kolushans now hold a feast for the dead they throw a little food in the fire for them and eat the rest themselves. [29]

The path to the land of the dead, according to Veniaminof, is swampy and wet for the souls of those whose survivors weep unduly, but for those to whom this does not happen, it is smooth and even. [30]

The Tlingit, according to Veniaminof, believe in transmigration of souls; the soul of a deceased person is supposed to return to earth and through a pregnant woman find its clan again. If a pregnant woman sees a dead relative in a dream she believes that his soul had entered her and if the newborn child has any birthmark that might identify him with the dead relative it is regarded as this person returned to earth and given the same name.

Therefore some Tlingit who are dissatisfied with their lot are supposed to express the wish that they may die soon so that they can start over again under more favorable conditions by being born into the clan of some envied chief. [31]

11. Shamanism

Characteristics of shamanism -- Appearance of the
shaman -- His effectiveness -- Preparation for the office of shaman -- The spririts of a shaman -- Veniaminof's account of the wonderful deeds of a Sitka shaman --
The petrified mask of a Chilkat shaman -- The calling of
the fish -- The account of the great shaman, Kaka, in
Sitka -- Unsociable life of the shaman -- The great shamanistic feasts -- The dances of the shaman -- Masks,
drums and rattles -- The various classes of spirits --
The discovery of witches through shamans -- The punishment of witches -- The initiation of a new shaman at
Klukwan -- The treatment of the sick by a Huna shaman
-- Witch hunt in Wrangell, Sitka and among the Chilkat -
- Superstitious beliefs -- Weather control -- Carved
wooden figures at Klukwan.

The religion of the Tlingit consists of shamanism, that is, a
belief in spirits which interfere with the lives of the people and
whose power can only be broken through the knowledge of a few,
the shamans. The shaman, called ichta,[1] is recognized by his
wild, dirty appearance, with hair loosely hanging in strands, or
bound in a knot at the back of his head, but never touched by a
scissors or comb. Even in the deepest mourning he will cut only
the front of his hair.[2] A shaman has in his possession all kinds
of decorative objects, such as carved bone spikes, face masks,
rattles, drums, etc. For each spirit the shaman has a special
mask, which he uses when he appeals to that spirit. The conjuring of a spirit consists of a wild dance around the fire during
which violent contortions of the body take place. The shaman
cures the sick by driving out evil spirits, brings on good weather,
brings about large fish runs and performs other similar acts.[3]
For these services he collects good pay and in fact always gets it
in advance. If his services are not successful he is not found with-

out an explanation; for instance, other bad spirits interfered and to drive them out would require another performance and another payment.

The manner in which a Tlingit becomes a shaman is thoroughly described by Veniaminof whose account is substantially given here.

The position of shaman is usually inherited by a son or grandson, with the masks, drums, etc. But not everyone who wishes to can become a shaman; only those who obtain spirits and have entered into rapport with them. Veniaminof heard of a shaman with two sons, one of whom wanted to become a shaman but could not see a spirit, while the other, in spite of the fact that he did not want to be a shaman, was followed by spirits and given no peace until he decided to accept, even though he went to the women who usually drove these spirits away. He then became a very famous shaman at Yakutat, whose influence prevented the great smallpox epidemic of 1836 from reaching his people.

Whoever wishes to become a shaman goes alone into the forest or the mountains far from human contacts for a period of from one week to several months, during which time he nourishes himself only on the roots of Araliaceae (Oplopanax horridum (Sm) Miguel, devil's club), which is plentiful in this region. The shorter or longer period in the wilderness depends on the appearance of the spirit. When he finally meets the spirit he can count himself among the lucky if he gets a land otter in whose tongue is contained the whole secret of shamanism. The land otter goes directly to the would-be shaman who, as soon as he sees the spirit, stands still and exclaiming four times a loud "oh" in various pitches, kills him. As soon as the land otter hears this sound he falls on his back and dies, with his tongue protruding. The shaman tears the tongue out, saying, "May I be successful in my new calling, may I conjure and dance well," and putting the tongue in a basket which he has prepared for the purpose, he hides it in an unapproachable place, for if an uninitiated person should find this "kuschtaliute" (otter's tongue), he would lose his senses. He pulls off the skin carefully and keeps it as a sign of his success while he buries the meat in the ground. On account of the belief in the powers of the land otter, no Tlingit dared kill one before the coming of the Russians, but this belief was overcome by greed and by the realization that no evil consequences resulted.

If the spirits will not appear to a Tlingit who has gone into solitude in the woods to prepare for shamanism, then he goes to the grave of a shaman and spends a night there, taking one of the teeth from the skull or cutting a small piece of the tip of the little finger, he holds this in his mouth to bring him success. He returns to his people very lean on account of his fast, and begins at once to practice his art. [4]

The ability of a shaman depends on the number of spirits under his control and if he is a good shaman he can gain great wealth, but if he does not maintain a proper rapport with these spirits, they may kill him.

Every shaman has his own spirits for whom there are special names and songs. He seldom inherits the spirits of ancestors, but they do occasionally appear to him and then the shaman makes a practice of entertaining them cordially. He also has the power, according to the beliefs of the Tlingit, to throw his spirits into anyone who does not believe in him; and these people then get cramps or fall into a faint. [5]

The belief in the power and pronouncements of the shaman, which is now weakening, was once universal among the Tlingit. It is said that a famous shaman in Sitka, according to Veniaminof, allowed himself to be thrown into the sea. With his relatives and friends he went out in a bay on Tschistych Island (at the foot of Mt. Edgecumbe), let himself be wrapped in a mat and tied with a strap of otter, his shamanistic power, and after four loud exclamations was lowered into the sea. The people with him at first had great fear for his life and had first refused to do it. Faster than a stone and faster than a whale which had been shot, he went to the bottom so that the line to which he was fastened could scarcely follow. At the end of this line, his boatmates had tied the bladder of a land otter. After they waited in vain for some time for a sign from him, they went ashore in order to mourn for their friend. The following day they went back to the place without seeing anything unusual. But when they returned on the fourth day they heard a sound like a shaman's drum and as they followed it, they saw the shaman hanging on a steep cliff without being tied down, his face streaming with blood, his head downwards, and small birds swarming around. With difficulty the friends got him into their boat in which he at once regained consciousness and returned home with them. All these wonders were due to the fact that the shaman had acquired a powerful new spirit.

A famous Chilkat shaman is supposed to have owned a mask of which the left half had turned into stone, while the right half was still alder wood of which masks are usually made. Also a part of the shamanistic staff and the ermine skins which hung from it were partly petrified. This shaman had a quantity of regalia which he stored in several boxes that were hidden in the woods and only brought out when he needed them.

The following miracle is told of one of the contemporary Chilkat shamans: two years ago the run of smelt, the oil fish, was very late and because of this the Indian population was in great need. So a shaman, after he had fasted for four days, went out to sea in a canoe with all his paraphernalia and let himself be lowered to the bottom on a twenty fathom line. When, after some time he allowed himself to be raised again, and he appeared with his rattles and bells which he had taken down with him, he announced that the smelt would come the following day. The next morning many seals and killer whales were seen which are certain indications of the arrival of the fish run and when they went to the river they saw the fish in great numbers.

Also to bring about better weather a shaman will go into the water; if his hair gets wet, it will rain.

I will give one more example in a story told in Chilkoot about the great shaman, Kaka of Sitka, even though several points in it will remain unintelligible to us:

In Sitka there lived a man who had two wives, the younger of whom was in love with another man. She was most anxious to put her husband out of the way so she put two rings in his ears, made of the sinew of land otter; then she let Kuchta who lives in the north and has the appearance of a large monkey change him into a land otter. Kaka drowned on a canoe trip but was saved by the land otter and taken to an island where he was enslaved and where he fell in love with the chief's two daughters. One day he met his aunt who gave him the advice to take the sinew rings out of his ears. He did this and then realized his plight. Before this he was happy but now he became sad and longed for home. Then his two uncles promised to take him back home, provided he would not pay attention to anything which happened on the way. They traveled only at night; once however the dawn appeared before they reached land and a constellation which looked like a fish appeared in the sky. The travelers started a mourning song and the canoe grounded and changed itself into a ray while they themselves jumped out and became land otters. Immediately, they tore out Kaka's tongue and through possession of it gained the power of a shaman. The ray covered him with seaweed so the ravens would not eat him. After sunset the land otters appeared again as humans and the ray assumed the shape of a canoe. So Kaka came to Sitka where he was immediately feted as a great shaman. One of his wives had remained faithful to him, but the younger one had married another man, and would not believe his identity even though everyone rushed to him. One day, however, she felt herself so drawn to him that she watched him through the smoke hole. So the shaman made her fall down into the middle of the house and she was so ashamed of herself that she committed suicide.

At the drowning of a shaman, his relatives fast for a number of days, and, as we have seen, his burial is also different from that of all other Tlingit. The body of a shaman is not supposed ever to decompose because one of his first spirits stays with him, so it dries like a dried salmon; also boughs are never supposed to fall on the grave of a shaman but always beside it; the posts upon which the grave is set are supposed to decay simultaneously so that the grave sinks evenly into the ground, neither the feet nor the head first.

The great shamanistic performances are given only in the winter during a new or full moon. The shamans call ceremonially upon their spirits so that they may bring luck and ward off illness for the village, for the shaman himself, and for his relatives during the coming year.

From the morning of the day set for the performance until the following morning the relatives who are helping the shaman may not eat or drink, and for several days before this they purify themselves with emetics which they drink in water and then vomit again by sticking a feather down the throat.

When the sun is setting, all who are going to take part in the performance go into the houses which are prepared for the purpose by being cleaned and some even by having new boards put around the fireplace. Singing in which both men and women participate starts at once with time beaten on a drum which stands to the right of the entrance. After the shaman has put on his ceremonial regalia he starts running around the fire in the same direction as the sun, and doubles up his body forcefully, keeping time with the rhythm of the drum and the songs until his eyes, which have been directed toward the smoke hole all the time, seem twisted in his head. Suddenly he stands still, looks at the upper side of the drum and screams loudly. Immediately the songs and the drum stop and all direct their gaze on the shaman, since the spirit which has entered him is about to speak.

After the conclusion of the performance the guests are served with tobacco and all kinds of food until dawn. [6]

Erman witnessed a great shamanistic feast which began on November 12, the first day of the full moon at eight o'clock in the evening. On the lower level of the house hundreds of naked men stood around a fire in the middle of the floor. Men and women wearing clothing sat along one wall only of the upper level (cp. p. 88). The majority of those who were on the lower level each held a beautiful dagger in his right hand, ready for action, and while a few of them made a circle around the fire, the rest moved toward the lower tiers of benches, leaving the circle standing free. The singing, monotonous and slow at first, increased in tempo and gradually emphasized its monosyllables in louder tones. After several drum beats, a curtain rose which separated the main part of the house from a space directly opposite the entrance. Here the shaman appeared with flying hair and many bright decorations hanging on his cape which could not be further described because of the speed with which he moved toward the fire. The singers swung their daggers and seemed, with melancholy cries, to be pursuing the shaman who through graceful leaps and twisting of the body eluded them. Among other things, he pulled a burning log from the fire and threw it toward the roof of the house, thereby increasing the efforts of his pursuers. They turned with a gesture of their daggers, now menacing the elders and high class people who sat in the front rows, now attacking the racing shaman, and finally they caught him in a net and tied him down. He was covered with a mat and some of his followers dragged him behind the curtain. One could hear him groan, while the chorus which still remained around the fire sang more softly and at a slower tempo.

The same performance was repeated a second time with only the difference that at each repetition the shaman assumed another character. His head was always enclosed in a helmet mask which the first time seemed to represent a deer or sheeplike animal in whose skin he was also dressed. In these costumes he circled the fire, as quickly and skillfully as earlier, but in accordance with his role, on all fours, until he was bound again and carried, groaning and gasping, from the scene. When he came out the last time he wore a mask of a predatory animal or perhaps a distorted human face in blue and red colors with large white teeth in its open jaws. During this appearance he ran upright sometimes, and then again on his hands and feet, sometimes forward and then backwards. After he was overpowered and carried away again, the singing stopped altogether. All the spectators in the front seats, who had sung with the chorus now strained forward while the shaman behind the curtain gradually changed from his groaning into short staccato sentences of a prophecy which the interpreter rendered as, "I see the 'Jek' -- he is on the sea -- his boat is coming to me," and more which he said he could not translate into Russian. [7]

The spirits or "jek" (according to Holmberg jekh, plur. jekch), with whom the shamans are in communication, can be divided according to Veniaminof, into three classes, the "kijek," the upper spirits, from the word "kina" meaning up, the "takijek" or land spirits, and the "tekijek" or water spirits. The "kijek" which always appear to shamans as warriors, are the souls of persons killed in war. They live in the northern heavens, which open to receive new souls and at that time can be seen by those who are near their own death.

The "takijek" or land spirits appear to the shamans always in the forms of land animals. They are the souls of Tlingit who die an ordinary death. They live in the far north at a place called "Takanku."

The "tekijek" or water spirits appear in the form of sea mammals and, according to several, are supposed to be the souls of such animals.

Every Tlingit has his own guardian spirit, called "tu kinajek" (tu = his, kina = top, jek = spirit) but an evil or unclean person is deserted by his spirit.

All spirits like cleanliness and the sound of the drum and the rattle. Therefore a shaman who wishes to summon the spirits must practice alone for three to twelve months and the house in which the performance is to take place must be carefully cleaned and the songs and dances practiced to the exact beat of the drum.[8]

The shamans declare that in their performances a number of different spirits of various classes and with different faces appear one after another in no set order. The shaman puts on the mask of the spirit which he sees and also changes his ornaments according to the attire of the spirit.

In addition to the great shamanistic feasts the shamans also practice their art on a number of other occasions in connection with little or no feasting. For example, it is within his province to expose witchès, that is, such persons as attempt to harm others through magic, or are the source of illness.

Witches, both men and women, are called "nakutsati"[9] and are supposed to have learned their skills from Raven while he lived on earth. When they wish to harm someone they try to obtain something from that person -- his hair, his spittle, a morsel of his food or some dirt from his body which the Tlingit often scrapes off instead of washing off. With this they go to a graveyard and put it, with the proper maledictions, on an uncremated body, or in the ashes of a cremated body, or near the body of a dog.

After a time, usually when the body on which these things were put has decayed, the person from whom they were taken becomes ill and is afflicted in that part of him from which the property was taken. If the sick person believes he was bewitched he sends a messenger to a shaman who calls through the door, "o! iguk-chuáti" which means, "for you." The shaman allows these words to be repeated four times while he tries to recognize in the voice of the messenger the voice of the one who has bewitched the patient. Then he dismisses the messenger with the answer that he will come the following day. The next day the shaman with his friends and relatives visits the house of the patient which has been thoroughly cleaned. He puts on his regalia and while his companions sing and beat time with their staffs he goes to the patient and manipulates his abdomen in the usual fashion. When the singing stops he goes to a relative of the patient and accuses him of witchcraft, thus completing his task.[10]

The accused person, if he was not protected by powerful relatives, was seized, and after his hands were tied together, palms out behind his back, he was dragged to an empty hut where he was kept without food or drink until he admitted his guilt or, as a result of torture including the drinking of sea water, died. If he admits his guilt, he is taken to the place where he said he hid the belongings of the sick person. These are supposed never to decay, even if the corpse on which they are laid has decomposed. As soon as the witch, who has been freed from his bonds, but is closely watched, has found the pieces he lays them on a piece of bark, a leaf or in the folds of his cape and shows them to the spectators who do not dare touch them. Then when they are convinced that they are the possessions of the sick person, the witch runs, accompanied by his guards, to the beach and wades knee deep into the water. He stands there and turns four times toward the sun, holding up in his two hands the bewitched property. At the fourth time he dips them into the water, while he himself wades out up to his neck and immerses himself four times, calling out that the sick person should become well and clean, as he walks back to shore. Formerly the relatives of one accused of witchcraft were supposed to kill him in order not to have such a hated individual in their group of kin. But if someone of high class was suspected of witchcraft, his relatives would go to him secretly at night and beg him to heal the sick person because they were afraid to seize him and tie him down.

The Tlingit believed that witches could fly and expected them to escape from the hut in which they were confined, leaving their bonds behind and going through the smoke hole. In the early dawn they were supposed to gather at the graveyard where they associated with the dead. [11]

I now come to those facts about shamanism and witchcraft among the Tlingit which we ourselves could observe and find out. The belief in the strength and skill of the shaman still is strong in cases of sickness and other circumstances in spite of the efforts of the missionaries and lip service to Christianity.

A few weeks before we visited in the Chilkat village of Klukwan in January, 1882, an old shaman of the Raven clan had died and was buried with the ceremonies described above. During our visit a new shaman was initiated. All the adults of the Raven clan fasted for four days, the children, only two days, while the new shaman fasted eight days with only a break on the morning of the fifth day when he received a morsel of food. The whole tribe was assembled in the house of the dead shaman and in the evenings ceremonial dances were executed in the light of the blazing fire, accompanied loudly on the drum. The participants, men and boys, stood around the fire, the boys nearer the blaze, all dressed in festive, clean clothing, decorated with fresh conifer twigs which were garlanded around the neck. In the background, and along the left wall from the entrance squatted the women with the small children, while the rest of the space was crowded with spectators. At the right of the entrance on a raised platform stood the leader of the ceremonial, who, with the help of several old Indians, gave

the beat for all the songs. On a rack close to him hung all the regalia of the shamans, heavy with teeth, beaks and other kinds of
rattles, which they wore around the neck, their headgear with its
ermine which cascaded down the back, the dance aprons woven of
mountain goat wool, various masks and many other things. Two
old shamans, recognized by their long, unkempt hair and fantastic headgear, were also present. The songs were sung in chorus,
accompanied by the drum and the beating together of wooden
sticks. The drum was a brightly painted wooden box with one
side covered with skin. It was pounded with the feet. Occasionally the songs were interrupted by the shouting of questions and answers; then all the participants resumed with greater enthusiasm,
shaking their clenched fists and stamping on the floor, as they
moved toward the fire and back again. All these movements were
carried out with extraordinary rhythm and great precision. These
were only short pauses between the individual songs, of which
four were sung with great earnestness and concentration by the
assembly. During the third song two wooden chests were lowered
through the smoke hole, and the masks, rattles and drums which
they contained were unpacked. Each mask was held near the fire
while the song was continued without interruption.

The fourth song was sung in a lively tempo. During the wildest
part, a young Indian, who had remained hidden among the back
rows of the dancers, plunged forward suddenly almost through
the fire toward the wooden drum and fell to the ground unconscious, after some convulsive contortions and when someone
near him had thrown one of the shaman's necklaces over his head.
This was the new shaman. For a time he remained apparently unconscious while the song continued as though nothing had happened. When he gained consciousness he withdrew into the rows
of spectators and soon thereafter the ceremony ended.

The shaman's regalia which was contained in the two chests
was removed in the same way in which it was introduced, namely
through the smoke hole, and as a conclusion to the ceremony
down, which had been lowered through the smoke hole, was blown
into the air. Then the spectators left the building, while the Rav-
en clan, men, women and children remained to begin a four-day
fast. On the evening of the third day the new shaman performed a
dance around the fire, wearing a gaily colored dance blanket and
holding a sharp knife in his hand. On the fourth and final night the
same ceremony which was enacted the first night was repeated,
but we noticed a great release of tension and excitement on the
part of the participants and many of the younger boys had left the
rows of dancers.

I will add here still another description of a curing ceremony
which my brother attended in September 1882 in a temporary
camp of the Huna on Lynn Canal. Songs could be heard coming

from one of the shelters, and as he entered he saw a crowd of people of both sexes who had gathered either as spectators or participants. On a mat beside the fire sat the patient, a five-year-old boy, and at his side was a shaman who looked very old with greying hair that hung in thick strands to his knees. [12] On his head he wore a crown made of wooden sticks, bent to resemble the horns of the mountain goat, which rattled as they struck each other through his movements. Around his neck hung a garland with many decorations. He was naked to the waist, about which was wrapped a brightly colored dancing·blanket. Squatting on his haunches he moved the upper part of his body with such convulsive violence that he soon broke out in a great sweat. In his hand he held a wooden rattle in the figure of a crane and he gesticulated with it as he accompanied his song which he often interrupted with wild groaning. He also used a pair of tongs about three diameters long with which he grasped the feet and then the head of the boy. After a while he took the boy's hands and laying them first on his hips and then his abdomen, and calling out the names of various animals, led him around the fire, first in one direction and then in the opposite one. Several men who were squatting in a circle around the fire beat time on a board with small sticks to a monotonous song and gave answers in one syllable to the sporadic questions asked by the shaman. The women were silent spectators the whole time, as was the father of the boy who had paid the shaman fifty marks (?) in advance for his services. The shaman led the boy around the fire several times more in various directions and after about an hour's work declared that the power of the bad spirits had been broken and the boy was cured. [13]

Witch hunts were conducted by the Tlingit until very recent times in spite of the efforts of the American authorities and the missionaries to discourage them. In the instances brought to our attention the accused were always women. In 1878 two girls were accused of witchcraft in Wrangell and submitted to the most gruesome tortures. They were dragged by the hair to the beach where they were held under water until they were nearly drowned and then laid, naked, on hot ashes. Through the efforts of the missionary one girl was saved from death but on the following night the other one was hanged. [14]

In the summer of 1882 two Chilkat women from Klukwan were accused of witchcraft. To persuade them to confess their guilt, of which they themselves seemed to be convinced, they were bound in such a way that the head was pulled back by tying their hands behind their backs to their braided hair. Then they were beaten with fir branches and thorny whips made of Fatsia horrida. [15] The unfortunate ones succeeded in escapting to the missionary who hid them until they could go south on a steamer.

Even in Sitka, under the very eyes of the American authorities two shamans tried in the winter of 1881 to 1882 to arouse the people to a witch hunt. The shamans were confined for several days in the jail and when they were released their long hair was cut off and hung up in the jail as a warning, but one night the Indians stole it.

The freedom of action which the Tlingit could have enjoyed because they were not restricted by external circumstances was inhibited by their superstition which prevented cultural development. Any departure from custom or anything extraordinary was called "chlakass" and considered as the cause for any mishap, like bad weather, illness, or misfortune in hunting or war. In this way the Chilkat believed that the continuous bad weather in the early months of 1881 was caused by the fact that the previous autumn, through the efforts of the missionary, two children were buried instead of cremated. Fault was also found in the fact that girls were no longer confined at puberty. Other causes for the bad weather were that girls combed their hair outside the house, that the missionary put his snowshoes on in the house, that the school children imitated the cry of wild geese in their playing, and that we washed off the pelt of a mountain goat in sea water and dragged a dead porcupine over the snow. Our Indian companion on another trip absolutely refused to do this, saying that a strong wind would result, and even though the animal was heavy, he carried it on his back to our camp.

Of the means which the Tlingit employ to bring about good weather we have observed the following. On canoe trips they spray water forward and hit the surface of the water with the flat paddle in order to get favorable winds. When bad weather threatened for the next day our Indian companion seized a firebrand from the campfire and swinging it several times around himself, cried "göss, göss" and then threw it behind him. When, on the following day, foggy weather developed he pulled up some plants and earth and bending over threw them behind him between his spread legs.

In the woods near Klukwan, away from a path, three male figures carved of wood stood near a tree trunk; the largest had its right arm raised as in the act of throwing a spear and the middle and smaller figures were near it. It seems that these figures were set out of the way here and were feared. Anyone who approached them stood in danger of death and actually, in a crowd of children who accompanied us, only a half-grown girl dared go near them. All around them were bushes thick with huckleberries while they had been picked almost everywhere else. It is said that in times of stress the Chilkat light a fire on the opposite side of the river from the figures and hope in this way to assuage their anger.

12. Neighboring Tribes

The Haida -- Settlements and tribes -- Physical appearance -- Loss of character through intercourse with
whites -- Clothing, painting and tattooing -- The lip plug
and other decorations -- Hunting and fishing -- Canoes -
- Trade with the Tsimshian -- Cultivation of potatoes --
The native tobacco plant -- Houses and totem poles --
The power of the chief -- Influence of the shaman -- Burial of the shaman -- The feasts of the Haida -- The stick
game -- Wedding customs -- Seclusion of girls -- Naming -- Slaves -- Mourning and burial rites -- Inheritance
-- Division into clans -- Values in trading -- Haida origin myths and the deeds of Ne-kil-stlas, the Raven --
The decrease of population among the Haida.

The Tsimshian -- Settlements and tribes -- Fort Mc-
Loughlin -- The lip plug -- Canoe building -- The ham-
etse or cannibal society -- Bad reputation of the Bella
Bella -- Earliest reports about the interior tribes, the
Gunanas -- Report from the ship's log of the Atuhualpa;
the reports of Veniaminof and Lütke -- The Koltschanen
or Galzanen -- Locations -- Trade relations -- The Ugalenzen and Atna -- The Kenai and Chugach.

The Tlingit are most closely related to their southern neighbors, the Haida and Tsimshian, with whom they have trade relations and also share almost completely their mode of life, customs, and habits. In addition to a slight difference in physical
appearance, it is principally the difference in language which separates these people -- a difference which is so great that Buschmann could see scarcely any likeness. [1]
The Haida[2] have had intercourse with the whites as long as the
Tlingit, but their relations have been limited to occasional visits
from trading vessels; factories and mission stations have only
been established in recent times. For this reason reports about

them are scarce and are scattered in various travel accounts.
The work of Dawson, <u>On the Haida Indians of the Queen Charlotte</u>
<u>Islands</u>, is the only nearly complete work on them, and we will
refer mainly to it for the following account.

The Haida live on the Queen Charlotte Islands which, according
to Dawson, they call Haida-kwea, the little Forrester Islands, and
the southern part of Prince of Wales Island. Those living at the
latter place are called Kaigani, [3] and according to tradition they
are supposed to have come there only about one hundred fifty
years ago.

The census of the Haida shows them to be less numerous than
the Tlingit. Veniaminof estimated eight thousand souls for the
Queen Charlotte Islands and for the Kaigani, including the inhabitants of Tschassin, one thousand three hundred and fifty souls.
Between the years 1836 and 1841 John Work counted six thousand
five hundred and ninety-three Haida on the Queen Charlotte Islands and one thousand seven hundred and thirty-five Kaigani;[4]
the American census in 1880 estimated the number of Kaigani at
only seven hundred and eighty-eight and the present population of
the Queen Charlotte Islands is given by Dawson as not more than
one thousand seven hundred and twenty to two thousand souls.
That the population was once greater might be assumed from the
many deserted settlements and the small numbers living in the
remaining ones. Dawson remarks that not a single village has
even one-tenth of the population its houses were built to contain.
The contact with the whites was also tragic for these gifted people, even though their relations were almost entirely limited to
trading and no invasion of the islands disturbed the lone possession of them by the natives.

The Haida, like the Tlingit, are divided into different tribes
and clans which have animals as totems.

We obtained the names of the following twelve tribes from Mrs.
Dickinson, so often mentioned, who had lived for some time
among the Haida:

Kaigani in the south of Prince of Wales Island. [7]

1. Ssokŏ̆ān hādē (Shaw-a-gan);[5] Shakan[6]
2. Chlen-kŏ̆-ān hādē (Kliuquan)[6]
3. Hau-kan-hādē (How-a-guan);[5] Howakan[6]
4. Gu-ai-hendlas hādē (Qui-a-hanless);[5] Koianglas[6]

Haida on Queen Charlotte Islands

5. Nē̆-kón hādē (Ne-coon)[5]
6. Māss hādē (Massett)[5]
7. Hā̆-jū̄ hādē

8. Kilkáit hādē
9. Kit-kādūss hādē
10. Kit-hai-uáss hādē
11. Rchau-ŭ-tass hādē
12. Kit-ŭïtsach hādē

Radloff makes a few remarks about the Kaigani which he gathered from the writings and conversations of Middendorff, for
many years the director of the magnetic observatory at Sitka.
The latter had obtained his information from a Kaigani, born at
the harbor of Kaigan, [8] named Kuku, who understood English.

According to Middendorff, the Kaigani call themselves Kaigani-
hatl. They use the word hátei, háttei, hátă, hăta as the generic
term for human being. This word hátei is used as a suffix to a
place name to designate the people, as an inhabitant of the Queen
Charlotte Islands (the stone pipe men of Ḵuku's) hátla hattei; the
Aleut, Kuttàks háttei, the Tlingit, Tlinkít hatei, and furthermore
their localities are differentiated, as Stakhin hátei, Hudz-naū
hatei, Heh hátei, Henga hátei, Tschilkàt hatei, T'ak hátei, etc.
The Russians are called Ljuschen-hátă, the English, Engeln-
hátei, the Americans, jèz háta, that is, iron men. [9]

The Haida are regarded as the tallest and most intelligent of
the Northwest Coast Indians. [10] They are distinguished from the
Tlingit by greater breadth of face, and they exceed at least the
southern Tlingit in waist circumference. Dawson describes them
as follows: The principal departures from ideal symmetry are
to be found in the coarsely cut mouth, the broad and prominent
cheek bones, and, in comparison to the body, an unusually large
head. The buttocks are large and long in relation to the legs, a
circumstance undoubtedly due to the fact that these people are
constantly in canoes and seldom travel on land. The hair is black
and coarse, and only among the medicine men did I notice that
the men also let it grow. A sparse mustache and chin beard covered the upper lip and the chin, especially among the old people,
who had given up the practice of pulling out the hair as it appears.
More frequently than among most coast Indians one finds among
them men as well as women who are pleasing in appearance and
even according to European standards have regular features. The
general physiognomy of the Haida points to a higher intelligence
and better comprehension than most Coast natives and closer acquaintance shows this assumption to be correct.

Unfortunately these gifted people have been demoralized
through contact with Europeans. The men have found a means of
income which appeals to their indolence in the prostitution of
their wives and daughters to the prospectors and traders; they
even go to Victoria and follow them to the Cassiar mines to carry
on their contemptible trade.

European clothing has been adopted by the Haida much more widely than among the Tlingit; only among the old people does one find the woolen blanket, that poor substitute for the former sea otter blanket. They paint their faces in the same way and on the same occasions as the Tlingit; also until recent years tattooing was common among them, the arm above the elbow, the leg above the knee, the chest, but never the face, bore the hereditary crest of the wearer. To do this cuts in the skin were filled with a charcoal that produced even blue designs. [11]

Likewise the practice of disfiguring the face with the lip plug has been completely dropped among the Haida as with the Tlingit. Only among some very old women is this custom still found, others content themselves with the silver peg and the younger ones have given it up altogether. Formerly the rim of the ear and the septum of the nose were also pierced, and ornamented.

Hunting and fishing were carried on by the Haida in the same manner as the Tlingit, only they are to a larger degree a fishing people depending for their support entirely on the coast and giving the interior of the islands no attention. They are also famous far and wide for their large and artistic canoes[12] and as courageous seamen they venture in them on the sixty kilometer trip to Prince of Wales Island and to the mainland through Hecate Strait. A number of their canoes which are made of the trunk of the Thuja gigantea are sold to the Tlingit and Tsimshian with whom they carry on active trade. A favorite import in return is the oil of the candlefish (Thaleichthys pacificus Gir.) which is called "tau" by them and not to be found on their coast. For a box which contains about one hundred pounds of fat, they pay six to ten woolen blankets or twelve to twenty dollars.

The cultivation of potatoes is carried on by the Haida more than by the Tlingit, but they give it little attention and produce only small poor tubers. Formerly they cultivated a tobacco plant, the so-called Indian tobacco. The leaves of the plant, which is almost unknown, [13] were dried over the fire and then ground in a stone mortar, which one still finds in almost every household, and finally made into pressed cakes. This tobacco was not smoked in pipes, but mixed with lime of burned shells, it was chewed and held in the cheeks. In consequence of the introduction of real tobacco the custom and the cultivation of this native tobacco was entirely dropped.

The houses of the Haida are built according to the same style as the Tlingit, but seem to be generally larger and more richly ornamented. Also the number of totem poles is much larger, so that there is an average of two to each house. [14] There is a distinction between the one at the entrance of the house, called "kechen" and those erected in memory of the dead, called "chat." At present a new pole is very rarely erected, and the numerous

208

fallen and rotten columns in abandoned or utterly deserted villages are a mute evidence of the rapid downfall of a noteworthy and remarkable culture.

Each village has its chief but his powers are very limited. At the death of a chief, the office goes to his next younger brother, or if there is none, to his nephew.

The influence of the shaman or medicine man who is called "Skā-ga" is greater. Whoever prepares himself for this calling goes alone into the woods and lives frugally on certain herbs, until as a result of his privation his body is lean and his spirit so alert that he sees visions. When he returns he tries his new powers at once in curing the sick by driving away the evil spirits which cause illness through drumming, singing and shaking rattles. Among the ever present paraphernalia of the "Skā-ga," in addition to the noise-making apparatus, is a hollow tube, open at both ends, decorated on the outside and inlaid with abalone. In this bone he captures the spirit, "ka-tlun-dai," when it leaves the body, by stopping both ends of the tube with cedar bark. [15]

Neither shears or a comb may touch the hair of a shaman. When he dies, he is buried in a remote place, designated by him. A shaman's grave investigated by Dawson consisted of a small square box, like a little hut, that on the side away from the water was covered with a well-made cedar bark mat. Against this the body was propped up in a sitting position, with the chin drawn down on the knees. A red woolen blanket covered the corpse; the long hair was carefully tied in a large knot on the forehead and secured with a pair of ornamented bone pins. A carved wand stood in one corner and in front of the knees lay a square wooden box which probably contained other insignia of the deceased.

The feasts which the Haida gave are similar to those of the Tlingit. Dances, songs, eating and the giving of gifts make up the procedure. Most of the songs are sung in the language of the Tsimshian, which points to the conclusion that they were adopted from them. According to Dawson there are six different kinds of dances, the Skā-ga, Ska-dul, Kwai-o-guns-o-lung, Ka-ta-ka-gun, Ska-rut, and Hi-atl.

The stick game is spread among the Haida as well as among all Indians of the Northwest Coast. A clean cedar bark mat is spread between the players who squat on the ground in a circle. Every one brings forth his bundle of clean smooth sticks which have different values according to the designs on them. They are shuffled in a bundle of soft cedar bark and withdrawn at pleasure.

The stick game is described in detail by Poole (Queen Charlotte Islands, p. 319) who compares it with "odd or even." Each person has forty or fifty sticks, highly polished, and ringed in red or black. One of the players takes a number of the sticks and covers them with some finely shredded cedar bark. Under this cover he divides the bundle in two parts which he then passes from one hand to the other, singing I-E-Ly-Yah. When he stops his opponent picks the bundle in which he thinks the right stick is. then the next one in the row plays until one side has lost all the sticks, which decides the game. [16]

Wedding customs of the Haida are as simple as those of the Tlingit. Polygyny is infrequent, only the chiefs occasionally having more than one wife. No high value is placed on chastity among the women, but some of the older authors state that formerly more rigid practices were adhered to. The custom of secluding girls during puberty was practiced by the Haida, but lately it has not been adhered to as closely as formerly. In the past a corner was screened off for the girl where she had her own fireplace. She had to leave the house by a special door in the back wall of the house; if she met any men she quickly covered her face with the corner of her woolen blanket. This seclusion lasted several months and sometimes half a year during which time she wore a headgear woven of cedar bark, round in contour and reaching down to her chest and with an opening for her face.

The first-born son usually receives the name of the mother's brother, the second child that of the next brother or another name of the eldest brother. If there are no brothers, the name of a friend is chosen or the name of the one whose spirit is reincarnated in the newborn child, according to the shaman. Just as among the Tlingit, the idea of reincarnation is common among the Haida. After naming, a ceremony follows when the nose and ears are pierced and at both occasions gifts are distributed. Four times the growing youth takes a new name, each time from his mother's relatives. At later name-giving ceremonies, tattooing is also done. At each ceremony, in addition to the usual dances and singing and gift giving, a new house is built. According to Dawson, the first house building is called "tuch-kucho," the second "ki-au-ni-gecha," the third "chaschl," and the fourth "tlo-cho-kĩs-til."

Formerly the Haida had many slaves, called "Elaidi." A slave was the exclusive property of his master who could do with him as he wished. In the past they were killed and buried under the corner posts of a new house. Also the children of slaves belonged to the master. Special expeditions were undertaken, particularly to the north, into Tlingit territory to get slaves. Now that war between Indian tribes on the west coast has almost disappeared, under the influence of the whites, these expeditions are infrequent and the price of a slave has risen to two hundred woolen blankets.

When a person falls ill, his brother, also the presumptive heir, invites the shaman and the friends of the sick man to a feast during which the shaman, through noise and a dance of exorcism, seeks to drive away the evil spirit with tobacoo. If the sick man dies, the body is put in a sitting position in a square box made of thin cedar slabs such as is used for household purposes, and set in a small grave house which is built to contain one body and generally is behind the house or close to the village. [17] If the deceased is an important person or a chief, the body is set up in his own house which has been cleared of other occupants and his possessions are spread out around him. There he remains on view for about one year and even the people from other villages come to see him. After the final burial of the body, a commemorative pole is erected for him, which is, however, not as artistically made as those in front of the houses. Often these are smooth pillars with a broad board on top on which there are some carved or painted figures. All this is done by the inhabitants of the village for which they are repaid by heirs at a feast when gifts are distributed. According to Dawson, the brother is the heir, or if there is no brother, the nephew, then the sister, and if none of these are at hand, the mother, who then adopts a remote male relative as her son in order to have someone to accept the inheritance. The widow receives a small portion occasionally. If the heir is unmarried he is obligated to marry the man's widow; if, however, he is married then the next of kin marries her.

About the social organization Dawson reports that the Haida are divided into clans which have as crests the eagle, the wolf, the hawk, the black bear, and the killer whale. Since the last two are united, there are only four different clans whose names, given in the same order as above, are Kūt, Kū-ji, Kit-ssi-naka, and Scha-nu-chã. In each tribe the members of these clans are equally represented. Here also the rule holds that a woman must always belong to a different clan from that of her husband and that the children follow the mother. As an exception, if it is desirable to strengthen the clan of the father, a child might be given to his sister to nurse and then be counted into their clan.

Because of their highly developed concepts of property and because a gift demanded a return, the Haida long ago arrived at a native currency. Dentalium, which they called "Kwo-tsing" and which was greatly prized by the Tlingit and other Indian tribes and used by them as currency, was not as highly regarded by the Haida. In contrast, slaves served as a unit of value, but even higher value was assigned to the native cooper which came from the north, probably from the Copper River and which was processed by them into plates of special shape and size, about one-half a meter long and one-fourth a meter wide; ten slaves are supposed to have been paid for such a valuable piece. Now, however, the value of these coppers has fallen because imitations made of ordinary copper have come into circulation, but still they carry a value of forty to eighty woolen blankets. Now among the Haida, as everywhere else on the coast, the woolen blanket is the common unit of value. The blankets made by the Hudson's Bay Company for trade have "points" woven into the border, the best ones having four and being called "four-point blankets," the poorest with only one point. As the common unit of value, the single two and one-half point blanket is used so that one speaks of a four-point blanket as worth so many blankets. Even the Hudson's Bay Company takes these blankets back from the Indians as payment if they are in good condition. Rich people possess several hundred of these blankets, which are carefully folded and laid away in large boxes.

The myths of the Haida are unfortunately not as well known as the Tlingit; however the short abstracts given by Dawson show their likeness to the latter. Because of its importance I will give here a word by word translation of the origin myth of the Haida according to Dawson.

Long ago there was a great flood in which all humans and animals perished except one raven. This raven was not an ordinary bird but, like all animals in old Indian tales, he possessed many human qualities. He could also take off and put on his feather cloak as he wished just like an ordinary garment. It was even told in one version of the myth that he was born of a woman who had no husband and she made a bow and arrows for him. As he grew up, he killed birds, of whose skins she made him a collar or mantle. The birds were the little junco with black heads and necks and the big black and red Mexican sparrow. The name of this being was Ne-kil-stlas. When the flood had run off, Ne-kil-stlas looked around, but he could find no companions nor a wife and he felt very lonely. Finally he took a pecten (Cardium Nuttallii) from the beach and married her, but he still brooded over the lack of a companion. After a while he heard in the shell a faint cry, as that of a newborn child, which gradually became louder, until at last a little girl came forth. Raven married her when she grew up and from this union came all the Indians and the land was populated. [18] At that time man still lacked many things; he had no fire, no daylight, no drinking water, no candlefish. All these things were in the possession of a great chief or a deity who was called "Ssetlin-ki-jasch" and lived at the source of the Nass River. First Ne-kil-stlas got water in the following manner: the chief had a daughter whom Ne-kil-stlas secretly courted. She took him as a lover and without her father's knowledge he visited her at night. The girl fell very much in love with Ne-kil-stlas and trusted him completely, as he had planned. When he thought the time had come to carry out his plans, he told her that he was very thirsty and would like a little drink of water. This the girl brought him in a tightly woven water basket. He drank only a little and, setting the basket beside him, waited until the girl was asleep, whereupon he put on his feather cloak, took the basket in his bill and flew through the smoke hole. Since he was afraid that the chief's people would pursue him he was in a great hurry. Here and there he dropped a little water from which the countless streams originated which one finds in the world today. Over the land of the Haida only a few drops fell like rain, and that is why there are no large rivers in their territory.

Ne-kil-stlas then tried to get fire which was in the possession of the same great chief or powerful being. He did not dare appear again in the house of the chief because he had also lost the favor of his daughter. Therefore, he assumed the form of a single fir needle and let himself down into the water near the house where his former sweetheart came to fill her cup. She scooped up the needle in her water and drank it without noticing it. Soon she became pregnant and after a while bore a child who was none other than the crafty Ne-kil-stlas, who thus gained entry into the house. One day when a favorable opportunity presented itself he got possession of a firebrand and flew with it through the smoke hole. Everywhere he spread the sparks, but one of the first places was on the northern end of Vancouver Island and that is why so many trees there have black bark.

Still people were without daylight and Ne-kil-stlas set it as a problem for himself to get that next. Now he looked for another ruse. He insisted that he also possessed light and stuck to his assertion even though the chief contested the truth of his statement. In some manner he brought into being something that resembled the moon and while the people were out fishing in the eternal night he let it shine a little from under his feather cloak. It threw a weak light over the water and the people and Ssetlin-ki-jasch thought it was the real moon. Angry that he was no longer the sole owner of light, he lost all pleasure in his possession and set out the sun and moon as we know them today.

One thing, however, still remained in the possession of Ssetlin-ki-jasch which the people wanted very much, the candlefish. The cormorant was the friend and companion of the chief and had access to all his wealth, even his supply of candlefish. Ne-kil-stlas now brought about a quarrel between the cormorant and the gull by telling each of them that the other spoke badly about him. Finally they met and after a lively battle of words, they followed his council and started fighting. Ne-kil-stlas knew that the cormorant had a candlefish in his stomach so he told them that they would fight better if they would lie on their backs and kick with their feet. They did this and finally the cormorant disgorged the candlefish which Ne-kil-stlas seized at once. Thereupon he made a canoe out of a rotten log and rubbed the scales of the candlefish all over the canoe and himself. When, during the night, he came to the house of the great chief he asked to be admitted because he was so cold. He said he had made a great catch of candlefish which he had left nearby. Ssetlin-ki-jasch replied that this was not true because he had all the candlefish, but Ne-kil-stlas challenged the chief to look at his canoe and his clothing. Since they were covered with scales, he was convinced that in addition to his candlefish others must exist and again growing angry because he was not in sole possession of the candlefish, he set them all free and said that every year they would come in great schools to honor his generosity and in memory of his name. This has happened since that time.

In the collection of Haida myths the thunderbird also plays an important role. When he needs nourishment he puts on his feather cloak and raises himself in the air so that his body darkens the heavens and the rush of his wings causes the thunder. Under his wings he hides a little fish which he has gotten out of the sea. He throws this with great force when he sees a whale and the snakelike tongue of the animal appears as lightning. [19]

Radloff reports that the Kaigani believe that the souls of those fallen in war (Tahit) appear to the living in the northern lights while those who die a natural death (zike-kaua) stay on earth. Therefore, it is said "hallgōa tahit kitzatlāng koān," "last night many tahits came," in other words, there was a strong northern light display. They also call them sa hatei or fallen people.

Time is reckoned by the Kaigani according to the phases of the moon and is counted not by days but by nights. [20]

The Tsimshian or Tsimshian Indians[21] live on the mainland between the Nass River and the Skeena River. They are divided into many tribes and number altogether about five thousand to six thousand, being as powerful as the Tlingit and Haida. In 1845 Lieutenants Warre and Vovasour at the request of the Hudson's Bay Company made the following report:

    4 tribes of Nass Indians with 1615 persons
    10 tribes of Chymsyan Indians with 2495 persons
    2 tribes of Skeena Indians with 322 persons

Veniaminof estimated their number about six thousand. According to information given us by a Tsimshian Indian woman, the Tsimshian are divided into fifteen tribes, as follows:[22]

On the Tsimshian Peninsula near Fort Simpson

    1. kīsch-păch-lă-óts
    2. kīts-āch-lă-āl'ch
    3. kīt-wulg-jats
    4. kīts-iïsch
    5. killūtsār

6. kittlĕān
7. kittandó
8. kĭn-nach-hangīk
9. kinnatō-iks
10. kit-wúlkse-bē
11. kittrālchlă

On the Skeena River and southwards

12. kĭtselāssir
13. kĭtkāĕt
14. kĭtraŭ-ai-iks

15. nüss-kā On the Nass River

The Tsimshian Indians wore the lip plug, but even in 1841 when
Simpson visited Port Simpson the custom was disappearing. The
Tsimshian are famous for their artistic work in stone, wood, and
bone. The houses here were better than elsewhere on the coast,
according to Simpson. [23]
   In consequence of the missionary activities of Duncan and Crosby, which will be more fully discussed in the following chapter,
the old customs have fallen into disuse and have almost been forgotten. In general the customs of the Tsimshian were probably
not very different from those of the Haida; however, here we encounter the trait of eating both dog and human flesh as a religious custom which is highly developed among the southern
tribes, especially on Vancouver Island, while among the Tlingit
and Haida nothing definite was observed along this line. About
this unusual custom we have only untrustworthy information from
which the true meaning cannot be discovered. The following description is reported by Mayne who took it from the accounts giv-
en by Duncan of his first years of missionary endeavor.
   "An old chief of the Tsimshian had an old female slave killed,
either to bring about the recovery of his daughter who had suffered a gunshot wound in the arm, or to serve her after death in
the next world. The body was thrown on the beach. Thereupon
two crowds of raving people appeared, each led by a naked man.
The two leaders moved forward, prancing like two proud horses,
and at the same time, alternating the right and left arm,
stretched it full length in a challenging position which they held
for some time. Simultaneously they threw their heads back so as
to shake their long flowing hair.
   "For a while they seemed to hunt for the corpse; but when they
found it they began to scream and run around like hungry wolves.
Finally they seized it and dragged it out of the water onto the
beach and there, as I was told, to tear it apart with their teeth.

Since the followers formed a close circle about the leaders, my vision of the scene was blocked, but after a few minutes they separated again and each of the naked cannibals had half of the corpse in his hands. After they had gone a few more steps away from each other they started with horrible howling on their even more horrible feast."[24]

Duncan further related that between eight and ten different societies of medicine men carried on their activities during the winter and that they could be divided into three classes; those who ate human flesh, those who devoured dogs, and finally those who did neither of these. Each of these societies initiate their novices, usually only one at a time. Early in the morning these novices go down to the beach where with constant screaming they crawl around and shake their heads until a crowd of men rush out, encircle them and start to sing. The dog eaters now bring along a dead dog which in dog fashion they tear apart with their teeth.

According to Dawson[25] there are four religions among the Tsimshian, which are called Sim-ha-lait, Mi-hla, Noo-hlem, and Hop-pop and which are independent of the divisions into tribes and clans. The first of these religiions is the simplest and has no striking ceremonies connected with it. The devotees of the second are supposed to worship a little black picture which is known as "the only one above." The Noo-hlem are the dog eaters and the Hop-pop, the cannibals, a name which they have because that is their cry when they go out in a real or fictitious rage to eat human flesh. As a consequence, all those who belong to the other religions try to stay out of the way of these maniacs, but those who belong offer their arms and allow pieces of flesh to be bitten out of them. A man can belong to more than one religion and as a matter of fact can be forced to join a second. [26]

About the origin of the Tsimshian we heard the following story: The Tsimshian came out of the interior down the Skeena River, but found the river barred by two glaciers that filled it from bank to bank. The river flowed through a dark cavern. They were ready to give up the journey when a man along in years offered to try to find a way. After he had sung the death song he went in his canoe into the cavern. From the glacier which some had climbed they saw him come out. Thereupon they went the same way and arrived safely at the mouth of the river where they settled.

While the Haida carry on active trade with the Tsimshian and, as Dawson reports, largely understand their language and have taken over their dances and songs, they are bitter enemies of the Bilballa or Bella Bella who live on the mainland further south and with whom they fight on their journeys to Victoria. [27]

The tribes of the Bella Bella are the following, according to information given us:

1. uúts-tá
2. kĭt-máchla-kach
3. kĭt-la-ōp (kit lope according to Schoolcraft)
4. kĭt-ă-mat (kit ta maat according to Schoolcraft)
5. kŏá-kŭlch
6. tlatlē-ssē-kŏ-lá
7. chlā-ūtsiss
8. jākŭlch-tăch

The Hudson's Bay Company founded Fort McLoughlin in Bella Bella territory. It was here that George Simpson, on his trip around the world in 1841-1842, saw the first lip plug. [28] The Bella Bella also are competent in canoe building. Simpson saw a canoe sixty feet long, four and one-half feet deep, and six and one-half feet broad which could carry one hundred persons and was made of one piece from stem to stern.

The chiefs are supposed occasionally to pretend insanity and rush into the woods, eat grass, and gnaw on the ribs of corpses. When they return they attack everyone they meet and bite a piece of flesh out of their arms and legs, which they swallow. [29]

According to Dunn the "Sebassa" who are identified as the Bella Bella were more active and enterprising than their southern neighbors, but also the worst thieves and robbers on the coast. Their villages were built by preference on high, steep islands or cliffs. The chief had numerous wives and many slaves; and these Indians also carried on energetic slave raids and trade. [30]

The earliest accounts of the neighbors of the Tlingit to the interior are found in the log of an American ship Atahualpa, published by the Massachusetts Historical Society. On August 25, 1802, it says: [31] "I had a conversation with Cou about several tribes who inhabit the country east of the Stikine. He had gotten his information from Cockshoo, the chief of the Stikine, who had been among them several times to trade. According to his description they resemble the local Indians, only they are larger. The men have short hair that hangs over their foreheads and the women are not disfigured with a lip plug or anything else. They are a frightened sex; at the approach of danger they flee into any kind of hiding and emit terrible screams. They dress in a mantle or kind of skirt and a trouserlike garment both of which being made of buckskin like the "Elammel" (armor) of the south. They live on venison, bear and other animals gotten by hunting for which they use bows and arrows, larger and better made than those of the coast Indians. They live in level country and are confirmed wanderers. When the ground is covered they use snowshoes.

"The language of these tribes is entirely different from that of the Stikine. They learned the use of iron only recently when the Stikine traded them knives, forks, etc. for food (what kind I

217

could not determine). "

The name Kunana or Gunana[32] applied to these people is first
found in Veniaminof. "The peoples who inhabit the mainland of
America," he says, [33] "are known to us under the name of tundra dwellers, but the Kolushans call them Kunana which means
'northern' or 'atakuan,' meaning 'in the north,' where the sky
touches the earth. The American tundra dwellers differ completely from the Kolushans in habits, clothing and speech, but,
except for the lip plug of the women, they have the same religion
and the same customs as the Kolushans." Lütke[34] speaks of a
people who live in the mountains to the north and whom the Tlingit call Konlan who differ from them in language and customs and
practice cannibalism. Formerly they had bows and stone-tipped
arrows, but now they have gotten guns and ammunition from the
neighboring Tlingit who trade them for fox and sable skins and
native copper. The Konlan are supposed to have connections
across the mountains with the natives of the Copper River and the
Chugach Sea. [35]

The Gunanas, who are called "Stick Indians" by the Americans
because of their custom of wearing a quill or skewer through the
septum of the nose, probably belong to the Athapascan or Tinne
tribes. We have not positively found out what they call themselves. Perhaps the Niharnies of Simpson and the Nehaunes of
Dall are the same people. [36]

They are a peaceful little group who have no fixed dwelling
sites and live by hunting. In trading with the Tlingit, as we have
seen, they are dealt with tyrannically and badly overcharged.

Wrangell says that westward from Cape St. Elias live the
Ugalenzen, [37] a small group of not more than thirty-eight families. In winter they stay in a little bay on Kajak[38] Island (not Kad-
jack, as Wrangell writes it), and in summer they move eastward
to the mouth of the Copper River for fishing. They are described
as a peace loving and amiable people who live entirely like the
Kolushans, specifically the Yakutat, with whom they are related
by intermarriage. Their language is supposed to differ from the
Kolushan but to have the same roots, so that both people should
be regarded as two different clans of one and the same tribe.
They are called Ugalenzen by the Yakutat as well as by the Atna,
the people who live on the Copper River. [39]

According to Veniaminof the language of the Ugalenzen is only
a dialect of Yakutat. Holmberg gives in the accompanying descriptions to his map the site Alaghanik in a bay northeast of the
mouth of the Copper River as the principal village of the Ugalenzen. It is the place which on the latest American map[40] is
marked as Alaghanik.

The neighboring Eskimo tribes call the Ugalenzen "Ugalachmut," a name by which they were mentioned by Shelikof. Neither

Ugalenzen nor Ugalachmut is the name by which they call themselves since the first has a Russian ending and the second an Eskimo ending for the name of a tribe, but both point to the name "Ugalach."

Dall's opinion that the Ugalenzen belong to the Innuit[41] not only contradicts Wrangell and Veniaminof but also disagrees with the linguistic research of Radloff, whose results cannot be doubted. He claims that the Ugalenzen are actually an independent people, however related to the Tlingit. "Even though the Ugalachmut," says Radloff, "through their geographical location and the description of their customs given by Wrangell, show themselves to be related to tribes which belong to three different linguistic groups, namely the Kadjaken and the Tschugatschen (Eskimos), the Atnahs, an Athapascan people belonging to the Kinai, and finally the Kolushans, their language shows little relationship to the first two. It can be stated with certainty that there is no relationship between the Eskimo dialect and Ugalachmut."[42]

However Radloff found among the one thousand one hundred recorded words of Ugalachmut from the vocabularies of Resanof about forty which bear phonetic and structural resemblance to Tlingit words.[43]

According to Wrangell, the Atna are related to the Kolushans. At that time there were about sixty families who had friendly relationship with the surrounding peoples. They knew how to make axes, knives, breast plates and other articles of the native copper in their territory. They are also supposed to have been the only ones who could work the iron which was received from the Russians. Their principal business was the hunting of caribou.

Their customs and myths, according to the meager information given by Wrangell, differ little from the Tlingit; even in their language there are resemblances.[44]

Veniaminof[45] related the inhabitants of the Copper River, whom he called Atachtani, to the Ttynai,[46] to which Radloff agreed. Dall, who also counts them among the Tinne tribes, became acquainted with them in 1874 at Port Etches where they come every year to trade, and according to him they call themselves Ah-tena.[47]

The Kenai are supposed to call themselves Tnaina (from tnai or ttenai, meaning human being) and live, with a population of about four hundred and sixty families, on the shores of Cook Inlet and on Iliamna and Kisshik lakes. They too, according to Wrangell, belong to the same tribe as the Kolushan even though there is scarcely any resemblance in their languages. The Kenai are also supposed to regard the Raven as the Creator; from various materials he created two women of whom one became the matriarch of five, the other, of six clans. The men must, according to ancient custom, take their wives from another tribe; the children are counted in the tribe and clan of the mother; inheritance is passed on to the sister's son.

After the wailing is over and his goods have been distributed among his relatives, the corpse is cremated in the presence of friends and the remains are buried. His successor prepares a memorial feast after one year at which the friends who helped at the funeral are the guests and receive presents. From this time on the name of the dead may no longer be mentioned.

The Kenai use birchbark canoes for transportaion on the rivers and lakes, like the people of the interior, which speaks again of their relationship. On the coast, however, they use skin boats which they undoubtedly borrowed from the Chugach or from the inhabitants of Kodiak. In addition to hunting and fishing they carry on an active trade with the Galzan. [48]

Buschmann regards the Kenai to whom he adds the Atna and Ugalents as a principal group of the Athapascans, which opinion Radloff shares. Dall[49] calls them, following Ross, Tehanin-Kutchin, but in accordance with the Atna they should call themselves K'nai'a-Khota'na. [50]

Even in the language of the Kenai many Tlingit words have been incorporated. [51]

Wrangell called the tribes who live in the river valleys to the north and east of the Atna Koltschanen or Galzanen, as well as those farther toward the other side of the mountains, who are however distinguished by the Atna as another people. The Atna called them Koltschanen[52] meaning "stranger." The closer ones came down along the river to the coast to sell caribou skins to the Russians. They are supposed to belong to the same tribe as the Atna and Kenai and understand them, even though they speak another dialect.

The more distant Koltschanen, whom the coast tribes only know by hearsay, are considered very cruel by them and are supposed, in case of need, to satisfy their hunger on human flesh.

The Kenai call these people Galzanen, meaning "guests." The Kenai meet them on the other side of the mountains during the caribou hunting season at the end of the summer and trade with them. From the Galzanen whose nearest settlement on the Copper River is called Nutatlgat, they are said to get caribou skins as well as European wares of English origin which they probably got from the Chilkat on Lynn Canal. [53]

From these accounts, meager as they are, it appears that the name Koltschanen as well as Gunana is used generally by the coast people for the various Tinne or Athapascan tribes of the interior. According to Dall, the Tut-chone-kutchin who live on the Yukon River from Deer River to Fort Selkirk and along the tributaries coming from the St. Elias range are the Koltschanen of the Russians.

At Prince William Sound (Chugach Sea) and on the coast of the Kenai Peninsula westwards to the entrance of Cook Inlet the Chugach live who belong to the Eskimo tribes and who are like the inhabitants of Kodiak both in language and customs. [54]

13. Missions and Efforts at Civilization

The first Russian missionaries, Father Juvenali and
Bishop Joasaf -- Shipwreck of the Phenix -- The efforts
at civilization by Resanof and Baranof -- Veniaminof in
Sitka -- The smallpox epidemic in 1835 -- Results of the
attempts at conversion -- Establishment of schools --
Unfortunate results of the change of government -- Mis-
sionary work in British Columbia -- Mr. Duncan at
Fort Simpson -- Founding of the mission village of Met-
lakatla -- The success of Duncan -- The Tsimshian at
Fort Wrangell -- The Rev. Dr. Sheldon Jackson and
Mrs. McFarland -- The Presbyterian school in Sitka --
Arbitrary rulings of the Commanders -- The Industrial
Home for Boys -- The mission among the Chilkat --
Mrs. Dickinson and Rev. Willard -- Missions among the
Huna, Taku and Kaigani -- The Russian church at Sitka -
- The Roman Catholic mission at Wrangell -- The re-
sults of missionary efforts -- Prospects for the future.

In 1793 Empress Catherine II at the request of Baranof and
Shelikof issued a ukase that priests should be sent to the new
American colonies in order to spread Christianity among the
heathen. As a result of this command the ship The Three Holy
Apostles was sent to the colonies with seven monks, among them
Joasaf, an Augustinian, through whose efforts in 1796 the first
Christian church was built on Kodiak. In the same year the Greek
Orthodox Church had to mourn her first and only martyr in the
colonies, Father Juvenali, who was killed by the natives at Lake
Iliamna. An even harder blow was struck at the newly founded
mission in 1799. Joasaf, who had become a bishop had gone to
Irkutsk for his investiture; when he was coming back to his territory from Okhotsk on the Phenix, it sank with all men aboard, including several clergy in addition to the new bishop. Through this
accident the colonies were left almost without any spiritual help.

Until 1809 the monk Athanasias was the only one who could perform sacred rites. Sitka remained until 1816 without any representatives of the church, in spite of the fact that since 1808 it had been the seat of the government. An officer of the Company undertook the spiritual functions until 1816 when the priest Sokoloff arrived, having been sent by the synod of St. Petersburg at Baranof's urgent request. [1]

With the establishment of schools, Chamberlain Resanof, who came to the colonies with the most idealistic intentions, really made a beginning. At his insistence a school was opened at Kodiak in 1805; he also gave impetus to the founding of a library at Sitka, which grew steadily under the directorship of Wrangell to about one thousand seven hundred volumes. Baranof constantly kept the conversion and civilizing of the natives in mind, but his efforts had only meager results among the Tlingit. In the last years of his administration he sent a prominent Tlingit, the brother of the chief Nauschket, together with others to Europe, but none of them returned. [2]

With the renewal of the privileges of the Company in 1821, at the request of the highest administration, three new clergy were sent to the colony from Irkutsk, among them Ivan Veniaminof, a man of remarkable talents and knowledge, who devoted himself with untiring energy and with great success to the education of the natives and who did not satisfy himself with entering their names on the rolls of the church through baptism but who sought to learn their characteristics, their customs, and their speech in order to understand them more fully. Veniaminof began his work on Unalaska in 1824. After he had worked with rewarding results for nine years among the Aleut where he was active in the spreading the Russian faith and the Russian language, he came to Sitka in 1834 to work for the welfare of the Tlingit, but as he himself tells it, with poor results in the beginning. "In spite of how well I became acquainted with the Tlingit and how friendly our intercourse was, a long period of time passed before they were satisfied as to my knowledge and ability. After I had been there three years, in 1834,[3] I tried without success to persuade them to use smallpox vaccine. In 1835 the smallpox epidemic came and decreased their population by almost half and while the Tlingit, knowing it to be contagious, wished that the Russians would also get it, not one Russian succumbed to the disease. Now they saw that the Russians had greater knowledge than they, and their own cures of ice and snow and the shamans' practice had not helped them, so they flocked in droves and from great distances to the Russian doctor in order that he might vaccinate them and their children. In one year two hundred and fifty Tlingits were vaccinated." So, as Veniaminof thinks, the smallpox epidemic of 1835, since it convinced the Tlingit of the obviously superior knowledge of the whites and shattered their faith in the shaman, became the turning point in their spiritual development.

Even though they allowed only a very few baptisms (until 1839 there had been only twenty), they in no way hindered those who wished it and did not cast them out of their society. Veniaminof thought that since they liked to attend the religious ceremonies of the Russians and through their good behavior and restraint from every kind of disturbance showed their reverence and listened attentively to the telling of Bible stories, the natives showed their inclination to Christianity. Still he feared that the apprehension, that acceptance of the religion would bring them under the domination of the Russians, as it did the Aleut, would prevent this step for a long time. [4]

In 1843 there were one hundred and two Christians among the Tlingit and that included, remarkably enough, two shamans. A church for worship in the native language was erected in 1849. Especially zealous in the spreading of Christianity among the Tlingit was the churchman, Litwinzof, who in the period of five years, 1847-52, baptized one hundred and fifty children of both sexes, thus increasing the number of Christians to three hundred and fifty souls. Still the attendance at church by the Tlingit during their fight against the Russians in 1855 showed that their reverence for their new faith was not very great. In 1860 there were four hundred and forty-seven Christian Tlingit, two hundred and twenty-one men and two hundred and twenty-six women. [5]

Veniaminof paid special attention to instruction in the schools. After he was appointed as Bishop in 1840 under the name of Innocent, he founded a seminar the following year which in 1842 had twenty-three students, creoles and natives; and after the transfer of the bishopric to Jakutsk in 1853 the seminar was located there also. [6]

In 1844 Veniaminof began assembling the children of the natives in the chapel in his home and teaching them Christian principles. His example was followed by all the clergy in the district and thus schools began in connection with all churches and many chapels in which the children of the natives received instruction in the Christian religion and in reading and writing as well. [7]

In addition to these religious schools there were also schools mainly for the officials and servants of the company maintained by the colonial administration. In New Archangel there was a boys' and a girls' school, the former founded soon after the beginning of the settlement, the latter in 1839. From these schools the best pupils were sent to St. Petersberg at the expense of the Company in order to be educated in the various arts and skills. In 1860 a special colonial school was opened for the children of the officers of the company. [8]

The constantly growing missionary activity and school development came to a complete standstill in 1867 when Alaska was taken over by the United States. The Russian schools in Sitka were closed and, on the part of the American government, nothing was done for the building and maintainance of new ones. Only ten years later, at the initiative of the Board of Home Missions of the Presbyterian Church, missionary activity was resumed in Southeastern Alaska.

The incentive for this was the successful missionary work which had been going on for a number of years in the neighboring British territory among the Tsimshian. It is timely to give some more details about this because it played such an important part in the development of all the Indian population of the Northwest Coast, on account of their active intercourse with each other.

In 1857 the missionary activity in British Columbia began, except for a few efforts of Catholic missionaries, who did not seem to have any particular success, when Mr. Duncan, a student at Highbury College in London, was sent out by the Church Missionary Society, started his activities at Fort Simpson, a trading post erected among the Tsimshian by the Hudson's Bay Company. In the beginning he truly had to combat great difficulties, but his ceaseless efforts succeeded, especially when he achieved some facility in the use of the Tsimshian language and could convince the natives of the superstitious nature of their beliefs. By the fall of 1858 he had triumphed to such a degree over the greedy nature of the Indians that he had their support and help in building a new schoolhouse. When he began instruction in the new house he had one hundred children and fifty adults as pupils. The winter season, however, brought new conflict. Only part of the Tsimshian were willing to forego the shamans' feasts; the others, with the principal chief at their head, insisted on the celebration and demanded of Duncan that he dismiss school during that time. Finally Duncan's diplomacy won over all difficulties and about 1861 he could at last carry out a plan he had long had in mind and with which he deservedly won great success. He had discovered that the vicinity of the fort was not a salutary place for Indian settlements and his own work there was hindered. There the Indians were exposed to the temptations of the liquor dealers, were witness of licentious living which took place on many ships that visited the fort, and constantly had the example of their heathen neighbors before them, reminding them of their old traditions and customs. Therefore Duncan decided to lead his faithful congregation to another place, and after careful investigation chose a place called Metla-Katla or Metla-Kah, [9] which lay on a narrow channel between the Tsimshian Peninsula and a small island, about twenty kilometers south of Fort Simpson. At this place there used to be the old village of the Tsimshian, but since the Hudson's Bay post was erected further north, because the narrow channel was not suitable for sailing vessels, the Indians had also moved their village site. But they themselves were not satisfied with the move and supported Duncan in his desire to lead them back to their old home which, in additon to their present needs, also had a roomy and sheltered beach for canoes and large pieces of land suitable for cultivation.

The move under Duncan's leadership constituted a complete break with their past on the part of all the participants. They had to pledge themselves to forego all heathen rites and put themselves completely at Duncan's disposal. Each man had to build his own house, not according to the customary plan of Indian houses, but like European dwellings. The necessary lumber was brought from outside, but the shingles for the roofs the Indians themselves prepared. In place of Indian clothing European garments came into use. The filth which is customary in Indian villages was not to be found here; Duncan was strong on cleanliness. For alien tribes who visited the new colony for trading purposes, a special structure was set up so that the visitors would not soil the dwellings of the colonists. After their departure, the space occupied by them was thoroughly cleaned and fumigated. A uniformed police saw to maintenance of order. To cover the cost of administration a tax was levied which could be paid in money, woolen blankets, or other goods. In addition adults were obliged to give their services for community projects, like the building of streets. In addition to his spiritual ministrations and his instruction, Duncan taught the Indians various handcrafts, took care of the business and trade enterprises, served as doctor, builder and judge, and conducted the administration of the place with such success that he raised the Indian settlement to being the model village of the whole coast, and made his own name known everywhere, even among the most remote tribes of the Tlingit. Duncan was appointed as justice of the peace by Governor Douglas and so was given authority over the white traders and prospectors, which he needed to protect his congregation. Also in recognition of his work, the government authorities were advised to support him in his efforts. [10]

In 1878 Metlakatla possessed its own schooner which made regular commercial trips to Victoria, a community warehouse, a merchandise store for alien Indians, a soap factory, a smithy, a sawmill, a schoolhouse which cost about four thousand dollars; a large building for public assemblies, courts and the care of strangers; a mission house, a church, a woolen mill, a rope and cord factory, a tanning establishment, a shoe factory and much else. [11]

The population was about eight hundred to one thousand. About one hundred and fifty children of both sexes in clean, neat clothes, were instructed at the school. In the beautiful church built by the

Indians under Duncan's leadership, there were places for twelve
hundred people. Reverend Collison and his wife helped Duncan in
his work; also Dr. Ridley, the Bishop of New Caledonia, had assumed his position. [12]

The success of Duncan stimulated missionary activity in other
places in British Columbia. The position vacated by Duncan's
move from Fort Simpson was filled by Reverend Crosby about
whose effectiveness favorable reports are at hand. [13]

From British Columbia, as was mentioned, the movement
spread to neighboring Alaska. In the spring of 1876 nine Tsimshian Indians came from Fort Simpson to Fort Wrangell in Alaska to cut wood for the military post. During their stay they celebrated each Sunday, according to their habit, with religious services, in which they were supported by the Commander of the station with the use of a proper room and the supply of hymn books.
When they were ready to return in the fall, the leader of these Indians, named Clah, also known as McKay, was asked to stay behind and open a school which was attended eagerly not only by
children but by adults. The eagerness to learn displayed by these
people moved the soldiers at the fort to write a letter to Major
General Howard, expressing the wish that some denomination
take it upon itself to send an accredited teacher. Through the publication of this letter in all the missionary journals general interest in Alaska was aroused. That same year, 1877, Dr. Sheldon
Jackson, a missionary preacher, undertook an exploratory trip
to southeastern Alaska for the Presbyterian Board of Home Missions, accompanied by Mrs. McFarland, a missionary, who at
once undertook the conduct of the school at Wrangell. The following year a girls' home, the McFarland Home, was founded in order to prevent the sale of girls by their own parents to the prospectors and traders. In 1882 the McFarland Home, which since
1879 had been housed along with the school in a two-story building, cared for about thirty inmates, while the school conducted
by Miss Dunbar had an average attendance of sixty day pupils. A
church was also completed in 1879; Reverend S. H. Young had
functioned as clergyman since 1878. For the children of the many
alien Indians Rev. Dr. Corlies had a school on the beach; the
adults were instructed by Corlies and Young in the evening. In
1878 a school was also opened at Sitka, but it continued only a
few months. In 1880 it was reopened under the direction of Mrs.
Olinda Austin and moved to the old Russian hospital. Through the
support of Captains Beardlee and Glass, who commanded the A-
merican warships stationed in the waters of southeastern Alaska,
this school became quite important, for Captain Glass ordered
compulsory school attendance of all Indian children between the
ages of five and nineteen, along with other judicious regulations.
In order to improve the health of the Indian village he ordered,

first, a thorough cleaning, the whitewashing of every house, and the provision of a drainage ditch. For better control of the community each house received a number and an accurate count was made of the inhabitants, adults as well as children. Further, every child had to wear a tin marker with the number of the house and his own number around his neck. Then if a child was found on the street during school hours, the Indian policemen looked at his tag and made note of it while the teacher could also

Mrs. Dickinson

easily find out what numbers were absent from each house. The following day the head of the house was summoned to account for the absence of the child from school, and if there was not sufficient reason for it, was fined a woolen blanket or a day in jail. Few punishments were necessary to bring all the children to school and in this way the attendance rose to an average of two hundred and thirty to two hundred and fifty daily. With the support of Captain Glass the old Russian hospital was remodeled into a training school which was called the Sheldon Jackson Institute. The building as well as the development of a garden was the work of the inmates themselves. Also the Lutheran chapel, built by Etolin, which, since the transfer of the territory to the United States, had stood deserted and half destroyed, was rebuilt by the Mission. When on a cold wintry night in 1882 the old hospital was destroyed completely by fire, a new "Industrial Home for Boys" was built in Sitka through contributions taken up in the eastern states and prepared for the care of one hundred inmates.

In the meantime missionary activities were begun among other tribes of the Tlingit. At the suggestion of Jackson, who frequently traveled in southeastern Alaska for this purpose, a school was opened in 1880 in Chilkoot, at the factory of the Northwest Trading Company, by Mrs. Dickinson, the Tsimshian wife of the trader, who is often mentioned in this book; and its direction in later years, after the erection of a dwelling as well as a school building, was turned over to a Presbyterian clergyman, Rev. Willard. According to the mission report, the school had seventy pupils in the winter of 1881 to 1882. A special school was next opened in the Chilkat village of Klokwan in a house loaned for the purpose by the Indians where a half-breed Indian named Paul and his wife, an Indian raised at Fort Wrangell, instructed sixty children. Also in connection with the factory of the Northwest Trading Company at Gaudekan, the Huna village on Cross Sound, a school was opened in 1880 under the leadership of a Mr. Styles; according to a report in March 1882, it was attended by eighty students. In the summer of 1881 Rev. Dr. Corlies conducted a school on Taku River above its mouth in a fishing village, and the following year he moved to a settlement of the same tribe just below Juneau. It is also mentioned that in 1881, under the auspices of the same Presbyterian Board of Home Missions, Mr. Chapman opened a school at Howkan among the Kaigani, the Haida living at the south end of Prince of Wales Island. After that, in the next summer, when school, church, and mission buildings had been erected, Reverend Gould took over the direction of the station.

The mission field in southeastern Alaska was, however, not left to the Presbyterian church alone; in Sitka a priest was supported by the Russian government and the so-called Creoles, that is, the offspring of Russian and Aleuts, as well as a portion of the Indians, adhered to the Greek Catholic faith. In Wrangell, finally, a Roman Catholic mission was founded and a Catholic church was built.

Here the relationship of the rival religious faiths was not uplifting, and the Indians who visited first one then the other church found pleasure in increasing the animosity through false statements. The situation was better in Sitka where the present Russian priest completely discontinued the proselytizing of his predecessors who persuaded the Indians, through a gift of a new shirt with a red cross, to allow themselves to be baptized two and three times. But nevertheless the revelation of the rich splendor

of the Greek faith found sympathetic appreciation among these Indians and made such an impression on them that a large number
of the natives became adherents exclusively of the Russian
church. For them it was a sign of the superiority of the Russian
church when in the winter of 1882 the Presbyterian mission
school burned to the ground and the house of the Russian priest
directly next door was untouched.

The Presbyterian mission had been erected and maintained
without state support; but in 1882 a request was made of Congress for $50,000 for educational work in Alaska.

According to the current reports of the missionaries themselves regarding their efforts, the possibility of further civilizing the Tlingit holds a great future, but these statements are all
too optimistic and highly colored. It is true that the Tlingit Indians in almost every place are favorably inclined to the building
of schools, but to every outsider it is obvious that selfish mo-
tives, above all, ambition to imitate the white man, are the driving forces behind this amiability. It is on the whole not difficult
to persuade the Indians not to work on Sunday, especially not as
it happened when a canoe accidentally overturned and this was
represented as a punishment of God for the breaking of the Sab-
bath. In the days of the fish run, however, as with herring and
salmon, where every loss of time means loss of food in consequence, the warnings of the missionaries, who foolishly demanded that work be stopped, were not heeded.

It satisfies the vanity of the Indians to go to church on Sunday
in ceremonious fashion, perhaps with white linen and a high hat.
With apparent attention he listens to the sermon, which he com-
prehends either not at all or only in part, but he still has the feeling that he is participating in a worthy cause. But, just as for
every other service, he expects a reward for it, and it was in accordance with true Indian custom when the Chilkat, after they had
gone to church for half a year and sent their children to school,
went to the missionary and complained that they had not been rewarded for their virtue and had not received boards to build their
houses as the Tsimshian had.

Whatever results the missionary endeavor has had, it is not of
great consequence. The Sitka, to whom the gospel was preached
during the Russian regime by men of such outstanding ability as
Father Veniaminof, now stand in the worst repute. Here as elsewhere the good influence which the teachers of the Christian
church have had was cancelled out by the damaging results of contact with civilization and intercourse with lawless whites who had
no regard for the rights of the natives.

The living habits of the Indians were also a great hindrance in
the civilizing process. If the missionary had achieved any results during the winter through regular attendance at school and
230

church, then he was certain that they would be lost again during
the summer when the inhabitants scattered for hunting and fishing. To this must also be added that fact that many persons were
attracted to the missionary work who were not suited to their
posts and had no understanding of the Indian character and customs and so satisfied themselves with superficial results. Only a
few made a serious effort to learn the language of the natives;
most of them contented themselves with the meager Chinook jargon, the common trade language of the Northwest Coast from the
Columbia River northwards to the Alexander Archipelago, which
is sufficient for trading purposes but totally unsuitable for the expression of religious and moral ideas.

Even though the efforts at civilizing the Tlingit have had slight
results, up to the present it is not hopeless, provided they are
carried forward in a sensible and systematic manner. Surely a-
mong the Tlingit and the other Indian tribes of the Northwest
Coast, like the Haida and the Tsimshian, better conditions exist
for such an ultimate goal than among the nomadic hunters of the
interior. Furthermore the former, at least since ancient times,
have been in permanent settlements in winter; also fishing is carried on in large groups. They are not adverse to changes in their
mode of life, everywhere potatoes are already grown in larger or
smaller amounts. Also these Indians do not flee at the approach
of whites; on the contrary they leave their village sites to settle
nearer the trading posts, the salmon fisheries, the gold mining
or other places where there are opportunities for easy gain. The
particular characteristics of the Tlingit which were unattractive
to the traveler -- his well-developed greed, his vanity, and his
distrust -- may well become a foundation for progress since they
tend to overcome their innate indolence.

The unfavorable climate and soil condition would have given the
natives an edge in the race with the white immigrants for a long
time, had not fairly rich finds of gold brought a stronger flow of
population. On the other hand, the material condition of the population is not unfavorable; famine is scarcely ever feared; also it
is not necessary to change the mode of life of the natives and introduce new ways of livelihood, but the oldest and most natural
resources of the country, namely, fishing and trade, promise
further development. But the problem of leading the native population toward civilization should not be left to individual missionary societies whose efforts are conducted from a one-sided and
narrow point of view, but it must become a matter for the state
to establish permanent agencies under whose care a slow and natural development can take place. The system of reservations and
Indian agents is frankly here even more out of place than in the
remaining territory of the Union where it has yielded very unsatisfactory results.

14. The Language of the Tlingit

The alphabet of the Tlingit language -- The pronounciation of the consonants -- Dialectic variations -- Literature on the Tlingit language -- The nouns -- The pronouns -- The verbs -- The adjective -- Numbers --
Time reckoning -- Vocabulary -- Samples of the language.

General Discussion

The alphabet of the Tlingit language consists of the following
sounds gathered from a test vocabulary: the vowels, a, e, i, o,
u; the umlaut ü and the diphthongs au and ai; also the consonants
g, k, h, ch, kw = q, l, m, n, r, d, t, ts = z, s, sch, tsch, w,
ks = x.

Between a and o there is a sound similar to the Swedish å and
that is indicated here by the same symbol. The sounds b, p and
f are entirely missing; l, m, o, kw, ks never appear as initial
sounds except in a few doubtful words.

There is especial difficulty in the pronounciation of k, the
sound with which most Tlingit works begin. Generally it is sound-
ed deep in the throat while the tongue is pressed against the teeth
of the lower jaw, nor does it merge with the following vowel so
that it really represents a syllable.

Veniaminof gives three ways of pronouncing k and t and intro-
duces special symbols for them. Since these differences are difficult to define and also since our ear can scarcely distinguish
them, I have contented myself with one symbol. Also t is preceded with a heavy throat sound and for this reason is often confused with k as our transcription and that of others shows. [1]

S at the beginning or end of a syllable is always sharp; we give
it as ss; ch indicates the ch in nacht, also at the beginning of
words; sch and tsch represent the same sounds as in German; only when preceded by a d, the sch becomes a little softer and is
pronounced almost like a French j, as in dscha-dschi, kadschin

and others.

W is similar in pronounciation to the English w; the diphthongs au and ai appear only in a few words.

The words in the following lists were gathered with few exceptions among the Chilkat; the words gathered at Huna, Killisnoo, and Sitka are designated by H, K or S, though only those appear in the vocabulary which were not gotten from the Chilkat or where they differ from the Chilkat. To what degree the Chilkat dialect differs from those of the other tribes the material we gathered does not allow us to judge. A comparison with the vocabularies gathered by Veniaminof, Wrangell and others from the Sitka[2] would indicate that the Chilkat use the soft rather than the harsh consonants; so we heard "Chtlingit" while Veniaminof wrote "Tlingit," also gedan which Lisiansky gave as keetan (English transcription). However, it is possible that this difference may be due to the different transcriptions of the various nationalities to which the observers belong since those Indian words recorded by an Englishman are often different to the point of not being recognizable as those recorded by a German or a Russian. Probably the dialectic differences in the Tlingit language, although there are minor ones, are however so slight that an easy understanding exists among the tribes.

An individual variation in the pronounciation, which may be due to a dialectic one, should be mentioned here, namely, the tendency of single individuals, men as well as women, to change n to l and to say "hil" instead of "hin," meaning water or river. Even more common is the tendency in the rendering of words of a foreign tongue to replace r with l, so that instead of saying "all right" they say "all light" and "leady" instead of "ready."

As has already been mentioned, we have a more or less complete vocabulary of Tlingit words, among others including that of Veniaminof which consists of about one thousand words and is the most complete and most trustworthy.[3] A larger work on the Kolushan language was done by Buschmann in 1856 in the Proceedings of the Academy of Science in Berlin in which everything which had been published up to that time was used and almost entirely reprinted. To this work which also discusses the relationship of the Kolushan language to other linguistic groups especially to the Aztec and Athapascan and in which the author determines that the Kolushan is an entirely independent linguistic type I refer those readers who wish to pursue the topic further; the following discussion consists only of the material gathered by ourselves and which in spite of its incompleteness nevertheless has certain points, especially in the grammatical structure, which may contribute to an understanding of the language.

The noun

The tendency to form "built up" words is characteristic. An object is seldom named alone, but usually in connection with another from which it is derived or to which it belongs or in connection with a possessive or demonstrative pronoun. So all the names for parts of the human body are prefixed with the word kā, meaning human, e.g., kā-schá, head, means human head; kā-dschín, hand; kā-chlū, nose; kā-gúk, ear; kā-wák, eye. Even shadow is kā-tschichrí and woman is kā-schát. To designate the parts of the body of animals dū is prefixed, so dū-schá, dū-chlū, dū-gúk, dū-wák, head, nose (bill of a bird), ear, eye of an animal.

To designate relationship the possessive pronoun is prefixed; so ach-iisch, my father; ach-tlā, my mother.

In reference to utensils, it is common to name the material of which they are made in a prefix or the figures with which they are painted or finally the name of the owner, as for example, tsāk-alchká, gaming sticks of bone; jēlch-tsik, dish with the symbol of the raven; íchta-gau, shaman's drum.

It seems that a declension of the noun does not take place, and singular and plural in most cases are the same. [4] Prepositions follow the noun, as Schítka-dĕ, to Sitka; Schítka-dĕch, from or out of Sitka; dĕkí-je, in heaven.

The Pronouns

The personal pronouns are:

chrăt	I
wŏé (ŭé) or wŏétsch (ŭétsch)	you
hu	he
uhán	we
ri	you
hasstu	they

The possessive pronouns are:

ach	my	Example:	ach-iisch	my father
i	yours		i-iisch	your father
tu	his		tu-iisch	his father
ha	ours		ha-iisch	our father
ri	yours		ri-iisch	your father
hasstu	theirs		hasstu-iisch	their father

The demonstrative pronouns are:

jatat   this; ja in combinations
              Example: ja-ān   this country
jutat   that; ju or juta in combinations
              Example: júta-ān   that strange country

Interrogative pronouns and adverbs are:

adūtse   who
chū-sse   how much
tā-ssé   what
gūch-ssé   where
gotk-ssé   when
             Examples: chū nā-ssé Tschilkat-kŏn jereti, how
                    many tribes has the Chilkat subdivision?

The Verb

The following table gives a summary of the conjugation of the verb in as far as it could be determined:

Infinitive	to be ill	atrá-to eat	see	kaūsk-to wash
Present				
1st per. sing.	chrăt janīk	at-chro-ch (r)á	chró-ssetin or chrátsch chró-ssetin	chro-daūts
2nd per. sing.	i janīk	at-i-chrá	i-ssetin or woétsch-i-ssetin	
3rd per. sing.	hū-janīk	hu-atrá		
1st per. plural	hā-janīk	at-u-chrá		
2nd per. plural	ri-janīk	at-ii-chrá	ri-ss(e)tin	
3rd per. plural	hass janīk	hass atrá		
Imperfect				
1st per. sing.		at-chro-ch (r) ágin	(chratsch) chro-chlatin	chro-daūtsin

2nd per. sing				
2nd per. plural				ri-daūtsin
Future				
1st per. sing.		at-ko-ch (r)a-chrá		
2nd per. sing.	ke-ī-chronīk			
1st per. plural	kē-ha-chronīk			
2nd per. plural				
Impera-tive			koschí	

This table, as well as the other scattered examples, shows that the personal pronoun in the third person singular and plural is simply placed before the infinitive form; the pronouns of the first and second persons as chrăt or chratsch, I; wŏé or wŏétsch, you; uhán, we and ri, you, are occasionally placed for emphasis, but the remainder of the persons are formed in the singular through chro or chra for the first person, i for the second, in the plural ha or u (?) for the first and ri or ii for the second, always appearing before the verb stem and after the object as: tā chrā-duha, sleep I will; ī-dschit-chro-atin, I gave you (something?); ī-chrā-chāwūts, you I ask.

The negative klēch or klēlch appears before chrŏ, i, etc., as klēlch chrō-ssetin, I do not see; chratsch klēch chro-áchtschk, I do not hear; klēlch atrā chrā-duha, I will not eat (not eat I will).

Interrogative forms are indicated by adding ge to the verb stem, as: ri-ssetin-ge, do you see? i-áchtsch-ge, do you hear?

A common occurrence in the first and second person is the combination of tū, "heart" or "being," with the possessive pronoun as: ach-tūú renik, I am sick, that is, my heart is sick.

The Adjective

The adjectives follow the nouns, as schetl klēn, the large spoon or the spoon is large; schetl katsko, the little spoon or the spoon is small. However in some cases adjectives also precede the noun, as: ssiāt ja-hīn, this water is cold; klēch retā ja-hin, this water is not warm; katlē-tsīchu ja-tlēk, these berries are sour; chlētsin ūschtscha, strong wind.

236

Opposites are generally indicated by prefixing the negative, as: jetálch, heavy; klēlch-utálch, light; jechlikáts, sharp; klélch-ulkáts, dull.

To designate color, generally, though not always, the word jéchati or échati is used which means something like our word "colored": klatl-jéchati, yellow; rchān-échati, red or flame color; tūtsch-jéchati, black; tsĭk-jéchati, blue or smoke color; tsū-jéchati, green or grass color. To this classification also belongs hĭn échati, wet or water colored or like water.

Similar derivatives from the noun are adjectives like chrotl-irk-utalch, light as a feather, featherweight; kot-irk-achat, round like an egg, oval; tultschan-irk-achat, round like a top.

The superlative is indicated by janach or anach, the comparative through kinchk, "less," e. g., jedŏk tu-tlāk du-anach-kolka, the boy is larger than his sister.

Numbers

1	tlēk, tlēch	17	tschinkat-ka- dachatuschu
2	dēch	18	tschinkat-ka-naskatuschu
3	notsk	19	tschinkat-ka-guschuk
4	dāch-un	20	tlēk-kā or dēch-tschinkat
5	kēdschin, kidschin	21	tlēka-ka-tlēk, or dēch-
6	klēd-ūschŭ		tschin-kat-ka-tlēch
7	dachat-ūschŭ	22	tlēka-ka-dēch
8	naskat-ūschŭ	30	notsk-tschinkat
9	guschúk	40	dachun-tschinkat
10	tschinkat	50	kidschin-tschinkat
11	tschinkat-ka-tlēch	60	klēduschu-tschinkat
12	tschinkat-ka-dēch	70	dachatuschu-tschinkat
13	tschinkat-ka-notsk	80	naskatuschu-tschinkat
14	tschinkat-ka- dachŭn	90	guschuk-tschinkat
15	tschinkat-ka-kēdschin	100	kidschin-kā
16	tschinkat-ka-klēduschu	200	tschinkat-kā

The number five is obviously derived from hand, ka-dschin. Four appears, according to Schott, to be a doubling of two; the numbers six, seven and eight seem to be correctly one, two and three plus five. If the supposition that kidschin means hand is right, then it stands to reason that tschinkat means two hands. The numbers from eleven to nineteen are then clearly ten and one, ten and two, ten and three, etc.

Tlēk-kā, twenty means one man, that is ten fingers and ten toes. For tlēk-kā, dēch-tschinkat, that is two times ten is also used, and from that twenty-one, dēch-tschinkat-ka-tlēch is formed, beside the customary form, tlēka-ka-tlēk. [5]

The tens from 30 to 90 are made by multiplying 10 by 3, 4, etc., at least so it appeared among the Chilkat and Huna. The Sitka Indians however, according to Veniaminof, formed these numbers in an entirely different way, namely, 40, 60, 80 from the analogue tlĕk-kā as 2 men, 3 men and 4 men were tach-ka, [6] nazk-e-ka and tachun-ka as against 30, 50, 70 and 90 which were 20 plus 10, tleka-ka-tschinkat; 40 plus 10, tachka-ka-tschinkat; 60 plus 10, nazkeka-ka-tschinkat; 80 plus 10, tachunka-ka-tschinkat.

One hundred appears everywhere to be kidschin-ka that is 5 men, 200 is tschinkat-ka that is 10 men. We were not given any higher numbers.

Tscha-tlē-nach ka, only one man or a single man, and dach-nach ka, two men, can be distinguished from tlēk-ka, twenty men, and dēch-ka, forty men, but nevertheless one says dach-nach jodok, two boys.

Reckoning of Time

The year (tāk, meaning winter) is divided into ten months (dis) of unequal length. Their names with their meanings were given us as follows:

August - October	1.	dīs-klēn, long month
November	2.	kokohá-dis, snow on the mountains
December	3.	schĕnach-dis, the first snow falls
January	4.	tauwok-dísse, the geese, tauwok, leave
February	5.	ssik-dísse, the bear, ssik, has young
March	6.	hīn-tānach-a-dísse, the first rain falls
April	7.	kĕrāno-dísse, the first flowers appear
May	8.	kachlat-ko-dísse, white flowers bloom
June	9.	átkadácha-dísse, the birds lay eggs (átkata)
July	10.	rchāt-dísse, the salmon, rchāt, appears

Since happenings in nature are used, and since these do not occur in the whole area at the same time, probably these names have only local use. The ones listed above were given us at Huna. The Chilkat call the second month, November, jekeri-kiēch, the dark days, and the third, December, red-kulch.

The days of the week, sson-dēchrat are called the first day, the second, etc.

Monday, tlēk-jekerikat; Tuesday, dēch-jekerikat.

Vocabulary

above (cp. heaven), dĕki, tlach-dĕki

adze (used in canoe making), chrutta

afterwards, later, behind, áit

again, tsūg

air, koúchtsche

all, (cp. every) tschaltakat

238

always (cp. all), tschatláka
amulet of bone, tsāk-ssēt
amulet of a shaman, tsāk-ssēt
  (S), (tsāk-bone)
and, kā
animal, male, kāá
animal, female, schitsch
answering, saying: Why don't
  you answer me? tāssé-ju
  klēlch ach i-retan
arm, kāchēk
armor of leather, chlŭch-tschi-
  nē
  the same but longer, kĕk-ke
armor of rods of wood, uónda
arriving: We will soon arrive in
  Deshu, uhān Dēschū-dĕ-jaidat
  katú-i-kuch
arrow, tschunēt
ash, kaniit
ask, to: I ask you, i-chra-
  chawūts (you I ask)
aunt: my aunt, ach-āt
autumn, jēss
axe, schinachaui
axe, little, schenacho jétti
axe or hatchet, schenagóje (cp.
  axe)
axe of stone, tajīs
back, kā-tēchr
bad, evil, tlēkuschkē, chla-kāss-
  taboo
bag, kăk, kåk (S)
bake, to: to roast, kachr-kánta
baking pan, kachr-kant-ráit
balance, jetáchli-at (H), (jetálch-
  heavy)
ball, kutschita
ball (musket ball), átkata
basket, for straining fish oil, kāk
basket of cedar roots, kātă-chúk
bathe, to: I take a bath, chtāk-
  ch(r)o-daūts (cp. to wash)
battle axe of bone, tsāk kēt-ú
battle axe of stone, kēt'-ú (the
  stone itself-tsū-ŭta, the wood-
  en handle, á-ssak-tic)

be, to: How are you? uásse-i-
  tú-eti? (How is your heart?)
  I am well, ka-dēn chro-denīk
be well, to: I am well, ka-
  denchro-denik, chletsinach
  tuu chrat, my heart is strong
bead, kawūt
beads, string of, worn by girls
  in their hair, kawūt-stchin
  (tschīn - braid)
beard, kā-chrattatsáje
bed, it, riēt
before, schichŏa
bell, gau
berries, tlēk(o)
  These berries are sour,
  katlē-tsīchu ja-tlēk
between, achkrák
bill, of an auk, rchēk-chlŭ-ú
  (S)
bill, of a duck, du-chlū - nose
bird, tsŭtsk, tsētsi
black, tūtsch, tūtsch-jéchati
  (H)
blanket (woolen), tlī
blind (cp. deaf), chlkūsch-tin
blood, schĕ
blue (cp. green), tsū, tsū-
  jéchati
  krēschk'ŭ (bluejay)
  tsīk-jéchati (tsīk - smoke)
  (H)
boat, andaiăgŏ
bodkin, punch, kē-na (S)
bones, atsáke, tsāk
bore, to: anachakanatúde (kan -
  wood)
borer, tul-chru
born, to be: Where were you
  born? gūch-sse ki-i-tstiren?
  When were you born? gotk-
  sse-ki-i-stīrin?
borrow, to: mu-hiss (because
  of its initial position the m
  is questionable)
both, atsū
bottle (of glass), ingrischā

bow, ssăks
bow net, kēit, chkētchk
box, kūk
box, four-cornered, of wood,
gā-kēne, kā-kă-né (S)
box, for rendering fish oil, tlăkt
box, oblong, with lid, kūk
box, for tools, chlítat ákă-kūk
(chlíta - knife)
box, for berries, chlăkt (S)
boy, jedăk, jedăk, jodŏk,
kessáne
the boy is small, jedăk katsko
the boys are sick, kessáne
janīk
boy, small, ridda-kátsko (H)
bracelet, kīss (cp. nose ring)
bracelet, silver, dāna-kīss
braid, tschīn (tachret-tschīn -
hair decoration of dentalium)
brain, ka-schán
brass, ore, īk
brave, tlitsinitú
bread, schenétsa
break, to: káwowut
breast, kā-chrētká
breasts, (ka)-tlā (cp. mother)
bring, to: to fetch, hatscháț
bring (imp.), hatschat, haditi
broken, utlīk
broom, chíta
brother, ikīk - your brother
ach-īk - my brother
brown, kachwēch-kahēni (color
of viburnum berries)
brush, kuchrīta, ku-chīta (S)
buoy (for whales), ju-dschin
burn, to: My hand is burned,
ach-tschīn wudekrécht
burning, cremation, aikané
bush, uóts
buy, to: awŭú
calico, kēsch-chit, klirk-atl
canoe, jăk
canoe, in Haida style, Haida-jăk
cap, matsích
carry, to: awaijá

catch, to: I catch (an animal)
chro-tli-schat
certain, kirkachá
chain, akákerki
chair, karkadschēt
cheek, kā-woschká
chief, gentleman, Mr., amkáu,
a-niáti
child: This woman has six
children, ju-schau-wot
klēduschu towåtkri
chin, ka-tejá
chisel, t'ījā
claws of a cat, du-chák
cleanly, chlulch-tūk
clear, aká-u-chatsk
cliff, steep, kēte (same as dog)
clock, jékeri-kwēri, gau
cloud, gūts
club for killing halibut, k'chūss
(S)
club with whale design, kīt-k'
chūss (kit - whale) (S)
coal (cp. ash), chúdsi, kān-íiti
(kān - fire)
cold, kussiāt
It is cold, kussă-át
This water is cold, ssiat ja-
hīn
This water is hot, klēch
ssiāt ja-hīn
I am cold, at-dēn ach-at-ūni
comb, chēdu (the same as
grave)
comb of whalebone, gåk-chēdu
(H)
come, to: hatkóatin
He comes, hāde-anagut
He came yesterday, hatnagūt
tātke
The steamship comes to
Gaudekan, gŭnten-jåk Gau
hāde-anakúch (H)
I will come tomorrow, hade-
koch-chra-gut sserkan
You will come, hade-krigut,
hade-kuch-ri-gut

We will come, hade-kuch-to-āt
You will come, hade-kuch-ri-
āt
They will come, hade-ha-ko-
ka-āt
Come! hagū
 I will not come, klēch ach-tu
 uássigu hatro-gutĕ
 Come very early, tsuwāk
 kinnaĕn haguchón
cook, to: atsĕ́é, utliuk
 The water is boiling, hīn utliuk
cooking utensils of tin, nassĕá
corner posts of house, gāts
count, to: dat-táu
crazy, tedla-kuschká, tlika-
 kuschkē
cut, to: kaját ch, nachasch,
 krēschētagot
dagger, double, schē-káts-tschŭ-
 chă-nát (S)
dagger, simple, tschŭ̈-chă-nát
 (S)
 dagger with carved bear head,
 chūts-tschŭ̈-chă-nát (S) (chūts-
 bear)
dance, to: atlēch
dance apron, nachēt
dark: It is not dark, klēch ká-
 utschē-kēt
darkness, ka-gēt
daughter, my daughter, ach-ssī̄
day, jekeri, iki-jĕ
daylight, kiā
day after tomorrow, sserkán,
 tlīrá, sserkán-tlira-káde
day before yesterday, tlirā tātke
dead, wŭ́ŭná, ŭŭná
 Mother Goose is dead (child's
 play) tá-wŏk-tlā ŭŭná
deaf, chkūtl-achtschk (achtschk -
 to hear)
deathly sick, near death, dēk-
 kŏná
deep, kadlān
dew, kokascha-chátl
die, to: ran-na-nān, kóg-kana

All human beings must die,
 tschaltakat chtlingit kóg-kana
His father died a year ago,
 tu-īīsch wŭŭná de klēk'tåk
The magpie died several
 days ago, tserkēne wŭŭná
 tlīra tātke
dirty, tschéchu, wul-tschēk
dish, tsīk
 dish with raven head, jēlch-
 tsīk (S)
 dish with sea gull head, kāch-
 tsīk (S)
 dish with seal head, tsā-tsīk
 (S)
 dish with beaver design,
 tsikēdi-tsīk (S)
dish of horn, chlīnēt-tsīk
dish with sloping sides, schŭ-
 chŏn-ka-tă-ā-tsīk (S)
dish of wood, tsegeschewu-tsīk
 long dish in shield form,
 kéchla, kálch-la (S)
dish of birch bark, at-tāgi-
 tsīk (S)
dollar, dāna (cp. silver)
done, made, jéussnē
door, chra-wūlch, chra-hāt
downstream, hīnik
dream, to: What did you dream
 last night? tāsse ī-redschūn
 nīs-tāt
 I did not dream anything,
 klēlch tāsse chro-adschūn
dressing: to put on a coat,
 kăch-kidatē
drink, to: ta-nāch
 to drink water, hīn-tanā
 to be drunk, kanoschū
drinking cup, gúcha
drop, kakástscha
drum, gau, a-tau-wŭtsch,
 atauwutsch-arī
 shaman's drum, íchta-gau
 (S)
 medicine drum, nak'-gau (S)
 chief's drum, a-niáti-gau (H)

241

dry, uchūt, ūwŭchuk, uschekétl
dull, klēlch-ulkats
dumb, chliŭch-ēsch-tank
dust, tūsk, kētet
each, tschaltakat
ear, a girl's, kā-gŭk
ear, a cat's, du-gŭk
his ear, tu-gŭk
ear drum, gūk-adschasch
ear ornament of wool, gūk-kátl
early, in the morning, kechrē
earring, gūk-át
earth, chtlingit-āni (tlingit -
human being, ān-village -
home of people)
east, chūn
eat, to: at-chrā, atrā
I eat, at-chro-chrā, atrochā
You eat, at-i-chrā
He eats, hu-atchrā, hu-atrā
We eat, at-u-chrā
You eat, at-ii-chrā
They eat, hass-atchrā, hass
atrā
The boy eats, jedŏk atrā
Both these boys eat, hass atrā
dachnách jedŏk
I ate this morning, kechré at-
chra-chágin (or atrachágin)
I will eat, at-ko-cha-chra
I eat and you drink, at-(ch)ro-
chā ué-kŭá at-i-taná
I drink and you eat, at-(ch)ro-
taná ué-kŭá at-i-ch(r)ā
I can not eat, klēlch at(ch)ra
chra-du-ha
ebb, ssūn
egg, gŏt
elbow, ka-t'eischu
end, to: renssénni
enough, kakugé
evening, chāna
every, each, stakát
exclamation of astonishment, a-
jách, a-jách kadán
exhaustion, schē-al-tuk (schē-
blood)

extinguish, to: to extinguish a
fire, k'rchān rakanaltitsk
eyebrows, kā-tsé
eyelash, kā-ŭchletrāni
eyes (human), kā-wák
eyes (of a cat), du-wak
family, jusniádi-danak
far, nalchlē (klēch-u-nachlē -
not far, near)
fast, towassijēk
fat, liquid, ich
fat, solid, atājé
father, isch, iisch
Father, Our, (in prayer), uhán
ha iisch or ha-isch-tlin -
our great Father
Is that your father? i-iisch
schekéju?
Is that your father? ri-iisch
schekéju?
fear, alarm, k'rān
fear or to create fear,
akulchrik
feather, chŏtl
feather of a duck, du-chótl
fell, to: a tree
I fell a tree, āss (ch)ro-
cháút
fight, to: kotlagáu
fill, to: to fill a spoon (cp. full)
tschetl-a-hik
find, to: I do not find my hat,
klēch, ka-chro-chaschi ach-
tsakŭ
Now I have found it, dē ka-
chro-cha-schi or dē chro-
ati-kochaschi
finger, kā-tlak, ka-tlíeki
thumb, kā-gusch
index finger, kā-djēchrē
middle finger, kā-tlēk-tin
little finger, kā-unekētsch-
ērkrē
finger nail, kā-chrak'(u)
fire, kān, k(r)chān
fire, on the, kān rajēk
fireplace, kān-dá

first, schichro-ánach
fish, fresh water, hīn-takat
fish hook, ht'ēch
fish spear (cp. salmon spear),
  kăt, tlakwā, klakwā
flame, kăn-ētlŭūt - tongue of the
  fire
flee, to: wutakēn
flesh (meat), tlīr
float for fish line, kīts
float in form of a bird, káts-hiss
flood, ēlkch
flown, ssanētsa, (cp. bread)
fog, kondigetsk
foot, kā-chŭss táchtlē, kā-chŭss
foot of a duck, dū-chŭss
footpath, way, dē
  smaller footpath, dē katsko
  larger footpath, dē klēn
for: for you, a-wŏé (wŏé - you)
forehead, kā-kāk
friend: my friend, ach-rŭni
fruits, also buds, kēkochwĕn
full, schau-hīk
garden, tār
garters on trousers, tsĭkadúch
girl, small, chat-kátsko
give, to: kadjiti
  I gave you, i-dschit-ró-atin
  (might be : i-dschin-chró-
  atin - I gave you the hand)
  (I gave you my hand?)
glacier, ssīt
  side moraine, ssīt wanechúwo
  terminal or end moraine, ssīt
    kachúwo
glimmer, micaceous, tatlák
glove, tsāg
go, to: nagō
  He goes, hu gut
  Go! noktè
  Go away! djŭk
  go into the woods, āss-kutu, āss-
    rŭ
goblet, kŭka
gold, gŭn, atu-tē (tē - stone)
good, jērk-ē, juk'ē

good morning, juk'-ē-ri-tsu-
  tāt
  very good, of the best, agan-
    rēka
good night, juk'ē-ri-tāt
grandfather, (ach)-ēlch
grandmother, (ach)-chlilchk(ŭ)
grasp: I grasp, ach-kā-āch-
  katti
grave, chēdu
grave house, depository for
  ashes, katakēdĕ
gray, chlawūch
gray (color of gull), kētl'-di-
  jētsa, ketl-di-ji-jētsi
green, tsū, tsū-jéchati (H)
guns, ū-na
hail, kadátst
hair, kā-scha-chawū, kā-schă-
  chāú
hair of a cat, du-chawū
hair of the mountain goat,
  dschenu chāúi
hairdress of women, scha-ka-
  ssīt
half, aschiū, aschiū-gu
  half past eight, naskat-úschū
  gau ka aschiū
halibut hook, năch (S)
  ssăksnăch (S), (ssăks - bow)
halibut hook with crane's bill,
  chlāch năch (S), (chlāch -
  crane)
halibut hook with the figure of
  a man, chtlingit năch (S),
  schetatsátĕ năch (S)
halibut hook with the figure of
  a sea lion, tan nach (S), (tan
  - sea lion)
hammer, tachke
hand, kā-dschin
  my hand, ach-tschin
  hollow hand, kā-tschin-tāk,
    kā-dschin-tāk-ieti
  right hand, to the right,
    schiīn-nach-anach
  left hand, to the left,

tsat-nach-anach
shake hands (greeting), hăndé-
i-tschin (hande - here)
hard, ret-ich
hat, tsāch, tsākŭ (S)
hat of bark fibers, kássēk
tsāch (S)
hat used in dancing, tāch-chá
chlach-kēt (S)
cylindrical rings on a hat,
schátă-kūch (S)
he, hu
head, kā-schā, kāschiú
head of a cat, du-schā
The head of (a bird) is red on
top, du-schā-kī chrān-
échate
head of a worm, a-schá
head ornament of bent wooden
rods, atrakú
headache, my head is sick, ach-
schān renik
hear, to: achtschk
heart, ka-t'ērch-ē, kā-t'ēchk,
ka-tu
heart, being (in combinations),
tū
I am well - my heart is well,
chlētsīn ach-tūŭ chrat
heartache, tachk-tsin
heat, kot-ār
heaven, dĕki gúts-tu (gūts - folk)
heavy, jetalch
help (cp. to help), ha-it, kóteschi
help, to: kūch-deschí
Help us (imp.), haíti-deschí
here or give it here, ha-dé
herring rake, jau-chitla
hew, to: chrut
to cut wood, gān chrut
hill, gūtsch
hook for salmon, gichra, t'ichrá
house, hīt
summer shelter of twigs,
tschāsch-hīt
shaman's house, gau-hit (gau -
drum)

how? uásse
How are you? How do you find
yourself? uásse-i-tū-eti?
uásse i-reti?
human being, chtlingit, t'lingit
hungry, chadrān-uhá
Are you hungry? ii-dek-
ránuha?
I am not hungry, klēlch atra
chra-duha, klēlch chra-
dan-uhá
hunt, at-lu-un
to go hunting, at-lu-un kagot
He goes hunting, hu-kagóet-
atlu-un
hunt, to: at-lūn-tsáeti
Are you going to hunt? at-
lūndre-gi-krigūt?
I, chrăt, chratsch, chra and
chro in the verb forms
I am here, chrat-ejá, chrat-
ajé
ice, t'ich
covered with ice, frozen,
wudli-t'ich
The ice melts, t'ich wulchlā
inside, in the house, nēlch-
acha
intestine, entrails of bears,
tsik-nássi (tsīk - bear)
iron, irkijēts (irk - copper)
joint, knuckle, kā-sche-tūch
kettle, redélch, kótl (probably
from the Russian)
knee, kā-kē-icha
knife, chlīta
pocket knife, kreschetagot
chlīta
stone knife, ta-chlīta
double pointed dagger,
gulchlá, kútla
know, to: I know, chra-ssi-kū
I do not know, klēch chra-
ssikū, klēk chra-ssikū
labret of wood, klū-ú chrēn-
tāch-a, kéntaga
ladder, dsēt

ladle with eagle head, tschāk-schin (tschāk - eagle, schīn - spoon)

lame, chlekátscht

lamp of stone, tsinā, tsinā-jit

lamp wick, tsinā katuchéje

land (as opposed to water - earth, ground), tlēkt, tlakt

land, occupied - village, an their own land, homeland, ja-ān

a foreign land, júta-ān

large, tlēn, k'tlēn, átlen big month (August and October), dis-tlēn

large spoon, schetl-klēn

large, of a tree (cp. long), kuát The pine is large, ssīt jēkulchkē

The boy is larger than his sister, jedŏk tu-tlāk du-anach-kolka

His sister is larger, tu-tlāk du-anach-kolka

M is larger than W, M. chligé, W. Janach

larynx, kā-chlētūch

later, sslitsa

laugh, to: at-schūk I do not cry, I laugh, klēch chro-kāch, at-(ch)ro-schūk

lead, gūch, gūch-tēch

leaf of a plant, ketkā, kajáni

leather lace or thong, chrēgotl

leather strips (cp. sinew), tassá

leg (of a cat), du-dschín (cp. hand)

leg (human), ka-chrūss, ka-chūss

light, k'agán (agán - sun)

light, light like a feather, klēlch utalch, chrotl-īrk-u-talch

lightning, chētl-iku (chētl - thunder)

lip plug, kāk'(u)

little, few, jēkugenk

live, to: Where do you live? -

Where are you? gūch-ssé-je i-reti?

I live far from here, nalchlē akch-je chro-dretige

long, large, jakuāt, jēkuat, jékutla

loud, kināch

love, to: I love, chro-ssrān You love, i-ssrān I love - my heart cares, ach-tu wassigu

make, to: jenessnē, a-ulch-jēch

make, to: to do, jenassni make fire! kān jenessne Who made this, a-dūtse wu-ulchēch je-at I cannot make this, klēlch ute-jēn-ka-ssa-nē-rit je-at

man, kā that man, ju-kā

marry, to: this man is married, ju-ka áwo-scha

mast spar, tsissa-to-āss (tsissa - sail, āss - tree) tsissa wuchli - crosspiece in boat for mast

mat, woven of cedar root, tālch (S)

measure, kā - man

medicine, nak'

medicine to drink, ta-na nāk'

mercury, gluchēni

metal, tōk'-ate

mica, tē-tetlák

mine, āch

moccasins, akuschtetîch

mollusk, edible, gåte

month, dis (moon) this month, jū-dīs-kat next month, jadach-dīs-kat two months, dēch dīs

moon, dīs half moon, dīs-schu (a-schiu - half) new moon, demtsakin ris-dīs

moon, new in the shape of a

sickle, dīs-akīje

more (to form the comparative), janách

morning, jekeri-schukuát

morning, early, tsū-tāt, kechré

mortar, of stone, tē-kajet

mortar, of wood, for pulverizing tobacco, kăcho-ka-jet (S)

mother, atlī

my mother, ach-tlā

mountain, schiā, schiāch

mouth, of a cat, du-chā

mouth, of a person, kā-chā

music, at-kaschi

nail, kachú

name: my name, ach-ssārī (H)

your name, i-ssārī (H)

his name, tu-ssarī (H)

name, to: or to call, What are you called, named, uásse-i-dŭĕ-ssagt

What is this called? uásse-dŭĕ-ssagt

neck, kā-ssét'a

necklace, pearl, sséké-kawút (kawút - pearl)

needle, richetaun

nephew, my nephew, ach-kálchku

net, kidát, digā

night, tāt

this night, ja-tāt

the past night, hīs-tāt

no, klĕk

northwest, tlakakāch

nose, kā-chlū, kā-chlŭk

nose of a cat, du-chlū

nose ring (cp. bracelet), chlĕk' o-kiss

nostril, kā-chlikŭtsch (H)

not, klĕk, klēlch

nothing, all gone, hŭtsch

nourishment, dochă-āt

now, at once, ridát

ocean, sea, hīn-chŏkŏá, etlká

once upon a time, long ago, chlīra tātke

one, tlĕk, tlēch

only: only one man, tschā-tlē-nach kā (H)

open, to: open the door, chrăhát hedeschutan, chrĕt-schr-schūŭtán (H)

The door is opened, chrăhát at-schuwatán

ore, brass, īk-nátsch (īk - copper)

our, hā

over all, tschaltakat - all, every

paddle, for ceremonial use, ŭū-tsa-gá

paint, to: to paint the face, rē-kot-taná

Have you painted your face? rē-ulch-ná-i-tsin

Why did you paint your face? tassé-rē-ril-chná

path, see footpath

peak, schiā-schekí (schiā - mountain, deki - on top)

pebble, white quartz pebble, nīch

pipe bowl, kstā-kēt (S)

pipe bowl with seal design, tsāch-ta-kēt

pit, in which fish is stored, átătl

plain, schetsch kanáko

pleasure, atschiuk

pocks, kuān

wind pocks(?), kuān-retki

poison, hích

powder, aktugáne

pretty, beautiful, ssik-gu, klēlch-uschku

pupil, kā-wak tagétse

quiet, be quiet! chla-kāss (see bad)

rage, to: to be angry, kchān

railroad, ták-cha gunten-jāk (gunten-jāk - steamship)

rain, ssīm

It is raining, rain is falling, ssúgi dagiússitán

rainbow, ketschanagat
raindrops, kokatách
rattle, tschē-schúch
  rattle with frog figure,
    chichtsch tschē-schúch
really, actually, tlach-ēka
red, rchān, rchān-échati (k'
  rchān - fire)
reef, ridge, hīn-akīdji, schel-
  tach
resin cakes - used for chewing,
  tăkle-kocho, koch'
right, tsumgussi
rind, bark, achláchē
ripe, kokăndlichon
rising, The smoke rises, tsīk
  kindējēūn
river, hīn
  large river, hīn-tlēn
  small river, hīn-katsku
roof, tsīre-tú
root, of a plant, ak'ē
  root of a fir (spruce) as bas-
    ketry material, chrat
    kassatuk
  the same, split, chrat-kaú
rough, kassich-ach
round, tultschan-īr-kachat, like
  a top, got-īr-kachat, like an
  egg
sack, guēlch
sail, tsissa
  lines for sail, tsissa-kajékajĕ
  sail yard, tsissa-jatsáke
salmon hook, gichra, t'ichrá
salmon spear, klakwá
salt, ēl-kechŭk
salty, chliētl
  These salmon are salty,
    chliētl ja-rchāt
sand, chlē-u
  fine sand, chlē-u kassaké
saw, chráscha
  little saw, chráscha kátsko
say, to: What do you say?
  uásse-chra-ri-ka
  Don't say a word, klēch-uásse-

chra-ri-ka-rek
scar, tīlch
scraper, to scrape off fat,
  krischá
scream, to: kāch
screw, kassīt
screw driver, una-kachētscha
sea, lake, āch, ā, āk'u
season, jech-kohá
see, to: I see, I saw (?)
  chratsch-chró-sse-tin,
  chratsch-chra-chla-tín,
  You see, woētsch-akē-i-sse-
    tīn
  I do not see, klelch chro-sse-
    tin
  Do you see this eagle? ri-
    ss(e)-tin-ge ju-tschāk
See! akákoschi, kōschi
sex, lineage, na
  How many lineages has a
    Chilkat tribe? chū nā-ssé
    Tschilkat-kŏn jāk jereti
  It has six lineages, klēdús-
    chu na awú
shadow, kā-tschĭchri
shamans, icht'a
sharp, jechli-kats
sharpen, to: to whet, jachitl
shinbone, kā-chrīss
shining, katle-ētscha
shoulder, kā-chrikscha
shovel - to remove hot stones
  in the preparation of fish oil,
  tachúnā
shut, to: shut the door, at-
  schitan
sick, renīk, jenīk (H), janīk
  I am sick, chradrenīk,
    chrătjanīk, chratrenīk
  My heart is sick, ach-tŭú-
    renīk
  You are sick, i janīk
  We are sick, ha janīk
  You are sick, ri janīk
  They are sick, hass janīk
  The boys (or children) are

sick, kessáne janik
I was sick yesterday, chrát
janik tätke
You will be sick, ke-i-chrenik
We will become sick, ke-ha-
chrenik
Are you sick? i-renik'u-gé
side beams of a house, chrange-
jēt
silver, dāna
silver plug for girl's lower lip,
kā-nŭch
sinew, also thread, tāss
sinew of caribou, wotsig-tāssi
sister: my sister, ach-tlāk
skeleton, kuchagē
skin, of a duck, at-tugú
skin canoe (baidarka), tschakúch
slave, kūchu
sled, ritagit
sleep, to: I sleep, di-chrŏ-tá
chrăt (H)
You sleep, wōétsch-di-k'ri-ta
(H)
Do you sleep? Are you going
to sleep? di-kr'-i-tá-ge (H),
ita-ge
No, I am not sleeping, klĕk,
klĕlch chro-tá
I am sleepy, tā-chrā-duha- I
want to sleep
You are sleepy, tā-k'-i-duha -
You want to sleep
sleep, to go to: nachto-chrĕch-ta
I go to sleep, dĕk-kotá
slow, sluggish, āútoka
slowly, takēna
small, kátsko
small saw, chráscha kátsko
small spoon, schetl kátsko
W is smaller than M
W. kussikā M. kinchk
smoke, tsik
smoke hole, gān
smooth, kāsche-riktl
sneeze, to: kaltsicha
snow, klēd

snow falls, It is snowing, klēd
arékadán, klēd dagiussitán
snow, melting, kanik
snowshoes, jād schi
snow water, klēd-hine
soap, ūdsch, ūtsá
soft, kāsche-rótlen
sole, kā-chüss-tāk
sole of foot (cp. hollow of hand)
kā-chūs-tāk-ieti
son: my son, ach-rit
song, raschiri
soon, jāidat
sour, katlē-tsichu
These berries are sour,
katlē-tsichu ja-tlēk
source, gūn (the same as gold)
south wind, gēlch-schā
speak to: I speak, chratsch
chro-cha-tán
You speak to me, woétsch
ach-i-re-tán
Why don't you speak to me?
tassé-ju klēlch ach i-re-
tán?
spirit, ghost, jēk, tsige-káo
spoon of horn, chlinēt schetl,
chlenet-schetl
spoon of lead, gúchti-schetl
(gūch-tēch - lead)
spoon of mountain sheep horn,
jēts-schetl - blue spoon
spoon with raven design,
jēlch-schetl
spoon with auk design, tschi-
schetl
spoon, large wooden, schin
spoon of wood or horn, schatl,
schetl
large spoon, schetl klēn
small spoon, schetļ katsko
Spring, tāk-iit, tāk-iiti (tāk -
winter)
star, kotrarennehá
star, falling, ajékatá
steamboat, gúnten-jàk
stick game, alchka, katŏk-

248

kítscha
stick, small, decorated with a
red encircling line, nak'-
alchká
sticks of bone, small, tsāk-
alchká
sticks of wood, small, ssaka-
alchká
stomach, akitscháje
stone, tĕ, tā
white stone (marble?), ītsch
storm, chletsin ūchtscha -
strong wind
straw for basketry, schāt
strike, to: awogóch
strong, chletsīn
stupid, du-schă-ret-ich (du-
schā - his head) klēlch ad-
risku - not smart
summer, kotān
sun, agán
the sun has risen, kenachich
agán
the sun has set, denachenchich
agán
the sun burns hot, agán táchē
the rays of the sun burn my
face, agán-tscheach-chráka-
ússigan
swamp, katli-hīni-ge
table, kāch-ato-chroat
tablecloth, kāch-ato-chroat
kakådschi
tail of a cat, du-chdlit
there, what is there, uásse dor
ssagt jut-at
therein, ali-jánache
they, hass, ha
they eat, hass-atrá
thigh, kā-chrēts
thirsty, to be: I am thirsty,
schekūch-chra-duhá
I want water, hīn-chra-duhá
(hīn - water)
this, játaga, jádŭ
What is this here? uásse dor
ssagt jat-at

this way, handé
throat, kā-tlēketschŭchu
through, digānach
throw, to: at-chīk
I throw, chratsch-at-(ch)ro-
chīk
You throw, woétsch-at-i-
jachīk
thunder, chētl
tobacco, kāntsch
today, jidát
toes, kā-chŭss-tlēk'e
the big toe, kā-chŭss-
kŭŭschi
tomorrow, the next day,
sserkán, ssirkán
tone, tsā, tsē
tongs, klat-tá
tongue, kā-tlŭŭt
tooth, kā-ūch
toothache, ach-ūchrenik
top (child's toy), tultochan
totem pole, kū-ti-ga
track, kā-chrē-tak
trade, exchange, barter,
assēch
trap for marmot, ssalk-ta'
ssa (ssalk - marmot; tāss -
sinew)
travel, to travel in a canoe (cp.
come)
We travel, u(h)an-tu-kŭch
Ssettin travels faster, Ssettin
janách haja-kŭch
Ssettin travels more slowly,
Ssettin-kinchk haja-kŭch
tree (cp. pine), āss
trestle of wood at the smoke
hole, gan-ēchli (gān - smoke
hole)
tribe, na
trousers, kăn, tāl-tsich,
tokatasch
tumpline, small one worn on
chest, chriaú
wide one, worn on forehead,
ka-kanchá

twig, branch, aschīri

twilight, the night comes on, rachinnā-át

two eyes (of a worm), dēch towak

uncle, my uncle, ach kāk

under, a'tagi

understand, to (cp. smart), he understands how to fight, kotlagáu tsāeti

he understands how to hunt, at-lūn tsāeti

undress, to take a coat off, kāt-kidatē

up, get up (imp.), ge-dán

upwards, kindatschūn (H)

valley, schiā-nách (schiā - mountain)

vessel for pouring oil, jēlch-schá-ta (jēlch - raven)

village, also every inhabited place, ān (also a ship)

violet, tsu-go-a-ta'tse

wall, ada-háti

want, to: What do you want? tassowé towassiku (H)

warm, hot, jēt'á, ret'á, kot'ár

It is warm inside (in the house), jēt'a nēlch

Your water is warm, ret'a ri-hīn

This water is not warm, klēch ret'á jahīn

wash, to: the body, tāk-kodaūts the hands, dschin-kaūts

wash, to: the face, achin-kaūts

I wash my face, rē(k)-koda-ūts

I wash my hands (?) schēk-koda-ūts

I have washed my face, rēch-ada-ūtsin

I have washed my hand, de-dschin-rach-ada-ūtsin

Did you wash your face? de-rē(k)-ri-da-ūtsin-ge

Did you wash your hand? tschin-ri-da-ūtsin-ge

water, hīn - river

The water falls, ja-kuchli-kuch hīn wúulchla (cp. the ice melts)

The water rises, hīn ūútá

waterfall, current, chrāss, wultichrāss

waves in fresh water, hāt in salt water, chrachásch, tit

breakers, chratlīk

we, uhán, ha

week, ssondēchrát

weep, to: kāch - cry, scream Why do you weep? tāssowé i-e-kāch

west, deki-nachēt

wet, wutatlak, hīn-échati

What is that called? uásse dor-ssākt jatat?

What is this called? uásse dor-ssākt jutat?

What is your name? uásse i-dūe-ssakt? (H)

when? gotk-ssé?

where? gūch-sse?

whetstone (also amulet), jin-na

whirlwind, jēlch-wuērsche

white, klēd - snow

who, adūtse

why? what? tāssé, tāssowé, uásse

wick, tsinā katuchéje (tsina - lamp)

wide, see far

windbreak at the smoke hole, gān-ēlchli

windy, The wind is blowing, arē-úteti

wing of a duck, du-chitsch

winter, tāk - year

wise, You are wise, at-kuk tsáeti, kotsch-i-reti

woman, see wife, ka-schát his woman or wife, du-schát

woman (also see wife), schau-wot

this woman, ju-schau-wot

wood, găn, kăn
wool (of mountain goat), gádli
wound, chrächek
wrist, ka-dschin-chlik'-itse
year - winter, tāk
  one year ago, de tlēk tāk
yellow, tsechone, klatl-jechati
  (H), (possibly: earth color,
  klātkt - earth)
yes, ā
yes indeed, hau
yesterday, tātke (tāt - night)
you, wŏé, wŏ-étsch (H)

you, ye, to her, of them, her,
  ri, hasstu, ii in verb forms
  these children of their father,
  ju achatku hass-tu iisch
your, tu
your (sing.), i
your father, tu-iisch
your father, i iisch
  Is this your father? i iisch
  schékeju
your father, ri iisch
  Is this your father? ri iisch
  schekéju
your name, i-ssári (H)

Personal names[7]

Men

Auktelchnīk (a shaman), is sup-
  posed to mean "Nobody bothers
  himself about his feathers."
Chlūnat
Dach-kā-ïsch, the father of two
  men
Dan-e-wăk, silver eyes[8]
Dūté (a slave)
Gytsch-kalsche-ïsch, father of
  Gytsch-kalsche
Jēlch-hagu, raven bones
Jēlch-kuchu, raven slave
Jēlch-tēlch, raven wood (tēlch -
  pitch)
Kaschgué

Kasko
Kaskoē
Ka-úschti (a boy)
Kin-tū-kā
Kïta
Kïtschk
Koltsūn (a Gunana)
Kudowān
Sach-a-hān
Schartritsch or Tschartritsch
Schédla-kā
Ssettïn
Tandegēk
Udechrā
Ūscha (a slave)

Women

Ratschenïtla
Kaskoé

Skēt-ú
Chtlingit tsāri, a tribal name

(For the names of clans and tribes see Chapter III)

Mythical personages and names of tribes

Kanuga, mythical person, rocks at Deje Fjord
Schā-kā-nā-ri or schkā-tā-hïn-āri, a mythical person on a totem
  pole

251

Gunakadēt, fabulous sea monster
Kūschta-kŏnē, otter people
Dē-kĭ-na, name for the Haida[9]
Gúnana, name for Indians of the interior who call themselves Kē-jik[10]
Tsugschan, name for the Tsimshian[11]
Waschten-kŏn "Washington people," name for Americans
Gūts-ta-kŏn people out of the clouds, name for all white people[12]

Villages
(an - village)

Klokwân	Jendēstáke
Gaudēk'-ân	Chlŭlchágu
Neltūschk'-ân	Chlachāik
Stacháti-āni	Chlowāk
Ān-gūn	Tsenta-ka-hīni
Ta-n-āni (ta, the white salmon)	Tagīsch
Katkwaltú	

Mountains

Gēlch	Dschenu-tēche, back of a
Gēissen	mountain goat
Schākdélchki	Krischa, saw, scraper
Gēlch-lak	Kotáss, the treeless plateau,
Komdsche hitkehĕ	the divide

Camps, fishing places, dangerous places, sandbanks, etc.

Dochrágu, a place where poplars grow (dok - poplar)
Tschatschēcha-chrágu, halibut's head (a rocky promontory), tschatsch - halibut, schá - head
Schichágu
Tājeis-scháku, Chrat-chágu, salmon place (chrat - red salmon)
Schā-schi-chratáku
Klechanū
Hoklen-tschuka-nū, a rocky prominence, comparable to a fortress
Dejē-chrā
Jēlch-ta-ka-chrāss
Anuk
Hutschi datūchku
Doktuschka, place where poplars grow
Sseatigūn
Dē-schu, end of the way (or halfways?)
Dachlakohōja
Ta-hĭt, stone house
Tandschēchkun
Scheltsāk
Kētl-ráchiē, the howling of dogs
Jēlch-áti
Kaschejĭk
Kadaschĭschkon

Islands

Altsáne
Chlachátsch
Chŭtsinŭ-ū, Bear Island (chūts -
   bear; nu - island)
Dachlatsūg
Jachlanissa

Inteje᷄
Kētl-di-káte, Sea Gull Island
   (ketl-di - sea gull)
Katagúne
Nechráje
Schikosseán
Schikuk

Bays and adjacent valleys

Dachanāch
Náchkŭ
Dejē-ssánke, Dejē-ssálke, near
   Dejē

Dejē
L'chtinigē
Jeochlitta

Rivers and valleys
(hin - river)

Ch'katse-hīn
Gatachage-hīn
Jēlch-hīni, Raven River
Jēlchta-katska-hīn
Kanadāri-hīn
Kaltséka-hīn
Kochtahu-hīni
Krota-hīni
Natage-hīn
Ta-hīni, salmon river (ta -
   white salmon)
Tak-hīn
Tatschants-hīni
Tislin-hīn
Tschilkat-hin
Tokásk-i-schanach-hīni, moun-
   tain brooklets
Schanach-hīni, mountain brook-
   lets

Schkā-tāri-hīn
Sseltat-hīn
Tlach-ka-hīniku
Hakoltseje-hīn
Ssergoit
Jŏkeách
Chraālch, wild mountain
   stream
Katschadēlch
Altsēch
Kuwakantessē
Katse-dajē
Kutenigé
Sakaeja
Anman
Tsirku
Ssidrajīk
Katla kuchra

Ravine

Jēlch-li-tā-jē, a place where ravens sleep

Lakes

Dana-áku, Silver Lake (dana - silver; a - lake)
253

Keïdēchligé
Kussŏ-ā, Narrow Lake
Tagisch-ájĕ, lake near Tagish
Tahīniwud
Tutscheá, Black Lake?
Schütlüchroā (supposed to mean "filled to the edge.")

Glaciers

Nāch-gel-ssit
Tsi-kach-kuéne-ssit ⎫
Ai-kach-kuéne-ssit ⎬ Blueberry Glacier
Ssit-kajē
L'kada-ssētsk
Jawūchl, glacier door?
Ssaksa-ēja, bow glacier? (ssaks - the bow)

Plants

blackberry	Rubus sp.	tūtsch-tlēkŭ
bracket fungus	Polyporus sp.	ass takádli
buffalo or soap berry	Shepherdia canadensis (L) Nutt.	hoklen
cedar, Alaska or yellow	Chamaecyparis, nut-kaensis Lamb. - Chamaecyparis Noot-katensis (Lamb.) Spach.	chlāch (the inner-bark - wŭd, the root-rchāt)
cedar, red	Thuja gigantea Nutt. - Thuja plicata Donn.	tī (not always distin-guished from yellow cedar)
crabapple, Oregon	Pirus rivularis Dougl.	kāk, kāk-wŭtsi, chrachk
cranberry, black	Empetrum nigrum	hidli wŭtsi
cranberry, rock	Vaccinium Vitis Idaea L.	nēgūn
currant, trailing black	Ribes laxiflorum Pursh.	chrachéwu, tlachēt
currant, swamp	Ribes lacustre Poir.	kaneltsuk, kaneltsák
devil's club	Fatsia horrida Benth. et Hook - Oplopanax horridum (Sm.) Miguel	áchta
dogwood, bunch-berry	Cornus canadensis L.	gaikachit

fern, licorice	Polypodium vulgare L.	ssātsch
fern, shield	Aspidium - Dryopteris	jēlch-koátl
fir, alpine	Abies subalpina Engelm. - Abies lasio- carpa (Hook.) Nutt.	kuchrēt
fireweed	Epilobium angustifoli- um L.	chokanágu
grass, long		schūkan, tschukán, ssūg
grass, short, lawn		tlachetse
hemlock, mountain	Tsuga Mertensiana Bong.	ijin, jin
hemlock, western	(Tsuga Pattoniana Engelm.)$\underline{13}$	tsĕch
huckleberry	Vaccinium ovalifoli- um Sm.	kanatá, kanatá wŭtsi
huckleberry, bog	Vaccinium uliginos- um	tsik-hāg, tsik'achk
kinnikinnick or bear berry	Arctostaphylos uva ursi	tinch
labrador tea	Ledum palustre - Ledum groenlandicum Oeder	ssek-scheltīn, ssetsch-katle-tsin
lichen, yellow thread - yellow moss	Parmelia vulpina Evernia vulpina	tsēchŭnē, ssechrŏni (H) (cp. yellow)
lupine	Lupinus śp. root	kantak
maple, dwarf	Acer glabrum Tor.	chralkrē
onion, wild	Allium sp.	jēlch-táche (raven- odor)
pine, shore or lodgepole	Pinus contorta Dougl.	tlaj, chlatl
sea lettuce	Ulva	tātsch
serviceberry	Amelanchier ovalis Ser - Amelanchier florida Lindl.	gawāk
servicetrees or mountain ash	Sorbus sambucifolia Cham. - Pyrus sit- chensis (Roem.) Piper	kaltschanēt (the fruit kāk)
snowberry berries are red to black. snowball?	Viburnum acerifolium L.	kachwēch, kachwēch- wŭtsi
spruce, sitka	Picea Sitchensis Carr.	ssit (the cones are called tsutsáne̅)

spruce, white	Picea alba Lk. - Picea glauca (Moench) Voss	Gunānā āss because this tree is found only on the far side of the passes to the territory of the Gunana

Animals[14]

bat		tsik-ē-di tān (beaver, sea lion, on account of the bat's teeth)
bear	(Ursus ferox) Ursus horribilis Ord.	chūts, hūts
bear, black	Ursus americanus	tsīk (s!īk-Swanton, RBAE 26:480)
caribou	Rangifer	wo-tsig
cat		dūsch
chipmunk	Eutamias sp.	ssalkūtsa
deer	Odocoileus hemionus	kookān, tschitlitsān (qowak'án, Swanton, p. 481)
dog		kētl (kel, Swanton, p. 481
dolphin, porpoise		tschītsch (tcitc, Swanton, p. 481)
ermine, weasel	Mustela sp.	dā (da, Swanton, p. 480)
flying squirrel	Glaucomys sp.	kukākinok
fox	Vulpes sp.	nakatsē
ground squirrel	Spermophilus sp.	ssälk, ssätl
hare	Lepus sp.	k'āch, gāch
horse		kudán
land otter	Lutra canadensis	kūschta, klēnikūchu, tlēnikūchu (kūcta, Swanton, p. 481)
lynx		kāg
marten	Martes americanus	ūch
mink	Mustela vison	nukschejān (lukcayán, Swanton, p. 483)
moose or elk	Alces or Cervus	tsüsk
mountain goat	Oreamnos americanus	dschénu
mountain sheep	Ovis sp.	towē
mouse		kuts-īn
muskrat	Ondatra zibethica	tsinn
porcupine	Erethizon dorsatum	ratlakatsch
sea lion	Eumatopias jubata	tān

seal		ssāch, tsā
shrew	Sorex	kakāk "any small mouse" (kagak, Swanton, p. 483)
squirrel	Sciuridae	kanaltsāk
whale	Cetacea	kīt
wolf	Canis	gūtsch

Birds

Blackbird, rusty	(Scolecophagus ferrugineus) Euphagus carolinus (Muller)	Gunanā jĕlchli
Buffle-head	(Clangula albeola - Glaucionetta albeola (L.)	bītschiú
Chickadee	(Parus)	ka-tū
Cormorant	Phalacrocorax	jó-ūk, jūk
Crane, sandhill	Grus canadensis	dūlch, duchlīk
Creeper	(Certhia familiaris)	āss-kantschádschi
Crow, western fish	(Corvus caurinus Baird)	jĕlchli
Duck, western harlequin	(Anas histrionica) Histrionicus histrionicus pacificus Brooks	tsutsk
Eagle	(Haliaetus) Haliaetus leucocephalus Washingtonii Audubon	tschāk
Eagle, young	same in juv. plumage	tschāk-jĕts
Goose	(Anser) Probably Branta, Anser as now constituted may not reach the area	táwok
Grouse, Canada spruce	(Canace canadensis) Canachites canadensis	kāchk, kāk
Grouse, dusky now blue	(Canace obscura) Dendragapus obscurus sitkensis	nŭk't
Guillemot	Cepphus	ssavón
Guillemot, marbled	(Brachyrhamphus marmoratus) Gmelin	tschī
Gull (several varieties)	Larus spp.	kĕtl-jádi, kĕtl-di kāch
Hawk, Goshawk	(Astur atricapillus) Accipiter gentilis	kedschŭk, ki-dschŭk
Hawk, Marsh	(Circus hudsonius) Circus cyaneus hudsonius	krēch, krēchk

257

Heron, North- western Coast Heron	Ardea herodias fannini Chapman	chlāch, tlāch
Hummingbird	(Selasphorus rufus)	takat-kījá
Jay, Steller's	(Cyanocitta Stelleri)	krēschk'
Kingfisher	(Ceryle Halcyon) Megaceryle alcyon caurina (Grinell)	tlachanēts
Horned Lark	(Eremophila cornuta) Eremophila alpestris	chā-katsīts-kuá, kawach-tūtli
Longspur, Alaska	(Centrophanes lappon- ica) Calcarius lappon- icus alascensis Ridgw.	hūts-tātsi
Leon, Common	(Colymbus glacialis L.) Gavia immer	kā-gīt
Magpie	(Pica hudsonica) Pica pica hudsonia (Sabine)	tserkēne, tserkēni
Mallard	(Anas boschas L.) Anas platyrhynchos platyrhynchos L.	kendetschunēt, kindatschūnet (H)
Merganser, American	(Mergus americanus) Mergus merganser americanus Gassin	jéwochran, jiwoch- rán
Merganser, red- breasted	(Mergus serrator L.)	hēnik-gáchu
Old-squaw	(Harelda glacialis) Clangula hyemalis	j'a-á-ŭna, ja-á-ŭne
Owl, great horned	(Bubo virginianus)	tsisk'
Owl, snowy	Nyctea nyctea (L.)- Nyctea scandiaca (L.)	kå̊k
Ptarmigan	(Lagopus albus) Lagopus lagopus	chretsowā
Puffin	(Lundā arctica) arctica is the eastern form; may be either or both the horned Fra- tercula corniculata and tufted Lunda cirrhata	chrīk, rchēk
Raven	Corvus corax	jēlch
Sandpiper	(Tringa, several varieties) Tringa was a large genus in older days including sand- pipers, knots and phalaropes	ajahīja, ajá-hiā

Scoter	(Oidemia sp.) Oidemia sp. or Melanitta sp.	kitsch-kawū
Scoter, surf	(Oidemia perspicillata) Melanitta perspicillata (L.)	gāch, kāch, tūtsch gach
Shoveller	(Anas clypeata L.) Spatula clypeata (L.)	kĭn
Snipe, Wilson's	(Gallinago Wilsoni) Capella gallinago delicata (Ord)	guts-retūchli
Sparrow, golden-crowned	(Zonotrichia coronata) Zonotrichia atricapilla (Gmelin)	Dēschū-tahī
Swallow	(Hirundo) The true Hirundo is the Barn Swallow; there are several swallows in Alaska, but all swallows were formerly called Hirundo	káschĕlatētl
Swan	Olor sp.	gokl
Waxwing	(Bombycilla)	hunkā
Woodpecker	(Picus) A number of genera were called Picus; now divided into Colaptes, Dryocopus, Sphyrapicus, Dendrocopus, and Picoides	kan-dā-ta-kūk

Amphibians, Fish and Mollusks

Blenny	locally called eels	chlūt, hīnichlūt
Chiton	(Chiton Stelleri Midd. and Chiton tunicata Wood) Probably the black chiton Katharina tunicata (Wood) and the two belong together	schau, jēlch-schau, kū
Chub or stone Perch		dūsch
Clam, butter	(Saxidomus squalidus Desh.) Saxidomus giganteus Desh.	gåtl
Cockle	(Cardium Nuttali Conr.) Cardium corbis (Martyn)	alkátsk
Crab	(Cancer sp.)	tsaúm
Crab	(Cancer sp.)	chrátle-kotla-tlak

259

Crab, box	(Lithodes sp.)	krēch, k'ēch
Dentalium or tooth shell	(Dentalium sp.)	tachrē
Devilfish or squid	class Cephalopoda	năk-náku, nākŭ
Frog		chichtsch
Halibut		tschātsch
Herring		jau
Mussel	(Mytilus edulis L.)	jāk
Salmon, humpback		k'rlūk, k'tlūk
Salmon, red		rchāt, chrāt
Salmon, white or spring		tā
Sculpin	(Cottus sp.) Cottidae, family name, since Cottus refers to fresh water sculpin	uérk', uérk'ch
Shark		tūss
Slug, land or snail	(Limax sp.)	tlúk'o
Smelt	(Thaleichthys pacificus Gir.) Thaleichthys pacificus (Rich). Also called Eulachon, there are several kinds of smelts	ssāg
Snail, sea	(Pachypoma gibberosum Chemn.) Astraea inaequalis (Martyn)	tāchr'-anūchu, tachr'-ū-tēje
Squid	see devilfish	
Stone perch	see chub	
Whelk	(Buccinum?)	tlalchk'u

Insects

Bee		kondoschajē
Beetle, snail eater or ground	(Cychrus longicollis)	ass-kotuiktschā (ass - tree)
leaf	(Lina sp.)	agan-schamētsi (agan - sun)
Butterfly		klēlch-lū
Dragonfly		kascheschráu
Grasshopper		kūk-ána
Intestinal worms of the porcupine		achrāni (a highly prized dish)

(The Tlingit believe that they come from the blackberries eaten in the fall)

Louse		wŏchūts

Spider   kassestān, katsestān
Worm   nēt

Song

Dul-chlūn kē-ut dultsijak ját-jēlch
ani-tūch-schē jawatuk tul-chlu-wu-ká
aschtsch-itīch-chī chlūt aut ti gūk ān kant dakīn
      hi, ha-hi, ha-ha-ha
      hi, ha-hi, ha-ha,
Jeko-ī-chrī kī-ssā-tā jīi jati-jēlch iko-ī-chri
ka-tu-ko-āch hīn-det-ka-at dak-tēt-kā-at

Free translation

     The raven invites all the animals, but on the
morrow he wants to kill them. So they flee, some
into the water and others into the woods.

Dirge

Hā-āni ssigū nak jēntsikit ach tlā hē
nachat-awū ach-tlā he naschat da
dacha kēragotsk
hī-jē
Tu-ani ssagū-rcha jēntsigit-ta (etc.)

Free translation

     How beautiful is our native country. My mother
flies away like a feather (and so on).

Notes

Notes for Introduction

1. U. S. Hydrographic Chart of Bering Strait. (Note: Under-lined footnotes are those of the translator.)
2. Between Cape Nuniano and Cape Krugugin.
3. Geographic Dictionary of Alaska, p. 178.
4. Spelling adopted by Swanton, RBAE 26.
5. Juneau (Geographic Dictionary of Alaska, p. 339).
6. Gaot!ā'k-ān, "Drum (or Bell) Town" (Swanton, RBAE 26: 397).
7. Chutsinu is the same as Killisnoo.
8. Redoubt Bay on Sitka Sound, Baranof Island (Geographic Dictionary of Alaska, p. 523).
9. Kruzof Island (ibid. , p. 384).
10. Klawak (ibid. , p. 371).
11. Henya (Swanton, RBAE 26:397).
12. Dejer or Dejah Inlet, now obs. It is Chilkoot Inlet at the head of Lynn Canal (Geographic Dictionary of Alaska, p. 523).
13. Probably Tagish Lake (ibid. , p. 611).
14. Ibid. , p. 405.
15. "The Athapascans whom they called Go'nana ('strange or different nation')" (Swanton, RBAE 26:414). They will hereafter be called Athapascans.
16. Klukwan (Geographic Dictionary of Alaska, p. 397).
17. Tlehini, now obs. , is Klehini (ibid. , p. 371).
18. Alsek (ibid. , p. 94).
19. Kusawa (ibid. , p. 389).
20. Ssergoit is the Takhini River, a left branch of Lewes River (ibid. , p. 613).

Notes for Chapter 1

1. All proper names in this chapter, unless otherwise indicat-

ed, are written according to Wagner in parentheses after Krause's spelling and then used in the modern form (Henry Wagner, The Cartography of the Northwest Coast of America to the Year 1800, Berkeley: University of California Press, 1937).

2. Krause's interpolation for which I can find no explanation.
3. Humboldt, III, 248; Grewingk, p. 374.
4. Legua, about 3.46 miles.
5. For discussion of these claims, see Wagner, p. 158.
6. The second of these double dates refers to the Russian calendar.
7. Avacha Bay is the body of water on which Petropavlovsk is located.
8. Chiniak (Geographic Dictionary of Alaska, p. 179).
9. Werst or verst, about .6629 miles.
10. Renntier is cervus tarandus L., which is Rangifer or caribou.
11. Horse mussel.
12. Identified by Golder as cow parsnip (Herecleum lanatum).
13. This same quotation is discussed by Birket-Smith and de Laguna, and the place is identified by them as Kayak Island (Birket-Smith and de Laguna, The Eyak Indians of the Copper River Delta, Alaska, 1938, p. 345).
14. A fathom is 6 feet.
15. Elle is 24 inches.
16. Identified by Golder as kelp (Nereocystis priapus).
17. Pallas, V, 155-167.
18. Kayak Island.
19. Grewingk, pp. 382-384; Baer, Beiträge, XVI.
20. Shumagin Island (Geographic Dictionary of Alaska, p. 573).
21. One of the Commander Group, Bering Sea (ibid., p. 129).
22. Alaska Peninsula (ibid., p. 92).
23. Greenhow, p. 135.
24. Humboldt, III, 251-252; Greenhow, p. 115.
25. See Wagner, p. 172.
26. Dixon Entrance.
27. Salisbury Sound (Geographic Dictionary of Alaska, p. 545). Wagner says this identification is doubtful because Bodega's location is 2" north and it may be Sea Lion Bay at the entrance of Salisbury Sound.
28. Bucareli Bay (Geographic Dictionary of Alaska, p. 150).
29. Perhaps Cape Knox.
30. Dixon Entrance (Geographic Dictionary of Alaska, p. 220).
31. According to Maurelle's diary in Pallas, III, 198-273.
32. Greenhow, pp. 117-124.
33. Lituya Bay (Geographic Dictionary of Alaska, p. 410).
34. La Perouse, p. 159.
35. Ibid., p. 162.

36. In the Sandwich Islands, "tohis" are stone axes made of nephrite or jadite. Since these have the blade crosswise to the handle, the traders had some like them made for their barter, and the name "tohis" was attached to them (Forster, II, 35n).

37. Shelikof Strait.

38. Not in the Geographic Dictionary of Alaska. Mentioned by Wagner, but not equated to any modern site.

39. Forster, II, 110.

40. Now Sitka Sound (Geographic Dictionary of Alaska, p. 578).

41. Western coast of Chichagof Island (ibid. , p. 508).

42. Compare mask, cat. no. 1347, in Washington State Museum, collected by Lieutenant Emmons from the Tlingit.

43. Forster, II, 400.

44. Douglas in ibid. , I, 324.

45. "On the May expedition the 'Washington' sailed north, and passing Cape Scott, which was named 'Cape Ingraham, ' stood up Hecate Strait to Derby Sound, which seems to have been Browning entrance on the mainland side. She then stood out to Dixon entrance, and Gray, discovering that the land to the west was an island, named it 'Washington Island. ' An effort was made to sail a little further north but the vessel could not get beyond 55° 43", having to take refuge in Distress Cove, which was probably Port Bazan" (Wagner, p. 209).

46. Humboldt, III, 255.

47. Ibid. , pp. 260-261.

48. Geographic Dictionary of Alaska, p. 684.

49. Humboldt, III, 261-265.

50. Vancouver, II, 122.

51. Geographic Dictionary of Alaska, p. 94.

52. Southeast shore of Baranof Island.

53. Frederick Sound (Geographic Dictionary of Alaska, p. 267).

54. Vancouver, II, 338-339.

55. Ibid. , p. 343.

56. Probably on Sumner Strait (Wagner, p. 245).

57. Skin-covered kayaks.

58. Kolushan (Handbook of American Indians, Bulletin 30, Bureau of American Ethnology).

59. Erman writes Tschilkat (Zeitschrift für Ethnologie, II, 303).

60. Shelikofs Reise von Ochotsk nach Amerika vom Jahre 1783 bis 1787, in Pallas, VI, 235-236.

61. Antlin, probably Aantlen (Geographic Dictionary of America, p. 79), but given also as Ahrn-klin on the Tongas National Forest map, Copper River Meridian, 1940, publ. U. S. Dept. of Agriculture, Forest Service. The other rivers in this group except the Alsek cannot be readily identified, but between the Aant-

len and the Alsek is the Italio, which might be the Kalcho, and near the delta of the Alsek is the Akwe.

62. Lituya Bay.

63. Chugach in Prince William Sound (Geographic Dictionary of Alaska, p. 511).

64. This attack is discussed by Birket-Smith and de Laguna.

65. Chliebnikof, pp. 16-17; Tikhmenief, I, 39.

66. Vancouver writes Portoff.

67. Tikhmenief, I, 41.

68. Chliebnikof names the following places as having been visited by Baranof: Chilcat, Kusnow, Kaknaut, Koukontan, Akku, Taku, Zultana, Stachin, Kek, Kuju. With the exception of the fourth and seventh, these are easily identified with present-day settlements. Koukontan is certainly the name of the clan (kagontan) which was misunderstood for the place (Chliebnikof, p. 81).

69. Lisiansky, p. 221.

70. Langsdorff, II, 95.

71. Ibid., pp. 102-117.

72. Only Larionof's wife, the daughter of a chief, and her children were allowed to live (Holmberg, Entwickelung der Russisch-Amerikanischen Compagnie, p. 59).

73. Chliebnikof, pp. 102-104.

74. Ibid., p. 100; Langsdorff, II, 192.

75. Chliebnikof, p. 115.

76. The term "Creole" is applied to people of part Russian and part Aleut or any other local native descent.

77. Tikhmenief, I, 240, 241.

78. Lütke, I, 165-166. Even Langsdorff, who saw everything in the colonies in the worst light, could not help giving Baranof unstinted praise (Langsdorff, II, 60).

79. Lütke, I, 165n.

80. Ibid., pp. 119-121; compare also Wrangell in Baer and Helmersen, Beiträge, I, 31-32.

81. Lütke, I, 122.

82. Ibid., p. 112.

83. Ibid., p. 129. According to Roquefeuil, the height of the English and American fur-trading period on the Northwest Coast was from 1804 to 1807, during which a total of 59,346 skins were taken to China, 17,445 in 1805 alone. In the following five years, from 1808 to 1812, the figure was 47,962; and in the two war years, 1813-1814, only 6,200; in 1815, 4,300; in 1816, 3,650; in 1817, 4,177; in 1818, 4,500 to 4,800.

The American traders generally made two trips and wintered either on the Northwest Coast or in the Hawaiian Islands. They figured on getting 1,500 sea otter skins besides others of less value. In 1820 a decree of the Russian government prohibited foreign nations from trading with the natives in the coastal stretch claimed by the Russians, that is, on the American side of Bering Strait north to the 51st parallel and on the Asiatic side to 45°40', or approaching the coast closer than 100 Italian miles (Roquefeuil, pp. 298-299). This order came too late and never could be enforced (Lütke, I, 128).

84. Lütke, I, 143.

85. Ibid., p. 145.

86. Ibid., p. 135.

87. Ibid., pp. 136-137.

88. Ibid., p. 137.

89. Baer and Helmersen, Beiträge, I.

90. Ibid.

91. Simpson, who also became acquainted with Veniaminof in Sitka, described him as follows: "His appearance, to which I have already alluded, impresses a stranger with something of awe, while, on further intercourse, the gentleness which characterizes his every word and deed insensibly moulds reverence into love; and, at the same time, his talents and attainments are such as to be worthy of his exalted station. With all this, the bishop is sufficiently a man of the world to disdain anything like cant. His conversation, on the contrary, teems with amusement and instruction; and his company is much prized by all who have the honor of his acquaintance" (Simpson, II, 191).

92. Veniaminof, pp. 119-120.

93. Baer and Helmersen, Beiträge, I, 322-323.

94. Martin, The Hudson's Bay Territories and Vancouver's Island.

95. Simpson, I, 226; II, 206.

96. Tikhmenief, II, 211.

97. Ibid., pp. 207-208.

98. Congressional Papers, House of Representatives, 40th Congress, 2 Sess., Exec. Doc. 177. Russian American, p. 73.

At first the natives were supposed to have harbored the idea that they would drive away the new invaders. They held a number of meetings for this purpose but were discouraged from any action by the chief of the Chilcats, probably Tschartritsch, who pointed to the fact that the new people had many cannon (Congr. Papers, Sen., 41st Congr., 2 Sess., Exec. Doc. 32. Report of Bryant).

99. Morris, p. 44.

100. Since there is no action of Congress on this at hand, the right of the government has been questioned several times. In 1875 the commander of the troops was asked to function as "Indian agent" (Congr. Papers, H.R., 44th Congr., 1 Sess., Exec. Doc. 135).

Notes for Chapter 2

1. Where the modern geographical name is only a slight variant, the correction is given in parentheses; when an explanation is deemed necessary, a footnote is added.

2. An obsolete name for "that part of Alexander Archipelago, west of Chatham Strait and south of Cross Sound and Icy Strait" (Geographic Dictionary of Alaska, p. 336).

3. Inlet on Admiralty Island. "This word comes from an Indian word, Khutzu'hu (bear's foot). The totemic symbol of these Indians is a bear. The obscure and difficult gutturals have produced great diversity in spelling. It has been called Hoochinoo, Hoosnoff, Houchnou, Hudsunoo, Kenasnow, Khutz-n'-hu, Kootsno, Koutsnou, Kutznoo, etc." (ibid., p. 379). Now known as Killisnoo.

4. Dall, Report on Mt. St. Elias.

5. The name of this mountain is written in various ways: Edgcumbe by Cook; Edgecumbe by Greenhow; Edgecomb by Holmberg; Edgecumbe by Dall (Translator's note: Edgecumbe is the present spelling (Geographic Dictionary of Alaska, p. 235).)

6. This reference is not found in Hofmann, Geognostische Beiträge, as Grewingk erroneously says, but in Lütke, p. 101n. Since Lisiansky makes no mention of an eruption, it seems doubtful (cp. Grewingk, p. 93n).

7. Lütke, p. 157; Blaschke, p. 29. The water of this spring contains sulphur, iron, chlorine, manganese. In addition to these, there are hot springs recorded from the Stikine River on the west coast of Chichagof Island, north of Portlock Harbor, and the long inlet that leads from Chatham Strait to Huna Strait.

8. Tikhmenief, II, 330.￼

9. Alsek River, written Alseck, Alsekz, Altsekh (Geographic Dictionary of Alaska, p. 94).

10. On the newest map of Alaska, U. S. Coast and Geodetic Survey, 1884, the Altsech or Altsek, as it is called there, is connected with a dotted line with the White River, a tributary of the Yukon. In a later notice (Science, Vol. III, No. 73) this supposition is withdrawn by Dall himself, but suggestions are made that the Altsech is a source of the Copper River. Since no definite information is at hand, we still hold to our theories which are based on Indian informants and agree with older Russian sources and are also given by Davidson.

11. The writing of this name, as with all taken from the native language, is variable. Of many variations we note the following: Stachin (Baer and Holmberg), Stickeen (Blake), Stikine (Dall, 1884); furthermore Stakeen, Stachine, Stahkin, Stychine.

12. An exhaustive geognostical-geographical description of Tlingit territory in Grewingk, pp. 87-111.

267

13. Blaschke, p. 36.

14. cp. Lütke, pp. 220-222.

15. This is not according to Smithsonian tables.The changes in the next paragraph are done according to these tables.

16. Langsdorff II, 88; Erman, Zeitschr. f. Ethn. II, 145.

17. It is questionable whether the Sitka spruce is the tree under discussion. All the attributes and uses listed by Krause are usually connected with the red cedar (Thuja plicata). On the same page Krause himself speaks of the confusion of Thuja plicata and yellow cedar, but I think he has also confused these with Sitka spruce.

18. Mountain hemlock.

19. Lodgepole pine.

20. Abies subalpina Engelm. has been changed to Abies lasiocarpa (Hook.) Nutt. According to Jones an alpine fir is more properly called a subalpine fir.

21. Thuja gigantea Nutt. is changed to Thuja plicata Donn.

22. Chamaecyparis nutkaensis L. has been changed to Chamaecyparis nootkatensis (Lamb.) Spach. The yellow cedar is called "chlach" by Krause (p. 254), but Swanton called it xa'i (RBAE 26:481) and calls red cedar lax (RBAE 26:480), which appears to be a more modern transliteration of Krause's "chlach." In Krause's list (p. 254) he also gives Western red cedar (Thuja gigantea Nutt.) as ti, stating parenthetically that the two trees are often confused.

23. Congr. Papers, H.R., 42nd Congr., 1 Sess., Exec. Doc. 5; Davidson, Coast Pilot, p. 30; Morris, pp. 109-110.

24. Acer glabrum Tor. is the dwarf maple.

25. Sorbus sambucifolia has been changed to Pyrus sitchensis (Roem.) Piper and is the mountain ash.

26. Fatsia horrida has been changed to Oplopanax horridum (Sm).

27. Lütke, I, 104.

28. Rubus parviflorus Nutt. is the thimbleberry.

29. Amelanchier florida Lindl. is the serviceberry.

30. V. membranaceum Dougl. is the mountain huckleberry.

31. Arctostaphylus alpina (L.) Spreng. is the Alpine bearberry.

32. Ursus horribilis Ord.

33. Enhydra lutris nereis Merriam.

34. Canis latrans lestes Merriam.

35. Tamiasciurus hudsonicus ssp.

36. Porcupine, E. epixanthus ssp.

37. Ondatra zibethica spatulata (Osgood).

38. Ovis dalli.

39. Oreamnos americanus (Kennedyi) Elliot.

40. Arctomys sp. Since two species of marmot may be found, it seems advisable not to use a species name. Modern term:

marmota.

41. Haliaeetus leucocephalus alascanus Townsend.

4̄2̄. Langsdorff II, 92.

43. Corvus corax principalis Ridjw.

4̄4̄. Lütke, I, 115.

45. Pica pica hudsonia (Sabine).

4̄6̄. Cyanocitta stelleri stelleri (Gmelin).

4̄7̄. Nyetea nyctea (L.) and Bubo virginianus saturatus Ridjw.

4̄8̄. Atna _ Copper River (Geographic Dictionary of Alaska, pp. 10̄8̄, 188).

49. From the many names by which this fish is known on the coast we list the following: smelt, candlefish, greasefish, hoolakin, eulachon, olihan, hou-li-kun (Mayne), oulican (Louthan), hoolakan (Macfie), ulicum (Colyer), ulikon (Dall). The Tlingit call it ssak. It is called candlefish by the Americans, because it can be dried and when lighted will burn like a candle. The name ulikon and its derivatives may come from the Tsimshian language, since the Tlingit and Haida have different terms.

50. Cardium Corbis (Martyn).

5̄1̄. Chliebnikof, p. 48; Lütke, p. 164, cites the loss of 150 persons; compare with Holmberg, p. 95; Davidof sets the catastrophe in 1797 and says that more than 80 succumbed, and that the survivors noticed effects of it in later years (Davidof in Moritz von Englehardt, Beiträge, p. 101).

Notes for Chapter 3

1. Point Whaley, the northernmost point of Revilla Gigedo Islan̄d (Geographical Dictionary of Alaska, p. 671).

2. May be a Sanya village. There are several small islands off C̄ape Fox.

3. There was a camp at Fish Creek on Douglas Island used by th̄e Auks (conversation with Dr. Garfield).

4. Hamilton Bay is on the Kupreanof Island side of Kekou Strait̄.

5. Compendium of the Tenth Census, Part II, p. 1427.

6. According to Veniaminof with the addition "antukuan," meaning "living everywhere" (Veniaminof, p. 28).

7. Langsdorff, II, 116.

8. Other readings are: Thlinkitt (Simpson), T'linkit (Dall).

9. Other ways of writing this name are: Koljuji, Koljuschi, Koloschi, Koljuschen (Wrangell), Koluschen, Kolush, Kaloschen, Kaljuschen, Koulischen, Koulisken, Kaloches (Lütke), Kalujes (Lütke), Kaliuches and Kaluscians (Anderson), Kalouches (Balbi), Koloshes and Koloshians (Ludewig). According to Davidof the Kenai call the Tlingit "Tos Koluschoch," and according to Doroschin they are called "Koluschuchtana" (Radloff's vocabulary).

Possibly the name Koluschi comes from the Kenai language, provided the words listed above are not late compounds.

10. Veniaminof, p. 28; Holmberg, p. 10.

11. Archiv, II, 489; Zeitschr. f. Ethn., II, 300-302.

12. In Pallas, VI, 28.

13. Zeitschr. f. Ethn., II, 303.

14. From Kodiak Island.

15. Holmberg, p. 11.

16. The word comes from a trade jargon on the Northwest Coast, known as Chinook, and is a corruption of the French "sauvages."

17. The same word, written by Swanton as qoan (RBAE 26:396).

18. Łaxayi'k, inside of Łaxa (an island) (Swanton, RBAE 26: 397).

19. There is no island in Yakutat Bay on any map examined which could be equated with this spelling; also no reference in the Geographic Dictionary of Alaska.

20. Tatshenshini River, a tributary of the Alsek (Geographic Dictionary of Alaska, p. 618).

21. Ugalakmiut are a tribe of Alaskan Eskimo living on the coast at the mouth of the Copper River. According to the latest writers, they have been so metamorphosed by contact with the Tlingit as to be more Tlingit than Eskimo (RBAE 26:396).

22. Pallas, VI, 231.

23. Dall classifies the Ugalentsen or Ugalakmut with the Innuits or Eskimo (Dall, Tribes of the Extreme Northwest, p. 21).

24. Alaganik is an Ahtena and Ugalakmiut village near the mouth of the Copper River (BBAE 30:35).

25. Not to be confused with the settlements along the Chilkat River, especially Klukwan.

26. Veniaminof, p. 100.

27. Veniaminof, p. 143.

28. Compendium of the Tenth Census, Part II, p. 1427. Translator's note: Corroborated by Swanton, RBAE 26:398.

29. Chilkat is a summer village near the Copper River (BBAE 30:985).

30. No village is mentioned at this location by Swanton, but Yaktag is given as a native name in the Geographic Dictionary of Alaska, p. 684.

31. Chilkat, BBAE 30, Part I, p. 267.

32. Klukwan, ibid., p. 750; Geographic Dictionary of Alaska, p. 373.

33. Five miles according to the Geographic Dictionary of Alaska, p. 347.

34. Qatq!wa' Ałtu (Swanton, RBAE 26:397); written Kalwattu in Geographic Dictionary of Alaska (p. 347) and means "Place of gulls," but Swanton translates it as "Town-on-the-point-of-a-hill."

35. The name obtained by Baker in 1880 from an Indian inter-preter was Gantegas-tak-heh, meaning "Village on right bank of river." In 1867 it was a village consisting of 12 large houses, and in 1880 of 16 houses and 171 people. It was situated at the mouth of the Chilkat River (Geographic Dictionary of Alaska, p. 270). Yendestaq!e (Swanton, RBAE 26:397).

36. Chilkoot (Geographic Dictionary of Alaska, p. 178); Djīiqot (Swanton, RBAE 26:397).

37. Point Retreat.

38. Gunana in Tlingit means "strange people" (Swanton, BBAE 30, Part I, p. 110).

39. Labouchère Bay is now called Pyramid Harbor, at the head of Chilkat Inlet (Geographic Dictionary of Alaska, p. 515).

40. The Auk are called Ak!uqoan by Swanton (RBAE 26:396).

41. "The old Auk village AntcgAltsu (abandoned town) was situated at Point Louisa, north of Douglas Island, and the modern town of Juneau is in their territory" (ibid., p. 412).

42. Dall, Coast Pilot, p. 172.

43. The Taku-kon are called T!aq!oqoan by Swanton (RBAE 26:396).

44. Simpson, I, 214.

45. Schoolcraft, V, 489.

46. Could this be the Sumdum of Swanton (RBAE 26:397)?

47. Gold Creek (personal communication from Dr. Garfield).

48. Chichagof Island is also known by the native name of Khuna or Hooniah (Geographic Dictionary of Alaska, p. 175).

49. Listed as gaot!a k-an, Drum or Bell Town by Swanton (RBAE 26:397).

50. Admiralty Island is Khutsnoi (Bear) Island of Tebenkof in 1848 (Geographic Dictionary of Alaska, p. 175). Also called Kenasnow Island on some maps.

51. Angoon, an Indian village on Admiralty Island, 2 1/2 miles north of Killisnoo, Chatham Strait.

52. Another form of Killisnoo, which is the same as Khutz-n'hu (see footnote 50).

53. Given by Swanton as Naŧtu'ck-ân "Town-on-outside-of-point" (Swanton, RBAE 26:397).

54. Other ways of writing are: Hoochinoo, Hudsunoo, Hoot-sinoo (Schoolcraft), Houchnou, Kootsnoo, Kutznou, Koutsnou (Bryant), Koutsnow, Hoosnoff, Kootznahoo (Meade), Koutsnu, Houtsnau (Roquefeuil), etc. Usually these designations are reserved for the village of Angoon. Kanas-nu or Ken-as-n'hu as Dall writes it, is supposed to mean "near the fort" (Dall, Coast Pilot, p. 175). Neltuschk-an is also written "Letuschkwin" by Dall.

55. British Admiralty Chart 2337 marks "Deep Lake" at this site (Geographic Dictionary of Alaska, p. 313).

56. Kake tribe also called Kekis or Kehons (Geographic Dictionary of Alaska, p. 344). Keq! (Swanton, RBAE 26:397).

57. Otherwise written as: Keku, Ḳekou, Kiku, Kake, Kekh.

58. Congr. Papers, H. R., 40th Congr., 2 Sess., Exec. Doc. 177. Congr. Papers, H. R., 42nd Congr., 1 Sess., Exec. Doc. 5; Morris, p. 147.

59. Kuiu is used as the name for both the island called Ku by Krause and the tribe, Kuju, Kuju-kon, and Kouyou (Geographic Dictionary of Alaska, p. 385).

60. The word "Smoket" which Vancouver and also Roquefeuil used for "chief" is not known in the Tlingit language. "U-en" might be identified with "tlen" meaning "big."

61. Congr. Papers.

62. Dall, Coast Pilot, p. 111.

63. Henya (Swanton, RBAE 26:397).

64. Tongass Island (Geographic Dictionary of Alaska, p. 631).

65. Buschmann finds that in the vocabulary of the "Tun Ghaase," which Scouler repeats from Tolmie, only 1/3 of the words are of Kolushan origin and 2/3 are foreign.

66. Sanya (Swanton, RBAE 26:397).

67. Swanton lists 14 geographical groups, all given by Krause with the Sumdum added.

68. Equivalent to s!itoqoedi of Swanton (RBAE 26:407).

69. The modern transcriptions are all from Swanton, RBAE 26, and the numbers following the words are the page references:

Raven	Wolf
Raven, yět (476)	Wolf, gōtc (476)
Frog, x̣ix̣tc (480)	Bear, xūts! (470)
Goose	Eagle, tcāk! (479)
Sea lion, tān (479)	Killer whale, kǐt (481)
Owl	Shark, tūs! (481)
Salmon, xāt (478)	Murrelet, tc!ǐt (415)

The only discrepancy is in the translation of tc!ǐt as "murrelet," as given above, and its use as tc!its!axu (p. 416), meaning "petrel hat."

70. Big House (personal communication from Dr. Garfield).

71. Grouse Foot (Dr. Garfield).

72. Swanton, RBAE 26:400.

73. Dr. Garfield.

74. Lütke, p. 195; cp. Lisiansky, p. 242.

75. Veniaminof, p. 29-30.

76. Archaeologia Americana, II, 302; Baer and Helmersen, Beiträge, I, 286.

77. Edinburgh New Philosophical Journal, XVI (1846), 83.

78. Schoolcraft, V, 489.

79. Holmberg, Ethnographische Skizzen.

80. Tikhmenief, II, 341.

81. Congr. Papers, H. R., 40th Congr. Exec. Doc. 177, p. 83. The same also in Morris, p. 67, and Colyer, p. 563.

82. Report of the Board of Indian Commissioners for 1869.

83. Historical Magazine (New York), VII (1863).

84. Probably Icy Point (Geographic Dictionary of Alaska, p. 318).

85. Scott reports the Hoods-na-hoos at the upper end of Chatham Strait and near Port Frederick (Cross Sound), clearly confusing the Chutsinus (Killisnoo) with the Huna.

Notes for Chapter 4

1. According to Erman's description (Zeitschr. f. Ethn., II, 314), the roofs of Tlingit houses are four-sided pyramids, and in Shelikof's Reise (Pallas, VI, 216) similar construction is mentioned for the Yakutat. We have not seen this anywhere, and it has not been observed by others, so it probably was an unusual type and used only for temporary buildings.

2. The word is supposed to come from the name of the ceremonial houses in Kodiak (Erman, Zeitschr. f. Ethn., II, 315).

3. Ibid., p. 318.

4. The word is taken from Algonquin and was introduced by Schoolcraft. According to Max Müller it means a "family symbol" and was originally pronounced "ote."

5. Erman described them as boxlike covered areas, on upright posts, about 10 to 15 feet above the ground, which could be reached by using a notched tree trunk as ladder. The space under these caches was used for drying salmon (Erman, Zeitschr. f. Ethn. II, 315). We did not see this kind of structure anywhere else but found storehouses built like little blockhouses.

6. La Perouse, I, 162; Kotzebue, II, 29.

7. La Perouse, I, 162.

8. Coleccion de documentos inéditos, XV, 284.

9. Erman, Zeitschr. f. Ethn., II, 383.

10. Lütke, I, 208.

11. Ibid.

12. Holmberg, p. 20.

13. The translator cannot determine this measurement, unless possibly between foremost points of molars, below the eyes. These terms were checked by Dr. Frederick Hulse.

14. Ibid.

15. La Perouse I, 165.

16. Forster, II, 124.

17. Ibid., p. 405

18. Marchand, I, 232.

19. Vancouver, II, 408.

20. Langsdorff, II, 98-99.

21. Holmberg, p. 21.

22. Erman, Zeitschr. f. Ethn., II, 316-318.

23. Erman, Archiv, VI, 532.

24. Lisiansky, p. 224.

25. Veniaminof, p. 99; Holmberg, p. 24.

26. Pallas, VI, 230. The second footnote 26 may be to this same reference. If not, it is misnumbered and no reference is given.

27. La Perouse, I, 164.

28. Holmberg, p. 19.

29. Compare the facial paintings with totemic designs recorded by Swanton (RBAE 26, Pls. 48-56).

30. Lisiansky, p. 146.

31. Marchand, I, 238.

32. Forster II, 159.

33. Probably abalone (haliotis).

34. Pallas, VI, 231.

35. Ismailof states that among the Yakutat the men do not cut the hair but bind it together in one place and paint it red and decorate it with feathers (Pallas, VI, 230).

36. According to our experience Lütke gives a rather exaggerated description of the Tlingit disregard of the elements when he says: "With his woolen blanket thrown over his shoulder, it seems he does not notice the wind, the rain, or the cold; if he is going to cross a stream, he undresses completely and sits down for a while in the water." He also asserts that one could find natives asleep beside a fire in the forest who were unaware of the fact that they were practically roasted on one side while on the other side they were covered with frost (Lütke, I, 201; cp. Kotzebue, II, 27).

37. Lütke, I, 217.

38. Veniaminof, p. 114.

39. The degree to which a superficial acquaintance with Indian character can lead to exaggeration is shown by this statement about the capability of the Tlingit, made by Indian Agent Vincent Colyear: "To sum up my opinion about the natives of Alaska, I do not hesitate to say that if three-quarters of them were landed in New York as coming from Europe, they would be selected as among the most intelligent of the many worthy emigrants, who daily arrive at that port. In two years they would be admitted to citizenship, and in ten years some of their children, under the civilizing influence of our eastern public schools, would be found members of Congress" (Vincent Colyer, Rep. for 1869, p. 560).

40. Lütke, I, 194n.

41. Erman, Zeitschr. f. Ethn., II, 379. In the report of

Krenitzyn and Levashof it is stated that the Aleut called men servants "kalee" (Pallas, I, 262). (Translator's note: The German word "Knecht" is used for "kalee"; if it is used for slave it is a very loose use of the word).

42. Veniaminof, p. 30.

Notes for Chapter 5

1. The statement by Kotzebue that the Tlingit generally ate everything raw is certainly false and is contradicted by many other authorities (Kotzebue, II, 29).

2. Probably spruce root, which was used for all cooking baskets. See Emmons, Basketry of the Tlingit, Memoirs, American Museum of Natural History, Vol. III.

3. Forster, II, 115.

4. Lütke, I, 214.

5. Langsdorff, II, 96.

6. In Morris' report on Alaska the spread of "Hoochenoo" or "Hootzenoo" is described as follows: "About in the middle of one end of a five gallon oil can a nozzle about 3 inches in diameter was attached and protruded about 3/4 of an inch. On this a lid was put which had a hole in the middle about 1 inch in diameter. Soldered to the lid of the nozzle was a lead tube about 6 to 7 inches long, occasionally straight but ordinarily crooked. The compound prepared for fermentation was this recipe: 1 gallon molasses, 5 pounds of flour, 1/2 box of yeast powder, and enough water to make thin broth. This mixture was set near the fire, and, when it had become warm and sour, it was poured in the can to 3/4 of its capacity and boiled. The tube was led through a cask of cold water in which the steam rising from the mixture was condensed. The drops gathered from the end of the tube were drunk while still warm. The smell and taste of this drink was repulsive" (Morris, p. 61).

Another recipe for the fermentation compound read as follows: "One takes beans, rice, potatoes, a few raisins, yeast or hops, pours some water over these, and stirs the broth, boiling it for about one hour and then leaving it to ferment after which distillation begins."

7. Ismailof speaks of an artist from Yakutat Bay who accompanied chief Ilchak on a visit to the Russians. He knew how to paint various articles made of wood and other materials with native colors (Pallas, VI, 233; cp. Erman, Zeitschr. f. Ethn., III, 158).

8. Lisiansky, p. 223.

9. Kotzebue (II, 31) gives a completely unbelievable instance of a father who was so annoyed by the crying of his infant in its cradle that he threw it into boiling whale oil. In the same place

we read another equally untrustworthy story. Four young men started quarreling over a girl and, when none of them would give up after beating each other for some time, they killed her. At the cremation a song was sung with the following words: "You were so beautiful that you could not be allowed to live. One need only look at you to become raving mad." We would not mention this story, if the name of the author did not give it a certain amount of authority.

10. Veniaminof, p. 110.
11. Forster, I, 324; Vancouver, II, 343.
12. Schabelski in Bull. geogr., 2nd Ser., IV, 208-209.
13. Simpson, I, 211.
14. Ibid., p. 212.
15. Belcher, I, 104.
16. A more accurate description of the stick game is given by Swanton, RBAE 26: 443.
17. La Perouse, I, 170.
18. Forster, II, 167.
19. See p. 19.
20. Lütke, I, 206.
21. Ibid., p. 202.
22. Erman, Zeitsch. f. Ethn. II, 314.
23. Ibid., p. 321.
24. Simpson, II, 196.
25. Belcher, I, 84. "How much the Tlingit expect a return for even the slightest service can be seen from the following incident. When we returned from a canoe trip at low tide, an Indian who was standing on the beach responded to our call and helped bring the boat in. Since it was already late in the evening we forgot to compensate him for the inconsequential service. Next morning we found the rawhide lacing of our snowshoes cut with a knife, and we all agreed that this Indian had done it because he had not received the compensation he expected. I remarked further, that he had not asked for anything and we had not otherwise been niggardly in the distribution of small gifts."
26. Ibid.
27. Lütke, I, 203.

Notes for Chapter 6

1. Thuja plicata Donn.
2. On Vancouver Island I saw a much better procedure for felling used by an English woodcutter. He used a wide horizontal drill bore in which he lit a fire and, placing two at angles to each other, used them as drafts. This method is much faster, and in as short a time as twenty-four hours he could bring down any of the giant trees for which those forests are famous.

3. The elbow adze.

4. 2 to 3 dm. is equivalent to about 6" to 9", which is very thick for the sides of a canoe. Compare with the measurements given on p. 120, 2 to 3 cm.

5. Lisiansky, p. 240.

6. Lütke, I, 212.

7. Holmberg, p. 27.

8. See footnote 4, p. 119.

9. La Perouse, I, 169.

10. Khart, "will not hold water," is the strainer basket. Emmons, Basketry of the Tlingit, p. 253.

11. Cp. Shelikof in Pallas, VI, 199; Holmberg, p. 31.

12. Cp. also La Perouse, I, 169; Langsdorff, II, 115.

13. Forster, II, 114.

14. Marchand, I, 249.

15. Cp. Langsdorff, II, 96; Holmberg, p. 22; Lütke, I, 118.

16. Holmberg, p. 29.

17. A discussion of the attitude toward bears is to be found in Hallowell, Bear Ceremonialism in the Northern Hemisphere, American Anthropologist, XXVIII, 1. The specific reference to the Tlingit which he cites is taken from Swanton, RBAE 26:455.

18. In the winter of 1861 the natives sold to the Russians in the market at Sitka 2,774 mountain goats. This unusually large catch was due to a heavy snow in the mountains which drove the animals to the beach where the hunters could get them easily (Tikhmenief, II, 238).

19. Holmberg, p. 29.

20. An example of native trading on the Northwest Coast is the spread of stone work. According to latest research it is not necessary to assume that all jadite and nephrite come from inner Asia or New Zealand, but they are still only found in a few iso-lated spots within the great area of its distribution.

21. Pallas, V, 198.

22. This date should be 1778.

23. Wrangell in Baer and Helmersen, Beiträge, I, 57-65.

24. Lütke, I, 138. The dentalia are secured, as we heard it, in this way: A dog's body weighted with stones is let down to the bottom of the sea on a long line. When it is raised again several days later, it is supposed to be covered with these animals. Similarly Dunn reports that some venison or a piece of fresh fish is lowered in the same way so that it can be raised again when the dentalia have fastened themselves to it (Dunn, p. 134). Davidof describes the same situation, only according to the information of the Tlingit the body of a slave especially killed for the purpose is used as bait (Davidof in Moritz v. Engelhardt, Beiträge, I, 94). According to Langsdorff the English traders tried to imitate the natural dentalia in porcelain, but, even

though they looked very real, they were regarded as false and ignored (Langsdorff II, p. 114). In British Columbia dentalia are called "haiqua" (Mayne) or "hi-qua" (Lord). Lord says they are fished up in Nootka Sound with long poles that have a crosspiece set with bone spikes, like a comb. The shells are strung so that 25 pieces, with ends meeting, should measure 6 English feet (Lord, II, 22).

25. Probably a potlatch copper.

26. Krause either means individuals with the flattened fore-head, common among the Chinook and Puget Sound tribes, or is using the term loosely to include the Kwakiutl, who have an elongated head deformation. It is quite certain he is not referring to the Flathead tribe of western Montana.

27. Lütke, I, 212.

28. Wrangell in Baer and Helmersen, Beiträge, I, 64.

29. Forster, II, 125.

30. Ibid., p. 126.

31. Malaspina, p. 288.

32. Lütke, I, 205.

33. Whymper discovered that the Indians from the Chilkat River traveled in the interior as far as Fort Selkirk and did the trip in 15 to 20 days, while the return trip took 50 days (?). Through the natives Captain Dodd of the Beaver received a mes-sage from Campbell, the trader at Fort Selkirk. Also a roughly drawn map of the trail was obtained from the Indians (Whymper, p. 228). In the winter of 1881 to 1882, which was marked by an unusually heavy snowfall, the Chilkat undertook only one trading expedition to the interior, which was shorter than was customary. The trip in took 6 days and the return, 4.

34. Among the clans of the Stikine listed by Swanton is the S!iknax'di, possibly the group referred to by Simpson (Swanton, RBAE 26:399).

35. A clan of the Stikine according to Simpson.

36. Simpson, I, 210.

37. Ibid., p. 216.

Notes for Chapter 7

1. Lütke, I, 125.
2. Does he mean bleached?
3. Cp. Emmons, Basketry of the Tlingit.
4. Evernia vulpina.
5. Cp. Emmons, Basketry of the Tlingit.
6. Probably abalone (haliotis) is meant.
7. Lisiansky, p. 150.
8. Belcher, I, 103.
9. Dawson, Pl. XI, Fig. 26.

10. Red top shell, Astraea (Pachypoma inaequalis (Martyn)).
11. Dawson, Pl. IX, Fig. 18.
12. Colleccion de documentos inéditos, XV, 287.
13. Forster, II, 166.
14. Cp. Holmberg, p. 101.
15. Veniaminof, p. 112.
16. Holmberg, p. 28.
17. Erman, Zeitschr. f. Ethn., II, 385-391.
18. Lisiansky, p. 150.
19. Dawson, p. 135 B.
20. See p. 19.
21. Morris, p. 34.
22. Ibid., p. 129.

Notes for Chapter 8

1. The statement by Holmberg that the mother is brought to this hut after the birth is probably not correct (Holmberg, p. 37). Kotzebue insists that the children have their heads compressed immediately after birth, but this is mentioned nowhere else (Kotzebue, p. 26).
2. Veniaminof, p. 90; Holmberg, p. 38.
3. Langsdorff, p. 131.
4. Lütke, I, 211.
5. Holmberg, p. 37.
6. Cp. Swanton, RBAE 26:429.
7. Lütke, I, 212.
8. Veniaminof, p. 90.
9. Lütke, I, 200; Langsdorff, II, 116.
10. Veniaminof, pp. 90-91; Holmberg, p. 41.
11. Holmberg, p. 38.
12. Erman, Zeitschr. f. Ethn., II, 318-319.
13. Veniaminof, p. 92; Holmberg, p. 40
14. Langsdorff, II, 114.
15. Langsdorff, II, 215.
16. Cp. Swanton, RBAE 26:428, 429.
17. Veniaminof, pp. 93-94; Holmberg, p. 34.
18. Cp. Swanton, RBAE 26:428-429.
19. Lütke, I, 211; Holmberg, p. 36.
20. Veniaminof, pp. 95-96; Holmberg, p. 35.
21. Veniaminof, p. 96.
22. Cp. Lütke, I, 211; Holmberg, p. 36.
23. Lütke, I, 211; Veniaminof, p. 96.
24. Langsdorff, II, 115.
25. Lütke, I, 202.
26. Krause probably means phratry. See Swanton, RBAE 26: 430.

27. Probably Grizzly Bear house.

28. Cp. Swanton, RBAE 26:429-434.

29. Morris, p. 80.

30. Simpson, II, 208.

31. Pallas, VI, 231.

32. Lisiansky, p. 240.

33. Malaspina in Coleccion de documentos inéditos, Vol. XV.

34. Schabelski in Bull. géogr., 2nd Ser., IV, 209.

35. Veniaminof, pp. 69-70; Holmberg, p. 71.

36. That this is not a description of a customary burial can be seen from the accounts of Ismailof and Malaspina, cited above, according to which the Yakutat also cremated their dead.

37. Dixon in Forster, II, 116. According to Lisiansky the head is removed only from the body of a person killed in combat and put in a special wooden box beside the one containing the ashes and remains of the bones (Lisiansky, p. 241).

38. A few grave houses even have windows through which one can see inside. They usually have one or more panes of glass. Cp. Morris, p. 76.

39. Holmberg, p. 43.

Notes for Chapter 9

1. Veniaminof, p. 100.

2. See p. 156.

3. The number 4 is important in the customs of the Tlingit.

4. According to Simpson, at one feast at Sitka six slaves were killed by placing them side by side with their necks over the sharp edge of a cliff, while a log was pressed down on them weighted at each end by an Indian (Simpson I, 243). The bodies of sacrificed slaves, according to Lisiansky, are cremated with their master, but the bodies of those offered at the building of a house are buried (Lisiansky, p. 241). Mertens, a companion of Lütke, found the body of a killed slave lying unnoticed in the underbrush in the forest (Kittlitz, I, 216). According to Veniaminof, generally only slaves who were sick and weak were designated for sacrifice. If they managed to escape, and some chiefs made it possible for them, they could return quietly after the ceremony without being punished for their flight (Veniaminof, p. 111; Holmberg, p. 51; Lütke, I, 196).

5. Holmberg, pp. 43-45; Veniaminof, pp. 100-101.

6. Holmberg, pp. 47-49; Veniaminof, pp. 103-106.

7. Holmberg, pp. 49-50; Veniaminof, pp. 106-108.

8. Veniaminof, p. 108.

9. House group.

10. Forster, II, 163; Vancouver, II, 389; Coleccion de documentos inéditos, XV, 268.

11. Belcher, I, 100.

12. When, in 1875 a Stikine chief, Fernandeste by name, committed suicide while he was being taken to Portland for a hearing because he became depressed on account of his circumstances, according to the report, his relatives demanded compensation of General Howard, claiming that the other Indians called them cowards because they had not taken revenge for his death. To pacify the Stikine, Howard gave them 100 blankets and delivered the body of Fernandeste. The reconciliation was celebrated the following night with a large feast at which, according to Howard, the departure, death, and return of Fernandeste, as well as the visit of the warship and the end of conflict, were symbolically represented (Congr. Papers, H. R. 44th Congr., 1 Sess., Exec. Doc. 83).

13. Compensation was demanded of the trader at Chilkoot for a woman who died on the way home from the trading post.

14. Lütke, I, 197-198.

15. Veniaminof, pp. 125-126.

16. Simpson, II, 204-205.

17. Lütke, I, 198-199.

18. Holmberg, p. 42; Lütke, I, 196.

19. Holmberg, p. 28; Forster, II, 386.

20. Erman, Zeitschr. f. Ethn. II, 386.

21. Lisiansky, pp. 238-239.

22. Holmberg, p. 42.

23. Veniaminof, pp. 97-99; Holmberg, p. 43.

Notes for Chapter 10

1. Veniaminof writes Элт, which equals El. (Translator's note: Krause writes Jēlch.)

2. Veniaminof, pp. 37-38; Holmberg, p. 42.

3. Pinart, who records the tales of Raven as of his own transcription, repeats here and elsewhere almost a verbatim translation of Veniaminof, but mentions his name only once.

4. The incidents in the following tales are all well-known parts of the Raven cycle, the long narrative of the adventures of Raven, the culture hero or trickster-transformer of the northern portion of the Northwest Coast. A similar collection of tales can be found in Swanton, "Myths and Texts of the Tlingit," Bulletin 39, Bureau of American Ethnology, and it would be pointless to note the occurrence of each separate incident. The spelling of the names of the characters is corrected to agree with Swanton and after the first appearance of the name the revised spelling is used without further reference.

5. Veniaminof calls her "kitchu ginsi, meaning daughter of a sea mammal."

6. Veniaminof says that Kitchuginsi went to the beach and a whale gave her advice.

7. Veniaminof reports that first he killed a large magpielike bird, Kuzgatúli, that is, bird of heaven, with a long tail and a very long, pointed shiny beak. He pulled the skin off this bird and through this obtained the power of flight. Another time he killed a large duck and gave his mother the skin, which gave her the ability to swim in the sea (Veniaminof, p. 41).

8. According to Veniaminof, the wife was also guarded constantly by 4 or 8 little red birds, called "kun," who left her at once to report if she turned her attention toward another man (Veniaminof, pp. 38-39).

9. Veniaminof indicates that, according to information from the Stikine, Raven fell on the Queen Charlotte Islands and from there, after he had taken a branch of cedar, called "tschaga," in his mouth, flew to the neighboring islands. Wherever he dropped a little piece of cedar this tree now grows (Veniaminof, p. 44). An exact translation of the Veniaminof version of the Raven myth is found in Erman (Zeitschr. f. Ethn., II, 372-374).

10. Lütke, I, 189.

11. Kit-ká-ositiyi-qā (Swanton, BBAE 39:3).

12. This may refer to either Baranof or Kruzof Island, since both were once called Sitka Island, but it is probably the latter because Sitka Point is located there.

13. Veniaminof does not make clear the relationship between this incident and the liver coming up from below.

14. Veniaminof tells only that Raven brought the gull and the crane into conflict with each other at a certain place, and thus obtained the eulachon (Veniaminof, p. 44). Cp. the far-fetched explanation of this myth in Erman (Zeitschr. f. Ethn., II, 376).

15. Veniaminof, p. 49; Holmberg, p. 63.

16. Veniaminof, p. 37; Holmberg, p. 52.

17. Veniaminof, p. 44.

18. Holmberg, p. 63.

19. Veniaminof, pp. 81-82; Holmberg, pp. 65-66.

20. Probably the crater is meant. For the volcanic nature of Mt. Edgecumbe, see p. 52.

21. These are the characteristics of Thunderbird in many Pacific Northwest mythologies.

22. Veniaminof does not say who the brother and sister are.

23. Veniaminof, pp. 84-85.

24. Ibid., p. 85.

25. Ibid., pp. 86-89. We heard from the Chilkat that they first tore the eyes from a bear which had been killed.

26. A Tsimshian village south of Fort Simpson.

27. Lisiansky, p. 166.

28. Veniaminof, p. 58; Holmberg, p. 65.

29. Veniaminof, p. 101n.
30. Ibid., p. 57; Holmberg, p. 64.
31. Veniaminof, p. 59; Holmberg, p. 65.

Notes for Chapter 11

1. íchet, according to Erman, Zeitsch. f. Ethn., II, 322.
2. The matted and feltlike appearance of the hair is probably quite natural without the use of any sticky substance as Erman supposed (ibid., p. 323). In the matted hair of a shaman Esch- scholtz found a peculiar bug, a Staphylinus, which he called Staphylinus pediculus, but it is uncertain whether this is an unusual or a regular parasite found in the hair.
3. According to Veniaminof the shaman's talents are also used in the discovery of theft (Veniaminof, p. 110).
4. Ibid., pp. 62-65; Holmberg, pp. 69-70.
5. Veniaminof, pp. 65-66; Holmberg, p. 71.
6. Veniaminof, pp. 70-73; Holmberg, pp. 72-73.
7. Erman, Zeitsch. f. Ethn., II, 324-326.
8. Holmberg, pp. 63-64; Veniaminof, pp. 56-57.
9. According to Veniaminof nākŭzáti from the word nāku, drugs, medicine.
10. The belief that the shaman has the power to identify witches who are supposed to be the cause of illness makes him an important and, at the same time, a dangerous person, for it gives him the opportunity to take personal revenge. Schabelski tells of a shaman at Sitka who accused a girl who had refused his suit of causing the illness of the chief. Her only brother immediately fell upon her and wounded her with his dagger, and only the intervention of the Russians saved her life. When, however, the truth of the matter became known, the shaman had to leave the neighborhood for a time (Schabelski in Hertha, XII, 182).
11. Veniaminof, pp. 74-80.
12. Erman saw a shaman whose hair reached to the calves of his legs (Erman, Zeitsch. f. Ethn., II, 323).
13. The Tlingit do not take all cases of illness to a shaman, for they also use special drugs, a few of which will be given here according to the information gathered by Blaschke. As a remedy for catarrhal and rheumatic fever they prepare a bed of hot stones on decayed fir or cedar wood, which is renewed every four days. For a chest inflammation due to catarrah, an effusion of Asplenium (spleenwort), and for inflammation of the lungs, an effusion of Coptis macrosepala (gold thread) and Cornicularia Richardsonii is used. For coughs a warm effusion of Osmorhyza brevistyla (sweet cicely) is used. For pleurisy an effusion of a variety of Artemisia vulgaris (wormwood) is used either internally or externally in steam baths. The same use is made of Pyrus

sambucifolius (crab apple). For diseases of the blood an effusion of the root of Spiraea Aruncus is used. For headache one holds one end of a hollow stem of Nereocystis Lütkeana (giant kelp) against the ear, while the other end is laid on a hot stone so that the steam which develops can reach the ear. For diarrhea the fresh juice of the Pinus canadensis is mixed with the tallow of mountain goat. For colic an extract of the roots of a variety of Oxytropis (locoweed) is used. For syphilis an effusion of the sprouts and bark of Pinus inops, Ledum palustre (Labrador tea), Thuja excelsa (cedar) is used internally, and externally the sores are treated with the resin of Pinus Mertensiana and Sitchensis mixed with the leaves of Claytonia alsinoides and the bark of Taxodium sempervirens (cypress). To heal open sores one uses Marchantia with shark oil, for gonorrhea the fumes of urine, and for inflammation of the testicles Heuchera divaricata (alum root). For skin ailments one washes in an effusion of Kalmia glauca (American laurel); mother's milk with Cladonia bellidiflora (sawgrass) is a remedy for eye diseases; while sores are treated with Nardosmia palmata (coltsfoot), the root of Boschniakia glabra, and the ash of Panax horridum (devil's club). For toothache one uses the warmed seeds of Pinus Mertensiana and Sitchensis. For external injuries, bullet wounds, and the like, as we observed, tight bandages are applied, and arms and legs strapped between boards. (Translator's note: Wherever possible, modern common names have been put in parentheses after the botanical terms, many of which are now obsolete.)

14. Wright, pp. 132-133.

15. The punishment of witches is often represented in sculpture. A Chilkat Indian brought us a small figure carved of alabaster (Translator's note: Probably the white marble found on Admiralty Island) in a squatting position with the arms tied at the back to the hair.

Notes for Chapter 12

1. Buschmann, Die Spuren der aztekischen Sprache, p. 678.

2. Other spellings are: Hyder, Hydah (Macfie), Haidah (Swan). The Tlingti call the Haida "De-ki-na." Tikhmenief writes it "Tekina" (I, 119).

3. Other spellings are Kegarnie (Dunn); Ky Gargey (Schoolcraft); Kaiaganies, Ky-ganneis, Kliarakans (Scott); Kygany (Anderson); Kyganie (Scouler); Kaigarny (Roquefeuil), etc.

4. Dawson, p. 172 B.

5. Work of Dawson, p. 173 B.

6. Report of Census for 1880, p. 1429.

7. These names are equated to Swanton, Contributions to the Ethnology of the Haida, MAMNH, p. 268n, as follows:

1, Sukkwan; 2, Klinkwan; 3, Howkan; 4, Q!we anḷas.

8. Baker, Geographic Dictionary of Alaska, p. 342.

9. Radloff, Bull. hist. phil., XV, 305-307.

10. Cp. also Poole, p. 309.

11. Cp. Swan, Smithsonian Contr., XXI, 3.

12. Poole describes a canoe which carried 37 men in addition to a load of 2 tons, and had 3 masts and large sails (Poole, p. 269).

13. This wild tobacco plant is probably Nicotiana pulverulenta Reush.which, according to David Douglas, was planted in cleared places in the forest after the tree stumps were burned and the ashes spread over the ground (Mayne).

14. Some of these totems, called totem or tomanawas by Swan, are over 15 meters high. They are made of a single log of cedar with the back side hollowed out slightly to decrease the weight. While among the Tlingit they usually stand to the side and a little away from the door, here they are directly in front of the door so that one must go around them, or through a round hole left at the base.

15. Usually called a "soul catcher."

16. Cp. also Swan in Smithsonian Contr., XXI, 8.

17. Occasionally the practice of cremation is still found among the Haida. Supposedly bodies of those dying on a journey are cremated so that they will not lie in a strange land (ibid., p. 9).

18. In another version of this myth it is told that out of two living mollusks, which he impregnated and kept warm, Ne-kil-stlas hatched a man and a woman who became the ancestors of the human race.

19. Swan in Smithsonian Contr., XXI, 7.

20. Radloff, Bull. hist. phil., XV, 308.

21. Other spellings are: Chim-sy-an (Schoolcraft), Chimpsain (Scott), Tsimsean (Swan), Simpsean (Macdonald), Tsimshean (Mayne), Chimsain, Tsimpsean, Chimsean (Anderson), Chim-mesyan and Chemmesyan (Scouler).

22. Schoolcraft counted 16 tribes of Tsimshian, Nass, and Skeena Indians which in the greater part agree with those given above. See also an untrustworthy census and estimate of Tsimshian tribes by Col. Scott in Congr. Papers, H. R. 40th Congr. 2 Sess., Exec. Doc. 177, p. 83.

23. Simpson, II, 206.

24. Mayne, pp. 283 ff.

25. Dawson, p. 125 B.

26. A very distorted account of the secret societies.

27. Poole, pp. 270 ff.

28. Simpson, I, 204.

29. Ibid., p. 205.

30. Dunn, p. 272.

31. Collections of the Massachusetts Historical Society for the Year 1804, 1st Ser., IX, 242.

32. Tlingit word for stranger, applied to the Athapascans.

33. Veniaminof, p. 27n.

34. Lütke, I, 215.

35. The Chugach Sea is probably Prince William Sound.

36. According to Mahony in Colyer the Chilkat call the inhabitants of the interior Si-him-e-na or Stick Indians.

37. Probably one of the many names used for the Eyak (Birket-Smith and de Laguna, The Eyak, p. 338).

38. Probably Kayak Island (ibid., p. 2).

39. Wrangell in Baer and Helmersen, Beiträge, I, 96-97.

40. U.S. Coast and Geodetic Survey, Alaska and Adjoining Territory, 1884.

41. Dall, Indian Tribes, p. 21.

42. Radloff, Ueber die Sprache der Ugalachmut, p. 25.

43. For a clarification of all these theories see Birket-Smith and de Laguna, The Eyak.

44. Wrangell in Baer and Helmersen, Beiträge, I, 97-100.

45. Veniaminof, II, 308.

46. Tanaina (?).

47. Dall, Indian Tribes, p. 34.

48. Wrangell in Baer and Helmersen, Beiträge, I, 103-116.

49. Dall, Indian Tribes, p. 35.

50. The Atna call any other people "Khota'na," so K'nai'a-Khota'na are the people from K'nai.

51. Radloff, Bull. hist. phil., XIV, 257.

52. Given by Osgood as one of six subdivisions of the Tatlatan who are one of two subgroups of the Ahtena. However, he says, "The last of the six groups (Kulchana) seems to be an erroneous generalized extension of the Ahtena people" (Osgood, Distribution of the Northern Athapaskan Indians, YUPA No. 7, p. 7).

53. Wrangell in Baer and Helmersen, Beiträge, I, 101-103.

54. Wrangell in Baer and Helmersen, Beiträge, I, 101-103.

Notes for Chapter 13

1. Tikhmenief, I, 296; Holmberg, Ent. der Russ. Amer. Co., p. 55.

2. Chliebnikof, p. 200.

3. According to Tikhmenief, Veniaminof came to Sitka in 1834 and the smallpox epidemic raged in 1836-37 (Tikhmenief, I, 298n, 311).

4. As an indication of the mounting influence of the Russians on the Tlingit, it was reported that in 1837, at the request of the former, the Stikine chief, Kuatche, gave a slave who had been designated for death his freedom. As a reward for this, he

received at the request of the highest administration, from the Emperor, a kaftan embroidered with thread of gold and a fur-trimmed cap (Tikhmenief, I, 299). As a result many slaves selected for sacrificial death had their freedom bought by the Russians, a trade in which the ever greedy Tlingit did not lose anything.

5. Ibid., II, 262-264.

6. Ibid., I, 310; II, 252, 273.

7. Ibid., II, 271.

8. Ibid., p. 274.

9. On the British Admiralty charts written Metlah-Catlah; by Scott, "Met-la-Kaht-la."

10. Cp. Mayne, pp. 307-348; Macfie, pp. 476-485.

11. Morris, p. 72.

12. Anderson, Report of the Inspector of Fisheries for British Columbia for the Year 1879. In consequence of an altercation with the spiritual leaders, Duncan was supposed to be removed from his position, but the Indians would not allow the new bishop into the church and forcibly held Duncan back.

13. Morris, p. 72.

Notes for Chapter 14

1. Rough throat and guttural sounds are characteristic of the language. Marchand comments in a possage cited by Buschmann, "The g and k preceding or following an l are pronounced with a roll which cannot be indicated by any symbol in French orthography and is almost impossible to pronounce if one is not trained to it in infancy (Marchand, I, 587).

2. Cp. Buschmann, Die Pima-Sprache und die Sprache der Koloschen.

3. Veniaminof, Bemerkungen über die koloschische und kadjakische Sprache. The other sources used by Buschmann are: Marchand, Voyage autour du monde, I, 587-591; Lisiansky, A Voyage Round the World, pp. 329-337; Archaeologia americana, II, 371; Davidof, Zweimalige Reise der Seeoffiziere Chwostow und Dawydow, I, App. pp. i-xii (in Russian); Krusenstern, Wörtersammlungen aus den Sprachen einiger Völker des östlichen Asiens und der Nordwest Küste von Amerika; Wrangell and Nossof in Baer and Helmersen, I, 271-274. A few newer vocabularies are in Volume I of the Contributions to North American Ethnology.

4. Cp. the contrary positions of Veniaminof as given by Buschmann, loc. cit.

5. Cp. Erman, Zeitsch. f. Ethn., III, 215-219.

6. According to Veniaminof's writing, without diacritical marks.

7. Discussion of personal names (Swanton RBAE 26:421-423).

8. A prominent Chilkat chief was called Danawǎq (Silver Eyes), referring to the eyes of the raven (ibid., p. 421).

9. Haida called Dekīna "Nation-far-out (at sea)" (ibid., p. 414).

10. Athapascans are called Go'nana (strange or different nation) (ibid., p. 414).

11. Tsimshian called Ts!utsxán by the Tlingit (ibid., p. 414).

12. All white people except Russians are called Lɛ̄t qoan (white or snow people) or Gūtsk!î qoan (people from the place where the clouds reach down to earth, i.e., horizon people) (ibid., p. 414).

13. Apparently a synonym of T. Mertensiana. Krause no doubt was attempting to refer (referred) to the two forms of hemlock, T. heterophylla and T. mertensiana. "To avoid confusion one has to bear in mind that T. heterophylla was known for a long time as T. Mertensiana and is still sometimes so called" (Rehder, p. 21).

14. The modern scientific names have been supplied by Mrs. Martha R. Flahaut, Curator of Biology at the Washington State Museum, University of Washington. The scientific names given by Krause are in parentheses.

Bibliography

(Author's note: In the following bibliography the publications available to the author in the preparation of this manuscript have, with a few exceptions, been marked with an asterisk. A more complete listing of the pertinent literature, especially in periodicals, can be found in Dall's works on Alaska and the surrounding territory.) (Translator's note: Dall, William, and Marcus Baker. Partial List of Books, Pamphlets, Papers in Serial Journals and other Publications on Alaska and Adjacent Regions, in Coast Pilot of Alaska, Appendix I.)

Anderson (Alexander Caulfield). Notes on the Indian Tribes of British North America, and the Northwest Coast. Historical Magazine. New York, 1863, Vol. VII, No. 3, pp. 73-81. (Translator's note: Excellent for Lower Fraser River; shipwrecks on coast.
---------. Report of the Inspector of Fisheries for British Columbia for the Year 1879.
Atahualpa (Voyage of the ship). Extracts from a journal kept on board the ship Atahualpa, bound on a voyage from Boston to the Northwest Coast and Sandwich Islands. Collections of the Massachusetts Historical Society. Boston, 1804. I Ser., Vol. IX, pp. 242-245. (Translator's note: One page on trade up the Stikine River.)
Baer (K. E. v.). Statistische und ethnographische Nachrichten über die russischen Besitzungen an der Nordwestküste von Amerika. Gesammelt von dem ehemaligen Oberverwalter dieser Besitzungen, Contre-Admiral v. Wrangell. In Baer und Helmersen, Beiträge zur Kenntnis der russischen Reiches und der angrenzenden Länder Asiens. Bd. I, Petersburg, 1839.
---------. Die Verdienste Peters des Grossen. In Baer Helmersen, Beiträge Bd. XVI, 1872.

Bancroft (Hubert Howe). The native races of the Pacific States of North America. 5 vols. Vol. I, Wild tribes. San Francisco, 1874.

Belcher (Sir Edward). Narrative of a Voyage Round the World, performed in H. M. S. Sulphur 1836-1842. London, 1843. 2 vols. (Translator's note: Pictures of Indians and Indian settings; trade.)

Bendel (Bernhard). Aus Alaska. Von Sitka nach dem Chilkcat-Fluss, 1868. Weser Ztg. 10 Okt. 1872.

*----------. The Alexander Archipelago. Proceedings of the Agassiz Institute, Sacramento, Calif., 1873. (Translator's note: Also in Daily Record, Sacramento, Feb. 15, 1873.)

Blake (William Phipps). Notes upon the geography and geology of Russian America and the Stickeen River from observations made in 1863. Congr. Papers, H. R., 40th Congr., 2 Sess., Exec. Doc. 177, Part 2. 8°. Washington, 1868.

Blaschke (Eduard). Topographia medica portus Novi-Archangelscensis. 8°. St. Petersburg, 1842.

Bongard (Heinrich Gustav). Observations sur la végétation de l'île de Sitcha. In Mémoires de l'Académie Impériale des Sciences de St. Petersbourg, VI Ser., Tome II, pp. 119-177. St. Petersbourg, 1833. (Translator's note: Plants collected by Dr. Mertens; 222 species listed with botanical descriptions. Excellent for historical botany.)

Bryant (Charles). Report as special agent of the treasury department. Congr. Papers, H. R., 44th Congr., 1 Sess., Exec. Doc. No. 83.

Burney (James). A chronological history of northeastern voyages of discovery, 8°. London, 1819.

Buschmann (Johann Karl Eduard). Die Pima-Sprache und die Sprache der Koloschen. Abhandl. der Kgl. Akad. d. Wissenschaften zu Berlin aus dem Jahre 1856. 4°. Berlin, 1857. (Translator's note: Comparative vocabularies of Tlingit, Haida, Athapascan and Aztec.)

----------. Die Völker und Sprachen Neu-Mexicos und die Westseite des britischen Nordamerika. Ibid., 1857. Berlin, 1858.

----------. Die Spuren der aztekischen Sprache im nördlichen Mexico und höheren amerikanischen Norden. Ibid., 2 Supplementband. Berlin, 1859. (Translator's note: Comparative vocabularies of Makah, Nootka; review of vocabularies from early voyages, p. 314.)

Caamaño (Don Jacinto). Expedicion de la corbeta Aranzazu al mando del teniente de navio D. Jacinto Caamaño á comprobar la relacion de Fonte. Collection de documentos inéditos para la historia de España por Salvá y Baranda. 8°. Madrid, 1849. Tomo XV, pp. 323-363.

Chliebnikof. See Chliebnikow (translator's note).

Chliebnikow (Cyrill). Lebensbeschreibung Alexander Baranows, Oberverwalters der russischen Kolonieen in Amerika. St. Petersburg, 1835 in Russian. (Translator's note: In Bancroft Library under Khliebnikov, Naval Printing Office.)

Colyer (Vincent). Report of the Hon. Vincent Colyer, U.S. special Indian commissionar, on the Indian tribes and their surroundings in Alaska territory, from personal observation and inspection in 1869. Report of the Board of Indian Commissionars for 1869. Washington, 1870. (Author's note: The part of this report which concerns Fort Wrangell was published with illustrations in the Congressional report H. R., 41st Congr., 2 Sess., Exec. Doc. No. 144.) (Translator's note: Historic pictures of the town of Wrangell; Indian-White relations; trade relations of Indians at Wrangell.)

Cook (James) and King (James). A voyage to the Pacific Ocean, undertaken by the command of his Majesty, for making Discoveries in the Northern Hemisphere. Performed under the direction of Captains Cook, Clerke and Gore in the years 1776-1780. 4°. London, 1784-1785. 3 vols.

Coxe (William). Account of the Russian discoveries between Asia and America, to which are added the conquest of Siberia and the history of the transactions and commerce between Russia and China. 4°. London, 1780.

Dall (William Healey). Alaska and its resources. 8°. Boston, 1870.

----------. Report on Mt. St. Elias. With map and view. In Coast Survey, Report for 1875. Appendix No. 10, pp. 157-188. 4°. Washington, 1878.

----------. Tribes of the extreme Northwest. In Powell, Contributions to North-American Ethnologie. Vol. I, Part 1, pp. 1-106. 4°. Washington, 1877.

----------. Coast Pilot of Alaska. Appendix I. Part 1. Meteorology of Alaska. Part 2. Partial list of Charts, Maps and Publications relating to Alaska and the adjacent region from Puget Sound and Hakodate to the Arctic ocean, between the Rocky and the Stanowoi Mountains. 4°. Washington, 1879.

----------. Pacific Coast Pilot, Alaska. Part 1. Coast from Dixon Entrance to Yakutat-Bay with the Inland-Passage. 4°. Washington, 1883. (Author's note: For the numerous other papers of more or less significance published by this author on researches on Alaska in the past twenty years, consult the bibliography listed above.)

Davidof. See Dawydow (translator's note).

Davidson (George). Report Relative to the Resources and the Coast Features of Alaska Territory. In Coast Survey, Report for 1867. Appendix No. 18. pp. 187-329. Washington, 1869.

August 7, 1869, at Kohklux, Chilkaht River, Alaska. Report
for 1869. Appendix No. 8, pp. 177-181.

----------. Coast Pilot of Alaska (First Part) from Southern
Boundary to Cooks Inlet. 8°. Washington, 1869. (Translator's
note: Information on shipwrecks and Indian population.)

Dawson (George M.). Report on the Queen Charlotte Islands 1878.
Appendix A. On the Haida Indians of the Queen Charlotte Islands. In Geol. Survey of Canada. Report of progress for 1878-
1879. (B) 103-171. Montreal, 1880.

Dawydow (Gawrila). Zweimalige Reise der Seeoffiziere Chwostow
und Dawydow nach Amerika. 2 Bde. 8°. St. Petersburg, 1810-
1812 in Russian.

----------. Reise der Russ. Kais. Flottenoffiziere Chwostow
und Dawydow von St. Petersburg durch Siberien nach Amerika
und zurück, in den Jahren 1802-1804. Beschrieben von Dawydow und aus dem Russischen übersetzt von Dr. Karl Joh.
Schultz. 8°. Berlin, 1816.

----------. Gawrila Iwanowitsch Dawüdovs Nachrichten von der
Insel Kadjak und den russischen Niederlassungen daselbst. In
Engelmann (Moritz v.). Beiträge zur Kenntnis Russlands und
seiner Bewohner. Bd. I, S. 71-142. 8°. Dorpat, 1818. (Translator's note: These names are spelled Khwostof and Davidof
in the Geographic Dictionary of Alaska, p. 15.)

Del Norte (nom de plume). Acquisition of Alaska. In Congr.
Papers, H. R., 40th Congr., 2 Sess., Exec. Doc. No. 177,
pp. 67-84.

Dixon (George). A voyage round the world; but more particularly
to the North-West Coast of America; Performed in 1785-1788
in the King George and Queen Charlotte, captains Portlock and
Dixon. 4°. London, 1789. (Translator's note: Cited according
to Forster's translation.)

Doroschin. Einige Beobachtungen und Bemerkungen über das
Goldvorkommen in den Besitzungen der Russisch-Amerikani-
schen Compagnie. In Erman, Archiv für wissensch. Kunde von
Russland. Vol. XXV, pp. 229-237.

Duflot de Mofras (Eugène). Exploration de l'Orégon, des Califor-
nies, et de la Mer Vermeille, 1840-1842. 2 vols. 8°. Atlas
fol. Paris, 1844.

Dunn (John). History of the Oregon Territory and British North-
American fur trade; with an account of the habits and customs
of the principal native tribes on the northern continent. 8°.
London, 1844.

Elliot (Henry Wood). A Report upon the condition of affairs in the
Territory of Alaska. Congr. Papers, H. R., 44th Congr., 1.
Sess., Exec. Doc. No. 83, pp. 1-277. (Translator's note:
Birds of Alaska, list prepared by Elliott Coues.)

Engelhardt (Georg). Russische Miscellen zur genaueren Kenntnis
Russlands und seiner Bewohner. 4 Bde. 8°. St. Petersburg,
1829-1832.

Erman (Georg Adolf). Archiv für wissenschaftliche Kunde von
Russland. 25 Bde. 8°. Berlin, 1841-1866. (Translator's note:
Contents of Erman listed in Dall, Coast Pilot of Alaska, App.
I.)

----------. Ethnographische Wahrnehmungen und Erfahrungen
an den Küsten des Berings-Meeres. In Bastian Hartmann,
Zeitschr. f. Ethnologie. 8°. Berlin, 1870, Bd. II, S. 295 bis
327 u. 369-393; 1871, Bd. III, S. 149-175, 205 bis 219.

Eschscholtz (Friedrich). Zoologischer Atlas, enthaltend Abbil-
dungen und Beschreibungen neuer Tierarten, während des Flot-
tenkapitäns v. Kotzebue zweiter Reise um die Welt 1823 bis
1826. fol. Berlin, 1829-1833.

Fleurieu (Charles Pierre Claret). Voyage autour du monde,
pendant les années 1790-1792, par Étienne Marchand. Précédé
d'une introduction historique (etc.) 4 vols. 4°. Paris, 1798-
1880. (Translator's note: A voyage round the World performed
during the years 1790, 1791, 1792 by Etienne Marchand. Trans.
from French by Fleurieu. London 1801. Long resume of voyages to the Northwest Coast.)

Forster (Johann Georg Adam). Geschichte der Reisen, die seit
Cook an der Nordwest und Nordostküste von Amerika und in
dem nördl. Amerika, selbst unternommen worden sind von
Meares, Dixon, Portlock, Coxe u. a. 8°. Berlin, 1792. 3 Bde.

Freimann. Bemerkungen über eine Reise (von Sitcha) durch die
Besitzungen der Hudsons-Bay-Compagnie. In Ermans Archiv,
Bd. VI, S. 226-240.

Furuhelm (Hjalmar). Notes on the Natives of Alaska. In Powell,
Contributions to North American Ethnology. Vol. I, Part 1,
pp. 111-116. 4°. Washington, 1877.

*Galiano (Dionisio Alcala). Relacion del viage hecho por las gole-
tas Sutil y Mexicana en el año de 1792 etc. 8°, Atl. 4°. Madrid,
1802.

Gallatin (Albert). A Synopsis of the Indian tribes within the
United States east of the Rocky Mountains and in the British
and Russian Possessions in North America. Archaeologia
Americana. Vol. II, pp. 1-422. 8°. Cambridge, 1836.
(Translator's note: Vocabularies in Chinook from mouth of
Columbia River, Queen Charlotte Islands; population figures.)

Gibbs (George). Notes on the Tinneh or Chepewyan Indians of
British and Russian America. Smithsonian Institution. Report
for 1866. pp. 303-327. 8°. Washington, 1872.

---------- and Dall. Comparative vocabularies (of native tribes
of Alaska). In Powell, Contributions to North American Ethnology. Vol. I, Part 1, pp. 121-156. 4°. Washington, 1877.

----------, Tolmie and Mengarini. Comparative vocabularies (of tribes in the northwestern part of the United States and in Brit. Columbia). In Powell, Contributions etc. Vol. I, Part 2, pp. 247-283.

Golowin (Paul). Ueber die russischen Kolonieen an der Nord-westküste von Amerika. Ermans Archiv Bd. XXII, S. 47-70.

*Golownin (Wasili). Reise um die Welt in dem Kriegschiff "Kam-tschatka" 1817-1819. 2 Bde. 4°. St. Petersburg, 1822 in Russian.

Greenhow (Robert). The history of Oregon and California and the other territories on the Northwest Coast of North-America. 2nd ed. 8°. Boston, 1845.

Grewingk (Constantin). Beitrag zur Kenntnis der orographischen und geognostischen Beschaffenheit der Nord-west-Küste Amerikas mit den anliegenden Inseln. Verhandlungen der Mineralog. Ges. zu St. Petersburg 1848-1849, S. 76 bis 424. (Translator's note: This is in the Russian series Vserossiiskoe mineralogicheskoe obshchestvo, Leningrad. The first 10 volumes are printed in German. A review of reports of early explorers with stress on physiographic features and minerals.)

Hofmann, (Ernst). Geognostische Beobachtungen, angestellt auf einer Reise um die Welt in den Jahren 1823-1826. In Karstens Archiv fur Mineralogie, Geognosie, Bergbau und Hüttenkunde. Bd. I, S. 243-315. 8°. Berlin, 1829.

Holmberg (Heinrich I.). Ethnographische Skizzen über die Völker des Russischen Amerika. Acta Societatis Scientiarum Fennicae. Vol. IV, pp. 281-421. 4°. Helsingfors 1856. (Translator's note: Author's notes refer to this volume reprinted as Part 1, Die Thlinkiten-Die Konjagen, pp. 1-141.)

----------. Entwickelung der Russisch-Amerikanischen Compagnie. In ibid., Vol. VII, pp. 37-101. 4°. Helsingfors, 1863. (Translator's note: Reprinted as Part 2 of Ethnographische Skizzen.)

Howard (Oliver Otis, Brig. Gen.). Report of his tour in Alaska in June, 1875. In Congr. Papers, Sen., 44th Congr., 1 Sess., Exec. Doc. No. 12, pp. 1-13.

Howard (Capt. William A.). Reports of. In Congr. Papers, H. R., 40th Congr., 2 Sess., Exec. Doc. No. 177, pp. 195-203, 206-214.

Humboldt (F. H. Alexander v.). Versuch über den politischen Zustand des Königreichs Neu-Spanien. 4 Bde. 8°. Tübingen, 1809. (Translator's note: It seems that Krause has the wrong place and date for this book. The earliest publication seems to be the French entitled Essai politique sur la royaume de le nouvelle Espagne, published in 2 volumes, 4°, Paris, 1811, as cited by Bayard Taylor in the bibliography (p. xvi) in his The Life, Travels and Books of Alexander von Humboldt, New

York, 1859. In the Bancroft Library, University of California, there is a 5 volume edition, 8°, published by F. Schuvell in Paris, 1811, with a foreword stating that the same work is also available in 4°, 2 volumes. In the advertisement it is stated that Humboldt had rewritten the work in Spanish during his sojourn in Mexico and given the first copy to the Viceroy in January, 1804. The first imprint of this edition was made in 1808. There is nowhere an edition of 1809 in Tübingen as listed, but in 1831 and 1853 other works of Humboldt were published in Tübingen and Stuttgart. He wrote in German as well as French.)

Jackson (Rev. Sheldon). Missionary work among the Indians of Alaska. Ninth annual Report of the Board of Indian Commissionars for the year 1877, pp. 41-47. 8°. Washington, 1877.

----------. Alaska: its scenery and resources, population, their customs and religions. 12°. New York, 1880.

----------. The neglect of education in Alaska. In Circulars of information of the Bureau of education. No. 2., 1882, pp. 61-75. 4°. Washington, 1882.

Kittlitz (F. H. v.). Denkwürdigkeiten einer Reise nach dem Russischen Amerika, nach Mikronesien und durch Kamtschatka (1826-1828). 2 Bde. Gotha, 1858.

Kotzebue (Otto v.). Neue Reise um die Welt in den Jahren 1823-1826. 2 Bde. 8°. Weimar, 1830.

Krusenstern (Adam Johann v.). Reise um die Welt in den Jahren 1803-1806 auf den Schiffen "Nadeshda" und "Newa." 3 Bde. gr. 4°. St. Petersburg, 1810-1812.

----------. Wörtersammlungen aus den Sprachen einiger Völker des östlichen Asiens und der Nordwestküste von Amerika. 4°. St. Petersburg, 1813.

Langsdorff (Georg Heinrich v.). Bemerkungen auf einer Reise um die Welt in den Jahren 1803-1807. 2 Bde. 4°. Frankfurt a. M., 1812.

La Pérouse (Jean François de). Voyage de La Pérouse authour du monde. 4 vols. 4°. Atlas fol. Paris, l'an V, 1797.

----------. Entdeckungsreise in den Jahren 1785-1788. (Author's note: From the French with annotations by C. L. S. 8°. Leipzig 1799. (cit.))

Lasaref. See Lasarew (translator's note).

Latham (Robert Gordon). On the ethnography of Russian America. In Jameson, Edinburgh New Philosophical Journal. Vol. XL, pp. 35-44. 8°. Edinburgh, 1846. (Translator's note: Important for relations with Northeastern Asia.)

*Lasarew. Reise um die Welt in der Schaluppe "Ladoga" 1822-1824. 8°. St. Petersburg, 1832 in Russian.

*Lincoln (David F.). Medical notes upon the aborigines of Alaska. Medical and Surgical Journal. Boston, 1870.

Lisiansky (Urey). A voyage round the world, in the years 1803-1806, in the ship Newa. 4°. London, 1814.

Lord (John Keast). The naturalist in Vancouver Island and British Columbia. 2 vols. 8°. London, 1866.

Lowe (F.) Weniaminow über die Aleutischen Inseln und deren Bewohner. Ermans Archiv. Bd. II, S. 459-495.

Ludewig (Ernst Hermann). The literature of American aboriginal languages. 8°. London, 1858. (Translator's note: The author's first and second name should be reversed.)

Lütke (Feodor). Voyage autour du monde, 1826-1829. Partie historique. 3 vols. 8°, Atlas fol. Paris, 1835.

Macdonald (Duncan George Forbes). British Columbia and Vancouver's Island. 8°. London, 1862.

Macfie (Matthew). Vancouver Island and British Columbia. 8°. London, 1865.

McIntyre (H. H.). Report of, as special agent of Treasury Depart. in Alaska. In Congr. Papers, H. R., 41st Congr., 2 Sess., Exec. Doc. No. 36.

Mackenzie (Alexander). Voyages through the continent of North America, to the Frozen and Pacific Oceans, in the years 1789 and 1793. 4°. London, 1801.

Malaspina (Alessandro). Viaje de Malaspina. In Coleccion de documentos inéditos para la historia de España por Salvá y Baranda. Tomo XV, pp. 268-320. 8°. Madrid, 1849.

Marchand. See Fleurieu (translator's note).

Martin (Robert Montgomery). The Hudson's bay territories and Vancouver's Island. 8°. London, 1849.

Maurelle (Franzisco Antonio). Tagebuch einer im Jahre 1875 zur Untersuchung der nördlich von Californien fortgesetzten Küsten geschehenen Reise (u. s. w.). In Pallas, Neue nordische Beiträge. Bd. III, S. 198-273. St. Petersburg u. Leipzig, 1782. (Translator's note: The date of the voyage should be 1775.)

Mayne (Richard Charles). Four years in British Columbia and Vancouver Island (1857-1860). 8°. London, 1862.

Meares (John). Voyages in the years 1788-1789, from China to the Northwest Coast of America. 4°. London, 1790 (cited according to Forster).

Morris (William Gouverneur). Report upon the customs district, public service and resources of Alaska Territory. Congr. Papers, Sen., 45th Congr., 3 Sess., Exec. Doc. No. 59.

Müller (Gerhard Friedrich). Sammlung russischer Geschichte. Bd. III, Nachrichten von Seereisen und zur See gemachten Entdeckungen u. s. w. 8°. St. Petersburg, 1758.

Pallas (Peter Simon). Neue nordische Beiträge zur physikalischen und geographischen Erd- und Völkerbeschreibung, Naturgeschichte und Oekonomie. 4 Bde. 8°. St. Petersburg und

Leipzig, 1781-1783.

----------. Neueste nordische Beiträge (u. s. w.). 3 Bde. 1793 bis 1796.

Pinart (Alphonse L.). Notes sur les Koloches. In Bulletin de la société d'anthropologie. Ser. II, Vol. 7. 8°. Paris, 1872.

Poole (Francis). Queen Charlotte Islands. 8°. London, 1872.

Portlock (Nathaniel). A voyage round the world, but more particularly to the Northwest Coast of America; Performed in 1785-1788. 4°. London, 1789. (Author's note: Cited according to Forster, Vol. II)

Powell (John Wesley). Depart. of the Interior. U. S. Geographical and Geological Survey of the Rocky Mountain region. Contribution to North-American Ethnology. Vol. I. 4°. Washington, 1877.

Radloff (Leopold). Einige kritische Bemerkungen über Herrn Buschmanns Behandlung der Kinai-Sprache. In Bulletin historico-philologique, Tom XIV, p. 257. 4°. St. Petersbourg, 1857.

----------. Ueber die Sprache der Ugalachmut. Bull. hist. phil. T. XV, p. 25. 1857.

----------. Einige nachrichten über die Sprache der Kaiganen. Bull. hist. phil. T. XV, p. 305. 1857.

----------. Leopold Radloffs Wörterbuch der Kinai-Sprache, herausgeg. von A. Schiefner. Mémoires de l'Acad. Imp. des Sciences de St. Petersbourg. VII Ser., T. XXI, No. 8. St. Petersbourg, 1874.

Ritter (H...). Land und Leute im russischen Amerika. Nach dem russischen Marine-Archiv (Morskoi Sbornik 1862, No. 1) bearbeitet. In Koner, Zeitschrift für allgemeine Erdkunde. Bd. XIII. Neue Folge. S. 241-270. 8°. Berlin, 1862. (Author's note: Report of Capt. Lt. Golowin.)

Roquefeuil (Camille de). Journal d'un voyage autour du monde, pendant les années 1816-1819. 2 vols. 8°. Paris, 1823.

Rothrock (Joseph Trimble). Northwestern North-America; its resources and its inhabitants. In Journal of the American Geogr. and Statistical Society. Vol. IV, pp. 393-415. 8°. New York, 1874.

*Russisch-Amerikanische Kolonieen. Bericht des Komitees über die Organisation der Russ.-Am.-Kolonieen. 8°. St. Petersburg, 1863 in Russian.

*----------. Supplement zu dem Bericht des Komitees über die Organisation der Russ.-Am.-Kol. 8°. St. Petersburg, 1863 in Russian.

*Russisch-Amerikanische Kompagnie. Berichte der Russisch-Amerikanischen Kompagnie. 19 Bde. 8°. St. Petersburg, 1845-1865 in Russian. (Author's note: Extracts from this in Erman's Archiv.)

Sarychef. See Sarytchefs (translator's note).

Sarytchefs (Gawrila), achtjährige Reise im nordöstlichen Siberien, auf dem Eismeer und dem nordöstlichen Ocean; übersetzt von J. H. Busse. 2 Bde. 8°. Leipzig, 1805-1815.

Sauer (Martin). Reise nach den nördlichen Gegenden vom russischen Asien und Amerika in dem Jahren 1785-1794. 8°. Weimar, 1803.

Schabelski. See Shabelski (translator's note).

Schelechofs Reise von Ochotzk nach Amerika vom Jahre 1783 bis 1787. In Pallas, Neue nordische Beiträge, Bd. VI. St. Petersburg u. Leipzig, 1793.

Schoolcraft (Henry Rowe). Information Respecting the History, Conditions and Prospects of the Indian Tribes of the United States. 6 vols. Philadelphia, 1852-1857. (Translator's note: This reference omitted by Krause.)

Schott (W.). Etwas über die Sprache der Koloschen nach Weniaminow. Erman, Archiv. Bd. III, S. 439-445.

––––––––––. Ueber die Sprachen des Russischen Amerika nach Weniaminow. Erman, Archiv. Bd. VII, S. 126-143. (Translator's note: Vocabularies collected by Sagoskin.)

Scouler (John). Observations on the indigenous tribes of the Northwest Coast of America. In Journal of the Royal Geogr. Soc. of London. Vol. XI, pp. 215-249. 8°. London, 1841.

––––––––––. On the Indian tribes inhabiting the Northwest Coast of America. In Jameson, Edinburgh New Philosophical Journal. Vol. XLI, pp. 168-192. 8°. Edinburgh, 1846.

Shabelski (Achille). Voyage aux colonies russes de l'Amérique, fait à bord du sloop de guerre l'Apollon, pendant les années 1821-1823. 12°. St. Petersbourg, 1826.
Extracts from this item by A. Tardieu in Bulletin de la Société de géographie de Paris, II Ser. , Tom. IV, pp. 201-220. The same in Hertha, Zeitschr. für Erd-, Völker- und Staatenkunde, von Berghaus und Hofmann, Bd. XII, S. 173-185. 8°. Stuttgart und Tübingen, 1828.

Shelikof. See Schelechofs (translator's note).

Simpson (George). Narrative of a journey round the world, during the years 1841-1842. 2 vols. 8°. London, 1847.

Stellers (Georg Wilhelm). Tagebuch seiner Seereise aus dem Petripaulshafen in Kamtschatka bis an die westlichen Küsten von Amerika. In Neue Nordische Beiträge. Bd. V. St. Petersburg u. Leipzig, 1793.

Sumner (Charles). Speech on the cession of Russian America to the United States. 8°. Washington, 1867.

Swan (James G.). The Haidah Indians of Queen Charlotte's Islands, B. C. Smithsonian Contributions to Knowledge, 267, Vol. XXI. gr. 4°. Washington, 1876.

––––––––––. Report on his cruise in Alaska in 1875. In Morris, Report upon the custom district. Appendix, pp. 146-150.

Tichmenew (P.). Historische Uebersicht der Organisation der russisch-amerikanischen Kompagnie. 2 Bde. St. Petersburg, 1861-1863 in Russian. (Translator's note: Spelling adopted in Geographic Dictionary of Alaska, Tikhmenief.)

Tikhmenief. See Tichmenew (translator's note).

Tytler (Patrick Fraser). Historical view of the progress of discovery on the more northern coasts of America etc. 16°. Edinburgh u. London, 1833.

Vancouver (George). A voyage of discovery to the north Pacific ocean and round the world, performed in the years 1790-1795. 3 vols. 4°, Atlas fol. London, 1798.

Veniaminof. See Weniaminow (translator's note).

Weniaminow (Iwan). Bemerkungen über die Inseln des Unalaschka-Distrikts. 3 Bde. 8°. St. Petersburg, 1840. Bd. 3: Bemerkungen über die atchinskischen Aleuten und die Koloschen in Russian.

----------. Bemerkungen über die koloschische und kadjakische Sprache. 8°. St. Petersburg, Kais. Akad. d. Wissenschaften, 1846 in Russian. (Translator's note: Spelling adopted by the Geographic Dictionary of Alaska, Veniaminof.)

Whymper (Frederick). Travel and adventure in the Territory of Alaska, formerly Russian America etc. 8°. London, 1868.

Woldt, (A.). Kapitän Jacobsens Reise an der Nordwestküste Amerikas 1881-1883. 8°. Leipzig, 1884.

Wrangell (Ferdinand), see Baer.

Wright (Julia McNair). Among the Alaskans. 16°. Philadelphia, 1883.

TRANSLATOR'S BIBLIOGRAPHY

Baker, Marcus. Geographic Dictionary of Alaska. 2nd ed. Washington, 1906.

Birket-Smith, K., and F. de Laguna. The Eyak Indians of the Copper River Delta. Copenhagen, 1938.

Dall, William, and Marcus Baker. Partial List of Books, Pamphlets, Papers in Serial Journals and Other Publications on Alaska and Adjacent Regions. Coast Pilot of Alaska, Appendix I.

Emmons, George T. Basketry of the Tlingit. Memoirs, American Museum of Natural History, Vol. III, Part 2. New York, 1903.

Garfield, Viola. Tsimshian Clan and Society. University of Washington Publications in Anthropology, Vol. VII. Seattle, 1939.

Hallowell, A. I. Bear Ceremonialism in the Northern Hemisphere. American Anthropologist, Vol. XXVIII, No. 1. Menasha, 1926.

Handbook of American Indians. Bulletin 30, Bureau of American Ethnology. Washington, 1907.

Osgood, C. Distribution of the Northern Athapaskan Indians.
Yale University Publications in Anthropology, No. 7. New Haven, 1936.

Swanton, John R. Contributions to the Ethnology of the Haida.
Memoirs, American Museum of Natural History, Vol. VIII.

----------. Myths and Texts of the Tlingit. Bulletin 39, Bureau
of American Ethnology. Washington, 1909.

----------. Social Conditions, Beliefs and Linguistic Relationships of the Tlingit Indians. 26th Annual Report, Bureau of
American Ethnology. Washington, 1908.

U. S. Hydographic Chart of Bering Sea. U. S. Coast and Geodetic
Survey 9302. Washington, 1941.

Wagner, Henry. The Cartography of the Northwest Coast of
America to the Year 1800. Berkeley: University of California
Press, 1937.

Index

Abalone (Haliotis), 95
Abies lasiocarpa (Hook.) Nutt. (subalpine
   fir). 268
Abies subalpina Engelm. See Abies lasio-
   carpa
Acapulco, 11
Acer glabrum Tor. (maple), 56
Achkani, 75, 178, 179
Admiralty Bay, 20, 21, 23, 25. See
   also Yakutat Bay
Admiralty Island, 26, 51, 53, 63, 68,
   69
Agischanak', 183
Ah-Tena. See Atna
Ak', Ako, Akku, Aks, Aku, Ark, Auk,
   37, 68, 69, 76, 265
Ak-kōn, 68, 78
Alaganik, 65, 218
Alaghanik. See Alaganik
Alaria esculenta Grev. (edible algae),
   58, 128
Alaska: transfer to United States, 46,
   225; Indian lands, 47; meteorology of,
   54-55; missions, 227
Alaska peninsula, 15, 52, 60
Albatross, 125
Aleutian Islands, 15, 19, 27, 42, 43, 52
Aleuts, 29, 30, 31, 32, 33, 34, 42, 43,
   60, 64, 72, 105, 213, 224
Alexander, ship, 33
Alexander I, Emperor, decree of, 39
Alexander Archipelago, 24, 27, 32, 48,
   108, 231
Alga fontinalis (moss), 13
Algonquin language, 273
Alláganak. See Alaganik
Alsek, 6, 28, 53
Altsēch, Altsek, Alzech. See Alsek
Amelanchier florida Lindl. See Amel-
   anchier ovalis Ser.
Amelanchier ovalis Ser. (serviceberry),
   57
Amkāu, 83
Amulet, 102

Anadyrsk, 127
Anderson, Alexander C., 77
Angaschi, 166
Angoon, 4, 69, 70, 88, 89
Angūn. See Angoon
Anian Straits, 12, 23
Antlin River, 28
Apollo, ship, 39
Arbusof, Lieut., 33
Arctomys sp. See Marmota
Arctostaphylus alpina (L.) Spreng. See
   Arctostaphylus uva ursi
Arctostaphylus uva ursi (alpine bear-
   berry), 58
Arteaga, Ignacio, 17
Artemisia vulgaris (wormwood), 283
Asplenium (spleenwort), 283
Astrolabe, ship, 18
Atachtani. See Atna
Atahualpa, ship, 217
Athanasias, 223
Athapascans, 108, 127, 134, 136, 137,
   167, 220. See also Gunana
Athapascan tribe, 218, 219
Atka, district of, 42
Atnahs. See Atna
Atna, the, 148, 218, 219-220
Atna River, 60, 220. See also Copper
   River
Atrevida, ship, 23
Auk. See Ak'
Austin, Mrs. Olinda, 227
Avacha Bay. See Awatcha Bay
Awatcha Bay, 12

Baer, Ernst von, 42, 54
Baidarkas (skin boats), 28, 29, 30, 31,
   32, 37
Baranda, 24
Baranof, Alexander, 4, 27-28, 29-38,
   57, 69, 72, 222, 223
Bassarguine, 73
Batavia, 38
Baux, 23

301